D1612767

INTO THE VALLEY

OF

DEATH

INTO THE VALLEY
OF
DEATH

THE LIGHT CAVALRY AT BALACLAVA

NICK THOMAS

Pen & Sword
MILITARY

AN IMPRINT OF PEN & SWORD BOOKS LTD.
YORKSHIRE - PHILADELPHIA

First published in Great Britain in 2021 by
Pen & Sword Military
An imprint of
Pen & Sword Books Limited
Yorkshire - Philadelphia

ISBN 978 1 52672 2 928

A CIP catalogue record for this book is available from the British Library

Typeset in Times New Roman 10.5/13 by
Sjmagic DESIGN SERVICES, India.

Printed and bound in the UK by
CPI Group (UK) Ltd, Croydon, CR0 4YY

Pen & Sword Books Limited incorporates the imprints of Atlas,
Archaeology, Aviation, Discovery, Family History, Fiction, History, Maritime,
Military, Military Classics, Politics, Select, Transport, True Crime, Air World,
Frontline Publishing, Leo Cooper, Remember When, Seaforth Publishing,
The Praetorian Press, Wharncliffe Local History, Wharncliffe Transport,
Wharncliffe True Crime and White Owl.

For a complete list of Pen & Sword titles please contact
PEN & SWORD BOOKS LIMITED
47 Church Street, Barnsley, South Yorkshire S70 2AS, United Kingdom
E-mail: enquiries@pen-and-sword.co.uk
Website: www.pen-and-sword.co.uk

Or

1950
E-mail

Contents

Acknowledgements

There have been many histories of the Charge and this latest naturally owes a great deal to all that have gone before. It owes even more to the veterans of the Light Brigade and the many eyewitnesses to the events of 25 October who recorded what they did or saw in such meticulous detail that they speak to us still, over 150 years on.

Of the modern historians, Canon William M. Lummis and Kenneth G. Wynn were trail-blazers. It was their work which first listed all of the members of the Light Cavalry Brigade and gave a profile of each man. They identified many of the Chargers and gathered together a collection of images of the heroes of the Charge – *Honour the Light Brigade* was one of my earliest purchases and is greatly treasured in my library.

Other seminal works include Roy Dutton's *Forgotten Heroes: The Charge of the Light Brigade* and Lawrence Crider's *In Search of the Light Brigade: A Biographical Dictionary of the Members of the Five Regiments of the Light Brigade from January 1, 1854 to March 31, 1856*, while the late Mr E.J. Boys built a vast library of information on the brigade, which his son, Philip Boys, and Roy Mills are currently putting on line. 'Lives of the Light Brigade' is a truly amazing archive, which has been made available to all.

The author freely acknowledges the invaluable work by these eminent historians and the many authors cited in the bibliography, from the Victorian journalists who had the foresight to record the words of living heroes, through to the twentieth and twenty-first century writers Cecil Woodham-Smith, Mark Adkin, Terry Brighton, James W. Bancroft, John Grehan, et al.

Sincere thanks are due to all.

Introduction

It is my intention to provide only a brief overview of the events leading up to the Battle of Balaclava, as well as providing a general account of the various phases of the battle itself.

The Battle of Balaclava was fought on 25 October 1854, following a build-up of Russian troops which threatened the harbour and fortifications previously captured by the British. Here the British landed both reinforcements and provisions for the siege of Sevastopol.

There survive many near contemporary accounts of the Charge penned by combatants and eye-witnesses while memories were still fresh. These include contemporary letters, personal diaries, official communiques and despatches, and early newspaper accounts from correspondents such as William Howard Russell.[1] His was not the first report to reach our shores. The advent of the 'electric telegraph' enabled war news, once it reached Belgrade, to be transmitted to Britain almost immediately. On 6 November *The Times* printed a translation of the report in *Le Moniteur*, and on 8 November *The Morning Chronicle* released a translation of an Austrian despatch recounting the Charge. On the following day (9 November) both *The Morning Chronicle* and *The Daily News* ran an official despatch from the British ambassador to Turkey, Lord Stratford de Radcliffe, which included a brief description of the Charge. On 12 November *The Daily News* followed up its earlier article when it published a short report by Lawrence Godkin, condemning Lord Raglan and describing the 'great loss of life' inflicted by the Russians on the Light Brigade. Raglan's official despatch of 27 October reached London on the same day but was held back by *The Times* which was preparing their own damning article by Russell and ran copy between the 14th and 17th, only publishing Raglan's words on the 18th. By then the casualty figures reached the press and the full enormity of the disaster began to hit home.

When quoting the many personal accounts featured in the appendices, I have made an attempt to redact the more repetitive information where editing does not affect the overall narrative. Many of these first-hand accounts evidently include details gleaned from other survivors and which quickly entered into the collective conscience of the whole brigade; this needs to be borne in mind when reading any account.

Where acquired knowledge appears to be misleading, inaccurate, or implies that the narrator has first-hand information, which cannot be so, this has often been omitted. Plausible discrepancies such as from whom commands were given, the carrying of gun spikes, and the disposition of forces and their numbers, are included in their original form – it is for the reader to decide which account is the more accurate.

In 1857 E.H. Nolan's book the *Illustrated History of the War against Russia* was published. It contained many inaccuracies relating to the campaign, and in particular the circumstances surrounding the Charge – these were to be magnified by later works and have become the accepted history of the battle.

One of the early well-informed publications to cover the battle was *Letters from Headquarters; or, The Realities of the War in the Crimea, by an Officer on the Staff.* The author, Colonel the Hon. Somerset Calthorpe, was Lord Raglan's nephew, and so was not without bias. He had a privileged insight into the conduct of the campaign, having served as an aide-de-camp on Raglan's Staff. He witnessed the battle from alongside Raglan on Sapouné Ridge. Much of his information was sourced from conversations and correspondence with the combatants. It was, however, not without errors, especially in relation to the conduct of the light cavalry division, making Lord Cardigan a scapegoat for all of its ills. Cardigan disputed these elements of the work, which led to litigation. While Cardigan was largely vindicated, he had left it too late after the first publication for a legally binding ruling.

The personal information provided by the affidavits in the Cardigan v. Calthorpe case relating to the Charge adds greatly to our knowledge, drawing on the experiences of individual witnesses. Their formulaic nature means that only representative examples are quoted, and these are quoted in a redacted form.

A more detailed account of the war with Russian was *The Invasion of the Crimea* by Alexander William Kinglake, published in eight volumes between 1863 and 1887. Kinglake's work includes much information drawn from interviews and correspondence with men of all ranks. Lord Cardigan, mindful of the earlier work by Calthorpe, wrote detailed accounts on *his* Charge in the hope of getting his views across. There was nearly a second liable case when the book was finally published, this only being averted by later editions carrying footnotes stating Cardigan's objections to some of Kinglake's assertions – the original text, however, was unaltered.

The significance of the Charge was recognised by its participants from the outset and the first anniversary was marked in the Crimea as well as at home.

After leaving the service, many of the veterans of Balaclava kept in touch. In 1875 their correspondence led to the forming of a committee whose role it was to mark the 21st anniversary with a dinner; annual get-togethers were held up until 1913.

Alfred, Lord Tennyson, immortalised the Charge in his poem *The Charge of the Light Brigade*, published in *The Examiner* on 9 December. The public's interest in the Charge did not decline and from time to time throughout the latter part of the century Chargers' accounts were quoted in the press. A small number of potted histories were printed, a few of which are more in-depth memoirs of real historical merit. Numbering among the latter are works by Private Robert Stuart Farquharson, 4th Light Dragoons, Private John Doyle, 8th Hussars, Private William Henry Pennington, 11th Hussars, Private Albert Mitchell, 13th Light Dragoons, and Corporal Thomas Morley, 17th Lancers. Extracts from some of these often vivid accounts are included in the appendices and liberally throughout the text.

Tables detailing the status of each Charger have been included within the appendices, along with tables detailing those who attended the 1875 Dinner and membership of the Balaclava Commemoration Society in 1877 and 1879. It is hoped that this information will assist future historians to successfully direct their research on establishing the names of the final 60-plus men whose names remain elusive.

While it seems churlish to have selected individuals for disctinction, when every man who charged expected death or injury, a number of men were granted both British and Foreign gallantry awards, including the Victoria Cross; nearly all were made according to official allocations rather than purely on merit. These medals and the circumstances that were cited for their award are included in the appendices – countless other well documented deeds went unrewarded, but may be found within these pages.

Chapter 1

The Road to War

The Crimean War (1854-56) was basically a clash of empires fought between Russia and the coalition of Great Britain, France, Turkey and, from 1855, Sardinia. This was the British Army's first major European conflict since Waterloo. It was marked by a series of blunders and won only through the supreme bravery, endurance and sacrifice of the ordinary servicemen and by the initiative and sound leadership of junior officers and NCOs.

Britain and France both wanted to stabilize the declining Ottoman Empire, Christened by Czar Nicholas I 'the sick man of Europe', and resist Russian influence in the Balkans, the eastern Mediterranean and the Middle East, and the Czar's search for an all-seasons port. For the British the greatest fear was that Russia might threaten their rule in India.

The Straits Convention (13 July 1841) between Britain, France, Prussia, Austria, Russia and Turkey, contained two main elements. One was that no nation's warships should pass through the Dardanelle Straits in peacetime – thereby bottling-up Russia's Black Sea Fleet. The other important clause was that no nation should seek exclusive influence within the Ottoman Empire – the Czar's troops had, in 1829, come within striking distance of Constantinople, retiring only in the face of international pressure. Czar Nicholas I, meanwhile, agreed with Austria that he would only seek influence in the principalities north of the River Danube, and the Balkans states, down to the Adriatic. The Convention maintained peace for over a decade, but it was only a matter of time before one of the major powers broke its terms in search of an edge over the others.

The flashpoint came in an apparently minor religious dispute between Roman Catholic and Orthodox Christians over the most important Christian sites – France supported the former and Russia the latter.

The power struggle was stepped up in 1852. Napoleon III demanded that the Ottoman Sultan Abdulmejid I (1823 – 25 June 1861) recognise France as the protector of Christian monks and pilgrims in the Holy Places. He used gunboat diplomacy and sent a warship up the Dardanelles, forcing the Sultan to cede to his demands to surrender the key to the main door of the Church of the

Nativity in Bethlehem to the Roman Catholics. The British Foreign Secretary, James Howard Harris, 3rd Earl of Malmesbury, remarked on 'the melancholy spectacle of such an unseemly diplomatic incident for exclusive privileges in a spot near which the heavenly host proclaimed peace on earth and goodwill towards men ... and rival churches contending for mastery in the very place where Christ died for mankind'.

In February 1853, Czar Nicholas I sent an ambassador extraordinary, Prince Alexander Sergeyevich Menshikov, to Constantinople to insist the letter of the Kuchuk Kainarji Treaty (21 July 1774) be adhered to and that Orthodox Christians' access be restored, with Russia acknowledged as the protector of the twelve million Orthodox Christians in the Ottoman Empire.

Prince Menshikov met the British Ambassador Stratford Canning, 1st Viscount Stratford de Redcliffe, for discussions about the future of the Ottoman Empire.

Through Britain's long-standing policy of maintaining the integrity of the Turkish Empire, Canning had access to the Sultan and encouraged him to refuse the Czar's demands, overstepping his brief by inferring British protection.

The Sultan duly resisted Menshikov's demands and in the summer he returned to St Petersburg; France had apparently gained the upper hand.

In 1844 the Czar had met Lord Aberdeen, George Hamilton-Gordon, while in England. When the Czar suggested the partition of the Ottoman Empire, Aberdeen made the mistake of not firmly denouncing the idea.

When Aberdeen became Prime Minister of the coalition government of 1852-55, Czar Nicholas I assumed that he would find an ally in Britain where there had recently been many outspoken voices against the French.

Russia's Black Sea fleet was put on alert at Sevastopol, and in June (1853) Britain and France responded by sending their fleets to the Dardanelles.

On 26 July the Russians invaded the autonomous areas of Moldavia and Wallachia (now Romania), which, under the terms of the Treaty of Adrianople (14 September 1829), were under the protectorate of Turkey.

Intense diplomacy followed in an attempt to avert war. The representatives of the four neutral Great Powers—Great Britain, France, Austria and Prussia—met in Vienna. A draft proposal was formulated but rejected by Abdulmejid I, who felt that it was open to interpretation. Great Britain, France, and Austria were united in proposing amendments to mollify the Sultan, but their suggestions were ignored in the Court of St Petersburg. In August Abdulmejid I declared that he alone would act on behalf of all Christians within his empire. The sultan gave Russia two weeks to withdraw and when they failed to do so, war was declared on 16 October 1853.

A Turkish army crossed the Danube in an attempt to liberate the principalities. On 30 November six Russian vessels entered the naval harbour of Sinope on the southern shore of the Black Sea under cover of fog. Here they destroyed a Turkish flotilla at anchor, using new explosive shells to devastating effect. The affair was reported in the British press as the 'Massacre of Sinope' and caused fever-pitch anti-Russian feeling among the public. The 'war faction' in the Cabinet feared a Russian threat to British naval dominance.

In January 1854, Britain and France deployed warships to the Black Sea with the intention of confining the Russian fleet to Sevastopol. Their arrival was quickly followed up by a British and French ultimatum to St Petersburg on 27 February, demanding a Russian withdrawal from the 'Danubian Principalities'. War was declared almost by default as a result of Russia's refusal to comply within the six-day deadline. Meanwhile, on 11 March the British Baltic fleet set sail to make their first patrol of Russia's northern waters – the war would be fought on many fronts.

The War Office sent a British contingent under Lord Raglan to support the Ottoman Turks. Lieutenant General George Charles Bingham, 3rd Earl of Lucan, was brought out of retirement to lead the Cavalry Division with his brother-in-law, Major General James Thomas Brudenell, 7th Earl of Cardigan, acting as his subordinate and commanding the Light Brigade. The Heavy Brigade would act under Colonel The Hon. Sir James Yorke Scarlett (becoming brigadier general on appointment, but most frequently referred to as General Scarlet) who similarly had no field experience, but who selected the greatly experienced Lieutenant Alexander James Hardy Elliot as his ADC.

Ironically, Lord Lucan's only field-service had been twenty-five years previously with the Russian army on the staff of Prince Menshikov, who would command the Russian forces in the Crimea. A lot had changed, including cavalry drill.[1] Remarkably, Lucan ordered that the Cavalry should revert back to the words of command and drill that he was still familiar with. Lord Paget, Commander of the 4th Light Dragoons, was able to persuade him to rescind this order which would have caused absolute chaos under war conditions.

To say that the nation was surprised at the appointments of Lord Lucan and Lord Cardigan would be an understatement, as it was well known that there was great personal animosity between the pair, who barely spoke. Indeed Raglan had protested but been overruled by the Duke of Newcastle, the Secretary of State for War. Major William Charles Forrest of the 4th (Royal Irish) Regiment of Dragoon Guards summed up the Cavalry's thoughts: 'If any mishap should occur to the cavalry, you may be able to form a correct idea how it happened'.[2]

By late June (1854), British and French armies were concentrated at Varna (Bulgaria) on the Black Sea, where they were strategically placed to defend Constantinople. The armies had initially been deployed to raise Russia's siege of Silistra. The Russians, however, had already been defeated by the Turkish army and, under pressure applied by Austria (which Russia had expected to remain neutral due to its support during the 1848 revolution), evacuated the disputed Balkan provinces in August, thereby belatedly fulfilling the terms of the earlier British and French ultimatum.

The British press and certain elements within the House of Commons demanded that the army should be used for further leverage.

The allies proposed punitive conditions for the cessation of hostilities, including: a demand that Russia give up its protectorate over the Danubian Principalities; that they abandon any claim to interfere in Ottoman affairs on the behalf of the Orthodox Christians; the revision of the Straits Convention; and that all nations were to be granted access to the Danube River. Russia refused to enter into negotiations.

The British government set the new objective of neutralizing the Russian fleet and deliver 'a blow that would cripple Russian naval power for a generation' by taking their naval base at Sevastopol. Lord Raglan, the commander-in-chief of the expedition, had already been briefed on this objective. The French and Turkish generals agreed and their combined force set sail for the Crimea. The first British contingent dropped anchor on the western side of the Crimea, near Eupatoria, in Kalamita Bay on 13 September.

A Brief Timeline of Events Leading to the Landings in the Crimea

1853

2 March	Prince Menshikov arrives in Constantinople with demands on the Porte
21 May	Prince Menshikov leaves Constantinople, breaking off relations
31 May	Russian ultimatum to Turkey
8 June	British Fleet approaches the Dardanelles
3 July	Russian army crosses the Pruth into Moldavia
5 October	Turkey declares war on Russia
28 October	Turkish army crosses the Danube at Kalafat
30 October	British Fleet enters the Bosphorus
4 November	Russians defeated by Turks at Oltenitza
30 November	Turkish naval squadron destroyed at Sinope

1854

4 January	Allied fleets enter the Black Sea
8 January	Russians invade the Dobruja
23 February	The Guards leave England
10 March	Baltic Fleet leaves Spithead

THE ROAD TO WAR

19 March	French troops sail for Turkey
20 March	French Baltic Fleet sails
28 March	France and Great Britain declare war on Russia
5 April	British arrive at Gallipoli
14 April	Russians besiege Silistra
18 April	Turkish victory at Rahova
20 April	Austria and Prussia declare their neutrality
22 April	Bombardment of Odessa
28 May	Embarkation of Allied force for Varna
23 June	Russians abandon the Siege of Silistra
26 June	Allied fleet arrives off Kronstadt
7 July	Russians defeated at Giurgevo
28 July	Russians withdraw across Pruth
	Russians defeat Turks at Bayezid in Asia Minor
13 August	Allies besiege Bomarsund
16 August	Surrender of Bomarsund
21 August	Bombardment of Kola, in the White Sea, by British squadron
30 August	British naval failure at Petropavlovsk
5 September	Allies embark at Varna for Crimea

Chapter 2

The Invasion of the Crimea and the Battle of the Alma

On 13 September 1854, the British and French fleets reached Kalamita Bay, thirty-three miles north of Sevastopol. Lord Raglan and Marshal St Arnaud, commanders of the British and French forces, decided to disembark the 64,000 allied troops and lay siege to the city; the allied fleets would form a blockade. Sevastopol was well protected on its seaward side, with stone-built forts bristling with heavy gun emplacements dominating the harbour. Russian warships added to these formidable defences.

Disembarkation commenced at dawn on the 14th, the first cavalry landing on the following day. Astonishingly, the Russians allowed the allies ashore unopposed, having decided to make a stand at the River Alma, fifteen miles to the south, en route to Sevastopol.

The 11th Hussars were the first cavalry deployed. Disembarking the horses was a slow process and continued until the 16th. Two days later, all 26,000 British troops, along with their 66 artillery pieces, had been landed. The British element consisted of the 1st, 2nd, 3rd, 4th and the Light Divisions, supported by one battery of horse artillery and ten field batteries. The Cavalry Division was represented by the Light Cavalry Brigade, the Heavies not arriving in the theatre until after the Battle of Alma.

Each of the five regiments of the Light Brigade was divided into two squadrons, and each squadron into two troops of 75 men. As each troop landed they mounted picquets inland.

The cavalrymen carried three days of water, rum and rations of salt pork and biscuit for themselves, with three days of corn for their horses; they would have to find fresh water for the horses as a matter of urgency. Cornet George Orby Wombwell, 17th Lancers, led a reconnoitre and found water after a six-mile trek.

Lord Cardigan led an unsuccessful reconnaissance, while a subsequent patrol made by the 13th Light Dragoons observed Cossacks torching barns full of corn. Other troops were more successful and brought back cattle and poultry. Captain Portal, 4th Light Dragoons, noted, 'The cavalry have been busy driving in bullocks, sheep and ponies, etc., all of which we pay for at our price, which is a very fair one.'

The advance ten miles south to the River Bulganak began on 19 September. The army marched with the 2nd and Light Divisions leading, the 3rd and 1st following, with the 4th Division to the rear, while the Royal Navy warships' 32-pounder guns supported the land forces' right flank as they moved parallel to the coast.

Lord Cardigan rode with the 11th Hussars and 13th Light Dragoons at the head of the army. The 8th Hussars and 17th Lancers rode out on the left flank with Lord Lucan in command. Lord Paget's 4th Light Dragoons were temporarily attached to the 4th Division, a role which he protested against, considering that it lacked the potential for glory.

Cholera and dysentery were brought from Varna and men fell out sick on the march. The infantry reached the Bulganak at about 2 pm when a 1,500-strong Cossack patrol was spotted on a ridge overlooking the river. Lord Raglan ordered Cardigan to take a squadron each from the 11th Hussars and 13th Light Dragoons and reconnoitre the opposite bank.

The enemy fired their carbines at extreme range before retiring; but it was a feint. Lord Lucan then rode to the head of Cardigan's force and was just about to order them to charge when General Richard Airey and his ADC, Captain Nolan, arrived with orders for their withdrawal; from his vantage point Lord Raglan had observed that the Russians had laid a trap, with 6,000 infantrymen and artillery support concealed just beyond the ridge; the enemy would outnumber them twenty to one.

The Russians moved across Lucan's left and were in position to charge his flank. General Airey therefore ordered Lucan to hold his ground until support from the 8th Hussars, 17th Lancers and a troop of the Royal Horse Artillery could cover the withdrawal.

Meanwhile, in their advanced position, the 11th Hussars and 13th Light Dragoons came under artillery fire, as Private Mitchell, 13th Light Dragoons, recalled:

'Several shells burst close to us. One struck a troop horse in the side, bursting inside the horse, cleaning him out as though a butcher had done it. Our Horse Artillery now galloped up and quickly came into action.'

An artillery duel commenced as the 8th Hussars and the 17th Lancers came up to support the withdrawal, orchestrated by Lord Cardigan. Among the casualties was Private James Williamson, 11th Hussars, who lost a foot, while Sergeant Joseph Priestly, 13th Light Dragoons, lost his right hand. Lieutenant Roger Palmer, 11th Hussars, reported:

'Williamson rode out of the ranks, his leg shot off and hanging by his overall. Coming up to me he said, quite calmly, "I am hit, may I fall out?"'

The British infantry mocked the Light Brigade for their retreat, unaware of the overwhelming force which had lain in wait to massacre them had they advanced. This loss of face would have grave repercussions.

The Alma, the second of the four rivers which the army needed to cross, was reached on the 20th. Here thirty-six Russian battalions held a steep hill on the south bank. It was anticipated that the strongly defended position would hold out for six weeks.

Captain George Maude, I Troop, RHA, made the following assessment of the situation:

'After advancing about six miles we came to a very strong position, where the Russians had entrenched themselves on the bank of the River Alma where the south side rises steeply to about 300 feet. Up the side of the steep slope the enemy had entrenched batteries with some very heavy guns. They began a tremendous cannonade on us when we came within 2,000 yards.'

Lord Raglan was no tactician. He launched a head-on assault, which entailed a march over open ground before wading across a fording-point, and advancing uphill straight at the muzzles of the enemy's guns. During the whole of the attack his troops would be exposed to heavy artillery fire from the 'Great Redoubt'. These guns were supported by mobile batteries and infantry, some of whom were concealed in rough terrain and brush, others held well-defended positions towards the top of the hill.

The French advanced against weaker opposition on the Russian left, but on crossing the river halted, leaving the twenty-seven British battalions to advance largely without support. The British 2nd and the Light Divisions lay flat under artillery fire for around 90 minutes, but once the French front stalled Raglan ordered them to their feet and to march up the slopes through a withering fire.

Meanwhile, the Light Brigade was held on the left to protect against a flank attack by Russian cavalry which was known to be in the area. They were ordered to retire when they came under artillery fire, because Raglan needed to protect his woefully small cavalry force, but this act further damaged their reputation.

The infantry, however, continued their advance, shoulder to shoulder and in perfect line through heavy fire, filling the gaps as their comrades fell. Private Timothy Gowing of the 7th Fusiliers wrote:

'They began to pitch their shot and shell right amongst us, and our men began to fall. I know that I felt horribly sick.'

The Russians were confident that their artillery would take its toll and that determined use of the bayonet would break the allies' resolve. But many of the British battalions were armed with the Minié rifle, accurate at a distance of 500 yards and far outranging the enemy's muskets. Their suppressive fire greatly assisted the advance.

The British infantrymen, depleted in number, scrambled up the steep slopes of the Great Redoubt against a hail of iron and lead, which became more concentrated with every step. Finally, both sides fired their last rounds before the British charged with fixed bayonets.

The bayonet and rifle butt were used to terrible effect as the British pushed forward. In the face of such a fierce assault, the gunners were ordered to limber up, signalling that the Russians were losing ground. Then, with victory within their grasp, someone sounded the 'Retire'. The bugle-call was picked up by other buglers and the men began to fall back. The Russians seized their opportunity and rallied.

In the face of possible defeat, the 1st Division, the Guards and the Highland Brigades remarkably pressed on in their ascent. In the rear, the Scots Fusilier Guards, the centre battalions of the Guards Brigade, had only just crossed the river. These men marched on uphill through the ranks of the men retiring all around them. The Grenadier and Coldstream Guards began to close on the enemy's summit positions. Their supreme discipline under fire had not only checked the retreat but many of the retiring troops had now formed up alongside them and returned back up the hill. The enemy fought bravely but were forced back, then turned and fled as their stronghold became overrun.

Despite heavy losses the British took the positions which commanded the Sevastopol road.

Lieutenant S.J.G. Calthorpe, ADC to Lord Raglan, later wrote that Marshal St Arnaud opposed an immediate advance on Sevastopol and, furthermore, failed to capitalize on the victory by not harassing the retreating Russians.

Raglan ordered the Light Brigade to escort the horse artillery into a forward position from where they could bombard the retreating army. He was conscious that he had less than 1,000 cavalrymen, while 3,000 mounted Russian troops remained in the vicinity. Furthermore, Raglan was concerned that Lucan might be drawn into combat as had nearly happened at the crossing of the Bulganak; the cavalry were given strict orders not to attack.

While Lord Lucan ensured that the artillery were escorted, he also sent forward two troops, one each drawn from the 11th Hussars and 17th Lancers, their role was to harry the retreating enemy. Tactically the cavalry's role was always to pursue a fleeing enemy, and this was Lucan's intent.

INTO THE VALLEY OF DEATH

Cornet Wombwell, 17th Lancers, recalled the scene:

'We went forward at a gallop, cheering and hollering as loud as we could. We could see the enemy running as hard as they could go, throwing away their knapsacks, arms and even coats to assist them in their flight. Morgan's Troop of my regiment were sent out to pursue and bring in prisoners, in which they succeeded very well, bringing in a good many.'

Lord Lucan's pursuit did not escape Raglan's notice. He twice ordered their retirement, which angered Lucan who showed his disapproval in a quite remarkable manner, by instructing the cavalry to release their prisoners and retire empty-handed.

Lieutenant Calthorpe recorded that the 8th Hussars also got in on the action, but with the same result:

'An officer of the 8th Hussars, who was somewhat in advance with his troops, and who had captured some 60 or 70 Russians, was ordered to let them go again, quite as much to the astonishment of the Russians who had been taken as of the Hussars who had captured them.'[1]

The British cavalry had played no part in the hard-fought victory at the Alma, and now could not even take defenceless Russians as prisoners – the officers and men of the Light Brigade wrongly blamed Lucan for their humiliation.

Captain Nolan, also ignorant of Lord Raglan's order, expressed his views to William Howard Russell of *The Times*:

'There was one thousand British Cavalry looking on at a beaten army retreating, within a ten minutes' gallop of them – enough to drive one mad! It is too disgraceful, too infamous. They ought to be damned!'

That night the men bivouacked on the heights where the worst of the combat had occurred.

Private Mitchell, 13th Light Dragoons, was among those who could not sleep:

'Then it was that we heard around us the groans of the wounded and the dying, some calling for the love of God for a drop of water. Others were praying most devoutly, well knowing this to be their last night in this life. We had already seen sufficient to harden our feelings, and make us callous to human suffering, but lay some time thinking very seriously and praying to God for protection from all dangers.'[2]

Lord George Paget too was moved by the scene, he wrote:

'The poor wounded must have had a terrible night of it, bitterly cold, and we could hear their moans all night for they were all around us …. Oh, war, war! The details of it are horrid. In one spot I found positively a pile of fifty Russians as they fell, a little further on another cluster of a hundred.'

It was a three-plus mile journey to embark the wounded for the hospital at Scutari, and no wheeled transport. The battlefield was strewn with Russian and allied casualties and the British spent two days burying the dead, only resuming the march south on the 23rd, reaching the River Katcha the same day. The Light Brigade – minus the 4th Light Dragoons – was sent forward to reconnoitre.

During the following day (24th) the army crossed the River Belbec. The horses had not been watered since leaving the Alma, but Lucan inexplicably ordered that they should not be allowed to drink. This and his actions at the Bulganak and Alma were genuine causes for concern. Cardigan, meanwhile, had written to Raglan complaining that Lucan rode with the Light Brigade and that he had previously enjoyed some autonomy – he was rebuffed in no uncertain terms.

The British advanced to within sight of Sevastopol. Raglan's engineering adviser, Sir John Burgoyne, successfully argued that the Russians would have expected an attack from the north; therefore the defences in the south would be weaker. Not even Burgoyne, however, could actually see any defensive earthworks, but he was able to persuade Marshal St Arnaud to attack from the south. Lord Raglan's orders were to maintain the alliance at all costs, and so fatally he gave way.

On 25 September the British began their flank march. The only map available indicated a single track cutting through the forest leading onto the Sevastopol–Simferopol road at Mackenzie's Farm.

The Light Brigade rode in advance, Raglan having sent one of his Staff Officers, Captain Weatherall, to show them the route. Lord Raglan and the artillery rode in the rear.

Prince Alexander Menshikov was charged with holding Sevastopol but anticipating an immediate assault had begun its evacuation. His troops had already travelled along the road past Mackenzie's Farm, his personal baggage train following on.

When the Light Brigade passed along the track they came to a fork and Weatherall sent them along the left track, Raglan and his staff officers reached the same point, taking the right fork which led to Mackenzie's Farm. General Airey was riding in advance and saw the Russians first, quickly doubling back before sending riders to locate the cavalry and to unlimber the artillery.

When the Light Brigade arrived they were, once again, not allowed to pursue, but formed a close guard for Raglan who greeted Lucan with the words, 'Lord Lucan, you are late!'

The captured wagons were hauled out of the forest to the army's bivouac near the River Chernaya and some of the munitions wagons blown up. The officers had the first choice of the booty, taking any silver, gold, jewellery, furs and other high quality clothing, along with some racy novels in French, before the other ranks were allowed to help themselves.

The cavalry managed to secure tobacco and cigarettes and stood around quietly smoking; they were more subdued than the infantry and artillery, still conscious that they needed to prove themselves.

Chapter 3

The March to Balaclava

The British advanced towards Balaclava on 26 September. The entrance to the deep-water harbour was dominated by the ruins of a fort manned by local militia who put up only a token defence.

On the advice of Admiral Lyons, Balaclava became the British depot, which meant they occupied the more vulnerable right flank of the siege operations, originally intended to be the responsibility of the French. Instead the French used the bays at Kamiesh and Kazatch on the western tip of the peninsula, establishing themselves to the west of Sevastopol on the Chersonese uplands. The British infantry advanced four miles further along the coast, where they occupied the hills overlooking the city and harbour, along with its naval base and dry dock. Sevastopol was garrisoned by 18,000 sailors, with 4,000 marines and reservists, but would be reinforced and resupplied throughout the siege.

Lord Raglan's long-term HQ was in a small farmhouse on a plateau adjacent to Balaclava, from where he had a direct route to the Sapouné Ridge (occupied by Bosquet's French Division) and could observe his vulnerable flank.

General Sir George Cathcart, commanding the 4th Infantry Division, observed Sevastopol's southern defences from the British lines. He wrote to Raglan:

'I am sure I could walk into it with scarcely the loss of a man at night or an hour before daybreak. We could run into it even in open daylight, only risking a few shots.'[1]

Raglan rode over to Cathcart to inform him that he proposed siege operations. When he added that heavy siege guns were to be brought up, Cathcart exclaimed, 'Land the siege train! But, my dear Lord Raglan, what the devil is there to knock down?'

The French, however, were determined to lay siege and Raglan gave way, even though he knew that the Russians' position was extremely vulnerable. In the meantime the allies began entrenching operations. Crucially, they lacked the resources to surround the city and a wide corridor along the Simferopol road remained open to the north. The seaward side was strongly defended by three fortresses, while twelve vessels were scuttled across the entrance to the harbour, preventing an allied landing.

Raglan understood the need to secure his supply line and created a force centred on Kadikoi whose brief was the defence of Balaclava and the Woronzoff road, which led towards Sevastopol. These men included the Light Brigade, and two troops of RHA (Captain Maude's I Troop, made up of four 6-pounder guns and two 12-pounder howtizers, and Captain Brandling's C Troop, consisting of four 9-pounder guns and two 24-pounder howitzers), along with the 93rd Highlanders and roughly 2,000 Tunisian troops who fought under the Turkish flag.

A chain of six redoubts were constructed at intervals of 500 yards along the Woronzoff road on the Causeway Heights. Four were completed by 25 October and occupied by the Turkish contingent. Each had an earth parapet around the perimeter, with occasional breaks for artillery pieces to fire through. The most strongly defended, No. 1 Redoubt, was constructed on an elevation dubbed Canrobert's Hill and had three 12-pound iron cannons. Both Nos. 2 and 3 Redoubts had two cannons, and No. 4 Redoubt three. These guns, which were in position by 7 October, had a range of around 1,200 yards firing round shot, a little more with shrapnel. Five gunners from Captain Barker's W Battery, RHA, were detailed to these Royal Naval guns. The redoubts provided each other with limited support, while the French guns of General Bosquet's 2nd Division, stationed on the eastern escarpment of the Sapoué Heights, were beyond the limits of their effective range. At best this outer defensive line could only ever buy time.

Balaclava's defence was strengthened by the arrival, between 1 and 4 October, of the Heavy Brigade; the 1st (Royals), 2nd (Scots Greys) and 6th (Inniskilling) Dragoons, and the 4th (Royal Irish) and 5th Dragoon Guards. Initially they camped adjacent to the Light Brigade, sharing the daily picquets and patrol duties.

Lieutenant Richard Temple Godman of the 5th Dragoon Guards wrote to his father on 3 October:

'We are harassed night and day with pickets [*sic*] and patrols, Our inlying pickets have just turned out in a great hurry after two squadrons of Cossacks, but the latter know better than to stand a charge of even a dozen of our men. They come near and shoot at us.'

Meanwhile, delays in construction of these redoubts, only Nos. 1 - 4 ever being effectively manned, caused Captain Nolan to write:

'No plan of defence has yet been fixed upon in Balaclava and the valley through which our communications [travel]. To guard these against infiltration [we need to] fortify the ridge and heights forming a natural bastion across the Valley of Balaclava.'[2]

One of the ways in which the cavalry was used to defend a position was by deploying picquets. There were two kinds, inlying and outlying. There were also regular armed reconnaissance patrols. An outlying picquet consisted of an officer and thirty to forty men, stationed on the approaches to their main encampment. It was their role to raise the alarm if the enemy were on the move. If possible the picquet was to hold a defensive line thus allowing the cavalry the time to strengthen their position. The inlying picquet was saddled up in camp and ready to provide immediate support. Stationed protecting routes of an enemy's approach there were also two-man vedettes. These formed a chain of spotters who communicated along their line using signals – the approach of infantry was signified by the troopers riding in an anti-clockwise circle, while moving in a clockwise circle indicated cavalry.

Patrols consisting of an officer and upwards of ten men went out beyond the outlying picquets to reconnoitre the enemy's disposition. British patrols encountered the enemy, usually Cossacks, if they crossed the Chernaya river. Lieutenant Godman mentioned these encounters in a letter to his father:

'We have daily skirmishes with the Cossacks; they nearly surrounded our patrol yesterday and drove them in before they saw them, but tho' supported by a considerable body of cavalry they did not even fire at us, though we were only about a dozen strong. Today our patrol was fired on, some shot and shell.'

Lord Raglan hampered the gathering of intelligence by forbidding patrols from crossing the river. Captain John Oldham, 13th Light Dragoons, was leading a patrol during which Sergeant Henry Alderson crossed the Chernaya and was captured by four Cossacks. Oldham was placed under open arrest. The fallout from this incident meant officers became extremely reluctant to break with Raglan's order, leaving the enemy free to bring up large numbers of reinforcements in relative secrecy.

Cardigan had reported sick on 5 October and so it had been down to Lord Lucan to call out the Cavalry Division whenever the alarm was raised. He did not, however, go on the offensive, being wary of a repetition of the Bulganak incident and therefore contented himself with observing the enemy's manoeuvres in the North Valley.

On 7 October eight infantry battalions supported by five cavalry regiments were observed towards the Mackenzie Heights and Captain Nolan was given permission to go forward with a troop of the 17th Lancers to make a reconnoitre.

15

Following Lord Raglan's orders, Lucan did not advance but maintained a defensive posture between the Russians and Balaclava, earning the inevitable nickname 'Lord Look-on'. Meanwhile, Captain Maude's I Troop, RHA, composed of four 6-pounder guns and two 12-pounder howitzer, fired a few rounds forcing the enemy to withdraw. Captain Shakespear, second-in-command to Maude, wrote:

'The finest opportunity for thrashing the Russian cavalry had been thrown away.'

Lieutenant Calthorpe added:

'I heard great blame given to Lord Lucan for not ordering the Light Cavalry to advance and charge the Cossacks.'

Lord Cardigan returned from sick leave on 12 October and on the following day his yacht, *Dryad*, anchored in Balaclava harbour. He received Raglan's permission to sleep and dine on this luxury vessel, so while Cardigan's command paraded daily two hours before dawn, he only arrived at the cavalry camp at about 10 am.

Meanwhile, to reduce tension between Lords Cardigan and Lucan, Raglan decided to transfer the Light Brigade's camp to a position below No. 6 Redoubt, with the Heavy Brigade remaining at Kadikoi. Lord Paget's observation goes a long way towards explaining the need for the move:

'There are Lucan and Cardigan again hard at it, and it is found desirable to separate them.'

Coordination of the defence of Balaclava had lain with Lord Lucan, but on 14 October Lord Raglan transferred authority to Sir Colin Campbell, commanding officer of the 93rd Highlanders. Lord Lucan outranked Campbell; he was allowed to retain independent command of the cavalry.

On the same day the 4th Light Dragoons were assigned to the Cavalry Division, having been attached to the 4th Division until a few days after it arrived before Sevastopol, transferring in turn to the 3rd and next day the 2nd Divisions; the Light Brigade was now at full strength.

The bombardment of Sevastopol, from both land and sea, began at 6.30 am on 17 October, continuing well into the night. Return fire from Russian guns stripped from vessels scuttled in the harbour detonated a French magazine, the destruction of which had a bad effect on their morale. British gunners were equally accurate and scored a direct hit on the magazine in the fortification known as the Great Redan, while the Russians also lost Vice Admiral Vladimir Alexeyevich Kornilov who was killed at the Malakoff Blue redoubt.

There now presented itself a clear opportunity to strike, but the French commander refused to mount an assault as the defences on their front remained largely intact. The Russians, badly shaken, had been ready to surrender and another potential opportunity to end the campaign was squandered.

Under the guidance of Lieutenant Colonel Franz Todleben, a Russian army engineer, work parties laboured through the night and by dawn had repaired, reinforced and extended the defences. This process continued in shifts by day and night throughout the siege.

Concentrated fire from the allies' artillery continued to wreak considerable damage on the city's defences, but without a complete siege, the defenders could be reinforced and resupplied at will. The general feeling among British officers was that far from becoming weaker as time passed, the Russians' positions were becoming stronger.

On 20 October three Russian infantry columns marched towards the Causeway Heights, attracting artillery fire from the redoubts. Lord Raglan saw the danger and sent an ADC to Brigadier Goldie requesting 1,000 infantrymen of the 4th Division be brought down from his position on the Chersonese plateau via The Col to Kadikoi. The redeployment did not begin until 3 am on the 21st, and took over three hours. Sir Colin Campbell, who commanded Balaclava's defence, immediately sent the reinforcements back, saying that he didn't need them. This cavalier attitude may well have had a bearing on Cathcart's attitude towards sending troops to Campbell's aid on the 25th. For the Russians, the manoeuvres provided invaluable intelligence on the poor construction of Balaclava's outer defences, their blind spots and the calibre of artillery in the redoubts. Moreover, they were held by Tunisian troops. Equally important, the delay in bringing up reinforcement cannot have gone unnoticed by the Russians and must have given them confidence in their future plan of attack.[3]

Cossack patrols continued to probe the British defences by crossing the Chernaya, leading to numerous false alarms which had already become the norm. Lord Paget recorded:

'We are now regularly turned out about midnight. Every fool at the outpost, who fancies he hears something, has only to make a row, and there we all are, generals and all. Well, I suppose 500 false alarms are better than one surprise, so there is no help for it.'

The frequency of such incidents is confirmed by Lieutenant Edward Seager, 8th Hussars, who wrote in a letter to a friend:

'The cavalry have been worked very much, as we do all the outpost duty, night and day. We cover Balaclava, being encamped in the valley leading to the town, and we have to find patrols, pickets [sic], and vedettes for all the country around our position. We are protecting the rear of our position from attack, and what annoys us the most is there is scarcely a day passes that it does not sound "turn out the whole", and away we have to go to look at a few Cossacks; perhaps to remain there for many hours.'[4]

Cornet Wombwell, 17th Lancers, wrote to his father of how these alarms arose:

'The way they keep turning us out is ridiculous. If a Heavy Dragoon or any other thick-headed individual sees a Cossack, he comes galloping into camp and instantly magnifies the Cossack to 500. So of course out we all go and by the time we all get there, not a soul is to be seen.'

The situation was exasperated by a lack of common sense – the cavalry on being turned out, whether a false alarm or not, remained in the saddle until first light. It was desperately tiring work. Private Robert Farquharson, 4th Light Dragoons, wrote:

'The nights were awfully cold, and the heavy dews would almost drench us, till the blood felt like ice, and what with outlying pickets [sic] and inlying pickets. Every day now the Russians loitering or moving in great masses about the Chernaya, keep us on the alert morning, noon and night.'

Major Augustus Willett, commanding the 17th Lancers, added to the hardships by refusing to permit his men to wear their cavalry cloaks. The night of the 21st/22nd was bitterly cold and he was taken ill with cholera brought on by exposure. Private Wightman said that 'Willett was a corpse before sundown on the following day.'

During 22 October there was yet another alert and that evening the cavalry was turned out again; they were not stood down until first light by which time the men were utterly exhausted.

Having tested Balaclava's defenses, Prince Menshikov finalized his plan of attack. He assembled his army at Chorgun, north of the river, from where he could launch an assault against the flank of the British infantry. Lieutenant General Pavel Liprandi (usually referred to, even by the Czar, as General Liprandi), commander of the 12th Infantry Division, was appointed to orchestrate the main attack force which included 17 infantry battalions, 30 squadrons of cavalry and 64 guns. Acting in close cooperation was Major General Zhaboritski with a further 8 infantry battalions supported by 4 squadrons of cavalry and 14 guns, making a combined force of 20,000 infantry, 3,400 cavalry and 2,300 artillerymen manning 78 guns.

Raglan's intelligence officer, Charles Cattley, had informed him on 22 October that two independent sources were indicating a large number of Russian reinforcements were headed from Odessa. Two days later, on the evening of the 24 October, a Turkish spy stated that an enemy force estimated at 20,000 were massed around Chorgun, and would advance on Balaclava from the east and north-east. The attack was planned for the following morning. The spy reported to the Turkish commander in Balaclava and was brought before Lord Lucan and Sir Colin Campbell. After carefully analysing the details via Lord Lucan's interpreter, John Blunt, both considered the account credible. Lucan sent his son, Lord Bingham, with an urgent message for Raglan who on reading the note simply said, 'Very well,' adding later, 'Let me know if there is anything new.' No action was taken to strengthen the British position nor additional patrols ordered.

William Howard Russell of *The Times* spoke to a number of officers in the cavalry camp during the evening of 24 October, from which he surmised:

'I was told that "the Ruskies were very strong all over the place", that reports had been sent to headquarters that an attack was imminent, and that Sir Colin Campbell was uneasy about Balaclava.'

Russell was leaving the camp for his quarters when Nolan caught up with him. The two rode together for a while during which 'he "let out" at the Cavalry Generals, and did not spare those in high places, saying that "We are in a very bad way I can tell you."'[5]

The start time for what the Russians called the Battle of Kadikoi was set for 6 am. Liprandi stood at the Tractir Bridge encouraging his troops, urging them to 'fight as well as they had done on the Danube!' The troops answered each salutation with resounding cheers.

Lieutenant General Ivan Ryzhov (usually referred to, even at court, as General Ryzhov) commanded the Russian cavalry which he concentrated on the Mackenzie Heights. His instructions were to follow on from the capture of the redoubts by engaging with the cavalry as a part of the main objective which was the capture of the area around Kadikoi and to cut off the British army from its supply base.

Chapter 4

The Fall of the Redoubts to the Signing of the Fourth Order

At about 5.45am on the 25th Captain Alexander Low, duty field officer for the Cavalry Division, was checking with the outlying picquets. On approaching the most forward picquet, towards the Kamara Heights, Low sighted a squadron of Don Cossacks, followed by the lead elements of Colonel Jeropkine's lancers, heading towards the village of Kamara. The picquet and their vedettes seemed unaware of the enemy's approach.

Low ordered the men to retire towards No. 1 Redoubt, also sending a warning that a Russian column was advancing close behind; signal flags were duly flown.

Not all of the vedettes had been caught off-guard, as Private Robert Farquharson, 4th Light Dragoons, later wrote:

'The vedettes were circling to right, and also to left, some of them being at a trot. These combined movements signalled to us that the enemy were showing with both infantry and cavalry.'

The speed of the vedettes' trot was noted by Troop Sergeant Major George Smith, 11th Hussars, to whom it was an indication that a large force was on the move.

Meanwhile Lord Paget, following the inspection of his own regiment, accompanied Lord Lucan, Captains Charles Beauchamp Walker (ADC) and Walter Charteris (ADC), Mr John Blunt (interpreter), and Trumpet Major Henry Joy (duty trumpeter) on his pre-daybreak tour of his command and of the Causeway Heights. Paget was alongside Lord William Paulet (assistant adjutant general), and Major Thomas McMahon (assistant quartermaster general), fifty-five yards to the rear of Lucan's party as they rode to the Kamara ridge. Unsighted by the adjacent hills, they remained unaware of the vedettes' movements; it was still a little before 6 am:

'"Hello," said Lord William, "there are two flags flying [from the Redoubt]; what does that mean?" "Why, that surely is the signal that the enemy is approaching," said Major McMahon. "Are you sure?" we replied. Hardly were the words out of McMahon's mouth, when bang went a cannon from the redoubts in question. Off scampered my two companions to their chief while I turned round and galloped back "best pace" to my brigade, which I at once mounted.'[1]

Lord Paget galloped back to the Light Brigade and the Brigade mounted. Lieutenant Colonel John Douglas, 11th Hussars, addressed his command in squadrons mounted in echelon:

'Eleventh, attention. Now men, in all probability we shall meet the enemy today. When you do, don't cut but give them the point, and they will never face you again.'[2]

Douglas had observed the battlefield evidence at the Alma where the Russians' garb had protected them from the cut and slash. The concentrated energy transmitted via the 'point', however, penetrated heavy clothing, even a hardened leather or metal helmet.

Meanwhile, having captured Kamara without firing a shot, Major General Gribbe quickly deployed his artillery overlooking No. 1 Redoubt, while the rest of the attacking force continued its advance. Moments after Douglas had begun his address the booms of heavy artillery from No. 1 Redoubt filled the air.

No. 1 Redoubt was at the furthest easterly point of Balaclava's outer defences. Its three 12-pounders had an effective range of about 1,200 yards, while their narrow field of fire was reduced by the rugged terrain. The advanced position of the redoubt further added to its vulnerability.

Sir Colin Campbell rode from Kadikoi in search of Lord Lucan who was heading towards the former's temporary headquarters. They met en route and quickly conferred; large numbers of Russian troops were entering the north-eastern end of the North Valley, crossing the Fedioukine Heights; other pressing towards the Causeway Heights. Both agreed that this was not a feint. A message was despatched via Charteris to Raglan on the Chersonese Uplands; the French too were notified. Campbell returned to the 93rd Highlanders near Kadikoi and Lucan rode over to the Heavy Brigade which he advanced towards No. 3 Redoubt, supporting their position by deploying Captain Maude's I Troop, RHA, to their right. The 6-pounder guns laid down fire on the enemy cavalry as they crossed the North Valley. The intention was to bolster the redoubts, but the Heavy Brigade's position, with the Light Brigade in echelon to their rear, was unseen by the enemy. The Cavalry Division was, however, in direct line of fire from the enemy's artillery, and took rounds that overshot the redoubts.

An NCO of the 1st Dragoon Guards wrote:

'We advanced to the end of the plain and within range of the Russian guns, which began to play upon us in a very rapid manner. A larger 32-pound shot passed through our squadrons, breaking the legs of two horse and we soon began to think it was time to move off, as in another minute a ball struck a man right in the head, and of course killed him instantly. Several other casualties took place in the right squadron, but I was too busily engaged in my own lot to take notice of all that passed.

'Our light field guns were no match for the immense artillery which the enemy bought against us; besides, our artillery began to suffer severely in men and horses.'[3]

Lord Lucan is reported to have turned to Blunt and commented, 'Those Turks are doing well.' However, his next move, seen by the troop fighting under the Turkish flag, may have hastened their capitulation. Without considering the consequences, he ordered the Heavy Brigade to retire to its previous position beside the Light Brigade roughly 440 yards away from No. 2 Redoubt.

The Russians' advance continued, with the assault on No. 1 Redoubt led by their south column. This was composed of three battalions of the 24th Dnieper Regiment, the Ingermanland Regiment, a Composite Uhlan Regiment (including Colonel Jeropkine's lancers and a squadron from the 53rd Don Cossacks), six light field pieces and four heavier cannons of the 60th Don Cossacks, commanded by Major General Gribbe. They had been the first to move off and advance south along the River Chernaya to the Baidar Valley, turning west and crossing the river bridge and capturing Kamara, along with the high ground overlooking the South Valley. They protected the left flank of the assault.

The Russians' Left Centre was commanded by Major General Semiakin. His force occupied the slopes to the north and north-east of No. 1 Redoubt and included four battalions of the Azov Regiment, the 4th Battalion of the 24th Dnieper Regiment, and one company of the No. 4 Rifle Battalion. Their artillery support was also composed of six light field pieces and four heavier cannons, but he had no cavalry. Their advance was along a track leading south-west from the start point at Chorgun to Kadikoi, crossing the Chernaya via a ford.

The Right Centre was commanded by Major General Levutski and his three battalions of the 23rd Ukraine Regiment, with artillery coming from four light field pieces and four heavier cannons. Levutski's objective was No. 2 Redoubt.

The Russian's Right column was under Colonel Skiuderi. Once across the Tractir Bridge his force of four battalions of the 24th Odessa Regiment, three squadrons of the Don Cossack Regiment, one company of No. 4 Rifle Battalion and eight artillery pieces of No. 7 Light Battery, marched on No. 3 Redoubt. In total the Russians deployed an overwhelming force of 14,000 men in the first phase of their attack, these supported by 36 artillery pieces.

THE FALL OF THE REDOUBTS

The bombardment of the redoubts began at 6 am, with Major General Gribbe's ten artillery pieces focussing their attention on No. 1 Redoubt. Major General Levutski's eight guns pounded Nos. 2 and 3 Redoubts. His heavier artillery had a range of 1,800 yards meaning that the redoubt's gunners were powerless to silence them. Softened up by Gribbe's and Semiakin's combined artillery barrage, the 600 Turkish defenders faced the onslaught of eight infantry battalions, totalling 8,000 men. The enemy advanced using natural cover to good effect. Meanwhile two other attack columns advanced on their right.

General Levutski's column approached No. 2 Redoubt while Colonel Skiuderi headed for No. 3 Redoubt. The main body under General Ryzhov advanced to the edge of the North Valley ready to act as support. A large force under Major General Zhaboritski were held in reserve on the Fedioukine Heights. This force included the 31st Vladimir and 32nd Suzdal Regiments, along with two companies of riflemen, one company of the Black Sea Cossacks, two squadrons of the 12th Ingermanland Hussars and 60th Don Cossacks, supported by four light guns and ten cannons.

The Turkish contingent in defending No. 1 Redoubt could only bring the five guns of the first two redoubts to bear on Semiakin's men. Captain Maude's I Troop provided support but soon came under heavy fire and he was 'horribly wounded'. As one of his officers said, 'What could 6-pounders do against 18-pounders at 1,800 yards.' With only sufficient rounds for one gun, Lucan ordered their withdrawal. Two guns of Captain Barker's W Battery under Lieutenant Dickson were deployed close to No. 3 Redoubt on Sir Colin Campbell's instruction.

At about 7.30 am, still before the fall of the redoubts, seeing the growing threat, Raglan sent word to both the Duke of Cambridge and General Sir George Cathcart before Sevastopol, to march their divisions, fresh from the trenches, the three-plus miles to support the defence of Balaclava.

Once the orders were acted upon it would take two hours to move the 1st and 4th Infantry Divisions into position.

The Turks meanwhile had withdrawn to the far side of No. 1 Redoubt; a British gunner braving the shrapnel succeeded in spiking the guns. In truth, the British gunners from W Battery could do nothing but spike the Naval guns in the redoubts, for which they were later to receive gallantry medals. Gunner David Jenks was nominated to the Médaille Militaire and Gunners Jacob McGarry and John Barrett were awarded the Medaglia al Valore Militare.

No. 1 Redoubt was stormed at bayonet-point by Colonel Kridener's Azov Regiment, one of whom later wrote: 'The loss of the enemy in this redoubt, in dead alone, amounts to more than 170 men.' The sight of troops scrambling over the ramparts, hotly pursued by the Russians, was the trigger for the occupants of Nos. 2, 3 and 4 Redoubts to abandon their posts.[4]

Private Albert Mitchell, 13th Light Dragoons, later recalled how, while retreating, some of the Turks put up resistance:

'Two Cossacks came over the ridge together. One of them lanced a Turk in the back. Another Turk being a short distance ahead, they both made for him, but before they could reach him, Johnny, who had his piece loaded and bayonet fixed, turned suddenly and fired at the foremost, knocking him off his horse. The other coming up made a point, but where it touched the Turk I cannot say; but in an instant he had bayoneted the Cossack in the body, and he also fell from his horse. Johnny resumed his journey at a walk.'

Lucan, seeing the Turkish contingent fleeing from their posts, sent his interpreter, Mr Blunt, down into the South Valley to encourage the fleeing troops to rally alongside the 93rd in front of Kadikoi.

The Russian artillery now occupying Nos. 1 and 2 Redoubts targetted the British cavalry. Meanwhile, Russian troops penetrated the Allied lines as far as the Cavalry Camp, where they savagely slashed at the sick and non-effective horses at the picket-lines.

A shell splinter struck Paget's stirrup. He exclaimed, 'What was that?' to which his orderly, Private Samuel Parkes, replied: 'Piece of shell my lord, pretty nigh taking your foot off.' Moments later a round shot bounded through the ranks and killed a horse in the front rank of the 4th Light Dragoons. Paget was too close for comfort: 'It [the round shot] completely whizzed him round, and I can well remember the slosh that sounded as it went through the centre of his [the horse's] belly.'

At about the same time, Cornet George Maxwell Goad, 13th Light Dragoons, was wounded and his horse killed (his brother, Thomas, 13th Light Dragoons, was killed in the Charge; both served in D Troop).

Lord Cardigan now arrived to take over command of the Light Brigade. Meanwhile, Lord Raglan and his staff were in position on the Sapouné Heights. Here too, overlooking the battlefield, were the French General Bosquet and his staff. Bosquet despatched two brigades into the western end of the South Valley below the Chersonese Uplands, with General d'Allonville leading eight squadrons of the 1st and 4th Chasseurs d'Afrique onto the North Valley.

Time had been against the allies, and the lack of close support meant that the loss of the redoubts was inevitable given the Russians' overwhelming numbers. With reinforcements two hours away only Sir Colin Campbell's command and the cavalry stood between the enemy and Balaclava, should the enemy decide to press home their advantage.

Captain Ewart arrived before General Cathcart's headquarters at about 8 am but was given a cool reception:

Ewart: 'Lord Raglan requests you, Sir George, to move your division immediately to the assistance of the Turks.'

Cathcart: 'It's quite impossible, sir, for the 4th Division to move.'
Ewart: 'My orders are very positive. And the Russians are advancing on Balaclava!'

Cathcart: 'I can't help that, sir. It is impossible for my division to move, as the greater portion of the men have only just come from the trenches. The best thing you can do, sir, is to sit down and have some breakfast.'

Ewart: 'No thank you sir. My orders are to request that you will move your division immediately to the assistance of Sir Colin Campbell. I feel sure every moment is of consequence. Sir Colin has only the 93rd Highlanders with him. I saw the Turks in full flight.'

Cathcart: 'Well sir, if you will not sit down in my tent, you may as well go back to Lord Raglan and tell him I cannot move my division.'[5]

Captain Ewart retired, but reconsidered, and after three attempts finally persuaded Sir George to relent.

Cathcart: 'Very well, I will consult [with] my staff officer and see if anything can be done.'

The 4th Division would not begin its march until around 8.30 am. Captain McDonald, who had been despatched to the Duke of Cambridge with a similar request of his 1st Division, initiated a more speedy response.

Raglan's instruction was that the 4th Division should avoid the Woronzoff road, the more direct route, this he intended leaving free for the 1st Division, which had further to travel. Instead they took the more southerly route via the Chersonese Uplands. Raglan had expected to see the first British reinforcements some time between 9 and 9.30 am, but only the Chasseurs and Brandling's C Troop arrived on the battlefield before the Light Brigade charged.

As I Troop retired towards Kadikoi it met up with Shakespear and the ammunition wagons. Shortly afterwards Lord Cardigan cantered up, asking: 'Where are you going, Captain Shakespear? Who gave you leave to retire?' Shakespear replied, 'We are going for more ammunition, my lord.' Lord Lucan came over and signalled for Shakespear to continue. Then the Cavalry Division slowly retired westwards by alternate brigades and regiments and halted near their camp, the Light Brigade to the north of their camp site on the Causeway Height between Nos. 5 and 6 Redoubts. On arrival Cardigan gave the order, 'Draw swords'.

From his vantage point Lord Raglan saw that Lucan had placed the Heavy Brigade in too exposed a position without infantry support. Consequently, at about 8 am, he issued his First Order to the Cavalry Division:

'Cavalry to take ground to the left of the Second Line of redoubts [formerly] occupied by the Turks.'

Captain Weatherall, one of Raglan's ADCs, took twenty minutes to pick his way down the slope to the plain to deliver the message. Lord Lucan knew that the redeployment would leave Campbell's men isolated but was obliged to obey. He requested that Weatherall remain close at hand to confirm Raglan's intentions. This was necessary as the order was vague. It should have included compass directions and not used 'left' or 'right', which are relative. In addition, there was no accepted first or 'second line of redoubts', simply a line roughly following the Woronzoff road. These defences were of course no longer occupied by the Turks.

As Raglan's ADC, Captain Weatherall carried the same authority as Raglan in explaining his orders and so Lucan acted quite correctly in executing Raglan's vague commands in this way. However, it might have been better in the long run if Raglan had been discreetly informed that his written instructions were nonsensical.

Lieutenant Calthorpe, watching alongside Lord Raglan on the Sapouné Heights wrote:

'Lord Raglan ordered the brigade of light cavalry to take post on the ridge, just at the foot of the plateau where we were standing. From this point they could watch and take advantage of any movement on the part of the enemy.'

It was now close to 8.20 am. The Light Brigade was positioned below the Sapouné Heights at the western end of the North Valley, adjacent to No. 6 Redoubt, but out of sight of the Russian forces. Their disposition is outlined by Paget who recalled that the Light Brigade was in two groups, one 'facing the end of the ridge of redoubts east' and the other 'placed in somewhat of a hollow and facing more to the left [north], looking towards the lower ground that separated us from the Woronzoff road, as it wound down from the old telegraph station on the plateau'.[6]

Contrary to Calthorpe's statement, visibility was severely restricted for both brigades. The Light Brigade's view of the North Valley was obscured by the eastward slopes of No. 6 Redoubt's location and the Woronzoff road, while the Heavies, to the south, were partly hemmed in by walled vineyards and the divisional camps. It would appear that neither brigade commander employed vedettes to inform them of enemy movements, despite their 'blind' positioning, although Lord Paget would later witness the Charge of the Heavy Brigade from the hill occupied by No. 6 Redoubt. This suggests that certain Light Brigade officers positioned themselves on high points from where they could observe the enemy's movements.

The main Russian cavalry force crossed the Tractir Bridge at a little before 8.30 am when General Ryzhov deployed his Cavalry Brigade of some 2,000 mounted men, including the 11th Kiev Hussars which fielded eight squadrons, and six squadrons each of the 12th Ingermanland Hussars and the 1st Ural Cossacks. His cavalry was supported by eight 6-pounders of the 12th Light Horse Battery, and eight guns of the No.3 Don Cossack battery. Ryzhov's command advanced to occupy the North Valley unopposed.

By 8.30 am, however, there was, as of yet, still no sign of the Russians in the North Valley; their troops remained concentrated on the Causeway Heights and in pursuit of the fleeing Turkish troops towards Kadikoi, Russian artillery peppering them as they crossed the open ground. Lord Raglan looked to reinforce Campbell's Highlanders and the Turkish troops he had gathered – in effect reversing his earlier command when he had moved the Heavy Brigade from this precise role. Raglan's ADC, Captain Hardinge, was sent with what became the Second Order to the Cavalry:

'Eight squadrons of Heavy Dragoons to be detached towards Balaclava to support the Turks who are wavering.'

Hardinge handed the order to Lord Lucan only a few minutes after his brigade had adopted their new position. Once again Raglan's order made little sense if taken literally – it made no mention of Sir Colin Campbell's 93rd Highlanders, nor gave the geographical location, which was the defensive line now formed at Kadikoi. Once again, it required Raglan's ADC to explain Raglan's intentions.

General James Yorke Scarlett led four of his Heavy Dragoon regiments riding in two parallel columns across the South Valley back towards Kadikoi. The left column, the nearest to the Causeway Heights, rode in open column of troops, the second squadron of the Inniskillings taking the lead position, with the Scots Greys following in the rear. The right column, marching in threes, was formed of the first squadron of the Inniskillings, with the 5th Dragoon Guards some distance in the rear. Behind them were two squadrons of the 4th Dragoon Guards. Two squadrons of the Royals were left adjacent to the Light Brigade. Once in their new position there would be a mile of separation between the two divisions.

Ryzhov's force, joined by three squadrons of the 53rd Don Cossack Regiment began to arrive in the North Valley at about 8.45 am.

The advance attracted artillery fire and at about 9.15 am elements of Ryzhov's cavalry ascended the Causeway Heights to the east of No. 4 Redoubt. One section of the advance, numbering some 400-plus of the 12th Ingermanland Hussars, peeled off and made for the position held by Sir Colin Campbell, who's men were sheltering on the reverse slope of a hill, having minutes earlier attracted artillery fire.

Sir Colin Campbell later reported: 'As I found that round shot and shell began to cause some casualties among the 93rd Highlanders and the Turkish Battalions on their right and left flank, I made them retire a few paces behind the crest of the hill.'

The main body of the Russian attack continued up the North Valley, turning to cross the Heights – they would be engaged by the Heavies.

Under the command of Sir Colin Campbell was a formidable force including 550-plus Highlanders, 100 Marines, and a regular Turkish battalion supplemented by troops who had escaped from the redoubts. A further 100 men under Colonel Daveney's command were on their way from the siege operations to Balaclava hospital. Significantly, Campbell was supported by four 9-pounders and two 24-pounder howitzers, Ryzhov's intended target; two long-range guns of the inner defences manned by the Royal Marines would also be brought to bear – the artillery's role in the action has been much underplayed.

As the Russian cavalry advanced to well within rifle range, Sir Colin Campbell's men, armed with the '53 Enfield, sprang to their feet on command. They stood in a long line two ranks deep instead of four, or in a hollow square, for decades the formation for receiving cavalry where an outflanking manoeuvre would prove decisive.

Private John Macdonald of the 93rd Highlanders wrote:

'We had to receive the Russian cavalry in line, for had the 93rd Highlanders formed a square the Russians might have ridden past us and set fire to our shipping and stores. Sir Colin Campbell, rode out in front of the regiment and said, "93rd, you are not to form square, we will receive the charge in line." Our cavalry at this time were not on the field.'[7]

The British artillery fired several volleys of grapeshot while the enemy was still some distance off. But with the Russian cavalry coming on at a gallop, some of the Turkish troops broke rank and fled. Sir Colin exclaimed:

'Men, remember there is no retreat from here. You must die where you stand.'

Private John Scott shouted the reply that Campbell wanted to know, but probably didn't expect to hear:

'Aye, aye, Sir Colin, and needs be we'll do that.'

As the Russian cavalry closed in Sir Colin ordered a volley, probably too soon, as not a single saddle was emptied. But it caused the enemy to wheel away to the left. This threatened Campbell's weaker right flank, where the Turkish troops had fled. A second charge came and was met by a more effective volley from the grenadier company of the 93rd under Captain Ross.

Private Donald Campbell had quickly reloaded after the first volley, and calmly awaited the order to fire again:

'The Russians coming again towards us, we opened fire on them the second time and turned them. They seemed to be going away. We ceased firing and cheered. They wheeled about and made a dash at us again. We opened fire on them the third time. They came to a stand, wheeled about and rode off at a canter. We ceased firing and cheered. Our heavy guns fired after them. They were soon back over the hill the way they came.'

Almost simultaneously as the Highlanders fired their volleys, W Battery raked the enemy with grape and case shot which wrought havoc among the Russians who turned further to the left and away from Kadikoi. Some of the Highlanders broke rank in pursuit, but Sir Colin Campbell checked them: 'Ninety-third, ninety third!' he shouted, 'damn all that eagerness!' Rallied, the Russians made one final bid to break the line, as described by Private Campbell, but it held and the cavalry pulled away. Captain Shakespear, I Troop, RHA, observed: 'The guns worked them with grape and case; the enemy fled in great confusion, as artillery-fire poured into the enemy formation as they rode back over the Causeway, the heavy guns joining in with a few salvos of ball.'

William Howard Russell, ignoring the important role played by the artillery and the numerical odds which had always remained in Campbell's favour, wrote: 'The Russians dash at the Highlanders. The ground flies beneath their horses' feet, gathering speed at every stride, they dash on towards that thin red streak, topped with a line of steel.' His words, misquoted as the 'Thin Red Line', became synonymous with this Pyrrhic victory.

The second prong of the attack meanwhile had continued up the North Valley before coming under fire from the French gunners on the Sapouné Ridge. I Troop RHA, stationed to the rear of No. 6 Redoubt, had gained Cardigan's permission to move forward to engage Ryzhov's cavalry, which wheeled to the south, crossing the crest of the Causeway Heights, descending into the South Valley where it would encounter Scarlett's men, who were still in the process of redeploying.

Lord Lucan called over to Lord Cardigan. His exact words are a moot point, but he claimed to have said: 'I am going to leave you. Well, you'll remember you are placed here by Lord Raglan himself for the defence of this position. My instructions to you are to attack anything and everything that shall come within your reach, but you will be careful of columns or squares of infantry.'[8]

29

Lord Cardigan's recollection was different, and if accurate explains his inactivity:

'I had been ordered into a particular position by Lieutenant-General the Earl of Lucan, my superior officer, with orders on no account to leave it, and to defend it against any attack of the Russians; they did not however approach the position.'[9]

Riding in a south-south-westerly direction, General Scarlett's men emerged from behind a vineyard adjacent to the Causeway Heights. It was his ADC, Lieutenant Elliot, having glanced to his left, who drew Scarlett's attention to the mass of lance tips just visible to the north-east, over the other side of the ridge near No. 5 Redoubt. The enemy cavalry was about to take the Heavies in the left flank and Scarlett had only moments to act. Ideally he would have wished to attack the enemy in two extended lines, but between his force and the enemy were the southern edges of the vineyard and the tented camp of the Light Brigade; the latter would still have to be traversed.

General Scarlett gave the order, 'Left wheel into line', turning the two advanced regiments of the 2nd Inniskillings and the Scots Greys into a single line facing the enemy (the Scots Greys now on the left). The regiments in the rear, the 1st Inniskillings, 5th Dragoon Guards and 4th Dragoon Guards, turned likewise to form a Second Line (the 4th Dragoon Guards on the left, the 5th Dragoon Guards taking the central position, and the 1st Inniskilling the right).

About 100 yards to Scarlett's front was a body of upwards of 1,700 Russians under General Ryzhov, who called his column to a halt. The wings of his formation were the slowest to come to a stop, which gave the effect of throwing out elements of the 1st Ural Cossacks to his flanks. Two squadrons of the 12th Ingermanland Hussars formed the front rank of the main body with the second and third ranks including 11th Kiev Hussars and more men from the 1st Ural Cossacks. Eight guns of the 12th Light Horse Artillery battery were in the rear. Ryzhov had a further eight guns of No. 3 Don Cossack battery.

Lieutenant Richard Godman of the 5th Dragoon Guards:

'A large mass of cavalry came over the hill, and would in a few minutes have been in our lines, when we got the order to advance. Their front must have been composed of three regiments, and a very strong column in their rear, in all I suppose about 1,500 or 2,000 while we were not more than 800.'

The Russians had both the numerical advantage and the slope on their side. An immediate charge would surely have routed the four regiments of the Heavy Brigade. But General Ryzhov's hesitation, possibly to allow his cavalry to draw and prepare their carbines, allowed the British to seize back the initiative. Lord Lucan, who had galloped over towards the Heavies, twice ordered his duty trumpeter, Trumpet Major Joy, 17th Lancers, to sound the charge, but the brigade's officers are said to have followed regulations and turned their backs on the enemy while their sergeant majors 'dressed' their lines. Scarlett's second-in-command gave the order, 'Eyes Front!' and the officers wheeled to face the enemy.

Scarlett restrained the Inniskillings with his outstretched sword, instructing, 'the line will advance at a walk,' before his orderly trumpeter, Trumpet Major Monks, 5th Dragoon Guards, sounded the 'Trot', 'Gallop' and 'Charge', in rapid succession.

Captain Henry Clifford of the Rifle Brigade:

'The Scots Greys [2nd Dragoons] and the Inniskillings [6th] Dragoons advanced in a slow, steady trot towards them, the Russians looked at them as if fascinated, unable to move. The distance between the two Cavalries at last decreased to about 50 yards, and the shrill sound of the trumpet, ordering the Charge, first broke the awful silence.'

The 5th Dragoon Guards, advancing some distance in the rear, were hampered by the guide ropes of the Light Brigade's collapsed tents, and some stumbled and fell, while the 1st Squadron of the Inniskillings were on the right flank. The 4th Dragoons, who were at the rear, peeled off to the left (north) to provide support; their progress was slowed by rough terrain. General Scarlett and his small group made up of Trumpet Major Monks, his orderly, Sergeant Shegog, and his staff officers, Colonel Beaton and Lieutenant Elliot, led the front line, a body of 300 men, two squadrons of the Scots Greys and the 2nd Inniskillings.

General Ryzhov ordered the charge and the Russians moved forward at the 'walk' to meet the Heavy Brigade, the British having the forward momentum. Lieutenant Godman wrote:

'The enemy seemed quite astonished and drew into a walk and then a halt; as soon as they met, all I saw was swords in the air in every direction, the pistols going off, and everyone hacking away right and left. In a moment the Greys were surrounded and hemmed completely in; there they were, fighting back in the middle, the great bearskin caps high above the enemy.

'This was the work of the moment; as soon as we saw it, the 5th advanced and in they charged, yelling and shouting as hard as they could split, the row was tremendous, and for about five minutes neither would give way, and their column was so deep we could not cut through it.'

The Russians in the front rank had fired their carbines and pistols as the two formations closed. Men were seen to go down, including Lieutenant Colonel Henry Griffith of the Scots Greys, shot in the head.

Scarlett and his small group, some fifty yards ahead of the front line, had entered the enemy's centre. Moments later, the Inniskillings, commanded by

Lieutenant Colonel Dalrymple, clashed with the enemy, followed by the Scots Greys, and a frenzy of cutting and slashing began as they pushed forward and were engulfed by the Russian formation.

In the tight mêlée there was scarcely room to wield a sword. Several Russians surrounded an officer but Sergeant Major John Grieve forced his way close and intervened, decapitating one would-be assailant, causing the remainder to back away from him.[10]

Major William Charles Forrest, 4 Dragoon Guards: 'My own attention was occupied by the hussar who cut at my head, but the brass pot [helmet] stood well, and my head is only slightly bruised. I cut again at him, but do not believe that I hurt him more than he hurt me. I received a blow on the shoulder at the same time, which was given by some other man, but the edge must have been very badly delivered for it has only cut my coat and slightly bruised my shoulder.'[11]

Now the 2nd Inniskillings slammed into the Russian's left flank. Then the 4th Dragoon Guards hit the Russians, driving deep into their right flank. General Ryzhov's horse was shot and fell to the ground and he was only saved through the bravery of an NCO of the 12th Ingermanland Regiment.

The Scots Greys and 2nd Inniskillings somehow forced their way through the mass of the Russian cavalry and emerged from the other side of the Russian cavalry and faced the Cossacks in reserve. The adjutant of the Scots Greys called out: 'Rally the Greys! Rally the Greys!'

The 5th Dragoons then hit the Russians' right wing. The Russians met them with a volley from their carbines.

On seeing the Russian cavalry's advance, Lieutenant Colonel Yorke had led the Royals across the valley with the intention of following the 4th Dragoons Guards into the enemy's flank but only exchanged a few blows before the Russians broke off the engagement and fled in disorder over the Heights. Cautious that his men might be drawn onto artillery fire or the enemy's reserve, Colonel Edward Cooper Hodge, 4th Dragoons Guards, ordered the rally and recalled his squadrons not a moment too soon, as suddenly the artillery on the Fedioukine Heights opened fire. The Russian cavalry's sojourn into the South Valley had all the appearance of a feint, as General Liprandi had stationed lancers from the Composite Uhlan Regiment, supported by artillery, just beyond the ridge ready to engage the Heavy Brigade had they continued the pursuit. Most of the British force present remained unaware of this fact.

Sergeant C. McGregor of the Scots Greys wrote in a letter to his brother, dated 2 November 1854, in which he summarized the events:

'The Heavy Brigade made the same charge up into them, swords in hand, waving them over our heads, and cheering as we went. When within two yards of our enemy, they fired upon us with pistols; but ere they could get them out of their hands, we [got] into them with our swords like very devils, laying them low at every blow. On both sides the fighting was severe and the slaughter dreadful; here and there might be seen one of our men surrounded by half a dozen Russians, and the next moment two or three of his comrades flying to his assistance, leaving them [the Russians] lying dead on their horses' necks or cruppers, for being strapped into the saddle, they could not fall from their horses; and after peppering each other for some time, they retreated.'

Despite the odds stacked against them, the British had been able to push the Russians cavalry back. Lieutenant Richard Temple Godman, 5th Dragoon Guards, wrote home giving his account of the Heavy Brigade's charge:

'At length they turned and well they might, and the whole ran as hard as they could back up the hill, our men after them all broken up, and cutting them down right and left.' Godman believed the pursuit took them about 300 yards, before the officers gave the recall and the British artillery opened fire. According to his account the Heavy Brigade had lost seven men dead but many more were wounded, some mortally. Godman described the scene:

'The enemy being gone, and we all right, had time to look round, the ground was covered with dead and dying men and horses…. The ground was strewn with swords, broken, and whole, trumpets, helmets, carbines, etc. There must have been some forty or fifty of the enemy dead, besides wounded, for I went over the ground today to look at it. All the wounded were of course immediately taken off. Lord Raglan who was looking down from a hill close by sent an A.D.C. to say "Well done the Heavy Brigade." This is some satisfaction after all we have gone through this summer.'[12]

Captain Brandling, commanding C Troop RHA, attached to the Light Division, was in the right rear (south-south-west) of the Heavy Brigade immediately before its advance. His two 24-pounder howitzers were quickly unlimbered south of No. 5 Redoubt:

'The Russians, however, halted short of the ridge, and their officers could be seen holding up their swords and endeavouring to rally them, and get them into order, which they very soon would have done, but C Troop now came into action, and fired forty-nine shot and shell at them, at a range of between 700 and 800 yards, with admirable results, the 24-pounder howitzers making splendid practice.'[13]

Maude's I Troop, along with three Turkish guns located in a defence-work on elevated ground near The Col, added to the barrage.

Following the enemy's retreat Brandling's C Troop ascended the Causeway Heights where it adopted a position a little to the south west of No. 4 Redoubt. It was from here that they witnessed the later Charge.

The Heavies, with artillery support, had routed a far superior body of cavalry and prevented the loss of the guns and a potential assault on Balaclava Harbour. The action was greeted with loud 'huzzas' from the staff and onlookers situated on Sapouné Ridge, as witnessed by William Howard Russell:

'A Cheer burst from every lip – in the enthusiasm, officers and men took off their caps and shouted with delight – and they clapped their hands again and again.'

Russell recorded in his *Despatches from the Crimea* that:

'Raglan at once dispatched Lieutenant Cuzon, Aide-de-Camp, to convey his congratulations to Brigadier-General Scarlett and to say "Well done!" The gallant old officer's face beamed with pleasure when he received the message. "I beg to thank his lordship very sincerely" was his reply.'

The 93rd gave out a great cheer as the enemy disappeared over the Heights and minutes later Campbell rode over to Scarlett's brigade, lifted his hat by way of salute and said: 'Greys! Gallant Greys! I am sixty-one years old, and if I were young again I should be proud to be in your ranks.'

Considering that the frenzied cut and thrust of close-quarters action had lasted something like eight minutes, there were surprisingly few casualties on either side. Russian swords picked up off the battlefield were largely found to be blunt. The British, however, found that the enemy's thick uniform was often their saviour, while cuts to the neck and head proved more telling. An anonymous member of the Heavy Brigade described some of the injuries:

'Some fearful sabre-cuts were delivered. I saw one man with his head cloven to the chin, through helmet and all, so that the head appeared in two flaps; and another with his arm lopped off as if it had been done by a butcher's cleaver; and a third having a deep gash into the brain from behind, severing the head nearly in two, yet this unfortunate man was alive, and several times sat up in great agony, actually holding his head together with both hands.'[14]

Sir Evelyn Wood's reminiscences, which appeared in the *Fortnightly* in 1894, tell the same gruesome tale:

'The Naval brigade sent doctors down to attend to the wounded, and they described to us that evening the effect of some of the sword cuts inflicted by our Heavy Dragoons on the heads of the Russians as appalling; in some cases the head-dress and skull being divided down to the chin.'

Major Forrest of the 4th Dragoon Guards: 'I don't know what the loss of the Brigade was but we had only one man killed and five wounded and I did not see more than two or three English on the ground. We had one horse killed and three wounded, there were about twenty Russians on the ground or perhaps rather more.'

Forrest's view of the overall British losses were inaccurate, as during the engagement the British had lost seventy-eight men killed or wounded, with an unknown number suffering minor wounds that went unrecorded. The Russian casualties were estimated at 270, including Major General Khaletski who was wounded.

Scarlett's 750-800 men had taken on a force of 1,700-plus Russians. Both sides had artillery support, but only the British used theirs. In both the action of the 'Thin Red Line' and the Charge of the Heavy Brigade the courage and professionalism of the ordinary soldier was unquestionable, but the use of artillery proved the deciding factor.

There was but one question: where was the Light Brigade?

And the answer was that throughout the action the Light Brigade were standing by their horses. Despite being within striking distance (only the Royals, who were originally adjacent to them exchanging blows with the Russians), Lord Cardigan remained at his station.

John Brown, regimental trumpeter to the 17th Lancers, later wrote that Captain William Morris was quick to react to the appearance of the Russians and ordered 'threes right' ready to attack the enemy cavalry's right flank. Brown was ordered to sound the trot, which illicited a rebuke for Morris. 'What are you doing, Captain Morris? shouted Cardigan, quickly ordering, 'Front your regiment!' Morris obeyed, but pointing towards the enemy, 'Look there, my lord,' extolling. 'Let me take the regiment on the attack.'

'Remain where you are, sir, until you get orders!' barked Cardigan.

When the enemy cavalry began to retreat Captain Morris asked for permission to detach his 17th Lancers and to pursue the enemy. He was denied.

Private James Wightman later recalled the moment:

Morris: 'My Lord, are you not going to charge the flying enemy?'

Cardigan: 'No. We have orders to remain here.'

Morris: 'But my Lord, it is our positive duty to follow up this advantage.'

Cardigan: 'No. We must remain here.'

Morris: 'My Lord, do allow me to charge them with the 17th. Sir, my lord, they are in disorder.'

Cardigan: 'No, no, sir. We must not stir from here.'

35

Captain Morris returned to his position in front of the 17th Lancers and slapped his leg angrily with his sabre and, probably within Cardigan's earshot he shouted, 'My God, my God, what a chance we are losing!'[15]

Private Albert Mitchell of the 13th Light Dragoons too was a witness:

'All this time we were expecting an order to pursue, but no order came, and soon the opportunity was lost. We all felt certain that if we had been sent in pursuit we should have cut up many of them, besides capturing many prisoners.'[16]

In the immediate aftermath of the Heavy Brigade's action Lord Lucan sent his son, Lord Bingham, with a cutting message for Cardigan, stating that 'he desired that Lord Cardigan would always remember that when he [Lucan] was attacking in front it was his [Cardigan's] duty to support him by a flank attack, and that Lord Cardigan might always depend upon receiving from him similar support.'[17]

Lord George Paget had a good view of the action. He had dismounted and was standing on a hillock near No. 6 Redoubt. He later wrote:

'Anyone who has ridden, or attempted to ride, over an old vineyard will appreciate the difficulties of moving among its tangled roots and briars, and its swampy holes. The Heavy Brigade had only just time to scramble over the dry ditch that usually encircled the vineyards when they came in contact with their foes. This has been called a charge! How inapt a word! The Russian cavalry came at a smart pace up to the edge of the vineyard, but the pace of the Heavy Brigade never could have exceeded eight miles an hour during their short advance across the vineyard. They had the appearance (to me) of just scrambling over and picking their way through the broken ground. They [the Russians] stop! The Heavies struggle – flounder over the ditch and trot into them!'[18]

It is not clear how much of the engagement Captain Nolan witnessed but historians have assumed that he was incensed by the opportunity apparently lost by the Light Brigade. His belief was that cavalry commanders must see a tactical advantage and act in an instant. Nolan was encountered by George Higginson, adjutant to the Grenadier Guards, while returning to the Sapouné Ridge, 'riding up from the lower ground, apparently in search of the adjutant-general [Estcourt]', having delivered a message. 'The impression he gave me during the short conversation we held together, that under the stress of some great excitement he had lost self-command.'[19]

But could the Light Brigade have played a more effective role?

When Scarlett charged, the Light Brigade were something like 500 yards away to the west. The Royals, who were in a similar location, galloped into the fray but were only able momentarily to strike at the left flank of the enemy; there was no opportunity to cut off the enemy, only to follow. Meanwhile, as the Russians retreated, Liprandi sent forward his reserve from the Composite

Uhlan Regiment, which immediately came under artillery fire and were ordered to retire. Had the Light Brigade followed the Royals and had both pursued the enemy it seems highly likely they would have come up against the Uhlans, as well as concentrated infantry and artillery fire. All was therefore not as it seemed, and the Russians had overwhelming forces in position ready to attack the British cavalry had they not been called to a halt and ordered to retire.

By 9.30 am the Russian cavalry had retired and the situation looked to have stabilized.

Lord Cardigan was desperately frustrated at not being able to engage the Russian cavalry and was heard to exclaim, 'Damn those Heavies! They have had the laugh of us this day!'[20] Despite the ongoing battle, Cardigan left his command and rode over to congratulate Scarlett and his senior officers on their victory.

The Russians' initial strikes towards Balaclava had been thwarted but the danger was still present, and at 9.45 am there was still no sign of the 1st and 4th Divisions. Lord Raglan despatched General Airey to General Cathcart and the Duke of Cambridge with orders to retake the Causeway Heights: 'Lord Raglan wishes you to advance immediately and capture the redoubts.'[21]

Little has been made of the fact that neither commander acted upon this direct order, their unwillingness to attack once they eventually reached the vicinity of the Causeway Heights being a contribution to the losses suffered by the Light Brigade.

The Russian cavalry re-formed in the North Valley (with elements of Colonel Bromben's Light Horse Artillery No. 12 Battery on their flanks) to the rear of eight guns of Colonel Prince Obolensky's No. 3 Don Cossack battery. Their position was further defended by eight battalions of infantry, supported by four squadrons of cavalry and fourteen guns located on the Fedioukine Heights, all under the overall command of Major-General Zhaboritski. Not only were Nos. 1-3 Redoubts in Russian hands, but the Causeway Heights were held by Russian infantry including the Odessa Regiment, with thirty-two artillery pieces largely on the south-facing slopes (some of these field pieces would be limbered up during the Charge and repositioned in time to fire on the Light Brigade). General Liprandi located a further six squadrons of Jeropkine's lancers strategically on either side of the valley, at the foot of the Fedioukine Heights and partially concealed in a ravine to the side of the Causeway Heights (these men would later engage the Light Brigade during its retreat).

Having updated his orders to the 1st and 4th Divisions, Lord Raglan now issued his Third Order to the Cavalry Division:

'Cavalry to advance and take advantage of any opportunity to recover the Heights. They will be supported by infantry which have been ordered [to] advance on two fronts.'

Once again Raglan's written order was lacking details. Presumably his words were to be explained by his ADC, Weatherall, although there is no indication that Lucan asked for further clarification. Evidently Lord Lucan believed that he was to await infantry support, a reasonable interpretation as cavalry only attacked fixed infantry or artillery positions in a support role, coordinated with an infantry assault. Military doctrine was clear: the taking and holding of a defensive position was the role of infantry.

In preparation for their attack against the lost redoubts Lord Lucan ordered the cavalry to mount. The Light Brigade formed up at the western end of the North Valley, with the Heavy Brigade in an adjacent position in the South Valley close to No. 6 Redoubt. Lord Lucan and his staff were roughly halfway between the two. Separating the brigades were the Causeway Heights. The French generals do not appear to have been given any orders relating to Raglan's plans but were on hand to go into action should they be required. The 1st and 4th Chasseurs d'Afrique were positioned at the western end of the North Valley to the north-west of the Light Brigade.

General Airey rode back up to Raglan's position bringing news of the impending arrival of the 1st and 4th Divisions. The Guards had forged their way ahead but were still twenty minutes away. General Cathcart was marching along the less direct route to take up station in the area of No. 4 Redoubt. Raglan by now was becoming impatient as the enemy remained in control of the redoubts and he wanted a speedy resolution.

The men of the Light Brigade were, by this time, in position but had been ordered to dismount. They were keyed up and waiting for orders to go into action. In the meantime they wanted to keep warm.

Looking down from his position Raglan could see that the Cavalry Division was dismounted. They were not looking to sit out the engagement, they were ready for combat but were simply resting their weary mounts. Private Albert Mitchell, 13th Light Dragoons, sets the scene, although writes with hindsight:

'We were now dismounted, and soon we could see the enemy had placed a number of guns across the lower part of the valley nearly a mile and a half from us. At the same time a field battery ascended a hill on our left front, where it was placed in a position facing us. They also placed a field battery on the slope between the redoubts and the valley on our right. The rest of the enemy's troops were placed in rear of his guns, except those who held the captured redoubts, and some others who were employed in carrying off the guns [*sic*] lost by the Turks, as also a battalion or two of infantry, who were extended along the slope towards the lower end of the valley.'[22]

Private John Doyle, 8th Hussars, recalled how Lieutenant Colonel Shewell (generally referred to as Colonel Shewell) had reprimanded a number of his men for smoking while they had their swords drawn. He then came across a sergeant holding a pipe and this was just too much for him:

'When a sergeant, named Williams [804 Sergeant William Williams], lit his pipe, Colonel Shewell ordered him to be made prisoner and his sword and carbine taken from him, and given to a private to carry on his saddle. The sergeant was not ordered to fall into the rear, so he came with us, and was cut to pieces. Poor fellow! Being unarmed, he was not able to defend himself.'[23]

The British troops remained in a defensive position and Raglan was agitated at their apparent inaction. At this moment one of his staff drew his attention to movement which appeared to indicate that the enemy was preparing to remove the captured guns from one of the redoubts – in an age when the life of combatants was seen as cheap, the loss of artillery pieces was the measure of defeat in battle.

The time was 10.45 am and it appeared as though the infantry's delayed response was going to cost Raglan dearly. The first infantry column remained ten minutes away, only Lord Lucan's command was immediately available to save the guns.

Lord Raglan now dictated his Fourth Order to the Cavalry, which was intended as an update to the Third Order to the Cavalry. Lord Airey scribbled down Raglan's words in pencil on a small piece of paper:

'Lord Raglan wishes the Cavalry to advance rapidly to the front – follow the Enemy and try to prevent the Enemy carrying away the guns – Troop Horse Artillery may accompany – French cavalry is on your left. R. Airey. Immediate.'

According to Lord Raglan it was always his intention that the lost redoubts should be attacked and taken by the Cavalry Division. Lord Paget maintained that had this order been correctly delivered, then the outcome of the Charge of the cavalry unsupported by infantry might have been similar to the Charge into the North Valley:

'If it be correct that the object of Lord Raglan's last order was that the cavalry should, instead of going down the valley, have made an advance along the Causeway Heights, to recapture the guns on the redoubts, then the nature of the ground must be considered, and I think I am right in saying that such an advance would have been attended with much difficulty, the ground being broken and uneven, and of such configuration that the cavalry would have acted on it at a great disadvantage.'[24]

Adye concurred with Lord Paget when he wrote: 'The writer is not, of course, advocating that the charge which took place was a sensible act of war, but the attack which Raglan thought he was ordering was surely of the same order of military lunacy. Even [re-taking] Redoubt "3" was a daunting task and

Redoubts "2" and "1" were much stronger. The only reasonable way to re-take the redoubts was by infantry, supported by cavalry and artillery, moving down the line of the Causeway Heights, attacking each fort in its turn, and this is indeed what Raglan had originally intended and ordered.'[25]

Colonel Fox-Strangeways, RHA, who watched most of the events of the day, was clear that: 'There was no other safe way of attempting to re-take the position than by advancing along the crests and slopes of the ridge, and winning it back bit by bit.'[26]

Some sources maintain that Raglan's nephew and ADC Lieutenant Somerset Calthorpe was the next in line to take despatches and it should have been he who carried the fateful order. But as Airey held it out, Lord Raglan intervened: 'No. Send Nolan.'

Others disagreed. It was Saul David who said that it was Raglan's 'duty aide, Captain Leslie' who should have taken the order.[27] Another witness suggests that it was always intended that Louis Nolan should take the despatch: 'then after he called General Airey and spoke with him. We saw the latter, taking his sabretache, using it as an improvised desk, to write a note in crayon. With the note written, the two generals exchanged some further words, and Raglan, calling Captain Nolan…entrusted him with the paper to carry to Lord Lucan.'[28]

If this were the case, then Raglan possibly considered that time was of the essence and Nolan was the more accomplished horseman. And, according to Lieutenant Calthorpe, 'Previous to his departure he [Nolan] received careful instruction from both Lord Raglan and the Quartermaster-General.'

Apart from when absent delivering an earlier despatch, Nolan would have been at Lord Raglan's side where he could follow the battle's progress, observing Raglan's strategy to counter the Russian threat – above all it was the role of the ADCs to follow, understand and clearly convey Raglan's intentions; they were not simply couriers.

As Nolan wheeled his mount to ride off down the ridge, Lord Raglan called out: 'Tell Lord Lucan the cavalry is to attack immediately.'[29] And with these words he sealed the fate of the Light Brigade.

There was an additional twist reported by Calthorpe. Brigadier General Hugh Rose, the British liaison officer with the French Army, was present on Sapouné Ridge and recalled that Nolan in a 'much excited' state replied, 'I'll lead them myself, I'll lead them on.' If this were true, Nolan was going against all military protocol and the mere suggestion of his usurping Lucan's authority ought to have led to his immediate recall by Raglan.

Nolan galloped off, taking, as Raglan had anticipated, the most direct route, riding almost straight down the steep escarpment, reaching the plain in fifteen minutes.

Chapter 5

The Charge of the Light Brigade

The Light Brigade was formed up in two lines at the western end of the North Valley. The front rank, from left to right, was composed of the 11th Hussars, 17th Lancers, and 13th Light Dragoons. The Second Line was made up of the 4th Light Dragoons and the 8th Hussars. Each regiment was in extended line, two deep.

Nolan reached the valley floor and rode through the gap between the 17th Lancers and the 13th Light Dragoons; the time was about 11 am. Private James William Wightman recalled the moment:

'Captain Nolan, of the 15th Hussars, suddenly galloped out to the front through the interval between us and the 13th, and called out to Captain Morris [Captain William Morris], who was directly in my front, "Where is Lord Lucan?" "There," replied Morris, pointing, "there, on the right front!" Then he added, "What is it to be, Nolan? – are we going to charge?" Nolan was off already in Lord Lucan's direction, but as he raced away he shouted to Morris over his shoulder, "You will see! You will see!"'[1]

Nolan galloped up to Lord Lucan, urgently handing over the hastily-written Fourth Order to the Cavalry, which Lucan read, but did not fully understand as he had positioned himself roughly halfway between his two brigades where he could only see the guns on the Fedioukine Heights and in the North Valley – remarkably his chosen location placed him out of sight of the Redoubts which had only recently been captured by the Russians and which Raglan's Third Order to the Cavalry had indicated was his objective. Furthermore, the Redoubts were from where he might anticipate the Russians would make their next move.

Lucan recalled the brief and stilted conversation which took place between the two men:

Nolan: 'Lord Raglan's orders are that the cavalry should attack immediately.'
Lucan: 'Attack, sir! Attack what? What guns, sir? Where and what to do?'
Nolan: 'There, my Lord! There is your enemy! There are your guns!'[2]

41

As had been the case with Raglan's previous orders, the written instruction made no sense from Lucan's perspective. The enemy was not retiring any guns that Lucan was aware of, while it was equally unclear as to what was meant by 'advance rapidly to the front'.

If Lucan were to follow Raglan's written order to advance to the front, he would have to send the Cavalry to two separate destinations: the Light Brigade fronted onto the North Valley, and the Heavy Brigade, the South Valley. When asked for clarification, Nolan had to gesture either to the North or South Valley. He could not have pointed to the Causeway Heights (i.e. the South Valley) and be mistaken for pointing to No. 3 Don Cossack battery, for which he would have pointed into the North Valley – two completely different locations.[3]

During the encounter between Nolan and Lucan, the latter was firmly left with the impression that he was to attack the guns at the eastern end of the North Valley. Those around Lucan had formed the same opinion.

Lord Lucan was in the company of his interpreter, John Blunt, and his ADC, Captain Charles Pyndar Beauchamp Walker, both key witnesses who were clear that Captain Nolan pointed to the location of No. 3 Don Cossack battery. Another eyewitness to the events was Lieutenant Henry Fitzhardinge Berkeley Maxse. As Cardigan's ADC he would have had privileged access to the dialogue between Lucan and Cardigan and he was clear in his mind that Nolan indicated that they should charge No. 3 Don Cossack battery.[4]

Captain Walker, as ADC to Lord Lucan, was also close at hand. He too was certain that Nolan indicated that the attack was to be made against No. 3 Don Cossack battery:

'An order was brought by an officer personally hostile to him [Lord Lucan], and received without the discretion fitting of an officer of high rank. Lord Lucan, instead of taking the order and exercising his own judgement as to how he carried it out, asked Captain Nolan what he was to attack, and was answered by his [Nolan's] pointing to the Russians drawn up across the valley, with the words: "There, my Lord, is your enemy, there are the guns."'[5]

John Blunt (interpreter) witnessed the encounter and noted Lucan looked 'Surprised and irritated at the impetuous and disrespectful attitude and tone of Captain Nolan. Lord Lucan looked at him sternly, but made no answer.' Lucan moments later gave Blunt the order for safe-keeping as he would not Charge – Airey had not made a copy for his own record and would later request one.

Although not within earshot, Captain Arthur Tremayne, 13th Light Dragoons, was within sight of Lucan when he received Raglan's order: 'I saw Lucan's evident astonishment at the message; Nolan pointed.'

When it was suggested to him that Nolan might have been indicating towards the guns on the Causeway Heights, Tremayne's response was direct and to the point: 'I think not.'[6]

Remarkably, Lord Lucan did not request that Nolan remain with him or his ADC to advise on the execution of Raglan's order, which he had done earlier in the day when instructed to carry out a far simpler manoeuvre – to redeploy the Heavy Brigade in support of the 93rd Highlanders. Having been dismissed by Lord Lucan, Nolan rode over to Lord Cardigan, then in front of the 13th Light Dragoons, to request permission to ride with the Light Brigade. A number of Chargers saw this exchange and believed that Nolan brought the order that led to the Charge directly to Cardigan.

Private William Butler, 17 Lancers: 'Captain Nolan, riding at full speed, came towards our Brigadier, Lord Cardigan, Major Morris (17th) and Colonel Dougherty, 13th Light Dragoons, [who] were talking together mounted, when the word to mount was given.'[7]

Having spoken briefly with Lord Cardigan, Nolan rode over to his friend Morris who granted him permission to ride with the 17th Lancers. It seems inconceivable that Morris would not have asked after their intended objective – perhaps most damning, therefore, was the fact that Morris never questioned that the Charge went in the direction other than that intended by Nolan.[8]

Private James Wightman, 17th Lancers, recalled the moment:

I distinctly remember that Nolan returned to the brigade, and having a mere momentary talk with Cardigan, at the close of which he drew his sword with a flourish, as if greatly excited. The blood came to his face – I seem to see him now; and then he fell back a little way into Cardigan's left rear, somewhat in front of and to the right of Captain Morris.

Corporal James Ikin Nunnerley, 17th Lancers, was within earshot when Nolan approached his friend and heard at least part of the dialogue between the two officers. He states that Nolan's words were, 'Now, Morris, for a bit of fun.'[9] Frustratingly, Morris' response, if any, is lost to history.

Lord Cardigan had not yet been officially informed of Raglan's 'wish', although there may have been an exchange between ADCs. Cardigan does, however, record the events surrounding Lucan, giving him the fateful order:

'Lucan came in front of my brigade and said, "Lord Cardigan, you will attack the Russians in the valley." I said, "Certainly, my lord," dropping my sword at the same time [in salute]; "but allow me to point out to you that there is a battery in front, a battery on each flank, and the ground is covered with Russian riflemen." Lucan, however, replied: "I cannot help that; it is Lord Raglan's positive order that the Light Brigade is to attack the enemy."'[10]

Each written instruction received by Lord Lucan throughout the morning had been vague and was little more than an aide memoir, Raglan's ADCs being required to furnish the exact details of the command. Although Lucan briefed Cardigan to attack the guns in the North Valley, he was aware of the earlier loss of the Turkish-held redoubts and the guns therein. Meanwhile, Cardigan respectfully pointed out that there were guns and infantry along the Fedioukine Heights so there were multiple batteries which could have been the cavalry's intended objective.

Lucan, therefore, knew that the Russians held strong positions on both flanks of the North Valley as well as the gun-line on its eastern plain. He was aware that on the battlefield there were at least three batteries, but Nolan's directions had been unequivocal.

Cardigan heard the bugle-call for the brigade to mount. There wasn't a moment to lose: 'I sent one of my aides-de-camp to reconnoitre the ground.'

Cardigan may have been mistaken here, as it was in fact Captain Walker, one of Lord Lucan's ADCs, who rode forward to examine the enemy's disposition on the Fediuokine Heights:

'Before they opened fire I saw these guns – or rather – I saw the horses – pulled out my glass, and in a moment saw what they were, and how completely they swept the whole length of our advance. I would not live over that moment for a kingdom.'[11]

This information would have been quickly relayed to Lord Lucan and to the Cavalry Division's senior officers.

Captain Walker's surveying of the battlefield was seen by Thomas Morley, 17th Lancers, who later confused the ADC for Cardigan in his account: 'Lord Cardigan galloped on perhaps three hundred yards to the front and to the right to a piece of slightly rising ground, evidently to reconnoitre the position of the Russian Army and the best ground for the brigade.'[12]

In Lucan's despatch to Lord Raglan, dated 27 October 1854, he says he ordered Cardigan 'to advance in two lines' and to do this 'very steadily and keep his men well in hand'. He later explained, 'I carefully divided the Light Brigade into three lines, to expose as few men as possible in the First Line, and that the First Line should be efficiently supported.'[13]

Cardigan later claimed to have been unaware that the 11th Hussars had been ordered to form a second line in direct support of the 17th Lancers, thus reducing the width of the front line to 154 yards, less than that of the eight guns (some eyewitness accounts state that there were as many as twelve guns at the west end of the valley, but most British historians refer to a single battery of eight guns. Two contemporary Russian sources, one by Staff Captain Yevgenii Arbuzov, and the other by an anonymous officer in No. 3 Don Cossack battery, state that on the right of No. 3 Don Cossack battery, were part of Colonel

Bromben's Light Horse Artillery No. 12 Battery. The latter account, however, includes a number of major errors) at twenty-two-yard intervals.

Meanwhile Lord Cardigan rode over to Lord Paget who was a little ahead of the 4th Light Dragoons in the Second Line:

'You will take command of the Second Line, and I expect your best support – mind, your best support.' This repetition rankled Paget, although Cardigan evidently appreciated the inherent difficulties in forming the second wave of attack under such circumstances. In the event Paget completely lost the shape of the Second Line, which arrived in separate waves, each regiment acting independently at and beyond the gun-line.

It may have been while Cardigan was speaking to Paget that Lucan ordered the 11th Hussars to fall back: 'Douglas, withdraw your Regiment and support the 17th Lancers.'[14]

Paget was also unaware that the 11th Hussars would fall back behind the 17th Lancers, tending to support Cardigan's account that he did not order this change in the brigade's formation and therefore was not in a position to inform his subordinate.

In the event, the divergence of the 8th Hussars during the Charge was a cause of some annoyance to Lord Paget as it materially damaged the impact of the Second Line. Paget would later write:

'It is an indisputable fact that the 8th Hussars were placed under my command by Lord Cardigan; that I ordered them to advance and named the 4th as the "regiment of direction" and that during the advance they became disengaged from the 4th, without, and contrary to my orders. It is fact, also, that my strict duty would have been to report Colonel Shewell's disobedience of orders, on my return from the Charge, and it is due to me to explain why I did not do so. This was because I knew the man with whom I had to deal – one of the most honourable, gallant, conscientious and single-minded men it had ever been my good fortune to be associated with. I therefore gave him credit for that which I felt sure would be his due – i.e. for acting to the best of his powers in the circumstances in which he was placed; and I determined, therefore, before taking any step, to talk the matter over quietly with him, and most amply was I rewarded for what I think was an act of forbearance on my part: for he then explained to me satisfactorily that he had acted in the emergency of the moment in the best manner that he could have done.'

Astonishingly, Lord Lucan did not use the French artillery on the Sapouné Ridge, although they fired independently. Nor, it appears, did he send orders to

C Troop RHA, then on the south side of the Causeway Heights (although they did act independently), while I Troop accompanied the Light Brigade part of the way but did not unlimber and deploy their guns, facts keenly observed by George Smith, 11th Hussars:

'Strange as it may seem, although 12 Horse Artillery guns were at this moment close at hand, the divisional general made no use of them before he ordered the attack. It had been the custom on brigade field days for artillery fire to precede a cavalry attack. Had this simple rule been followed out on the Causeway Heights for a few minutes before we moved off it would have been of the greatest advantage to us.'[15]

Had the guns of C and I Troops RHA engaged in a duel with the Russian batteries, they might well have taken a number of Russian guns out of action. Both troops would have required about five minutes to deploy. Equally importantly, the movement of the guns and subsequent artillery duel might have given Raglan the impression that his order was being carried out 'immediately'. These few minutes delay would have allowed the 1st and 4th Divisions to form up ready for an assault on the redoubts, while an ADC could have been despatched to liaise with the 1st and 4th Chasseurs d'Afrique, half a mile away, to the west, to coordinate their assault on the positions on the Fedioukine Heights. This was certainly the feeling of Cornet Fiennes Wykeham Martin, acting adjutant, 4th Light Dragoons:

'If we had waited ten minutes more for our own Infantry and the French Cavalry, we should have retaken all the forts and annihilated their army.'[16]

Troop Sergeant Major George Smith had been waiting with the rest of his troop in eager anticipation of action which seemed imminent, as he later explained:

'We had not been long in position when Lord Cardigan received the order from Lord Lucan to attack the battery of guns which was placed across the valley immediately in our front about a mile off. There was likewise a battery on the Fedioukine Hills on our left and the enemy had possession of the redoubts on our right, where another battery and riflemen were posted. This army in position numbered about 24,000 and we, the Light Brigade, not quite 700.'[17]

Waiting on their imminent orders, the men of the Light Brigade had observed the build-up of troops and artillery defending the North Valley – if they were to advance, there would be no escaping the carnage. Captain Thomas Hutton, 4th Light Dragoons, wrote: 'A child might have seen the trap that was laid for us, every private dragoon did.'[18]

The light cavalry had been ridiculed since their arrival in the theatre, and the men were aware that their senior officer might become reckless in search of glory. Private John Richardson of the 11th Hussars recalled: 'Every private soldier could see what a mistake was being made, but all we had to do was obey orders.'

Major de Salis, 8th Hussars, summed up the men's understanding of the impossible odds that they faced if they were to advance against No. 3 Don Cossack battery; and there was no indication from any officer that they were to do anything other than to charge down the valley – no officer ever wrote differently. De Salis recalled: 'When the order was received by the Light Cavalry to advance, there was not one officer or man but who felt there was certain death to all.'[19]

Cardigan gave the order: 'Draw swords'. He faced the brigade and in his strong hoarse voice gave the momentous word of command, as recalled by Private James William Wightman of the 17th Lancers:

'The Brigade will advance. First squadron of the 17th Lancers direct.'[20]

It would be the role of Captain White to provide the pace and direction of the Charge, maintaining five lengths (fifteen yards) distance between Cardigan and the front line. It was imperative that a steady pace was maintained. A cavalry charge would normally be delivered over a relatively short distance in response to an obvious weakness in the enemy's position. At Balaclava the horses would have to cover an unprecedented distance of one and a quarter miles, part of which was vineyards and ploughed land. Breaking into a gallop too early would have blown the horses and they would have arrived at No. 3 Don Cossack battery in penny packets. Cardigan was acutely aware that they needed to keep their cool; only by following Regulation speeds[21] could he deliver a tight formation to their objective.[22]

Lord Cardigan had the reputation of being pompous and difficult to get on with – he was better suited to Horse Guards than the theatre of operations – but with the prospect of almost certain death at the head of his brigade, he acted with dignity and supreme courage. Private Wightman described that as he led the Brigade Cardigan remained 'Calm as on parade – calmer indeed than usual on parade – stately, square and erect, with his stern face and soldierly bearing, master of himself, his brigade and his charger, Lord Cardigan looked the ideal cavalry leader.'

Cardigan positioned himself five lengths ahead of the First Line, and two (five yards) in front of his staff officers, Lieutenant Maxse and Cornet Wombwell. He turned to Trumpeter William Brittain and, according to Private Wightman, 'quietly said, "Sound the Advance!" and wheeled his horse, facing the dark mass at the far end of the valley which we knew to be the enemy. The trumpeter sounded "Walk"; after a few horse-lengths came the "Trot."'[23]

The calls were taken up by the regimental trumpeters. As he moved forward, Cardigan, not expecting to survive, muttered audibly, 'Here goes the last of the Brudenells.'

Among those gathered on Sapouné Ridge, aware that the Cavalry Division was going into action, was William Howard Russell of *The Times*. Looking down at his pocket-watch as the Light Brigade edged forward, he noted the time: 11.10 am.

The front line moved off together, the 11th Hussars delaying their advance before falling in behind the 17th Lancers, with 100 yards of separation. The Second Line proper, composed of the 4th Light Dragoons and 8th Hussars, maintained the same interval. On the Fedioukine Heights the 12-pounder guns and 18-pounder howitzers of the No. 1 Battery of Positions of the 16th Artillery Brigade prepared to fire into the Light Brigade's flank as soon as they entered their field of fire.[24] On the Causeway Heights, anticipating an attack on their positions, the Odessa Regiment and its artillery support began to pull back from the area around No. 3 Redoubt, towards No. 2 Redoubt where they formed into squares. At the far end of the valley General Ryzhov, 6th Hussar Brigade, had ridden forward to converse with Colonel Prince Obolensky, commander of the No. 3 Don Cossack battery (composed of four 6-pounder guns and four 9-pounder howitzers, with 22-yard intervals between each gun, and therefore presenting a 154-yards front).

The gunners manning the battery saw the Light Brigade was on the move and would come within range; it was not yet clear as to their objective.

Meanwhile the brigade's pace had increased and the First Line covered about 100 yards and, according to Troop Sergeant Major George Smith, the 11th Hussars were just in motion when the first volley burst harmlessly ahead of the brigade (both Private Wightman and Lord Paget thought that the front line had ridden 200 yards before the guns opened fire).

Captain Morris saw Nolan appear to force the pace by spurring his horse on and called out: 'That won't do, Nolan! we've a long way to go and must be steady!'

Nolan now rode across the front, drawing level and then slightly ahead of Lord Cardigan, waving his sabre in the air and shouting. Cardigan was only riding at a brisk trot and therefore was easily caught up with by Nolan who was said to be acting erratically and waving his sword in the air and shouting. However, neither Cardigan nor the officers in close proximity believed that Nolan was trying to attract their attention and change the direction of the charge. On the contrary, to his dying day Cardigan was adamant that Nolan was trying to lead the brigade and force the pace.

When Nolan was approximately five yards ahead of Lord Cardigan, an 18-pounder howitzer shell fired from the southern slopes of the Fedioukine Heights exploded, a splinter ripping into his chest.

From his position, Private Wightman had a clear view of the incident:

'I saw the shell explode of which a fragment struck him. From his raised sword-hand dropped the sword, but the arm remained erect. But all the other limbs so curled in on the contorted trunk as by a spasm, that we wondered how for the moment the huddled form kept the saddle. The weird shriek and the awful face haunt me now to this day, the first horror of that ride of horrors.'[25]

Corporal Thomas Morley was riding about seventy yards from Nolan, and to the rear of his position:

'Nolan rode away from the 13th at speed to the front of the 17th Lancers, reached a position in front of the centre of the 17th, gave his order "three's right" with his horse's head facing the regiment, at the same time waving his sword to the right, which signified "take the ground to the right," then turned his horse and galloped towards the Causeway Heights, still pointing with his sword in that direction. At that moment a shell exploded and a piece of it struck him in the left breast near the heart. He remained in the saddle until the horse had cleared the right flank of the first squadron of the 17th, in column of threes, when the horse, finding the rider had no control over it, turned sharply to the right – the way home – throwing the lifeless body head-first on the ground.'

Morley's recollection was of a far more controlled gesture and command, which was obeyed. Morley was seventy yards away, while others who were much closer heard no such command. According to Morley:

'The 17th had instantly followed his direction and gone "three's right." The 13th had gone straight on instead of checking, as they should have done to respond to our movements. They were perhaps 25 or 30 yards in front of us when Nolan fell. At that juncture I heard Sergeant-Major [Corporal] J. Nunnerley, of the 1st squadron, shout in a loud voice, "17th Lancers, Front forward!" (I belonged to the second squadron). We went three's left, the right flank of the second squadron lapping the left flank of the first one-fourth its front or more, so that the two flanks became merged together.'[26]

Morley's words appear to corroborate the account of Corporal Nunnerley, which had been put into print some eight years earlier (but still thirty years after the event), when he claimed to have corrected the Lancers' change in direction, giving the counter-command 'Front forward', bringing them back into line again.[27]

While these stories appear to support the idea that Nolan had tried to correct an error, this goes against all of the evidence concerning his relaying of the Fourth Order. Furthermore, Cardigan never looked back from the moment that the Charge began. He was only aware of Nolan's actions as he rode across and in front of him – as if to take command. This runs contrary to the accounts of Morley and Nunnerley, as Cardigan would surely have heard Nolan's command of 'three's right', had it been given.

Lord Cardigan's ADC, Lieutenant Maxse, was closer to the incident and was irritated when he read Kinglake's account, published in 1868, suggested that Nolan had ridden across the front of the brigade with the intention of redirecting the charge. His letter dated 'Heligoland, June 22' was published in *The Times* of 28 June 1868:

'I have no recollection of his divergence in the manner described by Mr Kinglake either by deed or gesture until after he was struck; then his horse took the line pointed out by Mr Kinglake.'

In a letter to his brother, Maxse was more categorical and damning of Airey's ADC: 'Nolan was killed close to me and Kinglake's account is absurd as to Nolan wanting to charge any other guns but those he did.'[28]

Lord Cardigan was convinced that Nolan was trying to force the pace when he was hit, and then immediately retired; he did not understand that Nolan was fatally hit, and was affronted at his actions and involuntary shriek: 'A shell fell within reach of my horse's feet and [of] Captain Nolan, who was riding across the front retreating with his arms up through the interval of the brigade.' He did not see or hear anything that might have led him to believe that Nolan was trying to redirect the brigade.

Nolan's body was thrown from his horse at the rear of the 13th Light Dragoons. Troop Sergeant Major John Linkon, who had moments earlier been unseated, mounted the former 13th Light Dragoon horse:

'We had gone some 500 yards when my horse was shot and I was in the unpleasant predicament of being shot by the enemy or ridden over by my own party, that was the Second Line. However as I retired the 1st squadron opened out and let us through, someone shouting "Don't ride over him". After which I looked rather sharply about me for I can tell you the faculties are very keen on an occasion of this sort.

'I saw about one hundred and fifty yards from me a loose horse. I made towards him no faster than my legs would carry me, mounted, galloped up and joined the squadron that had previously let me through, advanced to the attack with the 8th Hussars.'[29]

On the surface Morley and Nunnerley's version of events fits with that of Nolan suddenly realising the error and trying to prevent the Light

Brigade's destruction. The difficulty with this idea is that approaching the redoubts via the North Valley, which was surrounded by enemy batteries on three sides, was never a preferred option, while no other survivors from the ranks of the First Line featured this pivotal moment in their accounts. Meanwhile, none of the officers riding in the First Line or with Cardigan's staff ever countenanced that Nolan had intended that they retake the redoubts, or indicated a change in direction mid-charge.

Had Nolan needed to bring Lord Cardigan's attention to the mistake in direction, he would surely have done so the moment the brigade dressed to face the battery they charged. He would have been able to ride up alongside one of Cardigan's ADCs to relay the nuances of Raglan's order, or, at worst, alongside Lord Cardigan and requested permission to advise him on the correct objective. Nolan was acting as an ADC and therefore carried Raglan's authority and could act in a manner above his own rank. This, however, did not extend to taking command of the cavalry division. At the time that he broke ranks the brigade was only riding at a 'brisk trot' and so there was no need for Nolan to career across the front in the manner Morley describes.

Captain Nolan was riding with the 17th Lancers either left of the squadron or beside Captain Morris (although one source places him to the right-front of Morris). Nolan rode ahead of Cardigan for one of two reasons: he was either breaking with all military protocol and trying to force the pace – effectively usurping the Brigade Commander's authority (Brigadier General Hugh Rose's account claims that as he left Raglan's presence he shouted that this is what he would do[30]) – or he intended to change the direction of the attack. It would appear that in all probability, it was the former. The brigade needed to cover the one and a quarter mile distance between their starting point and the guns in good time, but not so fast as to lose formation. Captain White's squadron set the pace and direction of the Charge, Cardigan was the figurehead who could and did check the pace. It would appear that Nolan saw the first gun-flashes on the Fedioukine Heights and knew that the men needed to get out of their arc of fire as quickly as possible. It would therefore appear that Nolan's intentions were to force the pace and ultimately to lead the Light Brigade against No. 3 Don Cossack battery and the Russian Army in position.

The Russian gunners traversed their guns to try to match the motion of the front line, and the following volley from the Fedioukine Heights caused devastation in the ranks, as Private Lamb, 13th Light Dragoons, recalled:

'The next discharge tore wide gaps through our ranks and many a trooper fell.'

Private Albert Mitchell, 13th Light Dragoons, adds, as the advance continued:
'In a few moments several casualties occurred, for by this time the guns in our front [*sic*] were playing on us with round shot and shell, so the numbers of men and horses falling increased every moment.'

Lord George Paget, 4th Light Dragoons, reflected on the early stages of the Charge and how the Second Line lost its formation:

'The Second Line (under me) formed up in the rear of the First Line, (under Lord Cardigan). The First Line started off (down somewhat of a decline) at a brisk trot, the Second Line following though at rather a decreased pace, to rectify the proper distance of 200 yards [*sic*]. When I gave the command to my line to advance, I added the caution, "The 4th Light Dragoons will direct."'

This command did not properly register with the 8th Hussars, and for the next few minutes Paget fought a losing battle to maintain the line's cohesion, the 8th Hussars falling back and veering off to the right. As the Charge progressed the two regiments became completely separated and arrived at the gun-line at different times and locations.

Paget now increased his regiment's pace to match that of the First Line so that when they arrived at the guns they would be almost in line with the rear rank of the 11th Hussars, thereby creating a more effective Second Line:

'Before we had proceeded very far, however, I found it necessary to increase the pace, to keep up with what appeared to me to be the increasing pace of the First Line, and after the first 300 yards my whole energies were exerted in their directions, my shouts of "Keep up; come on", etc. being rendered the more necessary by the stoical coolness of my two squadron leaders.'[31]

It is not clear how quickly Raglan understood there had been a catastrophic mistake. Calthorpe's account suggests that this was fairly soon after the cavalry moved off – they were after-all in the wrong valley – perhaps as little as a few strides into the Charge. He quoted one onlooker as saying, 'We all saw at once that a lamentable mistake had been made – by whose fault it was then impossible to say.'

As they rode on, it quickly dawned on the rank and file of the First Line who had had any doubts, that they were to charge the guns to their front.

Private Henry Naylor, 13th Light Dragoons: 'The men on the right and left of me had seen many a hard fought field in India. They did not believe that we were going to attack the enemy in front of us, but they soon found out that we were; poor fellows, for that was their last [battle] field. Both were killed.'

As the brigade's ranks thinned, officers and NCOs desperately fought to maintain their squadron's shape, calling to their men to close up to fill the gaps – the cavalry needed to reach the guns *en masse* in close formation to be effective.

The left flank of the Light Brigade then came within range of the skirmishers and infantry around the Fedioukine Heights. These included a company of the Black Sea Foot Cossacks, two companies of riflemen, and the Vladimir and Suzdal Infantry Regiments under the command of Zhaboritski. Troop Sergeant Major George Smith of the 11th Hussars, which rode in direct support of the 17th Lancers and towards the right-hand side of the valley, nevertheless came under their fire: 'As we neared the battery, a square of infantry gave us a volley in flank. The very air hissed as the shower of bullets passed through us; many men were now killed or wounded.'[32]

Lord Lucan had ordered Lord Cardigan's Light Brigade, the faster of the two brigades, to lead the advance, with the Heavies to follow. Henry Joy later recalled: 'The Earl of Lucan had sent Captain Walker, aide-de-camp, to the officers of the heavy cavalry, commanding them to bring up the Heavy Brigade in support as quickly as possible, which was done, and they came in position in line on the same ground as that from which the Light Brigade had just charged down the valley.'

This manoeuvring took precious time. Cardigan's Light Brigade, accompanied by I Troop RHA, were riding down the valley at the trot. Although artillery support was available, not a shot was fired in advance of their charge to soften up the enemy or keep their heads down.

The Heavy Brigade adopted a similar formation to the Light. The front line composed of the Scots Grey to the left and the Royals to the right; the Inniskillings made up the Second Line; the 4th Dragoon Guards were on the left, and the 5th Dragoons on the right, making up the third.

Seated slightly ahead of his staff officers, Lord Lucan gave the command to Trumpet Major Joy, who sounded the 'Walk', which was immediately taken up right and left.[33] The First Line obeyed the command, a gap opening up before the Second Line followed, the third setting into motion upon the correct separation. But with each stride the distance between the two brigades became extended.

Soon, however, the Heavy Brigade were taking casualties from the Fedioukine Heights. A letter from one of the 1st Dragoon Guards which was published in the *Manchester Times* of 22 November 1854, illustrated the fire that the brigade was under:

'The heavy cavalry were advancing all the time, under the hottest and most destructive fire that ever was witnessed by Lord Lucan or any other man on the [battle] field. The long shot, with grape and musketry, came amongst us like hail, whistling through the air like a gale of wind through the rigging of a ship. I saw one huge shot drop on the left of our front, which I expected would sweep the whole line from right to left. Had it not been for the French cavalry, who stormed the battery on our left, and obliged them to cut and leave it [*sic*], we should all have been mowed down like grass. But fortunately, we retired with few casualties or broken limbs. I am sorry to say, my poor brother, George, got a shot through the thigh, which passed right through. If you remember, some person verily got his wish, for, I believe, after the first man of our regiment was killed, he was the next that had his leg shattered. Captain Campbell [Captain George Campbell], I am sorry to say, got shot though the shoulder. Captain Elmsall [Captain William Elmsall] and Mr Hurtoph [Cornet William Hurtoph] are wounded. We had several privates wounded. Two of them had their arms blown away. I got too close to one of the big shot myself for had I not reared my horse up just at that moment I did, I must have had it, for the officer riding alongside of me caught it in the chest of his horse, which dropped in a moment.'[34]

During the two-minute period that the Heavy Brigade were under fire they lost a number of men killed or wounded. Captain Walker claimed to have seen a single shell take out eight men. Lord Lucan's own horse was struck by several shell splinters and he was slightly wounded in the leg, while his staff officer, McMahon, was hit in the leg by a musket ball and his horse had two bullet wounds to the body.

Captain Walker, ADC to Lord Lucan, rode with the Heavy Brigade and recalled the events in a letter home dated 29 October:

'As soon as we came within range, they opened on us from a line of guns formed right across the valley [sic], from some more guns [sic] very well placed on their left, but which were partially occupied by the fire of our artillery [the battery commanders having taken it upon themselves to act], and on our left by a line of guns planted on the ridge of hills near the Black River [The Heavy Brigade would only have come under effective fire from the guns on the Fedioukine Heights]. My only consolation was seeing two squadrons of Chasseurs d'Afrique stealing on them up the hill, and after they had pounded us for about ten minutes [sic] they did succeed in dislodging them, but were themselves repulsed with some loss by a body of Russian infantry which was in support. I thought the fire on the 17th [17th September] was pretty heavy, but it was a joke [compared] to this, which certainly for eight or ten minutes [sic] exceeded my liveliest conception. I hope I shall not again get such a pelting.'[35]

Although the Fourth Order to the Cavalry advised Lucan that the French Cavalry was to the British Cavalry Division's left, as far as history records, he failed to liaise with its brigade commander, General Armand-Octave-Marie d'Allonville. Independently, however, General Morris had ridden down from the Chersonese Uplands and was in discussion with d'Allonville when the Light Brigade began its advance on their right. Seeing the Light Brigade's terrible predicament, Colonel Champeron and Major Louis Abdelal led four squadrons of the 4th Chasseurs d'Afrique in support of the British action. Riding in two lines, they rode in open formation and outside the arc of the gun's fire.

The Chasseurs advanced on the Fedioukine Heights under fire from Russian skirmishers and came in on the Russian gunners' right. Despite being caught in the flank, the Chasseurs succeeded in pushing the enemy back. In the face of the French onslaught, the guns soon fell silent as first the right half of the battery and then the left were ordered to retire. The Chasseurs fell on the gun teams and a fierce fight developed. Major Abdelal pushed the Russians back but came up against sharpshooters supported by infantry which had emerged from the scrub, quickly forming up into two squares. The infantry fired volleys into the Chasseurs causing a number of casualties. Indeed, most of the French casualties – thirteen killed (including two captains) and twenty-eight wounded – came during this phase of their action; this out of around 200 engaged. Zhaboritski ordered a counter-attack by the Vladimir Regiment which advanced and would force the French cavalry off the Heights.

The initial phase of the action was witnessed by Private James Lamb, 13th Light Dragoons who adds to the narrative his recollection of the eventual outcome of events:

'On turning around, I saw a body of horsemen charging down the valley on my right front, and thought they were a body of Cossacks coming down to cut off our retreat; but I quickly discovered that I was mistaken, and that the horsemen were two squadrons of French Dragoons [4th Chasseurs d'Afrique], charging down to silence a masked Russian battery that was firing on our left flank, whose guns were covered by a regiment of Polish Lancers. This battery gave the Frenchmen a warm reception by means of canister and grape, by which a number of saddles were emptied. But riding swiftly on, despite their losses, they charged right up into, and cut their way through, the Polish regiment, and wheeling round to their right flank, rode off and made good their retreat.'[36]

The Chasseurs d'Afrique undoubtedly saved the Cavalry Division from further fire from these guns, while significantly reducing the rifle and musket-fire from that flank. Their action was reported in *The Illustrated London News* of 25 November 1854:

'With fearful impetuosity, they dashed upon a battery on the left of our army, which had been telling severely upon our men, and cutting down the gunners… Of course there were some very narrow escapes. One of my friends in the squadron had his horse killed in the very [infantry] square – in the midst of the enemy; but was fortunate enough to catch an artillery horse, which he mounted, and got off safely with his companions.'

Troop Sergeant Major Smith, moments after his troop had suffered their first casualties, also looked over his shoulder and observed the French cavalry on the move: 'I saw the Chasseurs d'Afrique charging up the slope of the Fedioukine Hills at the battery that was taking us in the flank.'[37]

The Chasseurs d'Afrique were still in combat on the Fedioukine Heights, and below in the North Valley the Heavy Brigade were between Nos. 4 and 3 Redoubts, when Lucan turned to Lord William Paulet (assistant adjutant general of the Cavalry Division) and said, 'They have sacrificed the Light Brigade; they shall not have the Heavy, if I can help it.'

These were remarkable words, as Lord Cardigan, both in person and via his ADC, had made it clear to Lord Lucan that the Charge would face gun batteries in front and on both flanks, supported by riflemen and, to the rear, cavalry. It was with full knowledge of this that he sent 673 men to their almost certain deaths. Yet within two minutes of taking enemy fire, Lucan abandoned the Light Brigade to its fate.

Lucan ordered Trumpet Major Joy to sound the retreat. General Scarlett looked over his shoulder to see his brigade turning and countermanded the order before Lucan approached him and ordered for the Heavy Brigade's withdrawal, which he was obliged to obey.[38]

A member of Scarlett's Staff wrote:

'We galloped back and met Lord Lucan. It was he who had stopped the Heavies'. Confirming other accounts, he added: 'As near as I can recollect, Lord Lucan said to General Scarlett, 'We've lost the Light Brigade and we must save the Heavies.'[39]

The Heavy Brigade had already taken a number of casualties. The Royals' commanding officer, Lieutenant Colonel John Yorke, had been hit in the shin by a musket ball, with three other officers wounded, while 18 officers, NCOs and other ranks were killed, wounded, or had lost their mounts.

The London Gazette recorded the following casualties for the Heavy Brigade in the period 22-26 October inclusive and cover both charges; they confirm that the second action cost them minimal losses:

Staff – Lieutenant General the Earl of Lucan, wounded slightly; Brigadier General the Hon. J.Y. Scarlett, wounded slightly; Captain the Hon. W. Charteris, killed; Lieutenant A.I. Elliot, wounded slightly.

1st Royal Dragoons – Lieutenant Colonel John Yorke, wounded severely; Captain W. de Elmsall, wounded severely; Captain George Campbell, wounded severely; Cornet W.W. Hartopp, wounded severely; 2 rank and file, 10 horses, killed; 4 officers, 1 sergeant, 1 drummer, 5 rank and file, wounded.

2nd Dragoons – Lieutenant Colonel H.D. Griffith, wounded slightly; Captain G.C. Clarke, wounded severely; Cornet Lenox Prendergast, wounded severely;

Cornet H.E. Handley, wounded slightly; 2 rank and file, 14 horses killed; 4 officers, 5 sergeants, 48 rank and file, wounded.

4th Dragoon Guards – 1 rank and file, 1 horse, killed; 2 sergeants, 3 rank and file, wounded.

5th Dragoon Guards – Lieutenant F.H. Swinfen, wounded slightly; Cornet the Hon. G. Neville, wounded severely; 2 rank and file, 19 horses, killed; 2 officers, 9 rank and file, wounded.

6th Dragoons – 2 rank and file, 2 horses, killed; 3 sergeants, 10 rank and file, wounded.

The battery on the Fedioukine Heights had by this time already been silent although the Heavy Brigade continued to take casualties from musket-fire.

Captain Shakespear had accompanied the Light Brigade with I Troop RHA, but he was making little headway due to the rough terrain, while his horse teams were very vulnerable to enemy fire. Seeing the Heavy Brigade retire, he wheeled his guns around and joined them out of rifle range, near No. 4 Redoubt.

Shakespear wrote how it had become 'momentarily more and more apparent as the Troop trotted steadily forward that, before it could render any efficient service, the Russian fire would entirely cripple it: accordingly the word was given to go about and it retired to a position not far from the Heavy Brigade.'[40]

A little over three and a half minutes into the Charge, No. 3 Don Cossack battery fired its first volley.

Corporal Morley, 17th Lancers, recalled:

'At that instant, the Russian Artillery, in position across the valley, fired a volley into the 17th, which seemed to paralyse it, killing and wounding a number of officers and men. It seemed to me a troop of horses fell, myself and horse knocked down with them. I remounted and followed the shattered line... After that I simply scrambled on my horse and rode pell-mell.'

An anonymous 13th Light Dragoon who was cut down early in the charge:

'I was in the front rank of my regiment, the 13th Light Dragoons. As we galloped down the valley the Russian guns poured a continuous cross fire of grape and canister into our rank. My horse was killed, and I was wounded and rendered unconscious. On recovering, I found a number of shot holes in my uniform, the missiles grazing my flesh. My nearest comrade was lying dead, shot through the body.'[41]

Troop Sergeant Major William Barker, 17th Lancers:

'Just before we had finished the half league we received a tremendous volley from the enemy's twelve-gun [*sic*] battery in front, which emptied many saddles and laid prostrate numbers of gallant fellows who never rose again.'[42]

Private William Butler, also of the 17th Lancers, wrote in his memoirs:

'Just as we got to No. 1 Redoubt [*sic*], my right-hand man Walter Brooks was also shot. He was my comrade for over three years, from the time I went to the 4th Troop. We got a bit further, when my left hand man fell. My blood was up, and I began to wish to get near the enemy. Shot and shell were coming in all directions.'[43]

The Light Brigade was already at the point of no return and would soon disappear from the Heavy Brigade's sight into a thick pall of gun-smoke. Captain Godfrey Charles Morgan, 17th Lancers, recalled their progress:

'I do not recollect hearing a word from anybody as we gradually broke from a trot to a canter, though the noise of the striking of men and horses by grape and round shot was deafening, while the dust and gravel struck up by the round shot that fell short was almost blinding, and irritated my horse so that I could scarcely hold him at all.'[44]

Lieutenant Sir William Gordon, 17th Lancers:

'We, like Bulldogs who had been tied up all day – were only too glad to be let loose and off we went at a thundering gallop and cheering more like mad men than men with common sense.'[45]

Private William Nicholson, riding in the First Line as a member of 13th Light Dragoons:

'About half-way down the valley we could scarcely see one another, because, the ground being at the time very dry, the horses' hoofs and the shot and shell that were fired ploughed the ground making the air thick with dust and smoke. In consequence of this we could not see the enemy till we were close to them.'[46]

Private Albert Mitchell, 13th Light Dragoons, described the scene as they rode on, without proper artillery support, or Lord Lucan and the Heavy Brigade:

'In a few moments several casualties occurred, for by this time the guns in our front were playing on us with round shot and shell, so the numbers of men and horses falling increased every moment.

'I rode near the right of the line. A corporal [Corporal E.W. Aubrey Smith] who rode on the right was struck by a shot or shell full in the face, completely smashing it, his blood and brains bespattering us who rode near. His horse still went on with us.'[47]

Lord Cardigan and the First Line were by now close-on halfway down the North Valley and had already entered the extreme range of No. 3 Don Cossack battery. Meanwhile Lord Paget's Second Line continued to lose formation, with the 8th Hussars falling back from the 4th Light Dragoons and veering off to their right.

Paget later explained his difficulty in maintaining the line:

'The 4th Light Dragoons and 8th Hussars composed the Second Line, under my command. I led in front of the 4th (the directing regiment). After we had continued our advance some 300 to 400 yards distance, I began to observe that the 8th were inclining away from us, and consequently losing their interval. At the top of my voice I kept shouting, "8th Hussars, close in to your left", "Colonel Shewell, you are losing your interval", but all to no purpose. Gradually, my attention being occupied with what was going on in my front, I lost sight of the 8th.'[48]

Acting Adjutant, Cornet Fiennes Wykeham Martin was riding on the right of the 4th Light Dragoons. Hearing Paget he rode closer to Colonel Shewell, calling out, 'Lord George is holloaing to you to close in on the 4th.' Colonel Shewell responded: 'I know it, I hear him, and am doing my best.' Despite these efforts, the 8th Hussars continued to fall back and drift over towards the Causeway Heights; they would almost completely miss the gun-line.

Trumpeter James Donoghue's memory of events ran contrary to his commanding officer as regards the reason for the separation:

'I acted as Field Trumpeter in attendance upon Colonel Shewell, who was in command of the 8th Hussars, and my position at the time of the Charge was with Colonel Shewell in front of the centre of the Regiment.

'As we advanced the 8th Hussars became separated from the 4th Light Dragoons, in consequence of Colonel Shewell ordering us not to go too fast. I recollect Colonel Shewell waving us back with his sword on that account. The 4th Light Dragoons diverged a little to the left, and the 8th Hussars a little to the right, and an interval was left between the two Regiments.'[49]

Meanwhile, each man was fighting his own personal battle to get in amongst the gunners. Private James Olley, 4th Light Dragoons, was unhorsed but caught a riderless mount:

'About halfway down the man that was riding next to me was shot and fell on to my right leg. A little further on my horse was shot down. I caught one of the horses, which was coming back without its rider who had been shot out of his saddle.'[50]

The men around Cornet Fiennes Wykeham Martin, 4th Light Dragoons, riding some distance behind the First Line, were terribly cut up by flanking fire:

'We were enfiladed for half a mile by the hottest possible fire at about 30 to 40 yards distance.'[51]

At this point Private Matthew Keating caught sight of Lieutenant Houghton, 11th Hussars, retiring wounded. Houghton rode a chestnut mare similar in its markings to that of Lord Cardigan and it is thought that many in the Second Line mistook him for the Brigade commander:

'The 8th Hussars were slightly to the right rear of the 4th Light Dragoons, and they (the 4th) were about two or three hundred yards [*sic*] off the battery.'[52]

Meantime, Private William Bird, 8th Hussars, was unhorsed by small-arms fire as he approached the guns on the Causeway Heights but was able to re-join his regiment:

'Opposite the second battery, on the right of us, I lost my tired horse, which was shot dead; but, by skilful movement, I landed on my feet, and was not hurt. Shortly afterwards I caught a stray horse which was riderless, belonging to the Scots Greys, and rejoined my troop.'[53]

Captain The Hon. Godfrey Charles Morgan, 17th Lancers, described the scene as he drew ever closer to the guns at the end of the North Valley:

'On we went astonished, but unshaken in nerve over half a mile of rough ground, losing dozens of men and horses at every step, to attack horse artillery in our front, supported by three times [*sic*] our number of cavalry, heavy batteries on right and left flanks, backed by infantry, riflemen, &c.'[54]

Fire, particularly from the No. 3 Don Cossack battery and the Causeway Heights, was continuing to take its toll on the Light Brigade. At 11.14 am, under pressure from the ranks, the officers of the 17th Lancers tried to force the pace. Cornet George Wombwell: 'Every man felt convinced that the quicker he rode, the better chance he would have of escaping unhurt.'

At this point Captain White, who led the squadron of direction, drew almost level with Lord Cardigan, who calmly checked his pace by holding out his sabre across White's chest: 'Steady, steady the 17th Lancers!' According to the account of Private James Wightman, 17th Lancers, Captain Morris would also ride to within a yard of Cardigan, and received the same calm measured rebuke:

'Lord Cardigan, almost directly behind whom I rode, turned his head leftwards towards Captain Morris and shouted hoarsely, "Steady, steady Captain Morris!" '... [the 17th Lancer's squadron] was held in a manner responsible to the brigade commander for the pace and direction of the whole line. Later when we were in the midst of our torture and made to be out of it ... I heard again, high above the turmoil and din, Cardigan's sonorous command, "Steady, steady the 17th Lancers!"'[55]

Riding in support of the 17th Lancers, the 11th Hussars too had lost their station and had ridden off to the left. They were well within range of the Russian infantrymen on the Fedioukine Heights whose concentrated fire caused further casualties.

Private William Pennington explained how the adrenalin of the Chargers somehow numbed men to the horrors that faced them:

'To see a forearm torn by shot or shell, bleeding and dangling by the tendons which still held it to the upper joint, or brains protruding from a shattered skull, would in cool moments have been a soul-moving and sickening sight.'[56]

As the Second Line rode over and past the torn bodies of the casualties from the First; all were made acutely aware of the carnage as they rode through the arcs of fire of the Fedioukine Heights, No. 3 Don Cossack battery and the Causeway Heights. Paget recalled the scene:

'Bewildered horses from the First Line, riderless, rushed in upon our ranks in every state of mutilation, some with a limping gait that told too truly of their state. One was guiding one's own horse (as willing as oneself in such benevolent precautions) so as to avoid trampling on the bleeding objects in one's path – sometimes a man, sometimes a horse – and so we went on. "Right flank, keep up. Close in on your centre." The smoke, the noise, the cheers, the groans, the "ping, ping" whizzing past one's head: the "whirr" of the fragments of shells; the well-know "slush" of that unwelcome intruder on one's ears! – what a sublime confusion it was!'

The Russian View at 11.15 am: the guns on the Causeway Heights were not initially facing the North Valley.

Earlier, at about 8.30 am Captain Bojanov's No. 7 Battery of the 12th Artillery Brigade had stationed its six 6-pounder guns and two 9-pounder howitzers close to the location of No. 3 Redoubt. Bojanov heard the guns on the Fedioukine Heights open fire and realized that a cavalry attack was heading down the North Valley. Nearby, four battalions of the 24th Odessa Jaeger (Rifle) Infantry Regiment formed into squares ready to defend No. 7 Battery. Once the command had been given, it took only four minutes for Bojanov's gun teams to reposition ready to defend their position and to fire into the ranks of the British cavalry; the nearest would be only 550 yards away. As the First Line came within musket range the 24th Odessa Regiment fired off a volley before reloading and being ordered to fire at will. Meanwhile, No. 7 Battery's guns now in position, opened up on the First Line's right flank, as the fire intensified.

Albert Seaton in *The Crimean War – A Russian Chronicle*, confirms:

'The Odessky [24th Odessa Regiment], holding the high ground on the southern heights, as soon as they sighted the enemy, hurriedly fell back over the ridge of the Causeway onto No. 2 Redoubt and formed Square.'

This was accepted drill to receive a cavalry attack, forming into line would have given them greater fire-power, and so in this respect the British Cavalry were spared their full onslaught. With countless horrors unfolding around them, the men careering down the valley became fixated on reaching and silencing the guns, as an anonymous Charger of the 8th Hussars related:

'At that moment I felt my blood thicken and crawl, as if my heart grew still like a lump of stone within me. I was for a moment paralysed, but then with the snorting of the horse, the wild gallop, the sight of the Russians becoming more distinct, and the first horrible discharge with its still more horrible effects, my heart began to warm, to become hot, to dance again, and I had neither fear nor pity! I longed to be at the guns. I'm sure I set my teeth together as if I could have bitten a piece out of one.'[57]

Having pulled away to the right, the 8th Hussars were largely targeted by the Russian cannon and small-arms fire from the Causeway Heights. Lieutenant Edward Seager wrote:

'There were only about 100 of our regiment. We advanced at a trot and soon came within the crossfire from both hills, both of cannon and rifles; the fire was tremendous, shells bursting amongst us, cannon balls tearing the earth up and musket balls coming like hail. Still we went on never altering our pace, or breaking us up in the least, except that our men and horses were gradually knocked over... our men behaved splendidly.'[58]

As the officers of his Squadron fell – Lieutenant J.C.H. Fitzgibbon, Captain E.Tomkinson, Lieutenant D.H. Clutterbuck – Seager would find himself in command.

Corporal John Ashley Kilvert, 11th Hussars, had earlier lost his first horse to fire from the Fedioukine Heights, but quickly found another and joined the Second Line:

'I was in the Second Line and as we careered down the valley and shot and shell were flying about like hailstones, it was only the pace of the horses that carried us through at all. I don't think if it had been a body of infantry, that a single man could have reached the bottom of the valley. As we advanced, there was a hot fire from the Russian batteries on either side and we [who] survived, rode over the prostrate bodies of those who preceded us.'[59]

Private Robert Ashton, 11th Hussars, early on in the Charge, lost his first horse, later catching another, before rejoining the Charge:

'My first horse was shot under me a very short time after we started. After being dismounted, Sergeant Fleming [Private John Fleming] was near me, and I caught hold of the bridle of his horse. He said, "Leave go, or we shall both be killed." The bridle slipped out of my hand, and as the horse passed me I managed to catch his tail, to which I held on for a few yards; but the pace at which he was going was too much for me, and I was obliged to let go. Shortly afterwards I saw a horse belonging to the 4th Light Dragoons coming towards me, which, after some difficulty, I succeeded in catching, and, mounting it, I proceeded down the valley.'[60]

Corporal Thomas Morley, 17th Lancers, wrote how the discipline of the Russian gunnery and the lack of natural cover had helped increase the casualties:

'The Russian gunners were well drilled. There was none of that crackling sound where one gun goes a little ahead and the others follow, having the effect of a bunch of firecrackers popping in quick succession. In such case the smoke of the first gun obscures the aim of the rest. The Russian Artillery at Balaclava went off at the word of command, all together. One tremendous volley was heard with flashes of flame through the rolling smoke. While they reloaded the smoke lifted so that they could see and take aim again. There were probably twenty cannon at our right [sic] firing at us, and two batteries – twelve guns – in front [sic]. If we had been moving over uneven ground we should have had some slight protection in the necessary uncertainty of aim of the guns, but moving as we did in compact bodies on smooth ground directly in range, the gunners had an admirable target and every volley came with terrible effect... There is a natural instinct to dodge cannon balls. In such fire as we were under it changed to an impulse to hurry. There was no time to look right or left, and the guns in front were what I looked out for. They were visible as streaks of fire about two feet long, and a foot thick in the centre of a gush of thick white smoke, marking about every three hundred yards of the way, as they would reload in 30 or 40 seconds.'[61]

The enemy batteries on the Causeway Heights had a maximum arc of fire of about 650 yards. It has been estimated that the cavalry was subject to their fire for around two minutes, during which time the Russian gunners probably fired off 32 shots (24 round shot from the guns, and 8 shells from the howitzers).

The Light Brigade had already passed through the arc of fire of the guns on the Fedioukine Heights. Before they were silenced by the 4th Chasseurs d'Afrique, the gunners are thought to have poured shot and shell into the British Cavalry for about three and a half minutes, firing something like 70 rounds into their flank (30 shells and 40 round shot).

The British troopers had briefly entered a cross-fire from the Fedioukine Heights and the 8 guns of No. 3 Don Cossack battery, which would fire 32 rounds (8 shells and 24 round shot) in the two minutes the Chargers were subject to their murderous fire.

To those in the front ranks the sight of cannon balls hurtling towards them must have been terrifying; only the officers really had the room to manoeuvre, and some told of how they avoided certain death by the timely pull of a rein, others just trusted to luck. Godfrey Charles Morgan, 17th Lancers, recalled:

'I appeared to be riding straight on to the guns, and I distinctly saw the gunner apply his fuse. I shut my eyes then, for I thought that settled the question as far as I was concerned. But the shot just missed me and struck the man on my right.'[62]

The rank and file were less fortunate, as related by Private James Wightman of the 17th Lancers:

'We had not broke into the charging pace when poor old John Lee [Private John Lees], my right-hand man on the flank of the regiment, was all but smashed by a shell; he gave my arm a twitch, as with a strange smile on his worn old face he quietly said, "Domino! chum," and fell out of the saddle. His old grey mare kept alongside of me for some distance, treading on and tearing out her entrails as she galloped, till at length she dropped with a strange shriek. I have mentioned that my comrade, Peter Marsh [Private Peter Marsh], was my left-hand man; next beyond him was Private [Thomas] Dudley. The explosion of a shell had swept down four or five men on Dudley's left, and I heard him ask Marsh if he had noticed "what a hole that b- - - shell had made" on his left front. "Hold your foul-mouthed tongue," answered Peter, "swearing like a blackguard, when you may be knocked into eternity next minute!" Just then

I got a musket-bullet through my right knee, and another in the shin, and my horse had three bullet wounds in the neck. Man and horse were bleeding so fast that Marsh begged me to fall out; I would not, pointing out that in a few minutes we must be into them, and so I sent my spurs well home, and faced it out with my comrades.'[63]

Wightman's account continued: 'It was about this time that Sergeant [Edward] Talbot had his head clean carried off by a round shot, yet for about thirty yards farther the headless body kept the saddle, the lance at the charge firmly gripped under the right arm. Well, we were nearly out of it at last, and close on those cursed guns.'[64]

Troop Sergeant Major William George Cattermole, 17th Lancers:

'When about 200 yards from the guns, I received a graze wound on the knuckles of my sword hand, which caused the sword to fall from my grasp; but it being secured by the sword knot and by a handkerchief, I quickly regained my weapon.'[65]

Captain Godfrey Charles Morgan describes the fearful scene:

'On we went, the pace increasing, amidst the thickest shower of shell, shot, grape, canister, and Minié, from front and flanks – horses and men dropping by scores every yard. The whirling and cracking of shells was beyond all description.'[66]

Lieutenant Edward Lennox Jervis, 13th Light Dragoons, observed: 'The Lancers shaking their lances and waving them in the air like madmen, and all the time Cardigan bang in front, for all the world riding as if he were going down the park. And by this time the grape-shot was tearing holes in us.'[67]

Private Albert Mitchell, 13th Light Dragoons, maintained that his regiment was subjected to cannon-fire from all sides at once, but this was never the case:

'By this time, the ranks being continually broken it caused some confusion. Oaths and imprecations might be heard between the report of the guns and the bursting of the shells, as the men crowded and jostled each other in their endeavour to close to the centre. This was unavoidable at times, especially when a shell burst in the ranks, sometimes bringing down three or four men and horses, which made it difficult to avoid an unpleasant crush in the ranks. We were now fully exposed to the fire from all three batteries [sic] – front, right, and left – as also the infantry on our right, who were now able to reach us.'[68]

Captain Robert Portal of the 4th Light Dragoons on the deadly cross-fire:

'Shells fell like hail all round us, to say nothing of 18 lb shot, which whistled through our ranks, dealing death and destruction. The plain was soon covered with dead and dying horses, dismounted men, dead men, dead officers, in short, never was such a scene. On we still kept going, till at last we had all got so far that we had passed through this cross fire.'[69]

Sergeant John George Baker, 4th Light Dragoons added:

'A dreadful cross-fire opened on us from both sides and in front [sic], but it was too late to do anything but advance, which we did in a style truly wonderful, every man feeling certainly that we must be annihilated.'[70]

Captain Thomas Hutton, 4th Light Dragoons, added:

'We advanced in two lines at a full trot in the most perfect order possible through a concentrated storm of shot, shell, grape, canister, rifle balls & every missile that could be hurled at us; the ground was quickly spread with wounded men and horses.'[71]

The personal account of Private George Alfred Price, 4th Light Dragoons, highlights the toll of such fire on the rank and file:

'All Captain [Thomas] Hutton could muster of the old "E" Troop was twenty-eight, on the morning of the Charge. We came back numbering seven. I was one of the seven.'[72]

William Howard Russell wrote in his notebook:

'A more fearful spectacle was never witnessed than by those who, without the power to aid, beheld their heroic countrymen rushing to the arms of death.'

The time was 11.16 am and the First Line was closing to within 250 yards of No. 3 Don Cossack battery; Lord Cardigan increased the pace to the 'Gallop'.

The gun-smoke thinned momentarily before the next volley and Cardigan rode for what he thought was the central gun of the battery, thereby maximizing the possibility of the remnants of the brigade entering the full length of the battery.

As their objective drew nearer the enemy's fire only further intensified. Cornet Chadwick of the 17th Lancers wrote: 'My horse was seriously wounded by a ball received in the animal's neck and this had the effect of covering me with a shower of blood from the wound. After this I felt my chance of returning alive was hopeless.'

Private Henry Naylor, 13th Light Dragoons, was fast approaching the guns: 'The shot and shell flew like hail about us, our line began to get terribly thin by this time. My horse began to limp and I could not manage him. My off reins were cut in two. I managed to tie them; my curb was gone likewise, I received a stinging sensation about my left shoulder.' Naylor had been hit.

Now came shouts from the Lancers of 'Come on, Deaths! Come on!' – a reference to the regimental motto. But the 13th Light Dragoons were not to be outdone as Captain Arthur Tremayne related:

'The last thing I heard before I went down was one man saying to his neighbour, "Come on; don't let those bastards get ahead of us".'[73]
Captain Oldham's horse suddenly bolted. Two or three men riding immediately behind Oldham went with him; all were killed by a single shell. Captain Soame Jenyns witnessed their deaths:

'Oldham I saw killed by a shell which burst under his horse and knocked over two or three others. It blew his mare's hind legs off, and he jumped up himself not hit, when next moment he threw up his hands and fell dead on his face.'[74]

Lieutenant Edward Lennox Jervis, 13th Light Dragoons, reported a different version of events, such was the 'fog of war':

'One of our seniors [Captain John Augustus Oldham] was on a white horse, a rather curious mount, and he was literally blown up at this stage, so we found no trace of him afterwards.'[75]

The number of riderless horses was ever-increasing, many of them badly wounded and galloping wildly, others trotting or barely able to keep up a walking pace; many of the walking-wounded who lost their mounts were able to catch a spare or lightly wounded horse. The Second Line was in places broken by constantly having to change stride to avoid man and horse.

Leading his regiment and commanding the Second Line, Lord George Paget, 4th Light Dragoons noted:

'One incident struck me forcibly about this time – the bearing of riderless horses in such circumstances. I was, of course, riding by myself, and clear of the lines, and for that reason was a marked object for the poor dumb brutes, who by this time were galloping about in numbers, like mad wild beasts. They consequently made dashes at me [from] a considerable distance, at one time as many as five on my right and two on my left, cringing in on me, and positively squeezing me, as the round shot came bounding by them, tearing up the earth under their noses, my overalls being a mass of blood from their gory flanks (they nearly upset me several times, and I had to use my sword to rid myself of them). And so, on we went through this scene of carnage, wondering each moment which would be our last. "Keep back, Private So and So. Left squadron, close in to your centre." It required a deal of closing in, by this time, to fill up the vacant gaps.

'[Captain] Hutton was shot through the right thigh as he rode down the valley and reported the wound to Captain Low his squadron leader. "If you [can] sit on your horse," replied Low, "you had better come on with us, there's no use going back now, you'll only be killed."'[76]

Private John Whitehead, 4th Light Dragoons, whose horse fell dead and was forced to take cover behind its lifeless form, before eventually making his way back on foot:

'We advanced towards the enemy. The 17th Lancer's leading men and horses falling wholesale. About three parts down the valley a shell landed just in front of my horse. When it exploded it caught her fair in the chest and brought her down. I shot over her head for a dozen yards but my poor mare didn't move, being instantly killed. The shots from the Russian guns were so thick that I had to lie down behind my horse for protection.'

By 11.17 am the gunners of No. 3 Don Cossack battery were in full motion firing one round every thirty or forty seconds, the round-shot and shell wreaking havoc among cavalry's ranks, and with each volley creating a thick bank of smoke which engulfed the battery. But the men who survived came on all the more determined to take the guns. Captain Morgan recalled the moment that the 17th Lancers finally broke into the charge:

'The Lancers had cantered up to within 300 or 400 yards [*sic*] of the guns, when Major White hallooed out, "Charge, there." The lances came down to the proper position, Lord Cardigan then hallooed across to him, "You have now word to charge." I was close up and heard it; but as you might well imagine, before it had taken me the time to tell it the Lancers were amongst the guns, and there was no time to sound the trumpet at all.'[77]

Private James Wightman of the 17th Lancers:

'The minutes seemed like hours as the shot and shell ripped through them.... Cardigan was still straight in front of me, steady as a church, but now his sword was in the air; he turned in his saddle for an instant, and shouted his final command, "Steady! Steady! Close in!" Immediately afterwards there crashed into us a regular volley from the Russian cannon. I saw Captain White go down and Cardigan disappear into the smoke. A moment more and I was within it myself.'[78]

News of the fate of Captain White comes from a letter written on board Her Majesty's ship *Himalaya*, dated Balaclava Bay 27 October 1854 and published in the *Glasgow Herald* of 17 November 1854: 'The gallant Captain White, of the 17th Lancers, was lying on his back when we came up to him, with a round shot right through his leg.'[79]

Morris, leading the 17th Lancers, just behind Cardigan, declared of the brigade commander:

'Nothing could be better. He put himself just where he ought, about in front of my right squadron, and went down in capital style.'[80]

The First Line was nearly upon the guns. Men looked for the gaps between the cannons in the hope that they would survive the next volley.

Sergeant John Berryman of the 17th Lancers: 'And here a discharge from the battery in our front, whose guns were double-shotted, first with shot and shell, and then with case, swept away Captain [John Pratt] Winter and the whole division on my right.

'The gap was noticed by Captain [William] Morris, who gave the order, "Right incline," but a warning voice came from my coverer in the rear rank (Corporal John Penn), "Keep straight on, Jack; keep straight on." He saw what I did not, that we were opposite the intervals of the guns, and thus we escaped, for the next round must have swept us into eternity.'

Berryman looked over towards Private James Melrose, who exclaimed, 'What man here would ask another man from England?' Maybe Melrose foresaw his fate – he was killed in the next volley – he found his immortality as a Charger. 'We were then so close to the guns that the report rang through my head, and I felt I was quite deaf for a time. It was this round that broke my mare's off-hind leg, and caused her to stop instantly.'

The gunners had fired canister shot, which at the closing range created a devastating effect on the First Line (the shot from each gun would have a spread of 10 yards at a range of 150 yards, and every man and horse within that arc would be hit). It is said that some of the gunners loaded a round shot on top of the canister, firing a double-shot. No force of cavalry could possibly survive such an iron storm – and yet they did. Possibly they fired too late, or the use of ball and canister restricted the spread of the canister shot.

Captain Edwin Cook of the 11th Hussars: 'We went very steady, the fire was terrific, it seemed impossible to escape, we were in range of grapeshot on each side [*sic*] besides the barkers in front.'[81]

Captain Godfrey Morgan of the 17th Lancers:

'When about a hundred yards from the guns a gunner applying his fuse... the shot missed me and struck the man on my right full on the chest.'[82]

Corporal Thomas Morley of the 17th Lancers:

'Before we reached the guns, every officer of my squadron, the second, was either killed or wounded, leaving no one to command us.'

Private Albert Mitchell, 13th Light Dragoons, feared the end must surely be near as he prepared for that final salvo at near point-blank range:

'As we drew nearer, the guns in our front supplied us liberally with grape and canister, which brought down men and horses in heaps. Up to this time I was going on all right, but missed my left hand man from my side, and thinking it might soon be my turn, I offered up a short prayer: "Oh Lord, protect me; and watch over my poor mother." We were now very close to the guns, for we were entering the smoke which hung in clouds in front.'[83]

The First Line had only been thirty seconds from crashing into the gun-line; precious seconds which would allow the gunners to limber up and be ready to escape the inevitable slaughter. Colonel Obolensky had ordered one final volley with the British at under twenty yards. Ignoring safety precautions, the gunners had reloaded without swabbing the barrels, risking the possibility of their powder charge detonating on cinders from the previous shot.

Adkin observed that canister or shot fired at 110 yards would have a 23 foot diameter spread, while the gaps between the guns were roughly 22 yards. This meant that riders aiming for the interval between the guns would have a fighting chance of getting through, especially if the final volley was fired too late. Adkin suggests that not all the guns did fire canister as their last round, otherwise Cardigan and Captain Morgan, who were within yards of the cannon barrels when they were discharged, could not possibly have survived (at 20 yards the spread of shot would be approximately 10 yards).[84]

One account insists that Cardigan 'managed to keep the line and regulated charging pace until they were within 80 yards of the Russian guns at the far end of the valley. These guns then fired simultaneously, filling the air with thick smoke and flying metal.'[85]

The front line probably broke into the charge with around fifty yards to go, neither the command nor the bugle call was required as constant drilling meant every man knew instinctively the regulation distance at which to spur their mounts for the final dash, and bring their weapon to the 'Engage'.

All agree that the guns loosed their final volley at point-blank range and disappeared in an acrid cloud of smoke. The explosive roar brought death and destruction, the shot ripping and shredding the flesh of man and beast. But the thundering noise of horses' hooves went on and the ground beneath the gunners' feet shuddered. The gunners dived for cover or stood their ground to fight. A few turned and ran, and were lanced or cut down. About 150 men of the 13th Light Dragoons and 17th Lancers made it to the guns.

As the final volley had rung out, Ryzhov rode back and ordered his cavalry forward to defend the battery and prevent the guns from being carried away.

Cardigan, fifteen yards from the guns when the final volley was fired, was the first man to enter the gun-line. Cornet Wombwell, his Regimental ADC, and Lieutenant Henry Maxse, his ADC, riding only a yard or so behind. The latter recalled:

'Just as he [Cardigan] got close up to a gun, it went off, luckily without touching him, and not being able to see from the smoke he rode right up against the gun.'

Cornet Wombwell and Lieutenant Maxse were only a horse-length behind Cardigan and Maxse was wounded by grape-shot and Wombwell's horse was killed; Lord Cardigan went into the Russians' position almost alone.

Captain The Hon. Godfrey Morgan, 17th Lancers, was only a little behind Cardigan and quickly entered into a deadly mêlée with the enemy:

'Cardigan was 3 or 4 horses length in front of the centre of the line and on my right front. The Earl entered the battery a few yards distance from me. I then became engaged with a Russian Artilleryman and had no opportunity of noticing anything for some minutes.'

Lord Cardigan: 'We reached the battery in a very good line, and at the regular charging pace; and here many officers and men were killed. On leading into the battery a gun was fired close by my horse's head. I rode straight forward at the same pace.'[86]

Cardigan's account continues: 'I led into the battery and through the Russian gun limber carriages and ammunition wagon in the rear. I rode within twenty yards of the line of the Russian cavalry. I was attacked by two Cossacks, slightly wounded by their lances, and with difficulty got away from them.'[87]

Corporal James Nunnerley of the 17th Lancers was yet to arrive at the battery:

'When I was within a few yards of the Russian guns my horse was shot under me and fell on its head. I endeavoured to pull it up in order to dash at the gunners but found it was unable to move, its foreleg having been blown off. I left it and forced my way on foot.'[88]

Nunnerley was set upon by the Russian cavalry, through whom he cut his way.

Corporal Thomas Morley also of the 17th Lancers:

'The last volley went off when we were close on them. The flame, the smoke, the roar were in our faces. It is not an exaggeration to compare the sensation to that of riding into the mouth of a volcano.'

Captain Godfrey Charles Morgan, 17th Lancers, recalled the moment:

'Just as I came close to one, it went off, and naturally, round went my horse; I turned him round, and put him at it again, and got through; on we went, and passed the guns, and saw the cavalry retreating the other side.'[89]

As the 11th followed the 17th and 13th into the smoke and disappeared too, a number of officers and men who had been wounded and unhorsed faced another danger: being trampled by the Second Line.

Private Albert Mitchell of the 13th Light Dragoons rode to the right of the Lancers:

'I could see some of the gunners running from the guns to the rear, when just at that moment a shell from the battery on the right struck my horse, carrying away the shoulder and part of the chest, and exploding a few yards off. Fortunately, I was on the ground when it exploded, or some of the fragments would most likely have reached me.

'On my recovery from the shock, I found my horse was lying on his near side; my left leg was beneath him, and my right above him. I tried to move, but just at that moment I heard the Second Line come galloping towards where I lay, and fully expecting to be trampled on, I looked up and saw that it was the 4th Light Dragoons quite close. I called out, "For God's sake don't ride over me." Whether they heard me or not I shall never know. But one thing I do know: *He* in whose name I called to them did hear, and most mercifully answered my prayer for *He* guided them over me so that not a hoof touched a hair of my head. To *Him* alone be all honour and praise for *His* manifold mercies toward me.'[90]

The 13th Light Dragoons and 17th Lancers silenced No. 3 Don Cossack battery. The 11th Hussars, still off to the left, received heavy fire from the infantry on the Fedioukine Heights where a thick bank of smoke from No. 3 Don Cossack battery hung across the valley. While muzzle-flashes momentarily picked out the guns, once they had fired they disappeared in the growing bank of smoke and were hidden once more. The survivors of the 11th Hussars had drifted to the left and most rode to the one side of the battery; only those men on the extreme right of the regiment went in among the guns.

THE CHARGE OF THE LIGHT BRIGADE

Troop Sergeant Major George Smith of the 11th Hussars:

'As we neared the battery, a square of infantry that had been placed in advance of the left of the guns gave us a volley in flank, the very air hissed as the shower of bullets passed through us. Many men were now killed or wounded. I, at this moment, felt that something had touched my left wrist; on looking down I saw that a bullet, which must have passed close in front of my body, had blackened and cut the lace on my cuff. Private Glanister had his lower jaw shattered by a bullet entering on the right side, and a bullet passed through the back of Private Humphries' neck, just missing the spinal column [*sic*]. At this time we were at a sweeping gallop, in another moment we passed the guns, our right flank brushing them.'[91]

Lord Paget led the 4th Light Dragoons into the centre of the gun-line a little after the 11th Hussars. The battery was of course already silenced, so they were spared canister shot at short-range that had decimated the First Line. They had witnessed the carnage suffered by the men and horses of the First Line over the mile and a quarter of the Charge, but nothing could have prepared them for the sights of the last forty or fifty yards before the gun-line which were soaked with blood and gore, the aftermath of canister shot fired into concentrated ranks. The ground lay thick with the dead and dying, and although every attempt was made to avoid them some were trampled beneath the hooves.

Lord George Paget, leading the support line:

'This battery, owing to the dust and confusion that reigned, had not been perceived by us (by me at least) until we got close upon it, though we had of course been suffering from its fire on our onward course. The first objects that caught my eye were some of these guns, in the act of endeavouring to get away from us, who had by this time got close upon them. They had, I fancy, ceased to fire on our near approach, and the men were dragging them away, some by lasso-harness but others with their horses still attached. Then came a "View Holloa!" and a sort of simultaneous rush upon them by the remnants of the 4th and cut and thrust was the order of the day.'[92]

In the moments immediately following the arrival of the 4th Light Dragoons at the Russian guns, Lord Paget turned to Low saying, 'We are in a desperate scrape; what the devil shall we do? Has anyone seen Lord Cardigan?'

The 8th Hussars by this time were so far off to the right of the valley that when they reached the battery they charged into the smoke drifting out towards the Causeway Heights and almost completely missed the guns altogether, apart from, that is, a few men on their left flank.

73

Chapter 6

Behind the Guns

Scores of men and horses of the First Line had been eviscerated by the grapeshot fired in the final volley. Men were thrown as their mounts collapsed through wounds or exhaustion, others were pinned under their dead carcasses.

Colonel Obolensky believed that the final volley with canister would annihilate the First Line, but remarkably about 150 men entered the gun-line. Some of the gun-crews managed to hitch up their guns while the fighting went on around them; at least two guns were moved towards the rear. The survivors of the First Line went at the gun crews with vengeance. But some of the Russians fought back with sabre and carbine, even with ramrods and sponges. British blood was up and there could be no mercy, the battery had wreaked a terrible carnage among their ranks and they could not be permitted to continue to fire on the Second Line nor to carry the guns off.

The impact of the Charge was greatly reduced by the decimation of the 17th Lancers and 13th Light Dragoons. The Second Line regiments arrived at the gun-line independently of each other; the 11th Hussars closely followed by the 4th Light Dragoons, and finally the 8th Hussars, with elements missing the guns altogether.

Gun-smoke hung in the air, extending some eighty yards down the valley, beyond which were the Russian cavalry. It was into this white acrid cloud that the remnants of the First Line disappeared, engaging the 200-plus gun-crews, lancing, cutting, thrusting, and trampling them under their horses' hooves in a mad frenzy. The artillerymen found what shelter they could under the guns, limbers or harnessed horses.

Not all of the survivors of the First Line actually rode through the battery. Captain Morris led twenty of his squadron into the drifting smoke, missing the guns to the left, and riding past them and into the rear where they faced at least two squadrons of Russian cavalry. The other survivors of his regiment however found themselves among the gun-crews.

Private William Butler's squadron was in amongst the guns, but evidently he had lost his lance: 'What few reached the guns – and I amongst them – cut away like madmen and succeeded in taking and spiking them.'

Corporal John Penn pierced a gunner at the gallop but was unable to withdraw his lance. Penn drew his sabre and charged towards a Cossack officer who wheeled his horse about to flee, but Penn delivered 'cut six', which nearly decapitated him. Penn dismounted to claim the officer's pouch belt, sword and clasp knife as souvenirs. His own horse, however, had received a ball in the near shoulder.

Other men preferred to use the point, as exemplified by Private John Smith, also of the 17th Lancers:

'He found that the thick coat worn by the Russian soldiers was almost proof against his sword-cuts, so he used the point of his blade. Seeing a fellow trooper slashing for all he was worth at the enemy, he called out. "Don't cut 'em. man, give 'em the point." Many a comrade acted on this good advice, thereby lessening the number of the foe.'[1]

Despite the close attention of the 17th Lancers, the Russians made a determined effort to rescue the guns, as Corporal Thomas Morley explained:

'Those who did not fall were through the guns in an instant and full of fight. Our arrival at the battery [we] silenced it instantly, and the gunners began to try to move the cannon away. The gospel of Russian fighting was always to save the guns.'[2]

Cornet Archibald Cleveland, 17th Lancers, recalled the action at the guns. His horse had already been wounded and received a stab to the leg in one gunner's desperate attempt to escape. He could hardly get him to trot:

'Three Cossacks, seeing, as I suppose, the disabled state of my horse, came after me. I guarded the first fellow's point, and gave him a slight point, and he went on. The next ran his lance through my pouch-box, which is made of silver, and so saved me. The third caught me in the ribs, but the point of his lance being broken off, it only bruised my side.... I had, before that, other fortunate escapes of being cut down – only I was too sharp for them. My revolver was of great use to me.'[3]

Cornet and Adjutant John Chadwick, 17th Lancers, fought off several gunners until he was slashed across the neck and face, fell from the saddle, and was taken prisoner:

'When the attack was being made, Lieutenant [sic] Chadwick's horse was severely wounded by a ball received on the animal's neck and this had the effect of covering him with a shower of blood from the wound. After this, he felt that his chances of returning alive were hopeless. He would not leave his regiment however, but proceeded on in the face of heavy fire from 12-pounders.

'After the Charge, in which he was nearly unhorsed, he was surrounded by a number of the enemy, and had some difficulty in retaining his seat in consequence of his murderous assailants, each giving him a prod with their lances. He got his mare's head into the position towards our forces, when a Cossack advanced towards him with his lance in a threatening attitude. The captain [sic] at once prepared to meet his would-be assailant, but seeing his position, the latter retreated.

'At this moment he observed a Russian dragoon loading his carbine and suspecting his intentions the captain pressed on. While so doing the Cossack alluded to before had turned round to throw his lance, which hit the captain in the neck and threw him from his horse.

'The soldier recovered from his fall in a few moments, and on raising his head from the ground he saw the Cossacks behaving in a most barbaric manner, stabbing and wounding the English troops as they lay on the ground. Seeing one of these approaching, the captain bounded to his feet, and found that he was able to defend himself with his sword and revolver. In the hurry of the moment he threw the former away and presented the latter to the approaching Cossack, who, seeing this, turned away.

'While considering what was to be done, he observed six Ural Cossacks riding down on him. British pluck still animating him, he kept his assailants at bay with his revolver, but in a few minutes he was surrounded by some half-dozen or more Cossacks and dragoons, who called upon him to surrender.

'He was disarmed, and in this defenceless state he became the object of many indignities. One seized him by the belt, another gave him a blow with a knot across his back. At this time the captain felt indignant that, to use his own words, had he been armed he would have shot his assailant whatever might have been the consequences.'[4]

Troop Sergeant Majors John Linkon and George Smith of the 13th Light Dragoons saw the enemy dragging one of the guns away and shot the lead horse, which collapsed onto the mount of Captain Godfrey Morgan, 17th Lancers. To add to the irony, this officer's life was then accidentally saved by a Cossack, as he later related:

'In another minute I was on the gun and the leading Russian's grey horse, shot, I suppose with a pistol by somebody on my right, fell across my horse, dragging it over with him and pinning me in between the gun and himself. A Russian gunner on foot at once covered me with his carbine. He was just within reach of my sword, and I struck him across his neck. The blow did not do him much harm, but it disconcerted his aim. At the same time a mounted gunner struck my horse on the forehead with his sabre. Spurring 'Sir Briggs' he half jumped, half blundered over the fallen horses, and then for a short time bolted with me.

'I only remember finding myself alone amongst the Russians trying to get out as best I could. This, by some chance, I did, in spite of the attempts of the Russians to cut me down. When clear again of the guns I saw two or three of my men making their way back, and as the fire from both flanks was still heavy it was a matter of running the gauntlet again.'[5]

Lieutenant Percy Shawe Smith, 13th Light Dragoons, had arrived at the guns defenceless, as due to an accident to his right hand he was unable to use a sword:

'A Russian soldier rode alongside, and resting his carbine on the left arm, pressed the muzzle close to Smith's body as the two horsemen galloped, locked together.

'Smith presently finding the suspense intolerable, struck out with his maimed hand at the Russian's face, and the carbine going off, the bullet passed over Smith's head, his opponent then leaving him alone.'[6]

One of the many men pinned down by their dead horse about the gun-line was Private Mitchell, 13th Light Dragoons. Here he witnessed the fate of many as he came under fire from sharpshooters on the lower slopes of the Causeway Heights:

'I tried to extricate my leg, which, after a short time I succeeded in doing and stood upright, finding myself unhurt, except my leg, which was a little painful from the crush. I still had my sword in my hand and soon found there were numberless bullets lying around me which came from the infantry on the flank of their battery, who fired at any of us who were dismounted. Just at this time a man of my troop, named Pollard [Private Charles or Thomas Pollard], came to me, and throwing himself down beside the carcass of my horse for shelter from the bullets, called to me saying, "Come here, Mitchell; this is good cover." I said, "No; we had better make our way back as quickly as possible, or we shall soon be taken prisoners, if not killed, if we remain here." Upon this he jumped up, and we both started to get back, but had not gone many yards when a poor fellow called to us to help him. He was in a similar position to mine, and he belonged to our regiment. I took him beneath the arms, and Pollard raised the horse's forepart a little, so that I managed to draw his leg from under the horse; but his thigh was broken, and, besides, he had a severe wound on his head, which covered him with blood. On seeing his injuries, we laid him gently down.

He said: "You can do no more for me, I thought my thigh was broken before you pulled me out. Look out for yourselves." Now this incident had only been the work of a very short time during which our brigade had passed beyond the guns. The smoke having cleared away, for the guns were silent enough now, that is, the guns we had charged, so that we could see a number of men making their way back the same as ourselves. The number of horses lying about was something fearful.'[7]

With their officers killed or wounded, the NCOs and men had to take the initiative. Among the senior NCOs was Troop Sergeant Major Cattermole, 17th Lancers:

'When by the guns, I inclined to my left and crossed two or three of my regiment, who seemed so confused as to hardly know how to act, and, like myself, acted afterwards individually, the ranks being broken, and no officer left to command.'[8]

Cardigan had lost contact with his trumpeter and ADCs during the Charge and passed through the blanket of smoke alone, emerging some eighty yards behind the gun-line. Immediately in front of him he saw a mass of Russian cavalry.

Cardigan's Brigade Major, Lieutenant Colonel G.W. Mayow, recalled: 'As the line approached the Russian Artillery the smoke became so dense that we could see but little except the flashes of the guns and I then lost sight of Lord Cardigan.'[9]

Riding with the 17th Lancers, Private James Wightman was badly shaken by the concussion wave of a shell:

'A shell burst right over my head with a hellish crash that all but stunned me. Immediately after I felt my horse under me take a tremendous leap into the air. What he jumped at I never saw or knew; the smoke was so thick I could not see my arm's length around me. Through the dense veil I heard noises of fighting and slaughter, but saw no obstacle, no adversary, no gun or gunner, and in short, was through and beyond the Russian battery before I knew for certain that I had reached it. I then found that none of my comrades were close to me; there was no longer any semblance of a line. No man of the Lancers was on my right, a group was a little way on my left. Lord Cardigan must have increased his distance during or after passing through the battery, for I now saw him some way ahead, alone in the midst of a knot of Cossacks.'[10]

Lord Cardigan had ridden through the guns and by pure chance emerged from the dense smoke in front of Prince Radzivill, who recognized him from a pre-war meeting and detached a troop of Cossacks with orders for his capture. Cardigan maintained that it was 'no part of a general's duty to fight the enemy among private soldiers', and he tried to evade their lances using superior horsemanship: 'On being nearly surrounded by Cossacks, I gradually retreated until I reached the battery. I could see none of the First Line or of the supports. The First Line did not follow me.'

Restricted by their orders, all the Cossacks could do was to prod at him with their lances and try to force him into surrender. Cardigan later wrote that during this encounter he was 'slightly wounded' and only 'with difficulty got away from them'. Sergeant Johnson saw the wound inflicted and supposed it to be more serious, which it would have been if the Cossacks had not been constrained.

Cardigan always considered that he executed his duty to the full in leading the brigade to take the guns:

'I led into the battery and through the Russian gun limber carriages and ammunition wagons in the rear. I rode within twenty yards of the line of the Russian cavalry. I was attacked by two Russian Cossacks, slightly wounded by their lances, and with difficulty got away from them, they trying to surround me.' Cardigan then scoured the area immediately beyond the gun-line and found only the dead and dying and rode back towards the guns. 'On arriving at the battery through which I had led, I found no part of the brigade. I rode slowly up the hill, and met General Scarlett.'[11]

In some circles Cardigan was criticized for not rallying the remnant of the brigade. In his defence, Cardigan rhetorically asked Alexander Kinglake 'what was the duty of the Brigadier under such circumstances? In such a desperate mêlée to remain to be taken prisoner, or was it his duty to retire?'

Cornet George Wombwell, ADC to Cardigan, had his horse killed by grape-shot at point-blank range and caught a riderless horse and fought in amongst the guns. Only when his second horse was shot and he was surrounded by Cossacks did he surrender. Wombwell was roughly pulled down from his mount and taken back; he would later be held alongside Captain Morris. Meanwhile, as Cardigan had moved back towards the battery a number of men saw their brigade commander but chose not to rally on him. Corporal Thomas Morley, 17th Lancers, caught sight of Lord Cardigan: 'My first thought after we were through the line was to look for an officer to see what we were to do. I saw Lord Cardigan at first but I had no impulse to join him. I think no British soldier ever had. He led 670 [sic] and none relied on him. I saw troopers riding past him to the right and left. He was about 50 yards beyond the guns on their extreme left.'[12]

Crucially Morley too places Lord Cardigan well beyond the guns and over towards the Fedioukine Heights.

Cardigan's ADC, Lieutenant Henry Maxse, lost his horse before the battery. He pressed on towards the guns on foot and was nearly trampled by Private James Wightman's horse. Private Wightman recalled the action:

'At this moment Lieutenant Maxse, his lordship's aide-de-camp, came back out of the tussle, and crossed my front as I was riding forward. I saw that he was badly wounded, and he called to me, "For God's sake, Lancer, don't ride over me! See where Lord Cardigan is," pointing to him, "rally on him!"'[13]

Wightman believed that Cardigan had instinctively attempted to rally survivors: 'After passing the guns, I distinctly heard His Lordship give the order to rally inside the Guns in the space between those Guns and the Russian Cavalry in the rear.'

It is possible Wightman may have heard Lieutenant Colonel Mayow's rallying calls, although Private Richardson, 11th Hussars, claimed that Cardigan's voice was unmistakable:

'Lord Cardigan – he was a rough spoken man, was Lord Cardigan, but good hearted – he shouts [in the lead-up to the final moments of the Charge], "Give em the point lads; it's no use slashing at em." And he was right too, because they all wore those thick ulsters.'

According to his account Private Wightman did try to rally on Lord Cardigan but became involved in combat with a Cossack:

'I was hurrying on to support the brigade commander, when a Cossack came at me and sent his lance into my right thigh. I went for him, but he bolted; I overtook him, drove my lance into his back and unhorsed him just in front of two Russian guns, which were in possession of Sergeant-Majors Lincoln [Linkon] & [George] Smith, of the 13th Light Dragoons, and other men of the brigade. When pursuing the Cossack I noticed Colonel Mayow deal very cleverly with a big Russian cavalry officer. He tipped off his shako with the point of his sword, and then laid his head right open with the old cut seven. The chase of my Cossack had diverted me from rallying on Lord Cardigan. He was now nowhere to be seen, nor did I ever again set eyes on the chief who had led us down the valley so grandly. The handful with the guns, to which I momentarily attached myself, were presently outnumbered and overpowered, the two sergeant-majors being taken prisoners, having been dismounted.'[14]

Further evidence of Cardigan's exploits to the rear of the battery came from Lieutenant Percy Shawe Smith, 13th Light Dragoons, who witnessed Cardigan's exertions in evading capture: 'I saw one of the Cossacks who were drawn up in the rear of the guns cut at his Lordship with his sword and I recollect the circumstances, particularly as I observed that Lord Cardigan kept his sword at the slope and did not take any trouble to defend himself.'

Corporal John Daniel Robinson, 13th Light Dragoons, was also close by. He wrote to a friend in Leeds of his encounter:

'I did not ride many yards further before I saw our commander, Lord Cardigan, very nearly thrust off his horse and if it had not been for me the old boy's life would not have been worth a row of pins. I saved him, for I directly saw a Russian had marked him for he drew his lance and made at his Lordship, but I was too expert for the rascal. I parried, while the man struck, and then he bolted as if Old Nick were after him.'[15]

Another account states how a 17th Lancer saw Cardigan surrounded by hussars and intervened by running one of them through the neck with his lance before beating the others off.[16]

Sergeant Thomas George Johnson, 13th Hussars, also saw Cardigan was under threat:

'I passed however with some of the Second Line a second time through the Guns and on approaching the Enemy's Cavalry which I believe was drawn up some little distance in rear of the battery, I and a man named John Heeley [John Keeley of the 13th Light Dragoons] found ourselves within a few yards of Lord Cardigan who was also in the rear of the Battery and surrounded by and engaged in defending himself against four or five Cossack Lancers. Both Heeley and myself rushed to his Lordship's assistance but my horse on the moment received a severe wound which completely disabled him (and from which and other injuries he afterwards died) and I believe the man Heeley had his horse shot under him.'

Private James Olley, 4th Light Dragoons, also saw the earl at the rear of the guns:

'I saw several Russians dash at the Earl of Cardigan who was near the breech of a big gun; but his horse brought him safely over the limber towards us. I never saw him again in the battle.'[17]

Johnson's account continues: 'I then saw Lord Cardigan disengage himself from the Cossacks and ride away apparently unhurt but one of the Cossacks then made a right rear point at him with his Lance which I then believed and feared had passed through his Lordship's body [as mentioned in an earlier account].

'I then retreated towards the Hill as rapidly as I could and after a few moments I came up with some of Lord Lucan's staff who were saying that Lord Cardigan was killed. Someone present contradicted it which contradiction I then confirmed by telling them that I had just seen his Lordship's narrow escape and safety.'[18]

In the confusion of battle the men acted on their own initiative or following the orders of the few officers and NCOs who reached the guns; in the dense smoke it was difficult to assess the situation beyond a few yards. A junior officer of the 13th Light Dragoons, Lieutenant Edward Jervis, initiated an attempt to capture one of the guns which had been limbered up. Corporal Morley, 17th Lancers, was among the men who joined Jervis mistaking him for an officer of his own regiment. Morley informed Jervis that Lord Cardigan was nearby:

'Lieutenant Jervis was riding towards a cannon that was retreating to the rear. I galloped up to him and informed him that Lord Cardigan was above [sic], pointing my sword to the place. He replied, "never mind, let's capture that gun!" we raced towards it. He [Jervis] said, "Cut down the gunners!" He shot one of the horses in the head bringing it to a sudden stop. The gunners disappeared between the horse and the gun-carriage as we slashed at them. We both dismounted and took out the dead horse while more of the Brigade gathered about to assist us. Private John Smith [of C Troop] mounted one of the horses attached to the gun, and another soldier mounted another horse of the gun. We started back off the field at a gallop with the mounted cannon, and were near the place where I had seen Lord Cardigan, when a large body of Cossacks charged.'[19]

There were few survivors who observed Lord Cardigan at the eastern end of the valley after Johnson, Morley, Wightman and Maxse. While most of the Second Line had moved away from the gun-line, he appears to have made his way back towards the battery. Here the smoke was still dense and the other survivors remained largely unseen – those still attempting to take the guns neither saw nor heard him or chose to ignore him, while Cardigan saw no groups of men to rally. Cannon and small-arms fire filled the air rather than the noise of charging horses or shouts from great masses of troopers engaging with the enemy.

Cardigan had played no part directing the actions beyond the guns, as he had ridden through and well beyond No. 3 Don Cossack battery alone. He had been pursued back through the guns by Cossacks. Here no major elements of the brigade could be seen, only the dead and dying, nor did the Second Line arrive in any force. With the First Line now way in advance of the guns, the 11th Hussars having veered off to the left and the 8th Hussars to the right, only the 4th Light Dragoons had arrived near the centre of the line and it seems reasonable to suppose that he assumed that he was one of the few men of the brigade still alive. Deafened by the noise of the batteries and, perhaps, concussed from the shock-wave of the blast of the cannon that had gone off just to one side of him,[20] Cardigan was unaware of the survivors beyond his sight and believed there was hardly a man alive to rally. Indeed, he saw only 'the small broken parties retreating'. And so Cardigan began to pick his way back.

When later challenged as to why he did not rally the men behind the guns Lord Cardigan replied: 'The feeble remains of the lines of the brigade could have done nothing more under a general officer than they did under their own officers.' The Heavy Brigade supposedly charging in support of the Light Brigade was turned back because Lord Lucan believed that they would be annihilated at the guns. Cardigan did not look back during the whole Charge and only saw small numbers of survivors at and beyond the guns, the other troopers fighting in groups, both large and small, in the gun-smoke (between 190 and 200 shot and shell had been fired by the Russian guns) and beyond his sight. It was not unreasonable for Cardigan to believe there was no brigade left to rally. Lieutenant Colonel Mayow, second-in-command of the brigade, had frantically searched for Cardigan. Unable to find him, Mayow concluded, 'Lord Cardigan must be either killed or taken prisoner.' The command of the brigade fell on him and he called out, but only fifteen men of the 17th Lancers and twelve men of the Dragoons rallied on him, such was the reality of their situation.

As the smoke around Mayow thinned, he caught sight of the Russian cavalry formed up in line a hundred yards to the rear of the guns. Immediately realizing that these troops would decimate his small force if they retired, Mayow ordered the lancers to the fore and prepared to charge.

Ryzhov had ordered his cavalry forward to counter-attack and to cover No. 3 Don Cossack battery, but sent Cossacks rather than regular cavalry. This mistake proved decisive, as one officer explained:

'Frightened by the disciplined order of the mass of cavalry bearing down on them, [they] did not hold, but, wheeling to their left, began to fire on their own troops in their efforts to clear a route of escape.'[21]

The survivors of the front line were largely fighting at the gun-line, attempting to capture the guns, or had rallied under Mayow to charge the Russian cavalry. Each group was unaware of the other. A third party, about twenty lancers led by Captain Morris, had entered the bank of smoke drifting from the battery towards the Fedioukine Heights and charged by to their left.

Their momentum carried Captain Morris and his command through the smoke, emerging on the other side to confront an entire regiment of Russian hussars. Morris turned and called out: 'Remember what I have told you, and keep together.' Spurring his horse on, he headed straight at the enemy. Remarkably, facing only twenty or so Lancers, the Russians scattered in disorder.

Morris made for what he took to be a senior Russian hussar officer, charging with his sabre arm held straight out, dipping at the last moment under the enemy's defence and striking home. The two had clashed at full tilt and Morris's blade passed straight through the Russian's chest, right up to the hilt, half of its length protruded from the man's back. As the officer slumped back in the saddle Morris was nearly pulled from his horse. Morris later commented: 'I don't know how I came to use the point of my sword, but it's the last time I ever do.'

While Morris was still struggling to withdraw his sabre, two Russians slashed at him, one striking him above the ear, the other across his skull. Without the protection of a leather chapska (Morris had only very recently given up his staff role to assume command of the regiment and still wore his staff officer's blue frock-coat and forage cap with its gold braid trimmed peak), Morris felt the full weight of the blows, was unhorsed, and plunged to the ground.

Troop Sergeant Major Abraham Ranson saw this action:

'Then I saw an act of heroism; Morris was on foot, his head streaming with blood, engaging five or six Cossacks. I made the remark to Corporal Taylor near me that poor Captain Morris, I was afraid, was taken prisoner, there was so much odds against him.'[22]

Alexander Kinglake, having gathered statements from a number of eyewitnesses, recorded how 'Morris received a sabre cut on the left side of the head which carried away a large piece of bone above the ear, and a deep, clean cut passing down through the acorn of his forage cap, which penetrated both plates of his skull.'[23]

In a stroke of luck, and he needed one or he was a dead-man, as Morris fell his sabre came free. Despite his sight being obscured by his own blood, he regained his feet and took up his sword. The enemy bore down on him:

'Morris sought to defend himself by the almost ceaseless "moulinet" or circling whirl of his sword and from time to time he found means to deliver some sabre cuts upon the thighs of his assailants. Soon however he was pierced in the temple, which splintered up a piece of bone and forced it under his scalp. This wound gave him great pain and he believed that his life must be nearly at its end.'[24]

Morris undoubtedly owed his life to an English-speaking Russian officer who called off his men and offered Morris the opportunity to surrender.

Weak from loss of blood and probably concussed, he relented and offered up his sabre. This done, the officer moved on and Morris was beaten and his personal possessions stolen.

With Captain Morris having been made a prisoner, the remainder of his men fought for their lives against ridiculous odds. The Russians, realizing how few 17th Lancers faced them, attacked from all sides. Only a handful escaped to link up with Troop Sergeant Major Dennis O'Hara of their regiment who led fifteen-plus men back up the valley, weaving around the Cossacks advancing from the right flank who were skirmishing and attacking almost at random.[25]

Lieutenant Colonel George Mayow had already rallied a group of about twenty-seven men, who now linked up with a force now numbering thirty of the 17th Lancers led by O' Hara riding to his left front, and a dozen or so 13th Light Dragoons. Together they charged straight at the Russian cavalry formed up directly to the rear of the battery. The men behind him saw the extent of the enemy and knew that if they did not break, then not a man would survive.

They had silenced the guns and presumed that the Second Line, followed by the Heavies, were behind them. Not a man could have imagined that Lord Lucan had already turned back and abandoned them to their fate.

Why did the mass of Russian cavalry hold back? Despite their overwhelming numbers, the Russians turned and fled, some as far as the aqueduct close to the Chernaya crossing. It is possible that the Cossacks and hussars in the 17th Lancers' path believed that they were the vanguard and that the rest of the Light and Heavy Brigades were right behind them, obscured by the gun-smoke; a not unreasonable assumption, as it was what the men of the 17th Lancers believed. The Russians later claimed that this was a tactical move to draw the British into the trap, which was later sprung by their lancers. The Russians overlooking the scene however were critical of the withdrawal and recognized the chaotic scenes for what they were.

What the British troops reported was that the front ranks of the Russians turned and spurred their mounts; this was no orderly retreat. Mayow's group pushed them a further 500 yards back towards the Chernaya. The few who held their ground were quickly despatched.

The men who had rallied and fought under Mayow joined a squadron of 8th Hussars under Shewell, and the group, numbering around seventy, pushed on along the valley close to the Causeway Heights.

The Russians' panic was probably initiated by the shock and disbelief of witnessing a determined body of men charging through canister, shell, and shot. The British must have seemed like invincible madmen. The Russians had not expected a single man to survive the slaughter, and the emergence of a body of bloodied figures from the smoke – men who fought like demons – must have unnerved them and thrown them into disorder.

INTO THE VALLEY OF DEATH

Regarding the general retirement of the cavalry to the rear of the guns, Lieutenant Stefan Kozhukhov blamed the regular troops for fleeing first, which caused the Cossacks to quickly follow suit:

'Once through our guns the enemy moved quickly and bravely at a gallop towards our cavalry. This was so unexpected that before anyone realized it our cavalry had broken. First of all the hussars showed themselves unready to stand against the enemy cavalry, and after them the Cossacks, so that all our cavalry was soon retreating in disorder.

'It was chaos. Our cavalry outnumbered the enemy five times over, and yet it fell back in total disorder to the Chernaya, with the English coming hotly forward at the hooves of our horses. Then it became impossible for our regiments to escape and both bodies of cavalry came to a stop. In this tight space at the end of the valley, were packed four regiments of our Cossacks and hussars, and there inside this great mass, were the English, probably as surprised as ourselves at this unexpected circumstance.'

Back at the gun-line Lieutenant Jervis and his group had captured one gun and were leading it away. Corporal Morley wrote:

'We started back off the field at a gallop with the mounted cannon, and were near the place where I had seen Lord Cardigan, when a large body of Cossacks charged, who appeared from behind a hill and surrounded our group. I was riding on the right of the gun, the direction in which the Cossacks attacked us. In the mêlée I got through the wrong end and had to ride back again down the valley. I was pursued by seven of them until they fairly chased me into a body of Russian Cavalry with its back to me. There was no alternative but to ride through or surrender to the Cossacks. I put spurs to my horse and bolted into the line. I got through with a knock on the head from a Russian officer, that would have wounded me but for my dress cap, which I eventually lost, but the lines saved it.

'More members of the Light Brigade were riding about – some of them wounded – fighting as best they could. Corporal [James] Hall, of my own troop, had his lance trailing about and covered with blood. I told him to throw it away and wanted to pick it up myself, as I needed one, but there was no time. Hall was captured and died of amputation of the leg. During the mêlée, about 40 stragglers of the Brigade were driving a line of Russian Hussars down the valley in close column.'

From a letter by Thomas Morley addressed to Lord Wolseley, dated 12 November 1896, he continues the narrative:

'I rode from the right flank to the left flank of the rear rank calling to the men to fall back. Private Clifford of my troop rode into the column and was cut to pieces before my eyes. The Hussars came about and we were then between two large bodies of cavalry, one marching up the valley, the other down, so that the few of our Brigade who were farthest beyond the Russian guns were now completely hemmed in by a great body of Russians.'

Part of a petition submitted by Morley for the award of the Victoria Cross added:

'At this critical moment, when there was no officer to command us and we were apparently lost, I beg leave to introduce the words of a comrade still living describing my conduct.' Private James Wightman of the 17th Lancers was with a small group that fell in with Corporal Morley who was unlucky not to have received a gallantry award for his actions: 'We forced our way through ring after ring of enemies, fell in with my comrade Peter Marsh, and rode rearward, breaking through party after party of Cossacks, until we heard the familiar voice of Corporal Morley of our regiment, a great, rough, bellowing Nottingham man. He had lost his lance and hat, and his long hair was flying out in the wind as he roared, "Coom ere! coom ere! Fall in, lads, fall in!" Well, with shouts and oaths he had collected some twenty troopers of various regiments. We fell in with the handful this man of the hour had rallied to him, and there joined us also under his leadership Sergeant-Major Hanson and Private John Penn of the 17th.'[26]

Remarkably, this small band of survivors breached the Russian cavalry, but their ordeal was far from over and they still had a desperate time in reaching safety which lay a mile away. Men and horses were exhausted, wounded or both; there were marauding Cossacks looking to pick off easy prey; while artillery and musket fire still played across the valley. Many men stated that the fire during the retreat was worst than that during the Charge.

It was intended that the 11th Hussars should ride as direct support to the 17th Lancers. Unfortunately Lieutenant Colonel John Douglas and his regiment had ridden off to the left, even more so than Captain Morris and his lancers. Only those riding on the extreme right entered the gun-line, but they did so not long after the 17th Lancers and provided active support.

Private John Richardson, 11th Hussars, had his horse killed under him while at the guns:

'There was a lot of smoke about, and I couldn't see much. I remember after we got among the artillery and came to the hand-to-hand work, my horse was killed, and fell with me under him.'

Private Richard Brown of the same regiment was fighting on. He had lost his horse, mortally wounded by a cannon ball fired while closing with No. 3 Don Cossack battery. Fighting on foot, Brown attacked the gunners, slashing at one, defending against another coming at him with his ramrod, taking off his arm. In the frenzy, he nearly scalped a third. Cornered by two Cossacks, Brown fought back and killed both; one with a fierce body cut, the other with a vicious back-handed cut across his throat.[27]

Troop Sergeant Major George G. Gutteridge, 11th Hussars, also recalled his regiment's action against the gunners, particularly noting Sergeant Major Smith's attempts to capture one of the guns:

'As we approached the battery, which was formed across the valley, the fire was most terrific. After passing the guns, I observed a Russian field piece, drawn by six horses, being taken away from its position, and Sergeant-Major [George] Smith endeavouring to secure the assistance of a party to prevent it being carried off. He followed after it, but finding himself alone and unsupported, and a party of Cossacks led by an officer intercepting him, he returned to his place. I witnessed him encouraging the men to bear up and show a good front, calling out, "The better front we keep the better chance we shall all have." His example had beneficial effect.'[28]

Private Robert Ashton, another of the 11th Hussars who entered the battery a little after the 17th Lancers, stated the simple facts:

'We captured the guns, and killed as many of the gunners as we could; but of course we could not hold the battery.'[29]

In amongst the slaughter at the guns, Sergeant R. Davies, 11th Hussars, saw one of the gun teams limbering up at the end of the battery. Davies called over to Private John T. Bambrick riding beside him to follow him and together try to foil the gunners. Two enemy lancers rode to the gunners' defence, one of whom Davies shot with his carbine, the other shot Davies' horse, bringing him to the ground where he received a lance wound to the right thigh. Somehow Davies escaped, caught a riderless horse, and made it back to the British lines.

Members of the 11th Hussars who missed the gun-line galloped through the smoke beyond the guns. Here they were confronted by the same Russian hussars who had moments earlier decimated the lancers under Morris. The eighty survivors initially rallied on Captain Edwin Adolphus Cook, along with Lieutenants Dunn and Palmer. Lieutenant Colonel Douglas halted the men and shouted orders for them to 'Close in on the centre.' The carnage had created many gaps and they quickly re-formed their front.

Confusion reigned and once more the Russians hesitated and the British took the initiative. A Russian officer, 'decorated with several orders', came up to surrender his sword to Lieutenant Colonel Douglas, but he had too much to contend with at that moment and the offer was spurned, Lieutenant Palmer instead receiving the accolade. Douglas decided that to turn his back would prove fatal and that his only option was to charge the Cossacks.

Again the Russians reacted badly to the challenge and fell back with their comrades already fleeing the gun-line; the 11th Hussars in hot pursuit.

Lieutenant Colonel John Douglas explains how his small band threw the Russians back:

'As we came upon them they got into confusion and very loose order. My men got greatly excited, and we pursued at our best pace, they sweeping round the base of the hill to our left front, forming the end of the valley.'[30]

Troop Sergeant Major George Smith: 'We were now nearing the extreme end of the valley, about a mile and a half from our [starting] position, still pursuing this body of Cavalry. In their confusion, I saw one of their leading Cossacks fall from the bridge into the Aqueduct, there being no parapet. Near the bridge, was a moderately steep hill which formed the end of the valley, up which they rode a short distance, their rear being at the foot, close to us.'[31]

The 11th Hussars' gallant charge had pushed the Cossacks back into the unsuspecting ranks of the Ingermanland and Kiev regiments which were thrown into chaos and a general rout ensued. Some officers endeavoured to rally their troops but were cut down and these troops were pushed back as far as the gorge leading to the Chernaya.

Private William Cullen, 11th Hussars, had been left behind, but despite being isolated and in mortal danger, he went to the rescue of a comrade:

'When retiring, after driving the Cossacks into the River Tchernaya [Chernaya], I came up to poor Jack [Private John Flemming], who had three Cossacks attacking him. I had the pleasure of "skewering" one, when the other two bolted, not seeming to care about stopping in our company. We were then by ourselves, those of our comrades who were left having ridden on.'[32]

There were now two formed groups of survivors behind the Russian guns: Lieutenant Colonel Mayow with the remnants of the 17th Lancers and 13th Light Dragoons to the right, and Lieutenant Colonel Douglas with eighty men of the 11th Hussars between the left flank of the guns and the eastern end of the Fedioukine Heights, where they had pushed towards the track leading to the Traktir Bridge. Both groups had pursued the Russian cavalry to the Chernaya, and knew that they were only holding the enemy at bay because of their anticipated support. Meanwhile, the men still fighting at the gun-line had now been supplemented by a small number of men from the 11th. All expected the five regiments of the Heavy Brigade to emerge from the smoke and to sweep everything before them.

Private William Nicholson, 13th Light Dragoons, on pursuing the Russians to the Chernaya:

'When we got to the guns everything seemed in such confusion that we hardly knew what we were about. The Russians retired from the guns, and were pursued by some of us down to the River Tchernaya [Chernaya], into which many of the enemy was driven in their confusion.'[33]

Lord Cardigan had stressed to Lord Paget that he wanted his 'best support', but the unchecked pace of the 4th Light Dragoons had meant that the 8th Hussars had fallen behind; they had also veered off to the right. The 4th Light Dragoons had advanced straight down the valley into the centre of the gun-line, but engaged the enemy alone. As they reached their objective Private Parkes glanced over to his commanding officer: 'Come on, my Lord! It is time you were drawing your sword – we are on top of the guns!' Lord Paget drew his sabre and moments later they were in amongst the guns and he put it through the neck of a gunner. The 4th Light Dragoons found themselves apparently isolated, as Lord Paget looked around for the First Line, which had largely passed though the guns and were pushing the enemy back to the Chernaya:

'When I got to the Guns and saw all [of] their host [i.e. the Russia cavalry] advancing, I looked in vain for the First Line, and never could account for them till I came back.'[34]

Corporal James Devlin, 4th Light Dragoons, obeyed the rally call:

'We were well in hand on arriving at the guns. After seizing them the portion of the brigade then there was rallied by Lord George Paget.'

Private James Olley, 4th Light Dragoons, although already wounded, was soon in the thick of the mêlée:

'The first man I happened with at the guns was a Russian gunner who attacked me with a ramrod. I felled him at the muzzle of the gun he was defending with two strokes of my sword... I was attacked by a Russian gunner who I cut down with my sword.'

Olley was still at the guns when he received further wounds: 'I received two lance wounds, one in the ribs and one in the neck from behind. The Russian Lancer in the rear who stabbed me was killed by a comrade and I struck down the other. In this cavalry encounter, I was wounded with a sabre across the forehead by a Russian dragoon. He made "Cut 7" at me... I gave him point and stabbed him. The sword fell from his hand and the point penetrated my foot. We cleared the guns of the enemy.'[35]

The hand-to-hand fighting remained fierce. In the midst of it all Samuel Parkes, his sword up in the air, shouted anxiously, 'Where's my chief? Who's seen the Colonel?' Paget answered, 'Here I am, my boy, I'm all right,' and Parkes joined Hugh Crawford, the Colonel's trumpeter, at Paget's side.

Moments later, Paget sighted the Russian gun-crews trying to carry away three of the guns. He immediately ordered Captain John George Brown, 4th Light Dragoons, to take some of his men and to engage them, as Paget recalled in his journal: 'I observed twenty or thirty yards ahead two or three of the guns scrambling away, drawn by horses with lasso-harness, which it was evident had thus been attached so that they might be drawn away at the very last moment, upon which I said to Captain Brown, who was close to me. "There are some guns getting away. Take some of your men and stop them," which order I need not say, was promptly and very effectively obeyed.'

Now in among the guns his men dealt with the gun-teams. Some tried to cut the traces to prevent the guns being dragged to the rear, while others spiked the guns; the men were outnumbered by the enemy and were fighting for their lives. Private Dennis Connor, 4th Light Dragoons, dismounted at the guns:

'I was one of those who tried to cut the traces of the Russian guns. I used my pocket knife, but found that within the leather were chains of steel.'[36]

Meanwhile, a few men claimed to have spiked some of the guns, which appears to be corroborated by Russian accounts. Other Chargers, including Private Robert Grant, 4th Light Dragoons, however, were categorical in saying that none of the guns were spiked, not at least in their presence:

'When we charged into the guns I dismounted and could have used some gun spikes had I had them, but unfortunately none had been issued. I never saw a gun spike. We then disabled as many gunners and drivers as we could, to prevent them taking the guns, feeling they were ours. After some little time I found myself in the rear almost alone, the greater portion of my regiment having retreated. Seeing the 11th Hussars coming up the valley pursued by the Russian Hussars, I galloped towards them. In tracking onto their rear, a sergeant of the Hussars galloped at me and tried to cut me down, but I defended myself.'[37]

Private Robert Owen Glendwr, 8th Hussars:

'Looking round to see which course I had better take, being at this time in the rear of the guns, I saw the 11th Hussars down the valley, galloping towards me, pursued by a strong body of Russian cavalry. I galloped towards, joined and returned with them.'[38]

Another of those who latched onto the 11th Hussars was Lieutenant Percy Smith of the 13th Light Dragoons. His story was later told by Captain Arthur Tremayne, 13th Light Dragoons. Smith was unarmed but got the better of a lancer who had him cold:

'Lieutenant Smith found himself separated from his men and brought to a standstill by three Russian lancers, one on each side and one in the front. The lancer on his right hesitated for a moment and left him with only two to look after. The man on his left attacked first, but he contrived to turn his point off with the upper part of his bridle arm at the cost of a mere scratch from the side of the lance-blade. At the same moment almost, the man in front gave point at his chest.

'Smith saw he couldn't guard himself without dropping his reins, so instead of that, as he was mounted on a good hunter, he jumped right on his assailant. The lance-point luckily hit on a bone and came out as the Russian went down, and before the other two could renew the attack a party of 11th Hussars came to the rescue and the lancers had something else to occupy their attention.'[39]

Lieutenant Joliffe and Sergeant Short attacked a gun crew as they tried to save their gun:

'On arriving at the guns the Russians were retreating with them, and had retired some distance with them from their original position. The 4th endeavoured to take possession of the guns. Lieutenant Joliffe was then next to me. I went slightly in advance and attacked the drivers of the gun, while Lieutenant Joliffe shot with his revolvers the gunners sitting on the guns. I distinctly saw him do that. I state positively I cut down at least six drivers.'[40]

The combat at the guns remained frenzied. Private Robert Farquharson, 4th Light Dragoons, wrote how he saw one man unhorse six Cossacks, while Captain Alexander Low defended himself with his revolver when attacked by three Cossacks, shooting two and finishing off the third with the point: 'Much gore besmeared him.' Using his non-regulation sword to great effect he is said to have killed eleven gunners. While the true figure can never be known, it is clear that Low was heavily engaged with the enemy and acquitted himself well. Robert Ferguson witnessed the same action and wrote of Low's gallantry:

'I followed Captain Low up to the guns, which were then being carried away by the Russians, and were considerably to the rear of their original position. I was immediately behind him. I saw Captain Low knock over one or two gunners off one of the guns with his revolver; we got the gun completely into our possession, but could not bring it away, having no support to enable us to do so.'[41]

Captain Low's own account was penned in a letter to his father. This was seen by a journalist with the *Bath Press* who wrote an article for that publication based on its contents:

'After that terrible charge at Balaclava, in which he slew and unhorsed several of the enemy, dealing sabre strokes, every one of which carried death with it, he found himself alone amongst the enemy horsemen, three of whom bore down on the British cavalryman, one on each flank and one in front. Seizing his revolver, he shot the first two, right and left, and cut down the third with his sabre; his good horse [then] bounded over him, and although with a jaw broken by a grape-shot, carried his heroic rider safe into British lines.'

When interviewed for an article published in *The Illustrated London News* of 30 October 1875, Private Dennis Connor commented on the novelty of the revolver in action, 'They [the officers] fired five shots to our one, and that seemed to alarm the Russians.'

Private Robert Grant, also of the 4th Light Dragoons, added: 'Our officers had revolvers, and they did great execution with them. In fact, the officers altogether did a great deal more service than the men, because of the revolvers. Many of the Cossacks got shot foolishly like, for after one discharge they thought it was all over, but the revolver had several barrels. Those Cossacks were all for plunder, and they tried to surround our officers, but they got knocked down with the shots.'

Cornet George Hunt led three of his men in an effort to capture one of the Russian guns. While Hunt, Sergeant John Howes and Private Robert Ferguson dismounted and attempted to harness the cannon to get it away, Connor tried to cut the traces. Lord George Paget of the 4th Light Dragoons witnessed the men's endeavours:

'Cornet Hunt was close to my right, when he returned his sword, jumped off his horse, and began trying to unhook the traces from a gun! The only acknowledgement of this act of devotion being, I fear, a sharp rebuke, and an order to remount. He [Hunt] thus disarmed himself in the mêlée, amid hand-to-hand encounters, an act which he attempted would have been a most useful one, had support been near to retain possession of the gun which he was trying to dismember, though under the circumstances it was of course a useless attempt – but none the less worthy of record and of a Victoria Cross, for which he would have been recommended, had the choice lain with me.'[42]

Sergeant John Howes, 4th Light Dragoons, who had assisted Cornet Hunt, later wrote:

'I found myself amongst the Russian guns – a few of my troop, including our Troop Sergeant-Major Herbert (who was killed) surrounded one of the guns. He dismounted with the intention of cutting the traces. We killed all the men belonging to the said gun, and I went to the leading horses and turned their heads round with the view of bringing the gun away, but finding it impossible, I left them.'[43]

Having been ordered to remount, Sergeant Howes' only option was a 'brute of a horse', but it saw him back to the British lines, although he received a slight cut on the side of his head after an encounter with a Russian hussar.

Cornet Sparke and Troop Sergeant Major Herbert were also seen to dismount to prevent a gun from being carried away by the enemy, but were less fortunate, as Private George Alfred Price, 4th Light Dragoons, related:

'Captain Hutton led us up to the guns; it was poor Cornet Sparks [Lieutenant Henry Astley Sparke] and Sergeant-Major Hubert [Troop Sergeant Major Frank Herbert] who dismounted to cut the traces of the horses attached to the Russian guns. I saw them both fall.'[44]

Private Edward Grennan, of the same regiment, also recalled their valiant attempt to prevent the enemy from removing the gun:

'We went for the central battery, and when we got in there we found no one there but the gunners in charge of the six [sic] pieces. They fought well, but we cut them down on all sides. Some of them sat on their guns to the last, and were sabred on the limbers.

'Then we set to work to get the guns out. It was at this time that Sergeant Herbert and another sergeant, whose name I forgot, lost their lives very foolishly. They dismounted to try and cut a rope, which was holding one of the guns, and instead of holding the reins they let their horses go.

The rope turned out to have an iron core, and while they were hacking at it with their sabres they were attacked by a lot of Russians, cut off, and killed.'[45]

Private Matthew Holland, 11th Hussars, also reported the failed attempts to cut the traces:

'We attempted to cut the traces of the guns, but they were chains covered with leather, and in less than half an hour two-thirds of us were down and the order was given to retire. I only know I ducked my head on my horse's neck and came home.'[46]

As the fighting in and around the guns involving the 4th Light Dragoons continued, Private Samuel Parkes' horse was shot under him but he skilfully rolled safely away as it slumped to the ground. Nearby, Trumpeter Hugh Crawford was dismounted, only rising to his feet with some difficulty. Seeing the trumpeter wounded and disarmed, two Cossacks closed on this easy kill. Parkes immediately put himself between Crawford and the Cossacks and slashed at them with his sabre until they pulled back.

Parkes supported Crawford with his left arm – he could not walk unaided – while keeping the Cossacks at bay with his sabre, and together they headed slowly away from the battery. Having emerged from the smoke they were surrounded by Russian cavalrymen. Parkes swung his sabre viciously at them until a wound to the right arm disabled him, and both men were taken prisoner.

The scene, which earned Parkes the Victoria Cross, was witnessed by Private James William Wightman of the 17th Lancers:

'I then rode towards Private Samuel Parkes, of the 4th Light Dragoons, who supporting with one arm the wounded Trumpet Major [*sic*] (Crawford) of his regiment, was with the other cutting and slashing at the enemies surrounding them. I struck in to aid the gallant fellow, who was not overpowered until his sword was shot away, when he and the Trumpet Major were taken prisoners, and it was with difficulty I was able to cut my way out.'[47]

In the general mêlée one of the gunners swung his sabre at Private Farquharson, only succeeding in cutting open his horse's chest. As the animal dropped to the ground, Farquharson managed to kill the gunner. Like many of his comrades, he was left on foot among the guns.

With the gun teams now largely silenced Lord Paget pushed on to join the remainder of the brigade which he deduced was further down the valley: 'When those guns had been disposed of, which did not occupy a long space of time, the 4th (by this time resembling more a party of skirmishers than a regiment), leaving the disabled behind them, pursued their onward course in support of the First Line.'

The 4th Light Dragoons engaged the fleeing Russian cavalry, the Cossacks putting up some resistance, as was explained by Private Joseph Grigg:

'Beyond the guns, we went at the Russian cavalry with a rush. I selected a Cossack, who was making for me with his lance pointed at my breast. I knocked it upwards with my sword, pulled up quickly and cut him down across the face. I tried to get hold of his lance but he dropped it. As he was falling, I noticed he was strapped to the saddle, so that he did not come to the ground, and the horse rushed away with him.'

Lord Paget remained on the offensive despite his dwindling numbers:

'I here saw a body of Russian cavalry to my left front, and on the impulse of the moment I determined to attack them; my reasons were that I thought I could do it with very great advantage, being under the impression that I could jam them into the gorge of the valley, here forming a sort of cul-de-sac from which there would be difficulty in escaping, as the aqueduct and River Chernaya barred any hasty egress.' At this point he still believed the Heavy Brigade would arrive in support, expecting 'that shortly both infantry and fresh cavalry would come up.'

Last to enter the bank of smoke which denoted the enemy's front were Colonel Shewell and the fifty or so mounted men of the 8th Hussars. With the notable exception of the men riding on the extreme left, the regiment missed the by now silent battery altogether. Those who did enter the gun-line found the gunners among the right flank of the guns were still making a stand. An anonymous 8th Hussar recalled the scene:

'The first thing I did, once within the guns, was to cut clean off the hand of a Russian gunner who was holding up his sponge-staff against me. He fell across the gun-carriage glaring savagely, but I cared little for that. I had seen too much. Bodies and limbs scattered in fragments, or smashed and kneaded together, and blood splashed into my face.'[48]

A Cossack officer rode his men to the aid of the gunners under attack from the 8th Hussars and a mêlée developed. Private Doyle recalled: 'There was an officer who dashed into the centre of us when the Russian lancers came down on our left, and wounded a man named Kennedy [Private Richard Kennedy, 8th Hussars]; he took the skin off one side of his head; he had also wounded or killed several others, but I could not say how many. I had pointed him with a "right-rear point".'

Colonel Shewell who had led the remainder of 8th Hussars to the right of the guns, emerged from the thick acrid gun-smoke some hundred yards or more to their rear, placing his force between their right flank and the eastern end of the Causeway Heights. Here he halted the regiment, which had maintained its formation, saved from the carnage dealt out by No. 3 Don Cossack battery, but nevertheless under a murderous hail of bullets, shot and shell largely from the Causeway Heights for a full seven or eight minutes. The survivors took a moment to close their ranks. Shewell spotted Sergeant Reilly out of position and immediately remonstrated with him, closing only to see that his eyes were fixed and staring and his face was 'as white as a flagstone' – he was dead.

The Light Brigade was by now fighting in four main groups beyond the guns. Those under the command of Lieutenant-Colonels Mayow and Douglas and Colonel Paget had pursued vastly superior forces of Russian cavalry down the valley to the Chernaya. The majority of the 8th Hussars under Colonel Shewell had come to a stop on the far right between these groups and the guns. The turning point of this action, and perhaps the whole Charge, was the moment of recognition by both sides that these exceptionally brave men had been abandoned by Lord Lucan and were alone – they had braved bullets, shot and shell, reached and captured their objective against all odds, but there was no support.

At this moment Corporal William Taylor's horse, half mad with fright, bolted and carried him into a mass of Russian cavalry beyond the guns. Here Taylor of the 8th Hussars was wounded and taken prisoner.

Captain Edwin Cook of the 11th Hussars looked for the Heavy Brigade coming up in the rear: 'I got through safe up to the guns, cut down all that came within reach and then at the cavalry behind, but to our horror the Heavy Brigade had not followed in support and there was alarm that we were cut off in the rear, which was true.'[49]

The men in and around the gun-line remained under fire from both infantry and artillery, largely from the Causeway Heights. Small groups of Cossacks were pushing forward and capturing riderless horses, picking off isolated survivors and murdering men trapped under their horses or lying wounded on the battlefield.

Meanwhile, Lieutenant Colonel Douglas and the fifty or so men of the 11th Hussars gathered around him had slowed their pace and come to a halt. Assessing the situation they saw their predicament. The men looked to their NCOs and officers for the command.

Sergeant Major George Smith of the 11th Hussars:

'They [the Cossacks] now halted, but remained for a few moments with their backs to us, looking over their shoulders. Seeing there were so few of us, and without supports, they turned about, and we sat face to face, our horses' heads close to theirs. As we looked up at them they had all the appearance of a vast assemblage in the gallery of a theatre, the stillness and suspense during these moments was terrible; At last it was broken by their officers calling out to their men to follow them, and break through us, which they themselves attempted to do by driving their horses at our front rank, but their men failed to display the same courage as their leaders, and our men showed a firm front, keeping close together, and bringing their swords down to the right front guard, kept them at bay. Many of them now took out their pistols and fired into us, and the Cossacks began to double round our flanks, and get in our rear.

'Many of the flank men now became engaged, and several were killed. Our position became every moment more critical, for we were in danger of being surrounded, and must have been overwhelmed and killed to a man. But had a few more of our squadrons come up at this time, I am of the opinion that this body of cavalry would have surrendered to us, for we, numbering now not more than eighty sabres, held this Russian Hussar Brigade in a corner at bay for some minutes.'

The noise of battle and the thick wall of smoke that filled the valley offered only momentary glimpses of what lay beyond. Both friend and foe must still have half-expected to hear the thunder of horses hooves and see the massed ranks of the Heavy Brigade emerge in an overwhelming wave of horse flesh and steel, but every moment that passed confirmed the truth.

Russian Hussar officers had finally halted the retreat. Then, once their men wheeled about, the vulnerability of the pitifully small body of British cavalry became all too apparent. Now emboldened, the Russians gradually found their courage and edged forward. Lieutenant Colonel Mayow and his men of the 17th Lancers and 13th Light Dragoons withdrew reluctantly towards the gun-line. Colonel Shewell, who had been stationary further back with the 8th Hussars, still assessing the situation, moved his regiment across to reinforce them, bringing the Russians to a halt. Mayow too had seen only small leaderless bodies of British cavalry behind the guns and his first words to Shewell were: 'Where is Lord Cardigan?' Shewell had hoped that Mayow knew. The two officers surveyed the situation trying to decide what to do next. Mayow, as Brigade Major, had the lead, but for the moment neither man acted. Around them the men asked where were their support, where were the Heavy Brigade?

Lord Paget believed that the Russian cavalry could have been pushed back further and potentially routed. Taken aback by how poorly they reacted when confronted by even small bodies of determined British cavalry, he momentarily considered ordering his men, outnumbered by twenty to one, to charge them even without support:

'They received us with a sort of irregular volley of carbines… My first impulse was to charge; the word was almost out, but at the instant I saw how fruitless such a proceeding would be. I halted the regiment within forty yards of them, and gave the order to retire.'[50]

The Russians now pressed forward and Lieutenant Colonel Douglas was forced to fall back. Lord Paget, to his right rear, led his fifty or so men forward calling out 'Rally, rally!' as they rode beyond the gun-line, calling for survivors to form up to support the First Line, but seeing a dozen men of the 11th withdrawing the 4th turned to follow suit. Paget realised that with their backs to the foe, they would quickly be outpaced and overrun. The only chance that they had was to go against all instinct. Paget would, moments later, rein his horse in and order the small body of men to face the Russian cavalry.

One of those who rallied on Lord Paget was Troop Sergeant Major John Linkon, 13th Light Dragoons:

'In the mêlée I got separated from them [the 8th Hussars, with whom he rode after the loss of his first horse] and advanced to find my own regiment, but I was too late for them and was very nigh taken prisoner, a party of the enemy making a regular dash at me. I only escaped, having a splendid horse and making two of them bite the dust by shooting them and wounding a third in the bridle arm. I got quite clear and joined a small party I came into contact with under the command of Lord George Paget.

'The party of the 4th I had joined, about a troop or two-thirds, it could not be more. As we were returning, a strong party of the enemy were formed right across our retreat. They did not seem disposed to oppose us as they opened up and let us through as we rode at them.

'They ought to have taken the whole party prisoner if they had been plucky enough but they contented themselves in following us at about 40 or 50 yards interval and picking up those whose horses were shot or who were wounded.'[51]

Lord George Paget now picks up the narrative:

'The 11th had by this time been compelled to retire, and we consequently soon met their compact little knot retreating. When we met, the 4th hesitated, stopped, and without word of command 'went about', joining themselves to the retiring 11th. Masses of the enemy's cavalry were pursuing the latter, the more forward of them being close upon us. It now appeared to me that the moment was critical, and I shouted at the top of my voice, 'Halt, front; if you don't front, my boys, we are done!' and this they did, and for a few minutes both regiments showed a front to the advancing enemy.'

As Lieutenant Colonel Douglas' trumpeter, William Perkins was close at hand when his commanding officer and Lord Paget hurriedly conferred: 'When halted about 100 yards in right rear of the guns, I hear Colonel Douglas call out, "What are we to do now Lord Paget?" He replied, "Where is Lord Cardigan?" and galloped away.'[52]

Douglas had no idea of Cardigan's whereabouts. In the face of impossible odds, and with his limited command, including many wounded in its ranks, it was decided to continue the withdrawal. It is not clear as to whether they actually joined to form a single group under the command of the senior officer, Lord Paget, which is Paget's recollection, or whether they retired as separate regiments with Douglas in command of the 11th, which is how he described events. The Russian cavalry remained just in the rear, apparently content for the moment to follow and not to engage.

At the same time, and to the right of the valley, Colonel Mayow's party of the 17th Lancers and 13th Light Dragoons formed up with Colonel Shewell's 8th Hussars. Together they were still in a tense standoff, face to face with the enemy.

These were perhaps the first of the survivors to realize that the Russian cavalry had sprung a trap. Private William Pennington, 11th Hussars, who had become separated from his regiment and had joined this party explains:

'We numbered only some seventy well-mounted men. It was now discovered that some squadrons of Russian lancers had ranged themselves across the valley to our rear, thus interposed between us and the British lines. "Cut off" was the excited cry.'[53]

Lieutenant Koribut Kubitovich, Eropkin's Uhlans, was on the Causeway Heights. He was ordered into action by General Liprandi immediately before the remnants of the Light Brigade began their orderly retreat. It was Kubitovich's Uhlans that were mistaken for the 17th Lancers by some on both sides (some of the Russian infantry shooting into their ranks). Then, as the Uhlans engaged the retreating British cavalry, now in front of the guns, Russian gunners on the Causeway Heights, and possibly No. 3 Don Cossack gunners returning to the un-spiked guns in the valley, fired upon friend and foe.

It was Kubitovich's belief that of this party of survivors, very few escaped the pursuit, which continued at least as far as level with No. 3 Redoubt:

'The enemy came back down the valley and to give them their due they moved at a trot and in perfect order as if this were nothing but an exercise. My regiment then began to deploy. No.1 Squadron advanced to the right and then to the front, and dashed the foe. My squadron was next and I led it straight forward. No. 3 Squadron turned left and came on next. Brave Cornet Astafev, of my squadron, spurred ahead of us and charged into the enemy. This was a breach of discipline, but his bravery heartened our many recruits. I ordered my squadron to attack and even as I did the men of Astafev's platoon flew forward ahead of us, following their commander.

'The English fought with amazing bravery, even the dismounted and wounded fighting on until they dropped.'

By now the smoke to the rear of the guns had begun to disperse. Through pockets of haze Colonel Shewell could see that the gun-line was still being contested, with more Cossacks riding down to assist the gun-crews. At the same time, and more urgently, ahead of him lay a vast body of Russian cavalry. There was little time to act as the Russian infantry in squares on the Causeway Heights were picking off his men. Shewell's hand was forced; on the other side of No. 3 Don Cossack battery he sighted 300-plus of the Eropkin Uhlans sweeping down from the Causeway Heights ready to cut off their retreat.

Initially, however, as seemed to have happened so frequently during this phase of the battle, the enemy had been mistaken for the 17th Lancers, as related by Private William Bird, 8th Hussars:

'At the bottom of the valley we halted sometime, wondering what to do. I heard Lieutenant [Edward] Phillips shout to Colonel Shewell, "The Lancers are cutting off our retreat!" to which Colonel Shewell replied, "No, Phillips; it's the 17th coming to our relief."[54]

It was quickly established that Lieutenant Phillips was correct and the lancers were indeed Russian Uhlans. At this point it is said that Colonel Shewell saw that the only chance of escape was to break through the Uhlans and ordered his men to wheel round and charge them. Lieutenant Seager later claimed that it was he who urged his commanding officer into the decision:

'They afterwards gave us great credit for wheeling about and attacking the lancers. The Colonel gets the credit for it but Lieutenant Phillips, who was riding next to me, could tell you who it was that called to the Colonel to let us wheel about and attack them.'

In the heat of the moment, Colonel Shewell gave the wrong order, which caused confusion in the ranks at a moment when the utmost clarity was desired. Seager quickly corrected him and order was restored. Private William Pennington of the 11th Hussars recalled the moment, his account confirming Seager's claim: 'Colonel Shewell shouted, "Threes about!" There was some hesitation shown, for the withered ranks had kept together well, but lost their count by "threes". Seager interposed, "Excuse me sir; 'tis right about wheel." The Colonel then cried, "8th right wheel!" The 8th responded as if on home parade, and thus we faced the strong squadrons to our rear. This incident is vividly impressed upon my mind, but I have never seen a reference to it in any previous account.'[55]

Lieutenant Edward Seager's account of how the 8th Hussars broke though the Russian lancers appears in the regimental history:

'We dashed at them, they were three deep, with lances levelled. I parried the first fellow's lance, the one behind him I cut over the head, and as I was recovering my sword, the third fellow made a tremendous point at my body.

'I had just time to receive his lance's point on the hilt of my sword. Colonel [Shewell] and the Major [were] a long distance ahead, the batteries and rifles peppering them in grand style. On looking to see what had become of my men, I found they had got through and [were] scattered to the left.'[56]

The Russians had been convinced that the decimated ranks of British cavalry had no option but to surrender, as Lieutenant Syefan Kozhukhov explains:

Everyone thought that there was only one way out of the valley for the English – they had no choice now but to surrender. We watched for them to lay down their sabres and lances. But that is not what happened. The English chose to do what we had not considered because no one imagined it possible – they chose to charge our cavalry once again, this time heading back along the same ground. These mad cavalrymen were intent on doing what no one thought could be done.'

Private William Bird was not so fortunate and, having lost his mount, was taken prisoner. His account continues:

'Colonel Shewell, having wheeled us about, said, "Every man for himself and God for us all. Go into them, men!"

'We then made for the Lancers of the enemy, and they opened their lines for us to pass, but we did not feel inclined to go through. I did not think it was a trap for us, but there was a sort of feeling of devilment or courage in us at the time, and we would not avail ourselves of their opening, but cut our way past their right and left flanks.

'In this charge my second horse, which had been shot, fell on my left leg, and I remained on the ground until relieved from my painful position by some of the enemy's soldiers.'[57]

Private William Pennington of the 11th Hussars rode with the men led by Lieutenant Colonels Mayow and Shewell:

'We were obliged to pass through a strong body of the enemy's cavalry. Of course with our handful, it was life or death; so we rushed at them to break through them. With five or six fellows at my rear, I galloped on, passing with the determination of one who would not lose his life, breaking the lances of the cowards who attacked us in the proportion of three or four to one, occasionally catching one a slap with the sword across his teeth, and giving another the point on his arm or breast.'

Through the gap created by the charge led by the 8th Hussars also passed a small group of the 13th Light Dragoons which had rallied under Captain Jenyns.

As this action was taking place on the right of the valley, far to the left the second group of survivors under Lieutenant Colonel Douglas and Lord Paget was also withdrawing side by side, hotly pursued by the enemy. They soon encountered fresh units of the Russian lancers, estimated at between three and six squadrons, which had ridden down from the Fedioukine Heights. These troops had been placed between them and the British lines. Once again the Uhlans were initially mistaken for the 17th Lancers. As Lieutenant Colonel Douglas now called out: 'Threes about!', turning their backs on the Russian hussars they had until recently been pursuing, and faced the new enemy.[58] (Another account states that Lieutenant Colonel Douglas ordered Perkins to sound the "Reform" but at that moment it was seen that the line was a Russian one and Perkins sounded the "Rally". He was, after the break-though, struck by a spent ball and escaped on foot, his horse having been killed.)

Lieutenant Colonel Douglas explains:

'I saw two squadrons of Lancers drawn up. I instantly proclaimed, "They're the 17th. Let us rally on them." At this moment Lieutenant Roger Palmer [who had observed the green and white pennon below their lance tips] rode up and said, "Beg your pardon Colonel, that is not the 17th, that is the enemy".

"Well," I exclaimed: "we must only retire and go through them." So with the 4th Light Dragoons we charged the Russian Lancers and got past them with few casualties.'

Captain Edwin Adolphus Cook quickly arranged the remnants of the 11th, and as best he could, putting the men on strongest horses at the front, with the weaker to follow. If they were to have any chance of breaking through it was vital to advance as one compact body. As Trumpeter William Perkins put it, 'We were then close face to face with the Russian Cavalry.'

Douglas now issued the chilling command 'Charge!' and the remnants of the 11th Hussars galloped towards the Russian lancers. The enemy, who had begun to slowly advance, hemming the 11th between the two cavalry forces, started to slow their advance before they halted and swung into line, thus allowing the British Hussars to gallop along their front. As the two crossed, the 11th on their right parried their lances with their swords as they broke through.

Private Matthew Holland, 11th Hussars, was among the throng that escaped:

'We were yelling like demons, and this frightened the enemy, or I don't know what would have happened to us. Then it became a question of getting out of it again. I ducked my head and rode as hard as I could. The old horse got cut twice across his hindquarters and once across his head, but he kept on, and I was lucky enough to come out without a scratch.'[59]

In another account of this incident, Private Robert Ashton, 11th Hussars, recalled how men of his regiment and 17th Lancers had rallied:

'The colonel said, "Gallop, men, for your lives!" I was close to him when he said it; and we galloped away as fast as we could, for the enemy was surrounding us on every side. The plain was strewn with dead horses and wounded and dying men.'[60]

Pushing his mount as hard as he could, Captain Cook headed back up the valley:

'There was nothing left for it but to cut our way back the same way we came. The Lancers who cut us off made a very mild resistance, they seemed to be astonished at our audacity at charging them in the wretched confusion we were in; we got through them with very little loss. Just after getting through these beggars, I thought I heard a rattle behind, and by Jove, I was only just in time, we were pursued and on looking behind a Muscovite had his sword up just in my range and in the act of cutting down, I showed him the point of my sword instantly close to his throat, he pulled his horse almost backwards and gave me an opportunity of getting more forward. I now had nothing to fear, being on a good horse, except going through those infernal guns again.'[61]

Captain Godfrey Charles Morgan of the 17th Lancers, who rode with this party, used determined swordsmanship to get him through the enemy's ranks:

'We saw the enemy between us and home, and at them we went. I cut down one fellow and he ran one of my fellows through with a lance, and, digging my spurs in my horse's sides, he went at it as he has often gone at the big fences in Monmouthshire. I got through them with only a few lance pokes, which I managed to parry; but the number of men had diminished. We had to retire through a shower of Minié bullets, and we reformed in rear of the Heavy Brigade.'[62]

Private William Cullen, 11th Hussars, explains how the enemy's ranks opened up under their determined attack:

'The Polish lancers were extended right across the valley; we rode up to them, when they put spurs to their horses, and let us go through. All honour to them; for if they had opened fire on us there would not have been one left to tell the tale. We had then to go through the cross-fire to reach our lines.'[63]

Not everyone escaped unscathed, as Private John Smith Parkinson, 11th Hussars, recalled in an interview published in a Birmingham newspaper in 1906, this account also suggests that the Poles spared them:

'It seemed certain that we would be annihilated, for besides being outnumbered, there were probably 600-700 of the Poles, we were exhausted. We made a dash for it, and though I found afterwards I had been pricked slightly by a lance in the back of the neck, I cannot tell quite how I came by it, and certainly the majority of the Poles allowed us to pass without showing fight. Nearly all of us got through, whereas the Poles could have wiped us out.'[64]

Parkinson was lanced in the back of the neck, but the wound was not severe. Private James Elder was not so fortunate and came up against Russian Lancers, as was later reported by Sergeant Seth Bond: 'Just at that time a young man named James Elder fell from his horse, no doubt shot by the rifles pursuing us up the valley. I looked back for a moment and saw three Russian Lancers in the act of piercing him and heard his cry. "Oh, Oh, Oh," as the lances entered his body. I dared not look back again.'

Private Robert Grant, 4th Light Dragoons, tagged onto the 11th Hussars and made good his escape:

'After some little time I found myself in the rear almost alone, the greater portion of my regiment having retreated. Seeing the 11th Hussars coming up the valley pursued by the Russian Hussars, I galloped towards them. In tracking on to their rear, a sergeant of the hussars galloped at me and tried to cut me down, but I defended myself.'[65]

Private James Henry Herbert, 4th Light Dragoons, states in an interview published in 1912, 'Directly I got through I fell in with an old comrade named Thorne [Private William Thorne]. He was shot through the foot and terribly weak through loss of blood. As I galloped past him I seized hold of his horse's reins, he himself having [lost] command of his mount. I told him to hang on like grim death to the saddle and I would try to save his life. All this time the Russians were taking pot-shots at us; but I got him back alright.'

Inevitably several men fell behind as their mounts had tired or were wounded. Two, Sergeant William Bentley and Private Robert Levett, were saved by Lieutenant Alexander Dunn, who won the Victoria Cross for his actions.

Lieutenant Sir William Gordon was unarmed when he approached the Russian lancers and seemed certain to be killed or captured, yet somehow escaped:

'After being knocked out of the saddle he lay on the horse's neck, trying to keep the blood from his eyes. Eventually without sword or pistol he turned back, and, unable to regain his stirrups although a perfect horseman, rode at a walk up the Valley. He found between himself and our Heavy Brigade a regiment of Russian cavalry facing up the Valley. He was now joined by two or three men, and he made for the squadron interval. The nearest Russians, hearing him approach, looked back, and by closing outwards to bar his passage, left sufficient opening in the squadron, through which Gordon passed at a canter. He was followed and summoned to surrender, and refused, [and] would have been cut down had not his pursuer been shot.'[66]

Private Robert Ferguson stated that during the retreat Lord Paget, riding alongside the same force as Lieutenant Colonel Douglas, had also initially mistaken a party of the enemy for the 17th Lancers:

'After taking possession of the battery, and disabling as many of the gunners and drivers as we came in contact with, some of us passed a little beyond, but there being no troops there, and an alarm being given that the Russian lancers were intercepting us, we begun to retire, passing along their front as best we could, all order being lost. Lord George Paget then commanded us to form upon what he supposed to be the 17th Lancers. I looked round to my left rear and I saw that the cavalry behind were Russian Lancers, and not the 17th Lancers, and I told his Lordship so. His Lordship then said, "You are quite right; men, you must fight the best of your way back," and that he would find his own way back. We were then a good deal scattered, but we succeeded in retiring past the Lancers without being attacked by them.'[67]

Private Edward Grennan, 4th Light Dragoons, gives a slightly different narrative:

'Just then we saw some lance pennons coming on, and Sergeant Andrew [Corporal John Andrews, 4th Light Dragoons] sang out to Lord George Paget, "My lord, rally on the 17th." Lord George Paget, looking at the lance-pole, said, 'Yes, rally on the 17th.' He was deceived by the facings of the uniform, which were exactly the same as those of our 17th Lancers; but Sergeant Andrew sang out again, "My lord, it's a regiment of Polish Lancers," and sure enough it was, and precious ugly they looked. Lord George Paget called out, "Men, the only thing I can do is to tell you every man for himself. We must get through those fellows the best way we can." While he was speaking the Lancers had formed right across our front, but Lord George put spurs to his horse and rode straight at them, and we followed in close order. At the first shock we cut five or six of them down, and the rest of them opened out like a flock of sheep, and we rode right through them.'[68]

Paget's recollection of event was thus:

'Hardly, however, had we thus rallied [after the Charge], when a cry arose, "They are attacking us, my lord, in our rear!" I turned round, and saw a large body of Russian Lancers formed up, some 500 yards behind us and on the direct line of our retreat! On the impulse of the moment, I then holloaed out, "Threes about" – adding, "We must do the best we can for ourselves."'[69]

At which Captain Alexander Low of the 4th Light Dragoons said to Paget, 'I say, Colonel, are you sure those are not the 17th?' to which Paget replied, 'Look at the colour of their flags.'

Lord Paget ordered his men into the attack. Somehow the desperately tired horses once again picked up the pace and pushed on towards the enemy: 'Helter-skelter then we went at these Lancers as fast as our poor tired horses could carry us, rear rank of course in front …the officer…in rear, for it must be remembered that we still had pursuers behind us. As we approached them

I remarked the regular manner in which they executed the movement of throwing their right half back, thus seemingly taking up a position that would enable them to charge down obliquely upon our right flank as we passed them. Well, as we neared them, down they came upon us at a sort of trot (their advance not being more than twenty yards).'[70]

Paget led the combined force of seventy or less 4th Light Dragoons and 11th Hussars and pressed on in the face of a wall of fresh horses and men, all expecting the Uhlans to take them in the flank. Lined up as if ready for the charge, the Uhlans advanced with the right of the Russian formation edged ahead so that the line was at an oblique angle to the British. Suddenly the Russians stopped dead in their tracks, hesitating just before Paget's men came within striking distance. Blows were exchanged and casualties suffered on both sides, but once again the British got through. Paget later wrote:

'Strange as it may sound, they did nothing, and actually allowed us to shuffle, to edge away, by them, at a distance of hardly a horse's length.'

The men on the right side of the combined party of light dragoons and hussars found themselves subject to a half-hearted attempt at an attack, but managed to fend off the enemy lances with a simple parry, as Lord Paget explains:

'I can only say that if the point on my sword crossed the ends of three or four of their lances, it was as much as it did, and I judge of the rest by my own case, for there was not a man, at that moment, more disadvantageously placed than myself (being behind and on the right rear). Well, we got by them without, I believe, the loss of a single man. How, I know not! It is a mystery to me! Had that force been composed of English ladies, I don't think one of us could have escaped!'[71]

Among those who didn't get through was Private Thomas Lucas, 4th Light Dragoons, who was cut down a little before the break-through:

'When our line got to the guns I saw a few scattered parties of the First Line in front of us; the First Line was then completely broken up. A number of our regiment, numbering not more than twenty, together with Lord George Paget, went in support of the 11th Hussars. The Russians who were attacking the 11th fell back, and we then saw a regiment of Polish lancers to our rear. All that time I was within about four yards of Lord George Paget, and distinctly heard him call out loudly, "Where is Cardigan?" I did not hear any reply given, but immediately after I heard Lord George Paget say, "Eight and Left Incline;" I was at this moment cut down by a sabre wound from a Cossack, and was taken prisoner.'[72]

Captain Robert Portal, 4th Light Dragoons, killed one of the enemy barring the retreat, while the remainder broke ranks and allowed him to pass. He echoed many men's opinion of the Russian cavalry:

'I slew one Russian by running him through the vitals with my sword; several more were scratched a little. If they had had any pluck at all, not one of us, if we had been ten times as strong, could ever have come back again.'[73]

In his official report General Ryzhov claimed that the action to cut off the British cavalry was 'a brilliant success', but most of his officers and men knew that none of the British cavalry should have returned.

Lieutenant Stefan Kozhukhov was in awe of the gallantry displayed by the British. He wrote: 'These mad British cavalrymen raced along the valley floor littered with their dead and wounded from the advance, and now more of them were felled at every step, yet with a kind of desperate heroism they forced a path through our cavalry and rushed away, and not a single man surrendered.

'General Ryzhov called the Uhlans "brilliant". Those of us who watched the lancers noticed no brilliance at all. We did not even see a real attack. If General Ryzhov is correct, how do we explain the fact an exhausted enemy raced through our fresh cavalry and escaped us?'

Through shear grit and determination two groups had broken through the Russian line, one on the right of the valley and the other on the left. A few Cossacks did pursue the British, but largely the Russians turned back to pick off the isolated mounted and dismounted men, many of whom were wounded and easy prey.

Chapter 7

A Fighting Retreat

Troop Sergeant Major William Barker, 17th Lancers, had advanced beyond the gun-line despite his horse having been wounded. Eventually his mare collapsed, crushing his left leg and ankle. Barker managed to extricate himself and catch a riderless horse: 'Which I mounted without delay, and proceeded to assume the command of Lieutenant Thompson's Troop, whom I had seen but a few moments earlier shot dead and falling from his horse.

'As soon as I had taken the command, I saw at once that a squadron of the enemy's cavalry were encircling us, and I gave the rallying signal for my men to join me. But, unfortunately, only seven were able to respond; with these we made one desperate plunge through their ranks, and freed ourselves without a scratch.'[1]

Despite what must have seemed impossible odds, the men of the Light Brigade had taken their objective and gone on to push back Lieutenant General Ryzhov's cavalry but were now forced to retreat. Captain Thomas Hutton, 4th Light Dragoons, reflected the feelings of many when he observed:

'We succeeded in cutting down the gunners & dispersing a part of their Cavalry, capturing the guns, only the next moment being obliged to give them up for want of proper support.'

With both men and horses carrying wounds, they made for the British lines, and in so doing faced heavy fire:

'We had then again to retire through the same gauntlet of guns and crowds of Dragoons to oppose us… it was awful work, with a blown horse, and a wound in the leg which was weaker every moment, but I was determined to stick to my regiment and on my horse, as long as I possibly could, instead of trusting to the mercy of the Cossacks as some foolishly did.'[2]

In his account, Captain Robert Portal, 4th Light Dragoons, explains that his men had had to face two and in some placed three lines of enemy cavalry attempting to bar their retreat before fighting their way back in small groups:

'After going right through a regiment of Cossacks, a regiment of Lancers, and a regiment of Blue Hussars, we retired in perfect order towards our position that we had come from, of course at full gallop. To do this we had to again pass through this murderous cross fire that I have already told you of, and I certainly, with everyone else who saw what we had to do, never thought for a moment that the few remaining of the Light Cavalry Brigade would ever reach our own position. If anything, the fire upon us going back was more severe than before; the Infantry poured volleys of Minié balls [*sic*] into us while the heavy guns sent every species of shot and shell into us [the cannons and much of the Russian infantry at the west end of the Fedioukine Hills had been silenced by the 4th Chasseurs d'Afrique].'[3]

Private Robert Ashton, 11th Hussars, later found it difficult to describe the scene:

'Riderless horses were numberless, and many of the poor creatures were almost mad, the blood pouring out in great profusion from many of them, owing to the bullet wounds they had received. They rushed up and down the valley, sometimes even to the very mouth of the cannons, not knowing where to go or what to do; and this, as might be expected, added greatly to the confusion of a scene which was indescribable.'[4]

Private Albert Mitchell, 13th Light Dragoons, was making his way slowly back when he was approached by Lord Cardigan, retiring from the guns:

'As we went along we somehow got separated, and I got mixed up with some of the 8th and 11th Hussars, and in another minute found myself alone. Just then Lord Cardigan came galloping up from the direction of the guns, passing me at a short distance, when he turned about again, and meeting me pulled up, and said: "Where is your horse?" I answered: "Killed, my Lord." He then said in his usual stern, hoarse voice: "You had better make the best of your way back as fast as you can, or you will be taken prisoner." I needed no telling, for I was going as fast as I was able. He then rode a little farther down, and in a few moments returned past me at a gallop.'[5]

Watchers from the Sapouné Heights at first failed to recognize the Light Brigade as its remnants reappeared in small groups or individually made their way back. One – Fanny Duberly – exclaimed: 'What can those skirmishers be doing? Good God! It is the Light Brigade!'

The first men seen making their way back up the slight incline were those who had been wounded by fire from the Fedioukine Heights. Then there appeared from the smoke dismounted men who had lost their horses before reaching the guns. These men had been unable to catch riderless horses, were badly wounded, or were weak from loss of blood. Some were supporting comrades, others leading back wounded horses, with or without their riders in the saddle.

Many of the walking wounded were overhauled on their journey back by returning mounted men. A few dismounted to give over their horses to men who needed them more. Those mounted on less badly maimed horses were first to reach the safety of the British lines; each survivor had a harrowing story to tell.

Private James Mustard, 17th Lancers, was making his own way back when Private John Ettridge, 13th Light Dragoons, rode over towards him, calling out if he could lend him his sword, he having lost his own in the mêlée:

'I still had my lance, though the shaft had been chipped by a bullet. I turned to draw my sword to hand it to Hetrigde [*sic*], when to my amazement, I had neither sword, scabbard, nor belt. A canister-shot had caught me on the left hip, and cut away sword, belt, overalls, and pants, and laid bare a great patch of bleeding flesh. Another inch would have smashed my hip and killed me.'[6]

Private Mustard now joined forces with Privates Thomas Fletcher and James Wightman of the 17th Lancers. The trio were making their way back together, as Wightman relates:

'We were all three wearied and weakened by loss of blood; our horses wounded in many places; there were enemies all about us, and we thought it was about time to be getting back.'[7]

Private Robert Grant, 4th Light Dragoons, was closer to the British lines:

'I had passed them [the Russian lancers] some distance when my horse was shot under me. He was hit in the hind quarter. His belly was cut open, and his legs were broken. The shot came from a cannon that had a low sweep, and it struck him in the thick of the thigh. My leg was covered with blood. I could not get free from him for some time. Captain Portal passed, and said to me, "Damn you, get up; never mind your horse;" but I replied, "I can't, for he's lying on me." A private named MacGregor [Private George McGregor], of our regiment, however, came to my assistance. He asked me to get behind him on his horse, but I was not able, as I could not use my leg.'[8]

Once the last wave of cavalry had arrived, the Cossacks had been ordered down from the Heights to prevent the guns from being carried away by the enemy and to assist the surviving gunners. Some of the Cossacks were now appeared forward of the guns, spearing any unarmed or wounded men they found. Private John Richardson, 11th Hussars, encountered these scavengers and found them no match for him, even in his state of near exhaustion:

'I fought my way from among the guns, and then set out to return to the British line on foot. It was all over ploughed fields, and the Russians kept on firing on us all the time. A couple of Cossacks intercepted me on the way, and I settled both with my carbine. They were big cowards, the Cossacks. You had only to point a gun at them, and whether it was loaded or not, they would run.'

Troop Sergeant Major Linkon, 13th Light Dragoons, had only scathing words for the Cossacks too:

'The Cossacks are a cowardly set of villains. I never saw one of them who would fight unless they were three or four to one, most of our poor fellows at Balaclava when wounded or killed were mutilated in a shocking manner.'[9]

Many men reported how the Cossacks who picked their way through the men ahead of the guns were more intent on looting than engaging anyone who could defend himself. Lieutenant Percy Smith recalled that while making his way back to British lines he saw Cornet Denzil Chamberlayne, 13th Light Dragoons, sitting by the mutilated body of his horse 'Pimeto', stunned and uncertain what to do next. Smith advised him to retrieve the saddle and bridle and make the best of his way back: 'Another horse you can get, but you will not get a saddle or bridle so easily.' Chamberlayne was able to avoid the murderous attentions of the Cossacks probably because, carrying his horse's accoutrements, he was mistaken for one of their own.
    Private William Cullen, 11th Hussars:

'I saw poor Bob Lazell [Private Robert Layzell] lying wounded, with his horse beside him and several Cossacks murdering him. I could not assist him, though my heart was good.'[10]

The grisly progress of the Cossacks was seen both by those on the battlefield, desperately seeking safety, and by those on the surrounding Heights.

The witnesses to the whole affair on Sapouné Ridge remained helpless spectators. Among them was Henry Clifford who recorded the chilling sight of cold-blooded murder:

'Then the smoke cleared away and I saw our poor fellows lying on the ground, the Cossacks and Russian Cavalry running them through as they lay, with their swords and lances. Some time passed, then horses without riders galloped back, then wounded on foot, then a mounted body of 200 men – all that remained of the 600 [sic].'[11]

One anonymous 8th Hussar related his experiences in a letter written at Scutari:

'My old mare was smashed by a cannon round shot, and went down heavily on me, beating the breath and senses out of me; on recovering my recollection and trying to extricate myself, a Cossack put his spear into my shoulder – those vermin are always prowling about and act independently; I staggered away to the rear, having taken a shot at this same Cossack with my carbine, while he was plundering a dead man.'[12]

Private William Pennington, 11th Hussars:

'I bore well to the left, quite losing touch with the 8th. Thus separated from all aid, Russian lancers pursued me up the valley; but I kept them on my right and rear, my sword arm free to sweep around. With many a feint at cut and thrust (for I feared to check the gallant grey) I kept them at arm's length, foiled their attempts to get upon my left, where they might strike across my bridle-hand, and the grey mare gradually drew ahead. Balls from the causeway ridge raised up the dust around my mare's hoofs, but happily their force was spent.'[13]

Pennington's 'gallant grey' saved him. But by this time most of the horses were wounded or blown.

Private Albert Mitchell, 13th Light Dragoons, explains how even after breaking through the Russian cavalry lines and avoiding the Cossacks, men were still falling to both artillery and small-arms fire:

'By this time the mounted were making their way back as fast as they could, some singly and some in parties of two or three; but whenever the battery on our left could see anything like a party together, they would be sure to send a shell at them.'[14]

Throughout the retreat the men had to face the indiscriminate fire from the Heights for a second time. 'Many a poor fellow was laid low,' wrote Lieutenant E. Seager, 8th Hussars.[15]

One of those Seager might have been referring to was Cornet George Gooch Clowes, 8th Hussars, who, having wheeled about and broken through the Russian lines, had his horse brought down by grape shot. Clowes lay on the ground, wounded and bleeding badly. He noticed several Russians riding nearby and for a while played dead:

'I will only say I am very thankful that I did not share the fate of many of my brother officers for I had a pretty narrow escape, being hit hard in the back by a grape shot, but it only skimmed across, taking a few splinters of bone of my right shoulder blade.'[16]

Clowes later reported how he had realised that the Cossacks were systematically lancing the wounded and was forced to make a run for his life. Men unable to raise a carbine or get to their feet were murdered in cold blood.

Henry Clifford, referring to the general retreat, added:

'Some time passed. I can't say how much, but it was very long, waiting to see if any would return. Horses without riders, galloped back in numbers, and men wounded on foot and men not hurt, but their horses killed, returned on foot, and then saw a horse or a man fall, who wounded, had come as far as he could and then fell and died.

'At length about 30 horsemen dashed through a line of Cossacks who had reformed to intercept their retreat, and then another larger body came in sight from the middle of the smoke and dust. Two hundred men! I don't know the names of the officers who fell or were taken prisoner, but very few returned.'[17]

The valley floor was scattered with the grotesquely mangled body-parts of both men and horses. The less seriously wounded made their way slowly back stopping to try to rescue comrades pinned under their dead or crippled mounts, and carried or assisted men back as far as they could – by now all knew that to be left behind meant almost certain death at the hands of the Cossacks.

This was the fate of Captain Thomas Goad, 13th Light Dragoons, who was last seen unhorsed and wounded. Evidently Goad had seen the Cossacks killing other wounded men and was defiantly brandishing his revolver, determined to take as many of them with him as he could.

There were times during the height of the battle when it was a case of every man for himself, as illustrated by the story of Sergeant John Fitzgerald, 13th Light Dragoons, who had to make a split-second decision, which no doubt haunted him in later life:

'I had one horse shot under me at the very commencement and of course was running back to our own army the same as dozens of others when I saw a trumpeter of the 11th Hussars shot dead. He fell off his horse, poor fellow so I "borrowed" his mount and jumped on... There was another Sergeant of the 11th Hussars [John Jones or Thomas Jordon] running for this horse the same as I was, but I got there first and hopped into the saddle. I knew him well, poor fellow, and I can remember him saying, "Fitz, that horse belongs to us", but I paid no attention to him. I was sorry to hear they killed him, but everything is fair in war time.'

But for every act of self-preservation, there were many more of selflessness and bravery under fire. While retiring on foot, Privates Mitchell and Thomas Pollard stumbled across one badly wounded man who was lying on his back, apparently choking on his own blood. What he witnessed remained etched in Mitchell's memory:

'We had not gone many yards before we fell in with the man who had ridden on my left. He was lying on his back with his arms extended, and labouring very hard for breath. Each breath he drew brought up a quantity of blood, which, as he lay on his back, he could not clear from his mouth, and was almost choking. I could see death in his countenance, but turned him over, and placed his arm under his forehead, thinking he would be better able to relieve himself of the blood than by lying on his back. It was a good bit lower down the valley where I had first missed him from my side, so it is likely his horse was shot, and he afterwards [was wounded] in trying to make his way back, dismounted.'

Private James Olley, 4th Light Dragoons, already badly wounded, had made it through the line of Russian cavalry but was now hit by Russian infantry fire. He recalled the events:

'When we were retiring we met some Russian lancers. We made a charge and they fled to the left incline and rode past. Just after passing the cavalry I got a ball from the Russian infantry in my left. It went through my left eye, passed through my nostrils and the roof of my mouth and came out against my right eye. I did not know at the time that my eye was out. It was not painful at the time; afterwards the suffering was dreadful. After being thus wounded, I still kept the saddle though blood was pouring from my mouth and nostrils, as well as running from my forehead.'[18]

A shell entered the chest of the horse ridden by Private R. Evans, 13th Light Dragoons, which rolled over on him. The shell burst inside the animal, tearing it open from the shoulders to the hindquarters. The weight of the horse nearly suffocated Evans, while its death struggles inflicted severe contusions on his legs. Fortunately a man of his own troop and two lancers came along and released him; there were many stories in a similar vein.

One was recalled by Private Edward Grennan, 4th Light Dragoons. He relates how two men remembered one incident which occurred during the aftermath of the Charge, and how one man saved the life of another:

'Another man named Ford [Private John Ford] had his horse killed in the retreat, and was pinned by the leg by the [horse's] body. A dragoon called Farrell [Private John Farrell], who was coming along, also on foot and hard pressed by the enemy, stopped to lend him a hand, and managed to prise the horse off him. Both men reached our lines in safety, but every year afterwards, on the anniversary of the battle, Ford used to go to Farrell's quarters with a bottle, and they used to celebrate the escape.'[19]

Trumpeter R. Davis, 13th Light Dragoons, was trapped but managed to free himself. His account only came into the public domain after his death: 'He rode with his commanding officer between the guns without mishap, but on returning he had the misfortune to lose his horse, which was killed by round shot. For some time he lay beneath the animal, unable to extricate his foot from the stirrup. By hard struggling he eventually released himself, then ran as hard as he could to the rear, but owing to the smoke from the guns he had but little idea where he was going.

'While he was in this situation the short carriage of his sword belt, together with his trumpet, was shot away. For some time he was brought to a standstill, then he commenced again to run and soon succeeded in reaching the ground from which the advance had commenced.'[20]

Private Mitchell, 13th Light Dragoons, continued to struggle to make his way back to the British lines, coming across men who needed his assistance. By now he was beginning to tire: 'I looked up to try and measure the distance, when to my dismay I saw the Scots Greys, who had come part of the way down the valley to our support, where they were halted, and were now about five hundred yards from me, in the act of retiring at a trot. I thought there was no chance now, when our support was retiring at a trot at that distance ahead of us.'[21]

In avoiding the Cossacks some men pushed closer to the Heights and came within accurate range of the infantry; moving slowly they made easy targets. Troop Sergeant Major George Smith, 11th Hussars, accidentally walked into their field of fire:

'I now lost my breath, and began to give up all hope of escaping, when the thought occurred to me that by throwing myself down and pretending to be dead, I might recover myself. Then again, I thought, perhaps some of the infantry on my left might come, and on finding me alive, bayonet me, so I decided to keep on the move. I now walked a little distance and could occasionally hear a bullet pass close by me, so recommenced running.'[22]

There were still many riderless horses, galloping about the valley. Many of these horses were badly wounded, others were lashing out, or racing one way and then the next, mad with fear, not knowing which way to go to escape the carnage. Private Robert Farquharson, 4th Light Dragoons, caught a mount of the 17th Lancers. A little way on and his second horse was hit and he fell with it. Farquharson was attacked by an Uhlan while defenceless on the ground. Fortunately the lance tip pierced his trousers but did him no harm. Rising to his feet Farquharson avoided further blows and caught a Cossack pony on which he made to escape. Again he was singled out and a Russian horseman gave chase. Farquharson was forced to parry a blow and slashed back, cutting open the man's right cheek.

Another survivor who was seen making his way back on foot and managed to fight off the Cossacks only to be mowed down by riderless horses.

Captain John James Brandling's C Troop, RHA, had adopted a position a little to the south west of No. 4 Redoubt. During the retreat only one of C Troop's guns was on the ridge of the Causeway Heights, the remainder were positioned on the south-facing slope, but with British and Russian forces intermingled no clear targets presented themselves. The Troop's gunners however advanced and were able to lay down fire on the Russian batteries around No. 2 Redoubt until they became threatened by Russian cavalry and were forced to limber up and retired. Their most advanced position during the Battle of Balaclava was on the Causeway, midway between Nos. 3 and 4 Redoubts.

Cardigan is said to have ridden towards the guns of I Troop, which had ridden part of the way down the valley in the wake of the Light Brigade before retiring to join the Heavy Brigade. On reaching their position he spoke briefly to Shakespear who gave him a drink from his flask. Next he spoke to Raglan's ADC, Captain Ewart, and to General Cathcart near No. 4 Redoubt. Cardigan announced in despair: 'I have lost my Brigade.'

'After a great many wounded and disabled men had already passed it going to the rear, Lord Cardigan came riding by at a "quiet pace" close under the crest. He had passed the troop on his left for several horse-lengths, when he came back and halted within a yard or two of the left-hand gun, the only one fairly on the crest. He was not alone, but attended by Cornet Yates of his own old regiment the 11th Hussars, a recently commissioned ranker.[23]

'Lord Cardigan was in the full dress pelisse (buttoned) of the 11th Hussars, and he rode a chestnut horse very distinctly marked and of grand appearance. The horse seemed to have had enough of it, and his lordship appeared to have been knocked about but was cool and collected. He returned his sword, undid a little of the front of his dress, and pulled down his under-clothing under his waist-belt... He then in a quiet way, as if talking to himself, said, "I tell you what it is – those instruments of theirs", alluding to the Cossacks' lances, "are deuced blunt; they tickle up one's ribs!" [Referring to the slight wound given him by the Cossacks]. After this, he asked, "Has any one seen my regiment?"'[24]

'It was when Lord George Paget reached the British lines and found Lord Cardigan already there, not having seen him behind the guns, that he shouted "Hello my lord, were you not there?" Cardigan quickly replied: "Oh wasn't I, though! Here, Jenyns [Captain Soame Gambier Jenyns, 13th Light Dragoons], did you not see me at the guns?' Jenyns responded positively.'[25]

Captain Bradling provides the most informative account of the Brigade Commander's state of mind in the moments after the Charge:

'Having refastened his uniform, he [Cardigan] pulled his revolver out of his saddle-holster as if the thought had only just struck him, and said, "And here's this damned thing I have never thought of till now." He then replaced it, drew his sword and said, "Well, we've done our share of the work;' and pointing up towards the Chasseurs d'Afrique[26], in our left rear, added, "It is time they gave those dappled gentry a chance" – this had reference to the colour of their horses. After this he asked, "Has anyone seen my regiment?" and the men, thinking it was the regiment dressed, like himself, in the crimson overalls, answered, "No sir."'

Captain Brandling, however, bore witness to a disturbing scene which came about through the men's ignorance of Cardigan's role in the decision to charge and his actions beyond the guns. The events were later related to Whinyates:

'He [Cardigan] had turned backward from the gun [of C Troop] when the first cheer was given by some Heavies. He then halted, turned about as if to see what it was for, saw it was in compliment to the 8th returning, trotted towards them, turned about in front of Colonel Shewell, and took up the walk... And now occurred something rather painful to witness. As the 8th came into line of No. 6 Redoubt... Colonel Shewell was in front, and Colonel Mayow behind him on the left of the other officers. The moment Cardigan got his back turned round to the 8th, Colonel Mayow pointed towards him, shook his head, and made signs to the officers on the left of the Heavies, as much as to say, "See him; he has taken care of himself." Men here and there in the ranks of the 8th also pointed, and made signs... Colonel Shewell neither saw this nor took any part in it... Of course Cardigan did not know what was going on behind him while he was smiling and raising his sword to the cheers... He was thus, in a way, held up to ridicule.'[27]

The reason behind this rank insubordination may have been that some men of the Second Line had seen Lieutenant Houghton, 11th Hussars, retiring on his chestnut horse with white socks, and mistaken him for Cardigan riding his similarly marked chestnut mare 'Ronald'. Among those who thought they saw Cardigan come back there was, as Whinyates later wrote, a 'sort of tacit keeping away from him for a time; no congratulations on his escape were offered in the hearing of C Troop.'

The first words that Cardigan spoke to Scarlett were, 'What do you think of the aide-de-camp riding to the rear and screaming like a woman?' Cardigan was still smarting at Nolan's apparent attempt to lead the Brigade and his reaction to being wounded.

Scarlett cut him short, explaining, 'Say no more, my lord, for I have just ridden over his dead body.'[28]

Corporal James Nunnerley, 17th Lancers, had lost his horse and was forced to make his own way back. His account was later published:

'He then left it [his horse] and forced his way on foot through shot and shell, when he was attacked by the Russian Cavalry, through whom he cut his way, his more than ordinary height, combined with a powerful frame, proving at this crisis most advantageous to him.

'He had no sooner got clear of his foes than he was knocked down and ridden over by a number of riderless horses, together with a few hussars. Having regained his feet, he observed one of the 13th Light Dragoons under his horse, which had been killed, the rider (J. Malone) [Corporal Joseph Malone, 13th Light Dragoons] not being able to free himself. He dragged the horse off him, and set him to liberty, and accompanied him a short distance till he fell in with Sergeant John Farrell of his own regiment. He assisted Farrell to carry Captain Webb [Captain Augustus Frederick Cavendish Webb] out of danger on a stretcher, which had been brought to their aid by Sergeant [*sic*] John Berryman. He then returned [for] Trumpeter William Brittain, who was very seriously wounded; and, after having obtained water for him and the remainder of the wounded, he caught a horse belonging to the 8th Hussars, whose rider had been shot, which he mounted, and then joined his regiment.'[29]

It often proved impossible for the men on foot to catch unwounded horses, as they were gripped by sheer fear and running wild. However, occasionally the horses, not knowing what to do, fell back on their training and sought the company of recognisable uniforms; these, however, were often the most badly wounded animals.

Private Mitchell was unable to stop any of the riderless mounts which were racing hither and thither:

'There were several riderless horses galloping about the plain. I tried very hard to get one, but could not. I saw two officers' horses belonging to my own regiment. I could tell them by the binding of the sheepskins on the saddles. They appeared almost mad. I would have given a trifle just then to have had my legs across one of them, for I was getting tired; for we had been out since 4 a.m., and had nothing to eat since the day before. And to make it still worse there was a piece of ground that lay in my way which had been cultivated and was very loose, which made it heavy travelling... I could now see some Cossacks showing themselves in swarms on our right, thinking to cut some of us dismounted men off. As soon as I saw them approaching, I bore more away to my left front.'

Corporal John Ashley Kilvert, 11th Hussars, also described the frantic scene as men endevoured to escape the bloodshed, and how their plight could have been worse still but for the intervention of the Chasseurs d'Afrique:

'Horses were killed, others galloped about riderless and before long, order was abandoned and it was a desperate attempt to cut our way back through as best we could, as the Russians closed in on us. The Russian gunners were cut down and we started back to our own lines, but I do not know what would have happened had not one of the Russian flanking batteries been attacked and forced to retire.'[30]

As Troop Sergeant-Major George Smith rode slowly towards No. 4 Redoubt, he approached the position held by C Troop RHA; this would have been a little after Cardigan:

'A Sergeant-Major of the 11th Hussars came from the opening between the Redoubts and made for the Troop. On his arrival at the guns Brandling said to him, "Who on earth gave the order Sergeant-Major?" and the man answered, "Oh sir, God knows! We [just] heard, Come on! Come on! called out. My horse was shot when I was at the bottom of the plain; this is a loose horse of another regiment I am on, and this is a Russian loaded carbine I have been defending myself with against some Lancers who attacked and knocked me about."'[31]

With the Cossacks still posing a threat it was essential to keep on the move. Private Mitchell found a wounded man disorientated and uncertain which way to walk:

'As I came along he heard me, and calling out, said: "Is that an Englishman?" I answered: "Yes" and on going to him found he had been wounded by a piece of shell just between the eyes, which had blinded him. He had bled very much, and was still bleeding. I had a handkerchief in my breast pocket, which I bound round his wound, and taking him by the arm, led him along.'[32]

Meanwhile, Private William Pearson, 17th Lancers, was nearly killed by the Cossacks, three of whom tried to cut him off:

'...and he gave rein to his charger, which required no urging and would have cleared them, having beaten off all three with his lance, but a fourth appeared, wheeling right across his path.

'Pearson pressed his knees. He had taught his horse to do certain circus tricks. In response, the faithful animal reared itself and seemed as though it were to come down on the Cossack with its forefeet.

'The Cossack swerved and in a flash Pearson got through, not before, however, one of the three had jabbed him in the side with his lance. At the time he hardly felt the wound, although it had penetrated the left lung, and he reached the British lines in safety.

'Colonel White [Captain Robert White] was with another officer when he [Pearson] pulled up and heard him [White] say, "here's another back." Then Colonel White called out, "Are you hurt, my man?" Pearson replied "No, Sir," but fell off his horse from weakness. The air had got into his wounds and he writhed in awful pain. Till that moment he was unconscious of his injury.'[33]

As the minutes passed more survivors emerged from the smoke and settling dust, some riding their horses, others leading them:

'One of the 4th [Light] Dragoons came walking by me with his horse's head dreadfully cut. He told me that it was one of the enemy's horses, and that he had lost his own from under him.'[34]

The Cossacks continued their murderous journey along the valley while Russian infantry and sharpshooters fired upon the stragglers from a distance.

Orderly trumpeter William Brittain was mortally wounded and lay helpless on the battlefield. A mounted Cossack approached and attempted to scoop his bugle up with his lance as a trophy, but only succeeded in denting it. James Nunnerley noted in his memoirs: 'The bugle, which had been holed by a Russian Cossack, was battered and bent. I got the bugle out from under William Britain's body after placing him on a stretcher; the cord was under his back and to remove it would have given him great pain. So one of the men drew his sword and cut the lines which were under his back, from the bugle.'[35]

Brittain fell close enough to the British lines for him to be carried from the battlefield. At least one account records that he was a fairly early casualty, although this cannot be certain. It seems unlikely that he sounded the final 'Charge' if, indeed, the Charge was actually sounded, which was hotly disputed among survivors. Brittain was sent to Scutari where he was tended by Mrs Farrell and Sarah Terrot. He died on 14 February 1855.

'The trumpeter that sounded the Charge for Cardigan was a most pitiful case. He begged that his bugle not be taken out of his sight. Cardigan spent half an hour with him soothing him. He belongs to 17th Lancers, his name is Brittain, the Sergeant of the 17th calls him Billy and keeps telling him to pluck up and get out soon to sound another Charge but there never was any chance for him.'[36]

Sarah Anne Terrot, a Sellonite Sister who went out to Scutari with Florence Nightingale, wrote of Brittain:

'Lancers of the 17th – young innocent looking faces – the first was a handsome youth, badly wounded in both arms and leg in that disastrous Charge. A large ball was extracted from his thigh after it had lain there for almost three months and though for some time he appeared to be doing well, his appetite failed and he died, in fits, after four months severe suffering.'[37]

The earlier deployment of the Uhlans sent to entrap the survivors had been seen by those watching alongside Lord Raglan. When the two bodies of mounted men rode towards them, it seemed clear that they were doomed; the enemy were two ranks deep and both horse and men were fresh.

The French nobleman Vicomte de Noé, looking on from Sapouné Ridge, had witnessed the moment that the remnants of the Light Brigade broke through the Russian Lancers:

'A cloud of dust, from which came a chorus of British "hurrahs", advanced towards us; it was the unfortunate cavalry who were returning mutilated and decimated. The Russian artillery on the heights opened fire on the noble debris.'[38]

Private Dennis Connor, 4th Light Dragoons, was by now flagging. He had broken through the cavalry lines and made his way back, wary of being caught by the small groups of Uhlans who had broken to pursue the survivors:

'The Polish Lancers did follow us a little way up the hill, but they were cowards, and turned back again.'[39]

Private Thomas Dudley, 17th Lancers, was wounded during the early stages of the advance, but remained with his Troop and fought his way beyond the gun-line. Writing to his parents from hospital at Scutari he recalled:

'Well, I got out of the mêlée, but, in returning, my poor horse was shot down, and me under him... I got to my legs, and was fortunate enough to catch an officer's charger... I have thought it a very lucky hit for me in two respects: first, if it had been an inch further to my neck, it would have been all up with me; next it sent me here to be laid up in lavender – at least, compared with what the poor fellows are undergoing at camp.'[40]

The battery on the Causeway Heights had opened fire as soon as the survivors came within range. Lord George Paget of the 4th Light Dragoons, wrote: 'A ride of a mile or more was before us, every step of which was to bring us more under the fire from the Heights. And what a scene of havoc was this last mile strewn with the dead and dying, and all friends, some running, some limping, some crawling! Horses in every position of agony, struggling to get up, then floundering again on their mutilated riders!'

Mounted men at first clustered, but attracted cannon fire – those retiring singly were vulnerable to Cossacks. Retreating in two groups the mounted men who had moments earlier charged through the Uhlans now offered easy targets. Appreciating that they were now riding at a slower pace, which allowed the gunners ample time to find their range, some men including Private William Butler, 17th Lancers, struck out by themselves:

'Coming back I was attacked by two Cossacks. I engaged the one on my right, and despatched him at the time the other made a cut at me which just caught my nose, chin and bridle hand; but he never cut another, for I left him on the ground. Going a little further my horse was shot beneath me and I lay weltering in blood and swooned.'[41]

Lieutenant Edward Phillips, 8th Hussars, had several near misses and counted himself lucky to escape the enemy lancers during the retreat:

'I had not gone far when I found my mare began to flag and presently I think she must have been hit in the leg by a round shot, as she suddenly dropped behind and fell over on her side. I extricated myself as quickly as possible and ran for my life, the firing being as hard as ever. After going some distance I found myself cut off by some lancers who had got in my front... I was sure my time was come; I drew my revolver but seeing [this] they keep their distance, until an officer came up and ordered them back, as they were too far in advance, so I escaped this danger. Some little distance on I reached one of our poor fellows lying on the ground, dead or dying, his horse standing beside him; the saddle had turned round with what excitement and running for one's life I was so done that I had not the strength to right it, therefore undid the girth and by standing on the saddle managed to climb on his bare back. Never was I so happy as when I felt a horse under me again.'[42]

According to the *Chester Chronicle* of 18 November 1854, Captain Edwin Cook, 11th Hussars, 'had a regular run for his life of a mile and a half, pursued by the Russian cavalry. To avoid them he ran under range of the guns of their batteries.' Indeed, Cook made it back relatively unscathed.

Private Edwin Firkin, 13th Light Dragoons, had joined the group who had forced their way through the enemy lancers:

'By this time I could not see three men of our regiment. I of course thought I was lost but I turned my mare's head to try to get back if I could. I had only gone a few yards when I saw two Russian lancers coming towards me with clenched teeth and staring like savages. I prepared to meet them with as much coolness and determination as I could command. The first one made a thrust at me with his lance. It is a heavy weapon and easily struck down which I did with my sword thrusting it at the same time through the fellow's neck. He fell from his horse with a groan. The shock [of the impact] nearly brought me from my saddle. The other fellow wheeled round his dying comrade and made a thrust at me. I had not the strength to strike down the blow for my sword fell from my grasp, but my time was not yet come. One of our lancers seeing the attack made on me came to my assistance and thrust his lance clean through the fellow's body. I cleared myself of the saddle and my poor dying horse and succeeded – through a field of blood, and scrambling over dead and dying men and horses [in] getting out of gunshot.'[43]

Lord George Paget of the 4th Light Dragoons wrote: 'My wounded horse at every step got more jaded, and I therefore saw those in my front gradually increasing the distance between us, and I made more use of my sword in this return ride than I had done in the whole affair.'

Any rider who came close to the Heights ran the risk of having his horse shot by the infantry; then it was largely down to luck as to whether he was killed or taken prisoner; a few did escape on foot.

As Captain Thomas Hutton, 4th Light Dragoons, rode in the retreat nursing a wound to the right thigh received during the Charge, he was hit in the left thigh while his horse was shot eleven times.

Mentioned earlier in the narrative, a little after the first two groups had escaped through the line of Uhlans, Corporal Morley's small party had made a frantic dash against the same force. Remarkably most of them got through. However, in doing so they veered towards the side of the valley and onto the lower slopes of the Causeway Heights. Morley recalled:

'We came to a square of infantry on rising ground with muskets and fixed bayonets pointing at us. They yelled something in Russian, I suppose calling us to surrender. When they saw we was [*sic*] not going to surrender, they fired a volley point blank at us and at the shortest range. This was fearfully destructive, and only a few of my little squad were left, Wightman [Private James William Wightman] and Marshall [Private Thomas Marshall] together with others of the 17th were captured here, one with 13 wounds, the other with 9.

'We found the guns again re-manned and in position again across the valley, and after we had charged through them from the rear they opened fire on us again, as well as the infantry.'[44]

Private James Wightman, as Morley mentions, was soon to be captured. He had fought desperately against an attack by a Cossack who seemed determined to finish him off:

'My horse was shot dead, riddled with bullets. One bullet struck me on the forehead, another passed through the top of my shoulder; while struggling out from under my dead horse a Cossack standing over me stabbed me with his lance once in the neck near the jugular, again above the collar-bone, several times in the back and once under the short rib; and when, having regained my feet, I was trying to draw my sword, he sent his lance through the palm of my hand. I believe he would have succeeded in killing me, clumsy as he was, if I had not blinded him for the moment with a handful of sand.'[45] Remarkably Wightman survived the ordeal and was taken prisoner.

Parties of Cossacks and hussars had pursued the survivors, cutting many down. The Russian artillery on the Causeway Heights failed to realise that their comrades were endeavouring to cut off survivors who had broken through the Uhlans' line and they fired into the mass of men. Lieutenant Koribut Kubitovich witnessed this apparently indiscriminate fire which slaughtered both friend and foe, and which is referred to by a number of survivors:

'There was much frantic slashing, and it was then that our artillery and infantry reopened fire. The truth must be told, that this fire hit us just as it did the enemy, with as many men killed and wounded, and even more of our horses killed. The English fought with astonishing bravery, and when we approached their dismounted and wounded men, even these refused to surrender and continued to fight till the ground was soaked with their blood.'

Meanwhile, Lieutenant Edward Lennox Jervis, 13th Light Dragoons, found his path blocked by Russian infantrymen:

'As we pulled around, a body of infantry stopped the way and some of the cavalry came up. However, they opened ranks to let us pass, yet we were soon mixed up again, and our fellows were now few and far between. Then the guns on our left opened on the lot of us, Russians and all, and my mare's hock was shot away. I managed to catch another horse myself.'[46]

Not all of Morley's group got through, several were wounded and taken prisoner. Wightman was dragged away towards the rear, where he found himself beside Private Thomas Fletcher:

'Fletcher at the same time lost his horse, and, it seems, was wounded. We were very roughly used. The Cossacks at first hauled us along by the tails of our coatees and our haversacks. When we got on foot they drove their lance butts into our backs to stir us on... With my shattered knee and another bullet wound in the shin of the same knee I could barely limp and good old Fletcher said, "Get on my back, chum." I did this and then found he had been shot through the back of the head. When I told him of this his only answer was, "Oh, never mind that, it's not much, I don't think." But it was that much that he died of the wound a few days later – and here he was, a doomed man himself, making light of a mortal wound and carrying a chance comrade of another regiment on his back... I can write this; but I could not tell of it in speech for I know I should play the woman.'

Earlier the Russians were thrown into confusion when the rallied groups passed back through the battery. Captain William Morris, 17th Lancers, unable to act due to his wounds, nevertheless encouraged Cornet George Wombwell, also of his regiment: '"Look out, Wombwell! Look out and catch a horse!" Two or three of the loose horses instinctively came towards the men, recognizing uniform if not man. Buoyed by Morris's encouragement Wombwell acted immediately:

'I saw the 11th and 4th Light Dragoons coming back from the Charge, when I set off as hard as I could, luckily caught a horse, jumped on his back, and looking round to see what my friends who had charge of me were about and there they were in a great state but did not dare follow me (as if they had done so they would have run up against our troops) and then rode as hard as I could.'

In another account the young cornet admitted that he nearly came a cropper in his urgency to get away, as he 'vaulted so heartily that only the carbine kept me from going over on the other side. After this I had to get by a squadron of lancers who came up and attacked us in the rear, without any sword to ward off their thrusts, but thank God I escaped without a wound, only a little bruise on the arm.'[47]

Captain Morris had given Wombwell the courage to escape; now his time came. Believing his injuries to be totally incapacitating, the Russians were lax and in the confusion of the battle, despite being almost blinded by blood flowing from a severe scalp wound, he chased a loose horse and caught hold of its saddle, lifted himself up and rode pell-mell until his mount was shot, falling on him, trapping his legs. Drifting in and out of consciousness, Morris, who was by then suffering from a broken right arm and broken ribs, as well as the head wounds he received earlier, managed to extricate himself from under his horse. Staggering back up the valley, he reached within 100 yards or so of the brigade's starting point. Here he came across the crumpled body of his friend Louis Nolan. Then he collapsed and passed out. Troop Sergeant Major George Smith caught sight of him and reported that 'his face was covered in blood and he had a very wild appearance'. Elsewhere, Private William Butler, 17th Lancers, had made it back almost as far as the British lines when he passed out from loss of blood:

'I should think I must have lain there two or three hours before I came to. I did not know where I was until a French sentry challenged me, and I was taken to the French doctor, who dressed my wounds. I did not get to my own lines till next day and then I was made much of by the few who were left.'[48]

Throughout the retirement the Heavy Brigade had remained mere spectators. The 1st Chasseurs d'Afrique, however, rode down the North Valley past them, ready to cover the Light Brigade's retreat. Private Albert Mitchell, 13th Light Dragoons, recalled how 'a party of the Chasseurs d'Afrique showed themselves menacingly [which] had the desired effect of turning the Cossacks from the purpose' of murdering the wounded and those slowly making their way back to the British lines.

Troop Sergeant-Major John Linkon, 13th Light Dragoons, had nearly reached safety when he lost his second horse and was taken prisoner:

'I unfortunately had my 2nd horse shot about the same spot as my first was shot [500 yards from the starting point], my cloak and holsters were riddled and I thought it was up with me as the enemy was then close upon me. I turned round determined to do my best and the party halted, the officer motioning me to throw down my arms and after a moments consideration I did, as I saw the utter hopelessness of such a contest and he appeared a mild man.'[49]

At about this time, as the survivors were still withdrawing, Lord Cardigan's ADC approached Lord Lucan's party. Trumpet Major Henry Joy recalled the encounter:

'Some time afterwards Captain Lockwood, aide-de-camp to the Earl of Cardigan, rode up to me in a state of great excitement, without his busby, asking if I had seen Lord Cardigan. I replied, "Yes; he has just passed me," and I pointed in the direction which he had taken. The captain rode away, and I never saw that officer again.' Lockwood's fate remains unknown.[50]

Meanwhile, a number of mounted men had reached British lines and one of them called out to Captain Ewart, ADC to Lord Raglan, and informed him that a badly wounded staff officer was lying some distance back. Ewart had earlier accompanied General Airey in delivering a message from Raglan to Sir George Cathcart who had belatedly arrived with the 4th Infantry Division – they were to retake Nos. 1, 2 and 3 Redoubts. To Cathcart, this was madness. He knew well that if recaptured a redoubt, he would be required to vacate it again and return to the siege trenches in front of Sevastopol. Ewart now received Cathcart's permission to make a search for the officer, who turned out to be Captain William Morris.[51]

Riding down the valley at a gallop Ewart came across the body of Captain Nolan, almost level with No. 4 Redoubt; close by he found Captain Morris who was 'almost insensible' with blood running freely from a terrible head wound. Unable to move him, Ewart shouted to a mounted man of the 17th Lancers, Private George Smith, to send stretcher bearers to assist. Morris' rescue under fire was the subject of a Victoria Cross action.

Meanwhile, Colonel Paget came across Captain Hutton. Both he and his horse were struggling with their wounds, and Hutton looked faint. Paget rode over and offered his rum flask. In thanking his commanding officer, Hutton said in a very matter-of-fact way, 'I have been wounded, Colonel. Would you have any objection to my going to the doctor when I get in?'[52]

Lord Paget of the 4th Light Dragoons, who was still making his way back up the valley, having moments earlier encountered Lord Cardigan, recalled the encounter:

'With the continual application of the flat of my sabre against my horse's flank and the liberal use of both spurs, I at last got home, after having overtaken Hutton, who had been shot through both thighs, and who was exerting the little vigour left in him in urging on his wounded horse (which had eleven wounds and later had to be destroyed) as was mine… Well, there is an end to all things, and at last we got home, the shouts of welcome that greeted every fresh officer or group as they came struggling up the incline, telling us of our safety.'

Like many men who made it back Private William Pennington, 11th Hussars, was wounded and exhausted: 'I found that I could not dismount from the wound in my right leg, and so was lifted off, and then how I caressed the noble horse that brought me safely out.'

Lord George Paget spoke briefly again with Lord Cardigan: 'I then said to Lord Cardigan, "I'm afraid there are no such regiments left as the 13th and 17th, for I can give no account of them," but before I had finished the sentence, I caught sight of a cluster of them standing by their horses, on the brow of the hill, in my front.'

Nearly all of the mounted survivors had by now reached the British lines. The Heavy Brigade regiments cheered as they came in. Many of the men were wounded, as were nearly all of the horses, but still paraded.

The survivors re-formed close to the position from which the Light Brigade had set off some twenty minutes earlier – they made a sorry sight.

Private Daniel Deering, 4th Light Dragoons, recalled the scene:

'When we got back to where we started from, I saw Lord Cardigan in front of us; he rode up and said: "This has been a great blunder, but don't blame me for it."'

Private Robert Ferguson's account added: 'Some of the men, including myself, answered, "My Lord, we are ready to go back again." His Lordship said, "No, you have done enough today, my men!"'[53]

It would be a little while before the first roll was made. This would be to establish how many were still mounted and fit for duty and did not include those already being treated for wounds or those without mounts – it was possible that they might be required for further action.

Cardigan addressed the survivors, promising them, 'Men you have done a glorious deed. England will be proud of you, and grateful to you. If you live to go home, be sure you will be provided for. Not one of you fellows will have to seek refuge in a workhouse.'[54] Lord Cardigan, reflecting on the Charge, wrote: 'The whole affair, from the moment we moved off until we reformed on the ground from which we started, did not occupy more than 20 minutes. On the troops forming up, I had them counted by my Brigade Major [Mayow], and found that there were 195 men [198] out of about 670 [673].'[55]

Some of the walking wounded were still making their way back. Others, supporting wounded comrades or leading wounded horses arrived later and in ones and twos. Private Mitchell was still leading the blinded man: 'We met our commissary officer, Mr Cruickshank [Deputy-Assistant Commissary General Alexander Crowder Crookshank (later General, CB)], mounted on a pony with saddlebags filled with bottles of rum. He was making his way to meet any of the men returning from the Charge. He very kindly gave us a good drop each, which helped us along nicely… I could see a couple of ambulance waggons and two surgeons hard at work dressing wounds, etc... After seeing the poor fellow's wound dressed, and assisting him into the waggon, I bade him goodbye.'

The scenes at the British lines were incredible, as Lieutenant Seager wrote in a letter home, dated 1 November:

'Those that were left collected, shook hands and congratulated each other on escaping. We, about 5, sat down on the grass, and fared sumptuously on salt pork and biscuit, washed down by rations of rum, all brought on the ground by our quartermaster.'[56]

The Light Brigade was kept on alert until about 5 pm before being allowed to go back to their camp.

Not everyone made it back that afternoon, or even that day, some of the wounded lay on the battlefield for hours, some days, before they were found. One officer, Captain White, 17th Lancers, was initially reported dead, as a press article reveals:

'WHITE BELIEVED DEAD – ALIVE

'We are happy to be able to confirm our former statements of the safety of Captain White, reported killed at the battle of Balaclava. Letters have been received from the gallant gentleman himself, announcing his progressive recovery from the effects of a severe wound. His horse was shot under him, and he was for three hours on the field. He is not now considered in any danger.'[57]

But there were very few such happy outcomes and most of those posted as 'missing' were never heard of again, nor given a marked grave.

Chapter 8

After the Battle

The State of the Brigade

Twenty minutes of frenetic combat over the length of the North Valley had virtually destroyed Cardigan's Light Brigade. The action had resulted in over 250 casualties, with a further 58 men taken prisoner. Only 198 men remained effective, the remaining unwounded men were without mounts.

The Heavy Brigade, by contrast, remained a fighting force. Together with the composite Light Brigade force which now numbered the same strength as two troops, they were to hold their position.

Troop Sergeant Major George Smith had been ordered back to camp with a handful of unwounded survivors to find mounts and return to duty. Here they discovered that the Cossacks had callously wounded every animal they could find, including four horses from his Troop. Smith remained in camp; the Light Brigade was stood down at 5 pm.

Meanwhile, small parties drawn from the survivors, along with men who had been in Balaclava that morning or on forage duty, went about recovering the wounded and transporting them to Balaclava's makeshift hospital or to the docking area where some, including eleven men of the 13th Light Dragoons, were sent on board ship without seeing the surgeon.

Mrs Duberly's Diary

Mrs Duberly, who had witnessed the Charge from Sapouné Hill, later visited their camp enquiring after friends. She wrote in her dairy:

'Colonel Shewell came up to me, looking flushed, and conscious of having fought like a brave and gallant soldier, and having earned his laurels well. Many had a sad tale to tell. All had been struck with the exception of Colonel Shewell, either themselves or their horses.'

The entry then goes on to list the casualties among Mrs Duberly's friends and acquaintances, beginning first with the dead and missing: 'Poor Lord Fitzgibbon was dead. Of Captain Lockwood no tidings had been heard; none had seen him fall, and none had seen him since the action… Poor Captain Goad, of the 13th, is dead. Ah, what a catalogue!'

Of those who were wounded but made it back Mrs Duberly wrote: 'Mr Clutterbuck was wounded in the foot; Mr Seager in the hand. Captain Tomkinson's horse had been shot under him; Major De Salis's horse wounded. Mr Mussenden showed me a grape-shot which had "killed my poor mare."' News by then was still vague as regards those officers, NCOs and other ranks who had been taken prisoner, but the diary entry lists 'Mr Clowes' [Cornet G.G. Clowes] who was wounded by grapeshot and had his horse killed during the retreat. Mrs Duberly adds how 'Time would fail me to enumerate even the names of those whose gallantry reached my ears. Captain Morris, Captain Maude, both cut and shot to pieces, and who have earned for themselves an imperishable name!'

Raglan Demands Answers

Raglan had descended from the Sapouné Ridge in search of answers, according to Portal, as to why 'The Cavalry had been wantonly sacrificed'. He interviewed Cardigan first:

'What do you mean, sir, by attacking a battery in front contrary to all the usages of war and the custom of the service?'

Cardigan was able to respond, 'My lord, I hope you will not blame me, for I received the order to attack from my superior officer in front of the troops.'[1] This disarmed Raglan, who could not blame Lord Lucan's subordinates, Cardigan and the victor of the Heavy Brigade Charge, Scarlett. Lucan, however, had not covered himself in glory.

William Howard Russell of *The Times* reported that Lord Raglan was 'much moved with anger' and that 'he had given Lord Cardigan "a tremendous wigging" and had "given it hot" to Lord Lucan too.'[2] This was only partially true, as it was Lucan who was to bear the brunt of Raglan's anger at the loss of the Light Brigade.

Those Left on the Battlefield

Throughout the afternoon and into the evening parties of men continued to risk their lives to bring in the wounded. Indeed the rescue of Webb and Morris were later recognised with awards of the Victoria Cross. Most of the men's actions however, went unnoticed and unrewarded.

A burial party went out to Nolan, who had died close to the British lines, and his was the only officer's body easily found. The burial, on the lower slopes of the Causeway Heights, carried out by Bombardier O. Ormes and four gunners, was supervised by Captain Brandling of C Troop RHA: 'He [Brandling] looked about on the outer side of the [Causeway] ridge for the body. Having found it he came back and took with him Bombardier Ormes, and four limber gunners with spades to bury it. The bombardier, on his return, said that the poor fellow's chest had been quite broken away, and that the gold lace of his jacket very much burnt by the shell which killed him, and which must have burst close by; also that there was only one officer present, who appeared to be a friend, and was much affected, and who took off his watch and sword [which must have been attached to his wrist by his sword knot as witnesses saw him release it moments after he was struck]. The grave is in the outer plain, and there is a slight bend inwards in the ridge near that place. It would not be visited by the English for some months ... as the ground was abandoned that night, and for a certain period considered neutral.'[3]

Everything about Nolan became surrounded in controversy, even his burial. Colonel Fox-Strangeways, RHA, reported: 'The body was laid in the earth as it was, there was no time to dig a deep grave, as occasional shots were being fired.'[4]

Captain Edward Hamley, ADC to Sir Richard Dacres commanding the artillery, saw Nolan's body on the 25th and commented:

'Close to the ditch of the fieldwork on the last hill of the ridge on our side lay the body of Nolan on its back, the jacket open, the breast pierced by the fatal splinter. It was but an hour since the Division had passed him on the heights, where he was riding gaily near the staff, conspicuous in the red forage cap and tiger-skin saddle cover of his regiment.'[5]

There is another account of Nolan's burial which dates from August 1855. While riding over the battlefield in the company of the Duke of Cambridge, the duke pointed out the body of Captain Nolan to Captain Adye, with the words: 'The officer who brought the order lies dead in that ditch.' Nolan's body lay in the open and had not been buried, Adye was able to describe Nolan's wound.[6]

An unsubstantiated and anonymous source later claimed that on hearing that Nolan's body was to be retrieved and buried, Lord Lucan had exclaimed: 'He met his deserts, a dog's death – and like a dog let him be buried in a ditch'.

All That Was Left of Them
At dusk on the 25th the 11th Hussars returned to the camp where Sergeant Major George Smith assembled what was left of his Troop. Some thirty-two NCOs and men had paraded early that morning, now under half were present. As far as could be ascertained, of the absentees six were dead, ten wounded and two prisoners. Three of the wounded had lost their right arm and one his left. Two of the wounded died later. Captain Cook, the troop commander, was

wounded and Lieutenant Houghton mortally so. These casualty-rates were reflected across the brigade.

Even though the 8th Hussars had been in the Second Line and veering off course, which had spared them some of the cannon fire in front, they had still suffered twenty-eight killed and nineteen wounded. Other regiments fared worse, with the 17th in the First Line losing 31 men of all ranks killed and 53 wounded.

As Darkness Falls

As darkness fell the survivors tried to settle their nerves and get some rest in half-empty tents. Some went through the day's momentous events, wrestling with guilt, having escaped where their friends and comrades had been killed or terribly wounded. Others had faced the dilemma of leaving men behind to fall victim to the Cossacks. 'The camp seemed quite deserted, and the shadow of death lay heavy upon it.'[7]

As the pitifully few survivors of the Charge were settling down to try to get some sleep the order came for them to move camp 440 yards closer to the escarpment. Just to make their situation worse, another order came – 'No fires to be lit. No noise to be made.'

Cornet George Wombwell of the 17th Lancers probably summed up the thoughts of many: 'I want to see no more fighting, it has pleased God to keep me safe through what I have seen, and I am now anxious to get home.'

Many wounded horses had to be shot and at least six died in the night.

The Curious Story of Two Canine Heroes

The two dogs who charged with the Light Brigade were Jemmy, who ran the Charge with the 8th Hussars, and Boxer, with the 11th. Both returned with the first mounted men of their regiments. Jemmy had a slight neck wound and Boxer was unscathed. Private John Doyle, 8th Hussars wrote: 'We had a dog called Jemmy, the dog, which a man named Lennan [Private Martin Lennon] brought from Devonport. He used to follow the spent shot and shell, snap at the fuse and pull it out. A shell lodged under Captain Longworth's [Captain George Lockwood] horse, which would have blown him and horse into the air, but for Jemmy, the dog, who flew at it and pulled the fuse out'.[8]

After Relief Came Recriminations

After the relief of surviving such carnage and the joy of greeting fellow survivors, came reflection, and for some, recriminations. Sergeant Major George Smith was bitter at the lack of support for the Light Brigade. In his diary he wrote:

'And the world would ask: who was answerable for all this [lack of support for the charge]? The same man that ordered Lord Cardigan with 670 [*sic*] men to charge an army in position and then left them to their fate when he had at his command eight squadrons of Heavy Cavalry and two troops of Horse Artillery, besides a division of infantry with field batteries close in the rear. True, that he advanced two [*sic*] regiments of this brigade a short distance down the valley, but did he not follow on? What did this avail us, for as soon as he came under fire, he began to retire.'[9]

Smith's reading of the events was accurate in nearly every respect.

Cathcart and the Redoubts

The greatest irony, perhaps, was that Cathcart was correct, in that Nos. 1-3 redoubts were too isolated to be recaptured and held by the British, while for the Russians No. 4 Redoubt was considered too vulnerable to hold and they spiked and discarded the cannons before withdrawing. The men of the Azov, Ukrainian, Dnieper, and Odessa Regiments consolidated their hold on Nos. 1-3 Redoubts. Meanwhile, Ryzhov's cavalry held the eastern end of the North Valley between the Causeway and Fedioukine Heights which were occupied by Zhaboritski's men.

The Russians Celebrate a Famous Victory

Meanwhile, just as Raglan had feared, the Russians removed the seven captured Royal Naval cannons to Theatre Square, Sevastopol. Here they were exhibited as war booty, the church bells ringing in celebration. Writing his despatch to the Czar, Prince Menshikov raised this figure to eleven guns.

Russian casualties sustained in the battle were estimated at 300, although they were probably far higher, perhaps 550, but the capture of the guns and the Causeway Heights allowed them to claim a victory. With the loss of the Woronzoff road, the only metalled road, supplies bound for British troops besieging Sevastopol would have to be transported seven miles along a muddy track via The Col. This proved a major hardship during the winter of 1854-5.

In his official despatch Prince Menshikov wrote: 'The English Cavalry under Lord Cardigan charged 3 Don Battery, sabring some of the gunners, and attacked the hussar brigade of the 6 Cavalry Division, with unexpected recklessness. The enemy was taken in the flank by the Uhlan Regiment and the crossfire of riflemen and the artillery. Enemy losses are reckoned to be heavy.'

The Russians Command the Battlefield

Because the Russians commanded the battlefield, the first casualty returns for the Charge included the names of numerous officers, NCOs and men whose fate remained unknown; they were officially listed as 'missing or killed'.

On the 26th Raglan sent Captain Edward Fellows, 11th Hussars, and Trumpet Major Henry Joy, 17th Lancers, under a flag of truce to arrange for a ceasefire for the burial of the dead. They carried with them 'necessaries' for captured officers. The deputation was brought before General Pavel Liprandi, who was indignant, insisting that they were Christians and quite capable of doing what was necessary.

A second attempt to parley on the 27th was more successful and secured a list of the fifty-eight officers and men taken prisoner.

Lieutenant Seager: 'We sent a flag of truce to the Enemy on the 29th to find out the number of prisoners they had taken, and out of 11 officers missing belonging to the Light Brigade only two were prisoners, all the others killed and buried by the Russians.'[10]

The flag of truce was not always respected. Private Samuel Jamieson Murdock, 11th Hussars, was greeted with a hail of fire, bullets piercing the flag, smashing his leg, and taking the ears off his horse.

Informing the Next-of-Kin

The process of notifying the next of kin of casualties was ad hoc. Lord Paget wrote: 'On the 25th October that fateful date – in the afternoon I rode down to the Guards (to get something to eat) and had to tell them a sorry tale of some of their friends, and it was a strange coincidence that two of the first officers who rushed up to me were Bradford and Mark Wood, who each had brothers in our brigade though with different names, who had been killed; Goade [of the] 13th, being Bradford's brother, and Lockwood [Captain George Lockwood], Wood's brother, and their deaths were announced by me to their brothers without me knowing the relationship.'[11]

The men whose spouses had journeyed east with their regiment and were at Scutari or Balaclava were the first to learn of the dead and wounded. Some details were conveyed by letters written by the soldiers' friends, although the post took around a month to reach Britain.

The first official casualty list appeared in *The London Gazette* of 12 November, only the officers then being named. A more complete list was published on 17 November 1854. There were many mistakes in this and subsequent listings, while men who were listed as only being 'slightly wounded' were almost as likely to die as the grievously wounded.

Captains Morris and Nolan had exchanged final letters home. In error, Morris's letter, carried by Nolan, was forwarded to Mrs Morris.

The *Manchester Times* of 16 November carried details of an interview, which it claimed was 'with General Gortschakoff, in the valley of Balaclava, and ascertained that Cornets Clowes and Chadwick were prisoners and wounded, but well treated'.

Battlefield Burials

Despite General Liprandi's insistence that the dead would be given a proper burial, the Russians made only a half-hearted effort. This was evident from the report of members of C Troop RHA, who carried out exercises in the valley during May of the following year. The bodies had been buried in a small number of collective graves (trenches and pits). Many of the men and horses, however, had been terribly wounded by artillery and it was reported that pieces of uniform, along with limbs, bones and other scattered remains were visible in what was a truly macabre scene. The Turkish dead around Redoubts Nos. 1 and 2 had been piled high and left as carrion.

The Conduct of the Cossacks

The conduct of some of the Russian troops was brought under questions. In an article published in *The Daily Telegraph* of 16 October 1875, Private William Cullen, 11th Hussars, recalled how the Cossacks had murdered Private Robert Layzell in cold blood, which he had reported to both Raglan and Cardigan. The article claims the matter was raised with General Liprandi who responded that 'he would be answerable for his own soldiers, as they were Christians, but would not be for the Cossacks, as they were not paid, but employed in the time of war to harass the enemy of a night and to plunder and destroy all they possibly could. As for fighting, they were no good.'

General Liprandi and the PoWs

The bravery of the British was acknowledged by both friend and foe. A number of former PoWs related an interview with General Liprandi in a hospital hut. He asked how much they had been given to drink for them to 'come down and attack them in such a mad manner?' One account states that Private William Kirk, 17th Lancers, by then under the influence of several vodkas, insisted that if they had had a drink that morning 'we would have taken half Russia by this time.' Liprandi was amused and agreed.

Sergeant Major Fowler, 4th Light Dragoons, reprimanded Kirk for insubordination, assuring Liprandi that essentially what Kirk had said was true and that they had fought on empty stomachs that morning.[12] General Liprandi commended the 'gallant fellows'. Before leaving them, he ordered that they be provided with pens and paper so they could write home and inform their next-of-kin of their current circumstances.

Liprandi's conduct was typical of the officer class who generally treated the PoWs humanely; the same could not be said for the lower ranks and the Cossacks.

Private Farquharson's story was not untypical in the level of brutality meted out to British PoWs. Having surrendered he was bound so tightly that he almost fainted with the pain. Defenceless, he was repeatedly beaten and prodded with lances before being pulled along behind a horse. Then he underwent a mock execution, only being saved when a Russian officer intervened.

Death in Captivity

The British prisoners were force-marched off to Simferopol where they received medical attention. Among those requiring urgent hospital treatment was Private John Dryden, 11th Hussars, with thirty-six wounds of all types. Privates William Cooper and Robert Duke of the 13th Light Dragoons were little better off. Among the less fortunate were Privates Thomas Fletcher and James Normoyle, 4th Light Dragoons: both were badly mutilated and later died of their wounds.

Medical treatment was rudimentary and often more deadly than the wounds themselves. Private Wightman, 17th Lancers, recalled four men died one after another, only minutes after having a limb amputated without anaesthetic: 'It seemed a butchery job, and certainly was a sickening sight.' Of the nine men who underwent similar operations at Simferopol only one survived the hideous ordeal.

William Baynton, 13th Light Dragoons, suffered nine wounds, which included a serious injury to his leg. He died at Simferopol. Baynton had written to his brother, Harry Powell, stating how kind the Russians were and how well he had been looked after by the Sisters of Mercy. Another of the wounded was Private Thomas Cooke, 13th Light Dragoons, who had a severe gunshot wound. The bullet drove a button from his tunic into his chest. Often in such instances the foreign bodies in their wounds led to infections which could prove fatal – but he survived for many years.

As the days wore on the men's suffering from their wounds increased: 'At the time, owing to excitement and one thing and another, you don't feel the wounds that you receive: but when your blood has cooled down a bit, and you are in a calmer frame of mind, you begin to feel the wounds.'

Private John Bevin, 8th Hussars, recalled an awkward moment which occurred in Simferopol Hospital. He was having his wounds dressed when he noticed a Russian cavalryman staring at him. The man who had two sword cuts on his head and three fingers missing accused Bevin of causing the wounds. Bevin pointed to his head wound, explaining that the Russian had caused his injury – honour was even.

Bevin later wrote from captivity:

'I cannot describe the kindness of the inhabitants of this town (Simferopol). I am nearly recovered now, thank God; the only wound I have that will be discernible is a sword cut across my left ear. I had a great many lance wounds about my body, but they are all nearly well. There were about seventy [sic] of us taken prisoners. I hope you will not be grieved at my being a prisoner… the officers of the Russian army visit us every day and treat us kindly, and give us cigars and tobacco to smoke, and many times told us that we were very brave soldiers.'[13]

Cornet and Adjutant John Chadwick, 17th Lancers, who was in the company of Cornet Clowes, 8th Hussars, wrote to his brother Captain James Chadwick, from imprisonment at Karkoff on 2 April 1855. His letter, published in the *Reynold's Newspaper* of 13 May 1855, mentions the fates of a number of his men:

'Of the twelve men of the 17th Lancers who were taken prisoners on the same day that I was, five only are living. Corporal Hall and Private Jenner died at Simferopol, the former having had his leg taken off, the latter his arm; Private Wightman was left sick at Alexandrioski on the way here; and Private Marshall is here. Private McAllister has gone on for his destination. The seven dead are Privates Harrison, Ellis, Young, Kirk, Edge, Brown, and Sharpe. The latter two started quite well from Simferopol, but died on the journey. I wish you would write to Taylor, the riding master, at the depot, in order that he might cause their friends to be written to.'

The Russian officers generally allowed the PoWs to move around freely on their honour not to try to escape. The Light Brigade heroes became minor celebrities in the towns and villages they passed through and were permitted to receive visitors. One was even taken in by a wealthy lady and was reluctant to be repatriated.

Prisoner Exchange
And so the survivors had a chequered journey to Odessa, their final destination, from where they were exchanged, sailing on British troopships on 23 October (1855). The men arrived at Kadikoi on 26 October, from where they were transferred to the Cavalry Depot, Scutari, arriving there around 4 November.

The Times of 9 November 1855, carried the following announcement:

'Return of Prisoners of War, conveyed from Odessa, by the Steamship *Columbo*, and Her Majesty's ships:-

'4th Light Dragoons – Taken at Balaclava, October 25, 1854: Trumpet Major Hugh Crawford, Corporal Joseph Armstrong, Private James Bagshaw, James Bolton, Robert Farquharson, Charles Frederick, Thomas King, Thomas Lucas, wounded – lost left hand, unfit for service; Michael O'Brien, Samuel Parkes.

'8th Hussars – Taken at Balaclava, October 25, 1854: Private John Bevin, wounded in several places – well at present; William Bird, Patrick Horan, Richard Palfreyman [*sic*].

'11th Hussars – Taken at Balaclava, October 25, 1854: Private John Dryden, wounded severely – 27 wounds, suffers seriously at present; Nathan Henry, wounded; Henry Parker, William Pilkington [aka Private W.H. 'Tom' Spring], wounded.

'13th Light Dragoons – Taken at Balaclava, October 25, 1854: Troop-Sergeant-Major John Lincoln [*sic*], George Smith, wounded severely, Private George Cooper, wounded; Edward Hanlon, wounded; John McCann, wounded in several places – well at present; Charles Warren, Amos Harris, wounded.'

PoWs Tried by Garrison Court-Martial

On being repatriated the men had to go through the formality of being tried by a garrison court-martial for allowing themselves to be taken prisoner by the enemy. The court records for Samuel Parkes are dated 5-6 November 1855 and may be seen as representative.

Extracts from Regimental records of the 4th Light Dragoons:

'Scutari, 5th November 1855.

'Application for District Court-martial for the under-mentioned Non-Commissioned Officers and Men of the 4th Light Dragoons.

'No. 635 Private Samuel Parkes of the 4th Light Dragoons for having at Balaclava absented himself when engaged with the enemy on the 25th October 1854 and not returning till 26th October 1855 when he was exchanged.

'Proceedings of the Court-martial assembled by order of Brigadier General H.K. Storks, Commanding Troops on the Bosphorus, in accordance with the 30th Clause of the Mutiny Act.

'President - Captain H.E. Reader, 12th Lancers

'Members - Lieutenant Weir, 6th Dragoons, Lieutenant Preston, 3rd Light Dragoons, Lieutenant Blunt, 12th Lancers, Lieutenant Winstanley, 4th Light Dragoons.

'Scutari, 6th November 1855

'The Court having assembled and been duly sworn proceeded to enquire into the cause of the absence of No. 635 Private Samuel Parkes of the 4th Light Dragoons taken prisoner near Balaclava in the Crimea on or about the 25th October, 1854, and whom did not return until 26th October 1855, when he was exchanged.

'There being no evidence for the Prosecution and No. 635 Private Samuel Parkes of the 4th Light Dragoons being called upon for his statement states as follows:

'I was with the 4th Light Dragoons in the charge at Balaclava on the 25th October, 1854, when my horse was shot under me, I was at once surrounded and made prisoner, I was sent by the Russians to Simferopol where I remained until 27th August, 1855, when together with the other prisoners I was marched to Odessa from whence I was forwarded to Balaclava and reached that place on the 26th October 1855.'

'The Prisoner withdraws and the Court is closed.

'Finding

'The court having maturely considered the statement made by the prisoner, together with there being no evidence to adduce against him, is of the opinion that the said prisoner No. 635 Private Samuel Parkes of the 4th Light Dragoons, was not taken prisoner by the Enemy through wilful neglect of duty on his part, and returned as soon as regularly exchanged, and therefore recommends that the Prisoner No. 635 Private Samuel Parkes of the 4th Light Dragoons to receive the whole of such arrears of pay as may be due to him and further that he shall be permitted to reckon Service for the period of his absence.

'H.E. Reader, Captain, 12th lancers
President
6th November 1855.'

The Shameful Case of Private Perry
Not all of the returning PoWs were fairly treated. Private Thomas Perry, 8th Hussars, who was exchanged early, on 29 August 1855, due to severity of his wounds, was found guilty of allowing himself to be taken PoW.

Perry wrote to his parents from his hospital bed at Simferopol. His letter was published in the *Huddersfield Chronicle* of 24 February 1855:

'I myself was shot through both thighs, and through the right shoulder, at the top part of the arm, two sword cuts in the head, and two lance wounds, one in the hand and one in the thigh; so I leave you to think I was in a bad way. I was taken up almost dead by the Russians; but after got a doctor's attention I began to do well.'

Thomas Perry was sentenced to 84 days imprisonment, following on from which he was put before a medical board and discharged due to vertigo as a result of head wounds. This, of course, affected his army pension. Perry's was just one of the many terrible injustices suffered by the veterans of the Charge.

A Proposed Exchange

It later came to light that the captivity of the men of the Light Brigade might not have been so lengthy or harrowing, according to an entry in the diary of George Palmer Evelyn who noted on 31 October:

'Several flags of truce have lately passed on both sides on the subject of the prisoners – the enemy hold but two of our cavalry officers both wounded – Chadwick, 17th Lancers, and Clowes, 8th Hussars. Menschikoff offered to exchange the troopers for horses, valuing each biped at the rate of three quadrupeds.'[14]

It should be noted however, that by December 1854 the Cavalry Division could only muster 200 horses, about exactly the number required in exchange for the surviving PoWs.

The Recriminations

The recriminations over whose responsibility it was that the Light Brigade was lost began almost immediately. Cardigan had defended himself and placed the blame squarely on Lord Lucan. Raglan seemed to agree.

While the words 'charge' and 'attack' did not appear in the Fourth Order, Lord Lucan used the argument that General Airey's ADC's instructions were clear: the Cavalry was to attack No. 3 Don Cossack battery, and that the order was to be carried out immediately. Lucan recalled Raglan's rebuff: 'Lord Lucan, you were a Lieutenant-General, and should have therefore exercised your discretion and, not approving of the charge, should not have caused it to be made.'[15]

Raglan's actual plan was fanciful. He expected that the Russian forces, which vastly outnumbered the allies, would retreat from their fortified positions on the mere advance of the British Cavalry. The Russians had additionally defended their positions around the redoubts with heavy artillery, while they had overwhelming numbers in fresh infantry battalions and cavalry which supported both flanks.

Lord Lucan made it clear from the outset: 'I do not intend to bear the smallest particle of responsibility. I gave the order to charge under what I considered a most imperious necessity, and I will not bear one particle of the blame.'[16]

Lord Paget, another important eyewitness to the whole affair, recalled his meeting with Lucan on the 26th: 'Lucan is much cut up; and with tears in his eyes this morning he said how infamous it was to lay the blame on him, and told me what had passed between him and Lord Raglan.'[17]

During the evening of the 27th Airey was sent to Lucan to try to calm the situation, and reassure him he had read Raglan's despatch and that it did not to criticize him. Lucan seemed content.

Raglan's Despatch

Raglan's despatch, dated 28 October, was published in *The London Gazette* of 12 November:

'The enemy commenced their operations by attacking the work on our side of the village of Kamara, and after very little resistance carried it.

'They likewise got possession of the three others [ie. the redoubts] in contiguity to it, being opposed only in one, and that but for a very short space of time.

'The furthest of the three they did not retain, but the immediate abandonment of the others enabled them to take possession of the guns in them, amounting in the whole to seven. Those in the three lesser forts were spiked by the one English artilleryman who was in each.

'The Russian cavalry at once advanced, supported by artillery, in very great strength. One portion of them assailed the front and right flank of the 93rd, and were instantly driven back by the vigorous and steady fire of that distinguished regiment, under Lieutenant Colonel Ainslie.

'The other and larger mass turned towards Her Majesty's heavy cavalry, and afforded Brigadier General Scarlett, under the guidance of Lieutenant-General the Earl of Lucan, the opportunity of inflicting upon them a most signal defeat. The ground was very unfavourable for the attack of our Dragoons, but no obstacle was sufficient to check their advance, and they charged into the Russian column, which soon sought safety in flight, although far superior in numbers.

'The charge of this brigade was one of the most successful I ever witnessed, was never for a moment doubtful, and is in the highest degree creditable to Brigadier General Scarlett and the officers and men engaged in it.

'As the enemy withdrew from the ground which they had momentarily occupied, I directed the cavalry, supported by the Fourth Division under Lieutenant-General Sir George Cathcart, to move forward, and take advantage of any opportunity to regain the heights; and, not having been able to accomplish this immediately, and it appearing that an attempt was being made to remove the captured guns, the Earl of Lucan was desired to advance rapidly, follow the enemy in their retreat, and try to prevent them from effecting their objects.

'In the meanwhile the Russians had time to reform on their own ground, with artillery in front and upon their flanks.

'From some misconception of the instruction to advance, the Lieutenant-General considered that he was bound to attack at all hazards, and he accordingly ordered Major General the Earl of Cardigan to move forward with the Light Brigade.

'This order was obeyed in the most spirited and gallant manner. Lord Cardigan charged with the utmost vigour, attacked a battery which was firing upon the advancing squadrons, and, having passed beyond it, engaged the Russian cavalry in its rear; but there his troops were assailed by artillery and infantry as well as cavalry, and necessarily retired, after having committed much havoc upon the enemy.

'They effected this movement without haste or confusion; but the loss they sustained has, I deeply lament, been very severe in officers, men, and horses, only counterbalanced by the brilliancy of the attack and the gallantry, order, and discipline which distinguished it, forming a striking contrast to the conduct of the enemy's cavalry which had previously been engaged with the Heavy Brigade.

'The Chasseurs d'Afrique advanced on our left and gallantly charged a Russian battery, which checked its fire for a time, and thus rendered the British cavalry an essential service.

'I have the honour to enclose copies of Sir Colin Campbell's and the Earl of Lucan's reports.

'I beg to draw your Grace's attention to the terms in which Sir Colin Campbell speaks of Lieutenant Colonel Ainslie, of the 93d, and Captain Barker, of the Royal Artillery; and also to the praise bestowed by the Earl of Lucan on Major General the Earl of Cardigan and Brigadier General Scarlett, which they most fully deserve.'

Raglan had written a covering letter to the despatch, which was addressed to the Duke of Newcastle, Secretary for War. In it Raglan tried to salvage the events at Balaclava, but made it plain that Lord Lucan 'had made a fatal mistake', and that this had resulted in the loss of the Light Brigade. Raglan's damning observation was that 'The written order sent to him by the Quartermaster-General did not exact that he should attack at all hazards, and contained no expression which could bear that construction.'

Lucan's Despatch
Lord Lucan had not helped his own cause when he wrote his account of the battle in his despatch to Lord Raglan on 27 October:

'The Division took up a position with a view of supporting an attack upon the Heights when being instructed to make a rapid advance to the front to prevent the enemy carrying away the guns lost by the Turkish troops in the morning [i.e. those in the redoubts]. I ordered the Light Brigade to advance in 2 lines, and supported them with the Heavy Brigade.'

Lucan's Rage and Re-call

The British newspapers reached the Crimea in mid-December and Raglan's despatch and the press reaction to it left Lord Lucan in a rage. He wrote a letter which he wished to be forwarded to Newcastle stating his own position; Raglan tried to dissuade him but finally relented on 16 December.

Colonel Mundy, the Under-Secretary of State, on reading the letter and Raglan's covering note, summed up the opinion of the authorities:

'But even so the Lieutenant-General ought to have acted on the written orders of the Commander-in-Chief and not upon the oral ones of the aide-de-camp. It is evident indeed that he derived his resolution to attack at all hazards, and contrary to his own and Lord Cardigan's expressed opinion, not from Lord Raglan's note, which could by no possibility be construed in that sense, but from the hurried and as the Lieutenant-General says, "most disrespectful" remark of the Staff Officer.'[18]

Lucan's letter was critical of Lord Raglan, which would not be tolerated. It could only result in one thing, Lucan's recall. On 14 February 1855 Lucan sailed for home. Back in England, Lucan tried to rescue his reputation by requesting a court-martial on 2 March, the day after his arrival in England. He made a second request three days later.

A pamphlet was published which condemned him for being out of date and incompetent, even suggesting he had failed in his duty by not leading the Charge in person. Lucan published a lengthy reply.[19]

Lord Cardigan - The Unlikely Hero

The public's new perception of Lord Cardigan could not have been more different. He was hailed as the 'Hero of Balaclava' on his return. Earlier, on 20 November 1854 Lord Cardigan had written to Raglan saying that he would be 'obliged shortly to ask you for leave of absence on sick certificate. Were it not for bad health, I assure you I would have no wish to go, for you know you have no keener soldier in your army.' He then went on to try to get his sick certificate which he wished to do '...without having to explain my ailment in detail before a medical Board.'[20]

Raglan, however, insisted that he go before the Medical Board.

Two weeks later the Medical Board certified that Cardigan should not have to face a Crimean winter. On 8 December he left – he landed at Dover on 13 January 1855. He was agreeably surprised by his reception. A crowd on the quay gave 'Three cheers for Balaclava'. Even his charger, Ronald, was treated as an equine hero and the crowds that greeted Cardigan would try to pluck Ronald's tail for souvenirs! Cardigan was invited to Windsor Castle, where he had an audience with Queen Victoria on 16 January, sitting next to the Queen at dinner. Prince Albert requested that he give an account of the Charge, which he did, blaming Lord Lucan for the mistake in charging the wrong battery.

Cardigan continued to be feted a hero. Bands played *See the conquering hero comes* when he arrived at railway stations. Leicester gave him an illuminated address, Yorkshire a sword, and his home county of Northamptonshire a forty-yard-long testimonial made of sheets of paper signed by 5,000 individuals.

One of his engagements saw Lord Cardigan give a speech at the Mansion House on 15 February. Cardigan wore the uniform in which he Charged. His speech was transcribed and published in the press – it was both inaccurate and seen as boastful.

Before embarking on the campaign, Cardigan's career had been surrounded by controversy and many of his peers resented that he had become, in their eyes at least, an accidental hero.

It was not long before his critics tried to sully his reputation.[21]

In the meantime the Queen made him a KCB in the summer of 1855. This was during the period when Lucan was still struggling to redeem his reputation.

However, by January 1856 Cardigan's pull was beginning to fade. The findings of an 'Inquiry into the Supplies of the British Army in the Crimea' had been presented to both houses of parliament. Airey, Lucan and Cardigan were among those criticised. Cardigan demanded a further inquiry which became known as the 'Whitewashing Board'. It found 'the system' to blame.

Lord Cardigan's Reputation Challenged

In April, 1856, the war ended in a victory of sorts for the Allies and the troops came home. In December Raglan's former ADC, Calthorpe, published a book entitled *Letters From Headquarters*. It was woefully inaccurate and damaging to Cardigan's reputation. He demanded a retraction, which Calthorpe refused to give. Cardigan tried to have further editions stopped, but these efforts failed and he entered into litigation. The case was heard by Lord Chief Justice Cockburn, assisted by three other judges in Westminster Hall in June 1863.

Although there were a number of statements which Cardigan complained about, the most controversial were those surrounding the Charge. These included: Captain Morris's request to charge during the Heavy Brigade action; the allegations that Cardigan did not reach the guns; and that he did not rally his brigade beyond the guns.

The False Charges Against Lord Cardigan

The Literary Examiner 27 December 1856 quoted:

'Notwithstanding the favour with which Lord Cardigan seems to have been regarded at head-quarters, the staff officer's book [Calthorpe's publication] does not report favourably upon the military reputation of that hero. He makes notable appearance in the book only four times. First at Alma, where he was not in the battle, but helped thus in the pursuit of the defeated enemy:

"Lord Raglan now ordered the brigade of Guards, 2nd Division, and the 4th Division, who had taken no part in the action, up the opposite heights, which commanded the road to Sevastopol. The cavalry went in front of the infantry, and from some misconception of orders, Lord Cardigan would not allow any prisoners to be taken. An officer of the 8th Hussars, who was somewhat in advance with his troop, and who had captured 60 or 70 Russian soldiers, was ordered by Lord Cardigan to let them go again, quite as much to the astonishment of the Russians who had been taken, as to the Hussars who had captured them."'

In this instance it was Lord Raglan who forbade the cavalry from performing their usual role of pursuing an enemy in defeat. Lord Lucan disobeyed the command and sent elements forward, but on seeing this Raglan twice ordered their withdrawal. In disgust, Lucan ordered the prisoners to be released. Cardigan was blameless in this debacle.

The article continues:

'Secondly, at the Battle of Balaclava, where, of the serviceable charge of the Heavy Brigade, the staff officer writes:

"When Lord Raglan saw the successful manner in which the charge had been made he sent down an officer of his staff to say "Well done," to General Scarlett. It is much to be regretted that the brigade of light cavalry, under command of Lord Cardigan, did not attack the enemy in flank and rear when they first met the Heavy Brigade, as the defeat would have been more complete, and numbers of prisoners might have been taken. Captain Morris, who commanded the 17th Lancers, pointed out to Lord Cardigan the opportunity that offered of charging the enemy; but the earl said he was placed in that particular spot, and should not move without orders. In vain Captain Morris begged to be allowed to charge with his regiment alone. Lord Cardigan would not give his permission."'

Although he disputed the exact circumstances, it seems clear that Morris rode the 17th Lancers forward in readiness to charge, but that Cardigan overruled him. Lord Lucan claimed that his orders to Cardigan allowed him to use his initiative and attack any enemy that came within striking distance, but not infantry.

The Russians had previously set traps for the British and endeavoured to lure hot-headed commanders into deploying the cavalry – Lord Raglan had had to save Lord Lucan's command at Bulganak on 19 September and the Russians deployment either side of the North Valley could be seen as another such trap. Two squadrons of the Royals were near the Light Brigade at the time and raced to give support to the Heavy Brigade – they arrived only in time to exchange a few blows before the Russian Cavalry broke off the engagement and retired. Calthorpe's account practically vindicates Cardigan of the accusation he makes when he says:

'The Heavy Brigade were unable to pursue the Russian cavalry for any distance as they came under the fire from the redoubts captured by the enemy; indeed, as it was, we lost three or four men from the effects of their shot.'

The reporter from *The Literary Examiner* continues:

'And of the critical moment when the Light Brigade had arrived at the fatal guns, and needed to be extricated from their perilous position:

"This was the moment when a general was most required, but unfortunately Lord Cardigan was not then present. On coming up to the battery (as he afterwards himself described it), a gun was fired close to him, and for a moment he thought his leg was gone. Such was not the case, as he remained unhurt; however, his horse took fright – swerved round – and galloped off with him to the rear, passing on the way by the 4th Light Dragoons and 8th Hussars before those regiments got up to the battery."'

The accusation was clearly untrue and numerous eyewitnesses would place Lord Cardigan beyond the guns. Those who claimed that they saw Cardigan galloping back before the Second Line arrived at the guns most probably had seen Houghton of the 11th Hussars (Cardigan wore the uniform of an officer of the 11th Hussars) who also rode a chestnut mare and had suffered a mortal head wound and retired.

The reporter's attack continues:

'We next hear of his Lordship's desire to return home for the benefit of his health, and of its being granted on the report of a medical board, "that he is totally unfit to continue in command of the Light Cavalry". At home we remember hearing that he rode out as hero to a distribution of Crimean medals on the horse which carried him at Balaclava, and the horse was patted by the public little knowing what a coward it was, and how it had run away with his master and compelled him to desert his duty.'

In truth, after the Charge, the Light Brigade had ceased to exist as a fighting unit. Depleted in men and with the surviving horses either wounded or malnourished they were no longer an effective fighting force and took little real part in the Battle of Inkerman. The men found themselves in menial roles such as on forage parties, letter duty, etc. Reinforcements were on their way, but it would be months before they were back to strength. Cardigan had been ill leading up to the Charge, while he probably saw the writing on the wall as regards his relationship with his brother-in-law, which was now even further polarised after the controversies of the 25th.

Lord Cardigan Vindicated

Unfortunately Lord Cardigan had left it too long before initiating the liable case; he should have acted on publication. The court, however, established beyond doubt that Cardigan had reached and gone beyond the guns' positions. Nevertheless, his personal withdrawal before the bulk of his Brigade was still left open to unfavourable interpretation. By this time perhaps the feelings of many were summed up best by the diarist Charles Grenville when he wrote;

'The world is weary of Cardigan and his fanfaronades, and of the Crimean accusations and recriminations, and it is time that the subject should be allowed to drop.'

The Charge, however remained one of the most famous and infamous actions in the whole of the reign of Queen Victoria and became a symbol of British gallantry and selflessness – remarkably it encouraged enlistment into all of the regiments involved. The Chargers remained immensely proud of their part in the affair, and in 1875, the 25th anniversary, arranged the first major get-together to mark the event – from that year onwards the dwindling numbers of veterans met annually to celebrate their membership of the illustrious '600'.

Conclusion

Did Nolan intend to attack No. 3 Don Cossack battery?
From the eyewitness accounts of those privy to the encounter between Captain Nolan and Lord Lucan, it seems in all probability that he deliberately misrepresented Lord Raglan's order, with the intention of personally leading the Cavalry Brigade in a death or glory attack against the Russian army in position. Nolan would have known that such an undertaking could only possibly succeed if carried out with great daring and sound leadership, and therefore sought to assume the command of the Charge over Lords Cardigan and Lucan, both of whom he considered inept.

An ambiguous order provides an opportunity
Nolan had been a witness to the bungling of the British senior commanders. Not fully comprehending the back story to these events, he erroneously found Lords Lucan and Cardigan both culpable. Having seen opportunity after opportunity squandered he recognised the probability of a potentially protracted siege of Sevastopol decimating the army through disease. When Raglan instructed that Nolan should carry the fatally ambiguous order and called out to him that it should be carried out 'immediately', Nolan seized on the opportunity, and reportedly responded by shouting back that he would 'lead'.

Having delivered his version of Raglan's ambiguous command, and as the 673-strong Light Brigade (the strength of a Russian cavalry regiment) advanced at the trot, Captain Nolan raced forward in an attempt to usurp Lord Cardigan's position at its head, an unprecedented act by a junior officer but one which he must have felt would be vindicated by a glorious victory. Nolan's 'glory' was short-lived as he was killed by a shell splinter fired in the second volley.

There was no other logical reason for Nolan breaking rank in the manner in which he did. If he were intending to redirect the cavalry, as some theorise, then he would have done this before they moved off – indeed, before the two brigades formed up in the North Valley, the wrong position from which to best assail the redoubts. Furthermore, he would have acted through one of Lord Cardigan's ADCs (there are plenty of examples from all ranks acting with absolute restraint and following *Queen's Regulations* even when severely wounded or in great personal peril).

There remained ample time to redress the error, if error there was in Lord Lucan's understanding of the verbal order conveyed by Captain Nolan.

Nolan's realisation of the facts

The notion that Nolan at the last second understood the error is fanciful[1] – the brigades had formed up in the wrong valley from which best to attack the redoubts. Why charge across open ground where you could be under fire from the guns at the end of the valley, from the Fedioukine Heights, and the redoubts, their intended objective? Any commander-in-the-field would have known that to attack the lost redoubts it would be better to begin the advance from the South Valley and along the line of the Woronzoff road, retaking the redoubts one by one.

Raglan's written order – an aide-memoire

Too much emphasis has been placed on the exact wording of Raglan's order, which clearly could not be taken word for word. It was intended only as an aide-memoire, to support the word of the ADC to whom the commander's intentions had been divuldged. Earlier in the day Lucan had retained Raglan's ADCs in order to ensure that he carried out loosely-written commands exactly as Lord Raglan had intended his words to be interpreted. If Nolan had intended the advance to have been made on the correct locations, the redoubts, then he would have acted accordingly: he did not and so he allowed the attack to be made where he felt glory lay.

Misconception

The idea of a 'misconception' was one that was fostered by Lord Raglan in his official despatch and bitterly denied by Lord Lucan to the point of the near destruction of the latter's military career.

To understand why Lord Lucan was adamant that Captain Nolan intended that the Charge should go where it went, into the North Valley, one has to understand Lord Lucan's relative position to the battlefield when the order was verbally relayed. Lord Lucan was located between his two brigades, the Light Brigade being in the North Valley and the Heavy Brigade in the opening to the South Valley. This meant that there were two clear directions to go: into the heavily defended North Valley to attack No. 3 Don Cossack battery, or into the relatively lightly defended South Valley (and along the line of the Woronzoff road) to retake the redoubts. Following Nolan's instruction they went into the North Valley. From Lucan's position it was either left or right – and Nolan evidently indicated towards the North Valley. Therefore, from the two brigades' starting points Lord Lucan would not have led the Heavy Brigade to join the Light Brigade in the North Valley, and ordered them to ride into a field of intense fire, if his orders were to attack the redoubts which were accessible via the South Valley and the line of the Woronzoff road. If Lord Lucan had failed to grasp the intentions of Raglan's command as relayed by Nolan, then Nolan would have almost instantly understood this as the two brigades repositioned themselves in preparation for the attack.

The Lord Lucan v. Lord Cardigan Feud

The fact that there was long-standing feud between Lord Lucan and Lord Cardigan was well known, and this has been used to neatly explain why a 'misconception' was allowed to lead to disaster. But to suggest that this precluded the two senior officers conducting a reasoned discussion surrounding the order, as given verbally by Captain Nolan, and that this was materially to blame for the 'blunder' (if one ignores my first point), is all too convenient an answer to explain who was at fault, making both men scapegoats. It also lets Brigadier General Scarlett completely off the hook, as he too would have received the same order from Lord Lucan – no-one has questioned the relationship between these two commanders, nor blamed Scarlett for the events that followed.

Certainly the Lord Lucan v. Lord Cardigan feud often coloured their judgement, but in regard to the verbal command, Cardigan obeyed his superior's orders after respectfully and clearly expressing his observations on the enemy's disposition. Lord Lucan acknowledged this information, adding that they had no choice but to carry out Lord Raglan's wishes. There was no bickering between the men nor barbed words.

The notion that the Lucan v. Cardigan feud was the cause of the Charge also conveniently ignores the reality, which was that the discussion over the verbal order would have largely been conducted via their respective ADCs, and there were no issues between these men. There is evidence that following Lords Lucan and Cardigan's face to face dialogue, Lord Cardigan had despatched his ADC to reiterate the details regarding the enemy's disposition to Lord Lucan and subsequently his understanding of this information was acknowledged by the latter (Lord Lucan had also sent his own ADC some 300 yards down the valley to make a reconnoitre and he observed the enemy's disposition and reported this back, confirming Lord Cardigan's assessment).

Captains Nolan and Morris

Nolan had teased his friend Captain Morris (commanding the 17th Lancers) on his initial approach to the Cavalry Division's position with the order, and later gained his permission to Charge with the lancers – probably riding by Morris' side, although there were officially laid-down positions for non-regimental members to ride in formation (there may not have been time for this repositioning before the order to advance was given). One source even places Nolan in advance of the 17th Lancers at the commencement of the Charge - what better place to be if he intended riding forward to 'lead.' Morris, who survived the Charge, and might have been expected to defend his friend's actions, never once indicated that Nolan had informed him of any other objective than the No.3 Don Cossack battery.

No officer or ADC subsequently questioned the identity of their objective

Furthermore, no senior officer, ADC, nor any of the other officers or civilians (interpreters etc) who had first-hand access to Lords Lucan and Cardigan during the meeting which immediately preceded the Charge, ever expressed doubt that No. 3 Don Cossack battery at the end of the North Valley was their intended target, as the order was conveyed by Nolan. Clearly, then, there was no misconception as regards the verbal order given by Captain Nolan to Lord Lucan. When delivering an order, Nolan, acting as Lord Raglan's ADC, carried the same authority as Raglan himself – that was the nature of the role – and therefore Lord Lucan and Lord Cardigan had no option but to obey.

While Captain Nolan had been away from Lord Raglan's side from time to time during the run-up to the final order, he would have been made fully aware of the developments in the enemy's movements and would have known their disposition immediately before being handed the Fourth Order to the Cavalry – this was a crucial part of his duty as an ADC. Furthermore, several witnesses state that he was briefed before being sent to deliver the order.

Lord Lucan, meanwhile, may not have been fully conversant with the enemy's recent movements. He would, however, have been aware of the guns in the lost redoubts and the growing Russian presence in the North Valley. He would also have known, or been made aware of the enemy artillery's disposition and was therefore disbelieving that the order was to Charge into the North Valley. He questioned the order in disbelief, not in ignorance of the facts when he asked Nolan, 'What guns, where are the enemy?' If Lucan's words are taken literally, then it would demonstrate gross negligence – that he did not understand the developing battle around him, which had been going on for some hours. Even if this extreme view is taken, then it must be accepted that Lucan would have been fully aware of the enemy's disposition once he had addressed Cardigan and heard the report brought back by his own ADC who made a recconoitre immediately prior to the Charge. Following this relaying of the order, Cardigan, through his ADC, gave Lord Lucan the opportunity to revisit the order. Lucan then had the opportunity to send an ADC to Nolan for further confirmation of the order. But of course, if Nolan intended the Cavalry Brigade to charge into the North Valley, the outcome would have been the same.

CONCLUSION

British disposition – Lucan's use of resources

In carrying out Lord Raglan's order, as conveyed to him, Lord Lucan showed himself unable to command the cavalry. He was, in Nolan's eyes, tactically unaware. He did not call for artillery support during the advance, nor did he coordinate the attack on No. 3 Don Cossack battery with the Chasseurs d'Afrique to his left, who acted independently in silencing the guns on the Fedioukine Heights. He was slow in moving the Heavy Brigade off in their advance, having already let the Light Brigade gain too much ground on them, and then prematurely called the Heavies to a halt. He might have been better advised to coordinate with Cathcart's 4th Division and the RHA and at least put Nos. 2, 3 and 4 Redoubts under pressure thereby not only engaging the enemy troops on the Causeway Heights but also occupying the Russian field batteries, which would therefore not have been able to limber up and reposition themselves to bring their fire to bear on the Light Brigade. Similarly, the Russian cavalry at the foot of the Heights might consequently have had to be redeployed to support the redoubts and would therefore not have been able to try to cut off the survivors of the Charge.

It later transpired that Lord Cathcart had no intention of retaking the lost redoubts, the retention of which he considered a liability. Nevertheless, he still could have deployed his men in support of the cavalry's advance, thereby saving many casualties. The British infantry's Minié rifles had a longer range than the Russian's muskets, so they would have been able to fire on the Russians at their extreme range in an aborted attack or feint. They would, however, still have been within range of Russian Artillery.

Nolan's understanding of the use of artillery against a rapidly moving targets

Nolan was aware that the gunners would have experienced great difficulty in traversing their guns to track the rapidly moving target. Equally, setting the fuses would have been challenging. Although they inflicted the majority of the wounds and fatalities, the enemy's artillery did not destroy the Light Brigade. Maybe Nolan understood that if he pushed the pace, the cavalry would reach the Russian guns in sufficient numbers to capture and hold them long enough to be reinforced by the Heavy Brigade. Analysis of the eyewitness accounts confirms that around 500 of the 673 men who charged actually reached and captured the guns, with elements of these troops pushing the Russians back towards the far end of the valley, before being forced to abandon their objective due to lack of support.

The Russians had a total of eighteen guns on the Fedioukine and Causeway Heights, with a further eight guns of No. 3 Don Cossack battery at the end of the North Valley. It has been estimated that these combined batteries fired

190-200 rounds (round-shot and shell) at cavalry on the move – not their ideal target, as their gunners preferred slow moving infantry or, even better, static positions.

Meanwhile, No. 3 Don Cossack battery's vision was obscured by the smoke from their guns. All of the gunners struggled with constantly having to change the fuse settings, consequently many of their rounds exploded harmlessly.

Indirect route saves lives
Casualties to the British Cavalry were further reduced by elements of the 17th Lancers, 11th Hussars, and 8th Hussars veering away from the centre of the valley and the shot and shell of the guns of No. 3 Don Cossack battery, while also largely subjecting themselves to fire from only one flank by drifting away from the guns and small-arms fire from the opposite side of the valley.

Final volley
The final volley of canister fired by No. 3 Don Cossack battery should have utterly destroyed the front line, yet at least 150 men from these regiments survived to penetrate the gun-line; to be joined by over 300 men from the Second Line.

In the bitter fighting that followed, the enemy cavalry and gunners, with sword, lance and ramrod, took their toll on the British cavalry, particularly those who were wounded or had lost their mounts and were fighting or retreating on foot. Others were killed without mercy while pinned helplessly under their dead horses.

The Heavy Brigade in support
It was clear to many of the survivors of the Light Brigade that had they received the support of the Heavy Brigade and the other units that were on the battlefield, then there was every chance that the Russian cavalry would have been routed and massacred or forced to surrender for lack of an escape route over the Chernaya river. Despite the terrible odds, Nolan's death or glory charge was therefore not completely crazy, if executed with tactical awareness.

Statistics
Remarkably, over 250 of the men fought their way beyond the guns and on retiring forced their way through two lines of enemy cavalry drawn up across the valley, and made it back to the British lines without being significantly wounded. Around 200 Chargers (198) who returned were mounted and able to remain on duty. The total killed on the British side was 110, including those who died as prisoners of war, which means that 563 men survived the Charge, of whom only 130-150 were officially listed as wounded.

CONCLUSION

Mad idea nearly succeeds

In summary, Nolan's idea of attacking No. 3 Don Cossack battery head-on, mad as it seemed then and now, could have worked had Lord Lucan correctly deployed his own artillery to soften up the enemy while his men were on the move, had he requested the French Cavalry to provide support (which they did without orders) and had he sent an ADC to urge Cathcart to deploy his troops, who were by then close at hand, to attack the redoubts, even in a feint. The 'Thin Red Line' and Heavy Brigade victories were largely won through the support of artillery at crucial moments – Lord Lucan failed to grasp the significance of this and the need to properly support his own advance – cavalry and artillery always worked together during military manoeuvres, something Lord Lucan ignored in the heat of battle.

Lucan's failures to deploy for victory

Had Lucan continued to advance with the Heavy Brigade, rather than ordering a halt after taking only minimal casualties, the Russians could have been broken. Enough men of the Light Brigade reached and captured the Russian guns while others pushed the enemy back. Because these men were unsupported by the Heavies, the Russians were able to enter the valley on either side behind them and cut them off. The Light Brigade was not lost solely through a captain's lust for glory, but the ineptitude of one man – Lord Lucan – who failed to act on his ADC's reconnoitre of the battlefield (as did Scarlett), and to learn the importance of the use of close artillery support despite it winning two victories earlier that morning.

Troops act on their own initiative to support

The Russians had laid a trap at the Bulganak river which Lucan nearly fell into, and he now let his Light Brigade fall into one just as big by failing to understand the disposition of the enemy forces involved and failing to counter with the infantry, cavalry and artillery at his disposal.

Was there any victory in the Charge of the Light Brigade?

Despite being abandoned to their fate by Lord Lucan, did the Light Brigade win any sort of victory? It might be argued that if the Cavalry Brigade was deployed to prevent the Russians from using their gains as a springboard to take Balaclava, then it succeeded in this. If it were solely to prevent the loss of the Royal Naval guns from in the redoubts, then it failed, as the Russians retained control of the redoubts and paraded the captured guns in Sevastopol. More importantly they deprived the British of the use of the Woronzoff road, the only metalled road leading to Sevastopol. The loss of the road greatly hampered the supply of the British contingent before the city, increasing its suffering during the winter of 1854-5.

The British Cavalry's reputation

So much was the Light Brigade's reputation enhanced by its gallantry at Balaclava, that for a long time following the Charge the Russian cavalry would not engage even small numbers of British troopers. So, despite their greatly depleted numbers (the brigade could only muster 200 horses in December 1854) the British Cavalry remained a significant force, even if the reality was very different.

Appendix I

Medals

The Queen's Crimea Medal

The award of the Queen's Crimea medal, with clasps for the actions at Alma and Inkerman, was announced in *The London Gazette* of 5 January 1855 (with an extension of the medal to the next-of-kin made on the 23rd).

Not unnaturally there was consternation among the survivors of the Charge of the Light Brigade, that there was to be no clasp for this action. This found voice in England via the press. *The Examiner* of 20 January 1855 carried the following:

'The Heroes of Balaclava Unrewarded

'The complaints are general amongst the Light Cavalry, that while medals [*sic*] have been ordered for Alma and Inkerman, the "immortal" charge of Balaclava is altogether overlooked. An officer of the Light Dragoons who survived the Charge, expressed himself as follows:

'We are sending our claims for the Crimean Medal. Mine appears with the Alma [20 September 1854] and Inkerman [5 November 1854] [clasps]. I wish I could add [a] Balaclava [clasp]. We all consider it a great grievance that we are to get nothing for our Charge on the 25th of October. I confess I think it is "too bad." Our Allies are astonished. They said to an officer of the 8th a day or two ago "If we had made such a charge as that, every officer and man who came out would have been decorated." Lord Raglan said "the charge was made under a misconception". What have the officers and men to do with that? They were ordered to charge the Russian guns, and most gallantly did they obey the order." Another Cavalry officer says: "It was a most important action, for, if the enemy had succeeded in their attack, our army would have been hashed altogether, its base being cut off. Surely those who participated in the unparalleled gallantry which, unhappily, resulted from those blunders, should [not] be debarred from what all join in decreeing as justly their due.'

159

The dismay at the lack of a clasp for the Light Brigade led to a rethink at the War Office and the following appeared in *The London Gazette* of 24 April 1855:

'Horse Guards, 23rd February, 1856.

'THE Queen having signified her intention to confer a Medal for Service in the Crimea upon the Officers and Men, with Clasps for the Battles of the Alma and of Inkerman, and being further pleased to command that a Clasp shall also be conferred upon those who were engaged in the Action at Balaclava.'

A clasp was later added for the Siege of Sevastopol.

The Queen's Crimea medal was presented to many men in the theatre of the war, while others only received the medal on their return to Britain or during their next deployment.

The following Chargers received their medals from the hands of Her Majesty Queen Victoria at Horse Guards on 18 May 1855:

Staff
Major General the Earl of Lucan
Major General the Earl of Cardigan

4th Light Dragoons
Captain Thomas Hutton
Regimental Sergeant Major John Reilly
Corporal David J. Gillam

8th Hussars
Lieutenant Daniel Hugh Clutterbuck

11th Hussars
Lieutenant Harington Astley Trevelyn
Sergeant John Breeze
Corporal John Ashley Kilvert
Private Silvester Milburne
Private William Walker

13th Light Dragoons
Private John Keen

17th Lancers
Cornet George Orby Wombwell
Private William Dimmock
Private Thomas Magee
Private John Yates

The Queen's personal acknowledgement of the heroes of the Battle of Balaclava

'The following message from the Queen, conveying her Majesty's thanks to the army for their gallantry at the Battle of Balaclava, was communicated to the troops by Lord Raglan in general orders on the 5th ult:

'War Department, November 14, 1854

'My Lord, - I have the honour to acknowledge your Lordship's despatch, dated "before Sevastopol, October 28th." In which you give an account of a battle fought on the 25th of that month in front of Balaclava.

'I have laid that despatch before the Queen, and I have received Her Majesty's command to express to your Lordship her admiration of the gallantry and conduct of the troops engaged upon that occasion. Her Majesty has learnt with deep concern that the repulse of the enemy was not effected without a heavy loss of the division of cavalry, more especially of the Light Brigade: but the brilliancy of the Charge, and the gallantry and discipline evinced by all, have never been surpassed even by British soldiers under similar circumstances.

'To every officer, non-commissioned officer, and private engaged in this severe encounter with vastly superior numbers, the Queen desires me to communicate, through your Lordship, her approval and thanks. Her Majesty has not failed to remark the distinguished service performed on this occasion by Major General Sir Colin Campbell. Her Majesty has especially noticed the brilliant conduct of the division of cavalry under the command of Lieutenant-General the Earl of Lucan, and is deeply sensible of the gallant service of the Earl of Cardigan and the Honourable Brigadier General Scarlett, who commanded the two brigades of cavalry, and so nobly sustained the honour of that distinguished and important arm of Her Majesty's service.

'The conduct of the 93rd regiment, under the command of Colonel Ainslie, merits the greatest admiration, and materially tended to the repulse of the enemy from the position which was so vigorously assailed.'

'Newcastle.'

British Gallantry Awards

Six Hundred and Seventy-Three – Heroes All

The Officer Class
There was already provision for rewarding the officer class. Acts of bravery or valuable service were acknowledged by an appointment to one of the junior grades of the Order of the Bath or a brevet promotion (promotion in the field); a mention in despatches was the accepted recognition for lesser acts. This system generally recognised staff officers and the senior officers of the units engaged.

The awards for the Charge of the Light Brigade made under these provisions are listed below:

Staff
Major General James Thomas Brudenell, Lord Cardigan was mentioned in despatches (*LG* 30.11.54) and appointed a Knight Commander of the Bath (*LG* 10.07.55)
Colonel Lord George Augustus Frederick Paget was mentioned in despatches (*LG* 30.11.54) and appointed a Commander of the Bath (*LG* 10.07.55)
Lieutenant Colonel George Wynell Mayow was mentioned in despatches (*LG* 30.11.54) and nominated a Commander of the Bath

4th Light Dragoons
Captain John George Brown was appointed Brevet-Major (*LG* 12.12.54)
Captain Alexander Low was appointed Brevet Lieutenant Colonel (*LG* 01.12.54)
Captain Thomas Hutton was appointed Brevet-Major (*LG* 06.06.56)

8th Hussars
Lieutenant Colonel Frederick George Shewell was mentioned in despatches (*LG* 30.11.54) and appointed a Commander of the Bath (*LG* 10.07.55)
Captain Edward Tomkinson was appointed Brevet-Major (*LG* 12.12.54)

11th Hussars
Captain Edwin Adolphus Cook was appointed Brevet-Major (*LG* 12.12.54)
Lieutenant Colonel John Douglas was mentioned in despatches (*LG* 30.11.54) and appointed a Commander of the Bath (*LG* 10.07.55)

13th Light Dragoons
Captain Soame Gambier Jenyns was mentioned in despatches (*LG* 30.11.54), appointed Brevet-Major (*LG* 12.12.54) and appointed a Commander of the Bath (*LG* 10.07.55)

Captain Arthur Tremayne was appointed Brevet-Major (*LG* 21.08.55)

17th Lancers

Captain William Morris was mentioned in despatches (*LG* 30.11.54), appointed Brevet-Major for 'distinguished conduct' (*LG* 12.12.54) and appointed a Commander of the Bath (*LG* 10.07.55). Morris later unsuccessfully petitioned for the award of the Victoria Cross, having already been recognized for gallantry under this pre-existing system of military rewards.

NCOs and Other Ranks

The Crimea War was the first major conflict closely followed by the masses through reports filed by war correspondents in the field. Foremost among these were the perceptive and often critical despatches of William Howard Russell. He described the hardships faced by the troops and the many acts of valour performed by ordinary British servicemen. It was Russell's account of the Battle of Balaclava, published in *The Times* of 14 November 1854, which inspired Lord Tennyson's poem *The Charge of the Light Brigade*. The war correspondent's accounts were disseminated throughout the country via the provincial newspapers, which also published the official despatches as well as featuring vivid first-hand accounts of the Charge recorded in letters home. There remained no recognised gallantry award for the 'other ranks', although sergeants could earn the Meritorious Service Medal for either general good conduct or for a single act of bravery. The award of the Meritorious Service Medal brought with it an annuity 'not exceeding £20'.

The French, our allies in the Crimea, already had the Legion d'Honneur (first instituted by Napoleon in 1803), to which officers, NCOs and other ranks could be nominated (or promoted to a higher class of the order). For lesser acts by junior officers NCOs and other ranks, men could be nominated a Médaille Militaire. The French showed the way for their heroes of the Battle of Balaclava, and would later honour the British contingent too. The first nominations and promotions for the 4th Chasseurs d'Afrique were submitted on 28 December 1854 with four officers, NCOs and men nominated to the Légion d'Honneur and fifteen NCOs and other ranks being nominated to the Médaille Militaire. The 1st Chasseurs d'Afrique were similarly rewarded with four officers, NCOs and men nominated to the Légion d'Honneur and eleven NCOs and other ranks nominated to the Médaille Militaire.

The Distinguished Conduct Medal

There was a growing feeling among the public and in the Royal Court that more should be done to officially acknowledge the heroism of the soldiers who were fighting and, all too often, dying in the Crimea.

To this end the Distinguished Conduct Medal was instituted by Royal Warrant on 4 December 1854, and was for the non-commissioned men. The DCM came with a modest gratuity and/or pension.

It was ordered that:

'One Sergeant in each Regiment of Cavalry... shall be selected by the Commanding Officer and recommended to Us for the grant of an annuity not exceeding £20.'

Furthermore, it was stipulated that 'One Sergeant, two Corporals and four Privates, to receive a Medal and Gratuity, this to be in the instance of a Sergeant, £15, for a Corporal £10 and for Private £5.'

Official notification of the creation of the new award appeared a few days later in *The London Gazette* of 12 December 1854.

The Warrant continued:

'I am further directed to observe that in selecting individuals for the gratuities to be awarded for Distinguished Service or Gallant Conduct in the Field, you are not to be fettered in your selection by any consideration as to the length of service, the general good conduct of the individual being alone the qualifications to entitle him to the award.'

The following members of the Light Brigade are known to have been awarded the Distinguished Conduct Medal:

4th Light Dragoons
Sergeant Frederick Short
Corporal James Salamander Devlin
Corporal David John Gillam
Private (Saddler) Robert Ferguson
Private William Butler
Private Robert Grant
Private David Thomas

8th Hussars
Regimental Sergeant-Major Samuel Williams
Troop Sergeant-Major Michael Clarke
Corporal James Neal
Private Patrick Dunn
Private William Stephen John Fulton
Private Robert Moneypenny

Private Thomas Twamley
Private James Whitechurch

[NB. Private Patrick Dunn served on Lord Raglan's Staff; Private James Whitechurch is not considered a Charger]

11th Hussars
Sergeant-Major George Loy Smith
Hospital Sergeant George Archer
Sergeant John Breeze
Sergeant John Lawson
Private James Glanister
Private Robert Martin
Private Luke Oakley
Private Richard Albert Young

[NB. Private Luke Oakley was one of two orderlies to Dr John Burton St Croix Crosse, surgeon attached to the 11th Hussars at Balaclava, both of whom received the Distinguished Conduct Medal (DCM). Oakley was only appointed to the role on 20.10.54. The other was Hospital Sergeant George Archer.]

13th Light Dragoons
Sergeant John Mulcahy
Corporal John Allen
Corporal Matthew Long
Private John Keeley
Private John Keen
Private Joseph Moore
Private Joseph Priestly
Private Richard Rowley

[NB. Private Joseph Priestly had his leg shot off at Bulganak on 19 September 1854 and took no further part in the campaign. He received the Queen's Crimea medal without clasps.]

17th Lancers
Troop Sergeant-Major William George Cattermole
Sergeant Henry Joy
Corporal John Penn
Corporal George Taylor
Private John Bowen

Private Thomas Mason
Private George Smith
Private John Vahey

[NB. As Orderly Trumpeter to Lord Raglan, Sergeant Henry Joy sounded the
Charge of the Heavy Brigade (although contemporary accounts indicate that
his trumpet calls were ignored and those of the Heavy Brigade's trumpeters
were obeyed.)]

The Victoria Cross

On 3 March 1855, Queen Victoria visited several Light Brigade survivors at
Brompton Barracks. It is said that the Queen had used this occasion to announce
to those gathered her intention to institute the Victoria Cross.

There had been a growing awareness of the need for a higher decoration
which would be open to all, regardless of rank or previous service. In December
1854 Liberal MP Captain Thomas Scobell, RN (Retd) put a motion before the
House of Commons 'that an humble address be presented to Her Majesty to
institute an Order of Merit to be bestowed upon persons serving in the Army
or Navy for distinguished and prominent personal gallantry during the present
war and to which every grade and individual from the highest to the lowest may
be admissible.'

In January 1855 the Secretary of State for War, the Duke of Newcastle,
wrote a letter to Prince Albert:

'It does not seem to me right or politic that such deeds of heroism as the war
has produced should go unrewarded by any distinctive mark of honour because
they are done by privates or officers below the rank of major.'

Queen Victoria issued a Warrant under the Royal sign-manual on 29 January
1856 that officially instituted the Victoria Cross, a new award for individual
gallantry by officers, NCOs and other ranks of the British armed forces. It was
ordered that the award 'shall be styled and designated the "Victoria Cross",
and shall consist of a Maltese Cross [*sic*] of bronze with our Royal Crest in the
centre'. Qualification for the award was backdated to 1854 to include acts of
valour during the Crimean War.

Later that day the Duke was able to make the following announcement in a
speech in the House of Lords:

'Her Majesty had consented that a cross of military merit should be instituted,
which should be applicable to all ranks of the Army [and Navy] in future.

166

It was not intended in any way to affect the present order of the Bath, but that a separate cross of military merit should be granted for all ranks, attainable by every man from the highest general to the humblest private.'

Interestingly, the initial suggestion was that the award would be made following a selection process based on those engaged, rather than by the recommendation of an officer, which quickly became the established process: 'The cross would be awarded on the opinion of a jury of soldiers in the ranks as to the person on whom it should be bestowed.'

At about the same time, an official memorandum on the subject was circulated within the War Office setting out the details of a cross to be awarded for 'a signal act of valour'.

From the outset the standard for the award was exceptionally high. The Royal Warrant stipulated 'that the cross shall only be awarded for conspicuous bravery, or some daring or pre-eminent act of valour or self-sacrifice or extreme devotion to duty in the presence of the enemy.'

The War Office disseminated instructions for the appropriate regiments, units and vessels requiring the submission of the names of those recommended for an award. Without precise instructions on the allocation of awards, some commanding officers put forward dozens of names to the selection boards; others ignored the instruction. This lead to a situation where the 77th Regiment submitted no less than thirty-eight names, while six regiments, including the 8th Hussars, offered none at all.

The names of the first recipients were promulgated in *The London Gazette* of 24 February 1857 and included three Light Brigade Chargers: Private Samuel Parkes, 4th Light Dragoons; Lieutenant Alexander Dunn, 11th Hussars; Troop Sergeant Major John Berryman, 17th Lancers.

The first award ceremony was held in Hyde Park on 26 June 1857, during which Queen Victoria presented 62 of the 111 Crimean awards before a cheering crowd estimated at 100,000 people.

The final list of recipients was not published in *The London Gazette* until 22 June, four days ahead of the presentation ceremony, and Hancocks, the sole manufacturers of the Cross, had to work around the clock to engrave the names of the recipients on the Crosses.

Colonel Shewell died at Gosden, near Guildford, Surrey, on 1 October 1856 while on sick leave. It is thought that his premature death was the reason why no member of the 8th Hussars received a Victoria Cross for Balaclava – one man from each of the units involved was originally to have been selected.

No men of the 8th Hussars received the Victoria Cross for the action at Balaclava but one Charger went on to gain the award for the cavalry charge at

Gwalior on 17 June 1858, Lieutenant Clement Walker Heneage. At Gwalior a squadron of the 8th Hussars under Captain Heneage found themselves embroiled with a much larger enemy force trying to escape from Gwalior who they charged and put into confusion, winning the battle in 'one of the finest exploits of the war'. The awards to Captain Heneage, Sergeant Ward, Farrier Hollis and Private Pearson were announced together under the same citation.

They were promulgated in *The London Gazette* of 28 January 1859 under a heading dated two days earlier:

'Selected for the Victoria Cross by their companions in the gallant charge made by a squadron of the Regiment at Gwalior, on the 17th June, 1858, when supported by a division of the Bombay Horse Artillery, and Her Majesty's 95th Regiment, they routed the enemy, who were advancing against, capturing and bringing into their camp two of the enemy's guns, under a heavy and converging fire from the fort and town.'

The Balaclava VCs

Private John Berryman, Sergeant John Farrell and Corporal Joseph Malone, all involved in the rescue of Captain August Frederick Cavendish Webb of the 17th Lancers, were awarded the Victoria Cross. A fourth, Private James Lamb of the 13th Light Dragoons, was unsuccessful in drawing lots with Malone.

Private John Berryman, 17th Lancers
The hind leg of Berryman's horse was broken during the Charge to the guns:

'I debated in my own mind whether to shoot her or not, when Captain Webb [Captain August Frederick Cavendish Webb] came up to me and asked me, was I wounded? I replied, "Only slightly, I thought in the leg, but that my horse was shot." I then asked, "Are you hurt, sir?" He said that he was, and in the leg, too; what had we better do. "Keep to your horse, sir, and get back as far as you can." He turned and rode back.

'I now caught a loose horse and got on to his back, but he fell directly, the brass of the breastplate having been driven into his chest.

'Finding that Captain Webb had halted, I ran to him … his wound was so painful the he could not ride any further. Lieutenant George Smith, of my own regiment, coming by, I got him to stand at the horse's head whilst I lifted the captain off.'

Lieutenant Smith rode off on Webb's horse to find him a stretcher.

'By this time the Russians had got back to their guns, and re-opened fire. I saw six men of my own regiment get together. Seeing their danger, I called to them to separate, but too late, for a shell dropped amongst them, and I don't think one of them escaped alive. Captain Webb asked what I thought the Russians would do?

"They are sure to pursue, sir, unless the Heavy Brigade comes down."

"Then you had better consult to your own safety and leave me."

"Oh, no, sir, I shall not leave you now."

"Perhaps they will only take me prisoner."

"If they do, we will go together."

"Don't mind me, look to yourself."

"All right, sir; only we will go together, whatever happens."

'Just at this time I saw Sergeant Farrell [Sergeant John Farrell] coming by. I called to him. He asked, "Who is it?" When I told him, he came over.

I said, "We must get Captain Webb out of this for we shall be pursued."

'We made a chair out of our hands and lifted the Captain up, and found that we could carry him with comparative ease. [As they made their way back bullets and shot flew all about, a round shot taking off Farrell's chapska, but without harming him.]

'We had got about 200 yards in this manner, when the Captain complained that his leg was very painful. [Webb could see the men were struggling and ordered them to save themselves, but they refused to abandon him.] A private of the 13th (Malone) being near, I asked him would he be good enough to support Captain Webb's legs, until we could procure a stretcher?

At this point the party was approached by several officers on horseback.

'Sir G. Wombwell [Cornet George Orby Wombwell] said, "What is the matter, Peck?" (Captain Webb's nickname).

"Hit in the leg, old fellow. How did you escape?"

"Well, I was unhorsed and taken prisoner, but when the Second Line came down, in the confusion, I got away, and, seizing the first horse I could, I got away, and I find that it is Morris's"

'Sir W. Gordon [Lieutenant Sir William Gordon] made the same inquiry, and got the same answer.

'He [Webb] had a very nasty cut on the head, and blood was then running down his face. We had now reached the rear of the Greys, and I procured a stretcher from two Infantry band boys, and a young officer of the Greys gave me a tourniquet, saying that he did not know how to apply it, but perhaps I might.

'I and Farrell now raised the stretcher and carried it about fifty yards and again set it down. We resumed our patient, and got to the doctors (Massy and

Kendal). I saw the boot cut off and the nature of the wound, the right shinbone being shattered.'[1]

Captain Webb's leg was amputated on 5 November and he died in Scutari Hospital two days later. Writing to his wife Amelia, Captain Morris referred to Webb's operation: 'You will be grieved to hear that poor Webb had his leg amputated today, he was only partially under the influence of chloroform.'

The citation for Berryman's award was promulgated in *The London Gazette* of 24 February 1857:

'17th Lancer: Troop Sergeant-Major [rank at the time of presentation] John Berryman

'Served with his Regiment the whole of the war, was present at the Battle of the Alma, and was also engaged in the pursuit at Mackenzies's Farm, where he succeeded in capturing three Russian prisoners, when they were within reach of their own guns.'

'Was present and charged at the Battle of Balaclava, where, his horse being shot under him, he stopped on the field with a wounded officer (Captain Webb) amidst a shower of shot and shell, although repeatedly told by that Officer to consult his own safety, and leave him, but he refused to do so, and on Sergeant John Farrell coming by, with his assistance, he carried Captain Webb out of the range of the guns.'

'He has also the Clasp for Inkerman.'

The Register of the Victoria Cross carries the following reference to Berryman:

'On 25 October 1854 at Balaclava, Crimea (Charge of the Light Brigade) Troop Sergeant-Major [*sic*] Berryman, whose horse had been shot under him, stopped on the field with a wounded officer amidst a storm of shot and shell. Two Sergeants [*sic*] came to his assistance and between them they carried the wounded officer out of range of the guns.'

Berryman's VC was presented to him by Queen Victorian at a ceremony held at Hyde Park on 26 June 1857, he being the only one of his regiment present.

Sergeant John Farrell, 17th Lancers

Sergeant Farrell's horse was shot from under him, but he remained relatively unscathed. While retiring up the valley he came across the mortally wounded

Captain Webb of his own regiment. Despite a continual hail of shells, Minié rounds and musket balls, he remained on the battlefield and assisted Private John Berryman and Sergeant [*sic*] Joseph Malone in moving Webb until the pain of his wounds became too great, after which he remained with the officer until a stretcher could be found. Farrell is said to have carried the wounded officer a good 200 yards towards the British lines while under fire, having his chapska shot off by a cannon ball during the rescue.

The following recommendation was made for the Victoria Cross in respect of Sergeant John Farrell:

'On 25th October, 1854 at Balaclava, Crimea, Sergeant Farrell, whose horse had been killed under him, stopped on the field and amidst a storm of shot and shell helped a Troop Sergeant-Major [*sic*] (John Berryman) and another Sergeant [*sic*] (Corporal Joseph Malone) to move a severely wounded officer (Capt Webb of the 17th Lancers), who subsequently died, out of range of the guns.'

The citation for the award was promulgated in *The London Gazette* of 20 November 1857:

'795 Quartermaster-Sergeant [*sic*] John Farrell
Date of Act of Bravery, 25th
October, 1854.

'For having remained, amidst a shower of shot and shell, with Captain Webb, who was severely wounded, and whom he and Sergeant [*sic*] Berryman had carried as far as the pain of his wounds would allow, until a stretcher was procured, when he assisted Berryman and a private [*sic*] of the 13th Light Dragoons (Malone), to carry that officer off the field. This took place on the 25th October, 1854, after the charge at the battle of Balaclava, in which Farrell's horse was killed under him.'

Corporal Joseph Malone, 13th Light Dragoons

Malone's horse was shot during the Charge and he was trapped until Private James Nunnerley, 17th Lancers, dragged its body off him.

While making his way back towards the British lines he joined Private John Berryman and Sergeant John Farrell in assisting Captain Augustus Frederick Cavendish Webb of the 17th Lancers. During the rescue Private James Lamb of the 13th Light Dragoons also came to their assistance by helping to find water for the captain.

For his actions, Malone was awarded the Victoria Cross, promulgated in *The London Gazette* on 24 February 1857. Malone's citation was announced in the same publication on 25 September 1857:

'Balaclava, Crimea, 25 October 1854, Sergeant [*sic*] Joseph Malone, 13th Light Dragoons.

'For having stopped under a very heavy fire to take charge of Captain Webb, 17th Lancers, until others arrived to assist him in recovering that Officer, who was (as it afterwards proved) mortally wounded. Sergeant [*sic*] Malone performed this act of bravery while returning on foot from the charge at the battle of Balaclava, in which his horse had been shot.'

Malone was presented with the Victoria Cross at a ceremony held in the Quadrangle of Windsor Castle on 28 November 1857.

Private James Lamb, 13th Light Dragoons

Although not a winner of the Victoria Cross, Lamb played a part in the rescue of Captain Webb.

'I myself was struck down and rendered insensible. When I recovered consciousness, the smoke was so thick that I was not able to see where I was. When at last I made out my position, I found that I was among numbers of dead and wounded comrades. The scene I shall never forget. Scores of troopers and their horses were lying dead and dying all around me, many men severely wounded and unable to extricate themselves from their dead horses. Luckily for me, my horse was shot through the head, and falling forward, pitched me clear. My own wound was not a very severe one and I soon recovered sufficiently to endeavour to return to the British lines.

'Just as I made a start, I looked around and spied two companies of the Russian Rifles doubling out from the right rear of the position where their guns were stationed, and, as they dropped on one knee to fire a volley up the valley, I laid down close to my dead horse, having its body between me and the firers. I was not a moment too soon, as I had scarcely sheltered myself before the bullets came whizzing around me, and literally riddled the dead body of my horse and its saddle. After the volley, I ventured to look over my dead horse, thinking to see the enemy reloading to fire again; but, to my surprise, I saw them mustering together quickly, and running to the rear of their guns.

'I managed to get some distance up the valley towards our lines, and when near No. 3 Redoubt, I saw two men supporting a wounded officer [Captain Webb] of the 17th Lancers. One of the men was a trooper belonging to my own regiment [Corporal Joseph Malone], and the other was one of the

17th Lancers [Private John Berryman]. The officer was faint and exhausted from loss of blood, and was feebly asking for water. Neither of the men who were helping him had their water-bottles with them, and mine had been shot through in the cross-fire when the Russians first opened fire upon us. I retraced my steps, and was soon fortunate enough to find a calabash, half full of water, strapped to a dead trooper's saddle. I had to get along as sharply as I could, for the enemy were again on the move; but I succeeded in reaching the wounded officer and gave him the water, which he gratefully acknowledged, and, turning to us, said, "Men, leave me here, and seek your own safety." But we would not leave him, and the two other troopers carried him off the field while I limped along by his side, ready to render any assistance I could.

'As we were moving painfully along I saw a trooper of another regiment [17th Lancers] who had been severely wounded, and another endeavouring to get him off the field. I went to their assistance. My comrade and myself managed to get the wounded trooper safely into our lines [Lamb carrying him on his back for a while].'[2]

Lieutenant Alexander Robert Dunn, 11th Hussars

During the retreat Lieutenant Dunn risked his life to rescue Sergeant William Bentley and Private Robert Levett, both of his own regiment.

The remnants of the 11th Hussars rallied on Lieutenant Colonel John Douglas after passing through the gun-line. Having pushed back the enemy cavalry, their commanding officer ordered his men to re-form on what he believed to be the 17th Lancers.

Sergeant William Bentley recalled: 'I drew his [Lieutenant-Colonel Douglas'] attention to the circumstances of their being Russians, and not our lancers, when we got his order "Fight for your lives," thereupon all retired. On passing them [the Russian lancers] I was attacked by an officer and several men, and received a slight [neck] wound from a lance. I was pursued by them, and cut the officer across the face.'[3]

Bentley's horse was blown and refused to move any further, while Bentley received a further wound when a bullet grazed his calf, probably as a result of the rifle fire emanating from the Fedioukine Heights. Bentley was then knocked from his saddle by one of three Russian Dragoons who closed in from behind ready to finish him off. Lieutenant Dunn saw Bentley's predicament and turned back. He carried a personalised sword, several inches longer than the regulation; this Dunn used to great effect.

An extract from the *Canadian Legion Magazine* takes up the narrative:

'Prancing, side-wheeling, rearing his thoroughbred, he parried, thrusted and slashed at the assailants, felling them all in a matter of minutes. But Bentley was still in dire straits, desperately hanging on to his horse by one of the stirrups, so Dunn dismounted, lifted Bentley back into his own saddle, then belted the horse on the rump to send it galloping towards the British lines.'

One of those who witnessed the gallant defence was Trumpeter W. Perkins, 11th Hussars: 'When engaged with the Lancers I saw Lieutenant Dunn, with one stroke of his sword sever a Russian Lancer's head all but off.'

Dunn, like all officers in the brigade, carried a pistol, which he used to equally good effect. On the 26th the diarist George Palmer Evelyn wrote: 'Visited the 11th and saw Dunne [*sic*], who related his adventure – his horse was hit yesterday – he killed 2 men with his sword and three with pistol.'[4]

Instead of saving himself and heading back up the valley, Lieutenant Dunn then intervened to save the life of Private Robert Levett, who had lost his horse, killing another Russian Hussar and allowing him to escape on foot. Sadly, Levett died of his wounds.

Lieutenant Alexander Roberts Dunn was elected by his regiment to receive the Victoria Cross.

The citation for the award was promulgated in *The London Gazette* of 27 February 1857:

'11th Hussars Lieutenant Alexander Roberts Dunn – For having in the Light Brigade Charge on October 25th, 1854, saved the life of Sergeant Bentley, 11th Hussars, by cutting down two or three Russian Lancers who were attacking him from the rear, and afterwards cutting down a Russian Hussar who was attacking Private Levett, 11th Hussars.'

Alexander Dunn received his Victoria Cross at an investiture held in Hyde Park on 26 June 1857.

Private Samuel Parkes, 4th Light Dragoons

'We reached the guns and cut down the gunners and drivers, and succeeded in silencing the guns. While we were so engaged, we observed that the 11th Hussars were being cut up by the enemy, and a number of the 4th Light Dragoons, together with Lord George Paget and myself, charged down to their support.

'We then observed the Russians to fall back, but at same time we saw a regiment of lancers to our rear. Lord George Paget thought they were the 17th Lancers, but on discovering they were the enemy's troops, he called out to some officer near him, "Where is Lord Cardigan?" and I then heard someone (who I have always believed was Captain Low) say, "Lord Cardigan has gone back some time."

'Lord George Paget then ordered us to get through the Russians the best way we could, and we then retreated through the Russian cavalry, who opened out right and left, let us pass, and showed us no resistance. When we were retreating, and just after I had passed the left redoubt, my horse was shot, and I was attacked by Cossacks.

'I defended myself for a long time, but at length while engaged with a Cossack a shot struck the hilt of my sword and wounded my hand; two Russian officers galloped up to me and took me prisoner.'[5]

As Lord Paget's orderly, Parkes rode in close support to his commanding officer throughout the Charge, so too did Lord Paget's trumpeter, Hugh Crawford. Both men lost their horses in quick succession. Crawford's horse collapsed of exhaustion trapping his sword under its frame. Two Cossacks saw he was defenceless and closed in. Parkes whose mount was killed under him, saw Crawford's predicament and ran to his assistance, placing himself between the defenceless Crawford and the enemy. Parkes helped Crawford to his feet, supporting him with his left arm while using his sword to drive the Cossacks off; at length they retired, looking for an easier kill.

Moving back up the valley, endeavouring to find cover, the two men were joined by Private John Edden, from the same regiment. Soon afterwards Lord Paget's second-in-command, Major John T. Douglas Halkett, was spotted lying mortally wounded by a shell splinter in the chest. Captain Low's party evidently had seen Halkett a little earlier, when he called over to them: 'Take my money for the married women at home.' However, the severity of Halkett's wounds and the very close proximity of the enemy had meant the 4th Light Dragoons were forced to move on and leave their major. Halkett now instructed the men to place his sword in his hand and leave him, but the trio ignored his order.

Edden lifted Major Halkett onto Parkes' back and they moved slowly on as best as they could until they were attacked by seven or more Cossacks. Halkett ordered Parkes to put him down and try to save himself. He gently eased the major down to the ground before taking up his sword once more. Halkett told them to take his money belt, rather than let it fall into the hands of the murderous Cossacks, and to place his sabre in his hand, so he could defend himself.

As Crawford and Parkes inched their way up the valley they were descended on by the marauding Cossacks whose strikes were parried by Parkes. As further Cossacks were drawn into the fray, Parkes continued in his single-handed defence. Tiring every blow, it was inevitable that he would be overcome.

An English-speaking officer shouted to them, 'Give yourself up, and you won't be hurt.' Parkes refused and continued to fight on until a shot struck the hilt of his weapon and wounded him in his right hand. Parkes and Crawford were forced to surrender, but in the confusion Private Edden had been able to make good his escape.

Making their way to the rear as prisoners of war, the unhappy pair passed the looted dead body of Major Halkett.

A number of survivors of the charge at Balaclava gave first-hand accounts as to Parkes' conduct on that day and, as a result the story was gradually pieced together. *The London Gazette* of 24 February 1857, carried the following entry:

'Samuel Parkes, No 635, Private, 4th Light Dragoons, in the Charge of the Light Brigade at Balaclava Trumpet-Major [*sic*] Crawford's horse fell, and dismounted him, and he lost his sword; he was attacked by two Cossacks when Private Samuel Parkes (whose horse had been shot) saved his life by placing himself between them and the Trumpet-Major and drove them away by his sword.

'In attempting to follow the Light Cavalry Brigade in their retreat they were attacked by six Russians, whom Parkes kept at bay, and retired slowly fighting and defending the Trumpet-Major for some time until deprived of his sword by a shot.'

Parkes was presented with the Victoria Cross in Hyde Park on 26 June 1857.

Several late awards were made in association with the Light Brigade's Charge.

The rescue of Captain William Morris, 17th Lancers

Two men were awarded the Victoria Cross for assisting Captain William Morris from the battlefield while under fire; one of these was a surgeon attached to a regiment of the Heavy Brigade, the other was Sergeant Charles Wooden, 17th Lancers, who was not initially recommended for the award, but made a successful petition.

According to the account of Assistant Surgeon William Cattell (attached to the 5th Dragoons):

'Pte. George Smith informed Sergeant O'Hara of the spot where Morris lay and [Brigadier General The Hon. Sir James Yorke] Scarlet sent the staff surgeon with Troop Sergeant Major [*sic*] Wooden to bring him in. They found a trooper trying to arrest the bleeding from the scalp. Presently some Cossacks attacked the party and the doctor, Mouat, said he had to draw his sword, which he described as a "novel experience".'

Surgeon James Mouat, 6th Dragoons

Surgeon Mouat bandaged Morris' head wounds and, together with Sergeant Wooden, 17th Lancers, carried him out wrapped in a cavalry cloak. Private George Mansell, also of the 17th, ready to fend off the Cossaks.

John Blunt saw Morris being carried in by Mouat and Wooden. Morris was semi-conscious and Blunt heard him cry out, 'Lord have mercy on my soul'.

For this action, both Mouat and Wooden received the Victoria Cross. The latter petitioned for his award, having initially being overlooked.

The citation for Mouat's award in *The London Gazette*, 2 June 1858 reads:

'For having voluntarily proceeded to the assistance of Lieutenant Colonel Morris, CB [*sic*], 17th Lancers, who was lying dangerously wounded in an exposed situation after the retreat of the Light Brigade at the Battle of Balaclava, and having dressed that officer's wounds in the presence of, and under a heavy fire from the enemy. Thus, by stopping a serious haemorrhage, he assisted to save that officer's life.'

Mouat was also nominated to the Legion d'Honneur (5th Class), *The London Gazette*, 4 August 1856, and was appointed a Commander of the Bath, *The London Gazette*, 5 February 1856.

Sergeant Charles Wooden, 17th Lancers:

Sergeant Wooden went out with Surgeon Mouat to the assistance of Captain Morris, and together they carried him to a place of relative safety. Initially he was not recommended for the Victoria Cross, but was nominated to the Medaille Militaire.

When he learned that Surgeon Mouat had been awarded the Victoria Cross, Wooden wrote to him saying that if Mouat was to receive the higher award, then so should he as he had been at Mouat's side during the rescue (so, potentially, had Private George Mansell). Luckily for Wooden, Mouat agreed and wrote to Horse Guards supporting Wooden's claim.

The reply from Horse Guards read:

'His Royal Highness [the Duke of Cambridge] feels very unwilling to bring any further claim for the Victoria Cross for an act performed at so distant a period, but as the decoration has been conferred on Dr Mouat for the part he took in the rescue of Lieutenant Colonel [*sic*] Morris, and Sergeant Major [*sic*] Wooden appears to have acted in a manner very honourable to him on the occasion, by his gallantry, been equally instrumental in saving the life of this officer, His Royal Highness is induced to submit the case.'

The citation for Wooden's Victoria Cross was promulgated in *The London Gazette* of 26 October 1858:

'17th Lancer Sergeant Major [*sic*] Charles Wooden.

'Date of Act of Bravery, 25 October 1854.

'For having, after the retreat of the Light Cavalry, at the Battle of Balaclava, been instrumental, together with Dr. James Mouat, CB, in saving the life of Lieutenant Colonel Morris, CB, [*sic*] of the 17th Lancers, by proceeding, under heavy fire, to his assistance, when he was lying very dangerously wounded, in an exposed situation.'

Foreign Gallantry Awards

A number of foreign gallantry awards were granted to Chargers, beginning, of course, with the officer-class. Permission to wear these and other honours was granted by the Queen on 10 May 1855, the announcement being made in *The London Gazette* on the following day.

A further announcement was made in *The London Gazette* of 2 March 1858:

'War-Office, March 2, 1858.

'THE Queen has been pleased to give and grant to those Officers, Non-Commissioned Officers and men of Her Majesty's Army who, with the sanction of Her Majesty, have been allowed to receive Medals conferred by His Majesty the Emperor of the French, His Majesty the King of Sardinia, and His Imperial Majesty the Sultan, for services during the late War, Her Majesty's Royal permission to wear the same.'

The following officers and men were nominated to the Légion d'Honneur

Staff:
Major General James Thomas Brudenell, 7th Earl of Cardigan
Colonel Lord George Augustus Frederick Paget
Lieutenant Colonel George Wynell Mayow

4th Light Dragoons:
Captain John George Brown

8th Hussars:
Major Rodolph de Salis
Lieutenant Edward Seager
Lieutenant Colonel Frederick George Shewell
Sergeant John Atkins Pickworth
Trumpet Major William Gray

MEDALS

11th Hussars:
Captain Edwin Adolphus Cook
Lieutenant Colonel John Douglas
Private H. Ash
Private John T. Bambrick

13th Light Dragoons:
Captain Arthur Tremayne[6]
Sergeant Thomas George Johnson

17th Lancers:
Lieutenant Sir William Gordon
Captain W. Morris
Sergeant James Duncan recommended (unsuccessfully), awarded Al Valore Militaire
Trumpeter John Brown

The following NCOs and other ranks were nominated to the Médaille Militaire

4th Light Dragoons:
Corporal John Andrews
Private Thomas Guthrie

8th Hussars:
Private Charles Macaulay
Private John Martin
Trumpeter James Donoghue

11th Hussars:
Troop Sergeant Major Patrick Rourke Teevan
Sergeant-Major George Loy Smith
Private Robert Harrison
Private Cornelius Teehan

13th Light Dragoons:
Sergeant Thomas George Johnson
Trumpeter Richard Davis
Private George Dearlove
Private John Fenton

17th Lancers:
Sergeant John Shearingham
Sergeant Charles Wooden

Corporal James Ikin Nunnerley
Private Charles Watson

The Sardinian Medaglia al Valore Militare was presented on behalf of the Sultan of Turkey to members of the Allied forces of Britain, France and Sardinia who were recommended for distinction as a result of their service during the Crimean campaign.

The following received the Sardinian Medaglia al Valore Militare in connection with the Charge of the Light Brigade:

Staff:
Colonel Lord George Augustus Frederick Paget
Lieutenant Colonel George Wynell Mayow

4th Light Dragoons:
Lieutenant Colonel Alexander Low
Captain Robert Portal
Troop Sergeant-Major William Waterson

8th Hussars:
Lieutenant Colonel Rodolph de Salis
Major Edward Tomkinson
Trumpeter William Wilson

11th Hussars:
Cornet and Adjutant John Yates
Sergeant Robert Davies

13th Light Dragoons:
Captain Percy Shawe Smith
Corporal William Gardiner

17th Lancers:
Sergeant James Duncan
Troop Sergeant Major Abraham Ranson

The Order of the Medjidie

The London Gazette of 2 March 1858 announced the bestowal of the Imperial Order of the Medjidie on a number of Officers and one NCO in connection with the Charge of the Light Brigade, the awards being listed under the general notice that: 'His Imperial Majesty the Sultan hath been pleased to confer upon them as a mark of His Majesty's approbation of their distinguished services before the enemy during the late War.'

The following officers, and one NCO, were granted permission to receive and wear the Order of the Medjidie:

Staff:
Major General James Thomas Brudenell, 7th Earl of Cardigan
Lieutenant Colonel George Wynell Mayow
Colonel Lord George Augustus Frederick Paget
Lieutenant Henry Fitzhardinge Berkeley Maxse

4th Light Dragoons:
Captain John George Brown
Captain Thomas E. Hutton
Captain Alexander Low
Captain Robert Portal
Cornet George Warwick Hunt

8th Hussars:
Major Rodolph de Salis

11th Hussars:
Lieutenant Colonel John Douglas
Lieutenant Harington Astley Trevelyan
Assistant-Surgeon John Henry Wilkin

13th Light Dragoons:
Captain Soame Gambier Jenyns
Lieutenant Percy Shawe Smith
Captain Arthur Tremayne
Regimental Sergeant-Major George Gardner

17th Lancers:
Captain William Morris
Captain Robert White
Lieutenant Sir William Gordon
Sergeant James Duncan

Appendix II

Personal Accounts by Regiments

Staff

Major General James Thomas Brudenell, 7th Earl of Cardigan

An extract from Cardigan's affidavit filed in his defence in the Cardigan v. Calthorpe case reads:

'The Light Cavalry Brigade was suddenly ordered to mount; and Lord Lucan then came to our front and ordered me to attack the Russians in the valley – I replied "Certainly Sir but allow me to point out to you that the Russians have a Battery in the Valley in our front and Batteries and Riflemen on each flank" – Lord Lucan said "I cannot help that, it is Lord Lucan's positive order that the Light Brigade attacks immediately" – I instantly moved off to the Brigade, the formation of which Lord Lucan had previously altered. I had placed the 13th Light Dragoons, 17th Lancers and 11th Hussars in the front line – Lord Lucan ordered the 11th Hussars back to support the left flank of the 17th Lancers. The 4th Light Dragoons and 8th Hussars formed the original Second Line under the Senior Officer Lord George Paget – The Brigade therefore attacked in three lines – I was in immediate command of the First Line consisting of the 13th Light Dragoons and the 17th Lancers; the 11th Hussars under the command of Lieutenant Colonel Douglas (and supporting the left rear flank of the 17th Lancers) formed the Second Line: and the Third Line consisting of 4th Light Dragoons and 8th Hussars was led by Lord George Paget.

'The distance from the point from which we moved off to the battery in the lower part of the valley in front of us, was quite, if not more than, a mile and a quarter. We advanced directly upon and in face of the Battery which directed a murderous fire on the whole Brigade advancing. On coming at a steady pace within about 80 yards of the Battery which consisted of about twelve or fourteen of heavy ordinance [*sic*], a fire was opened upon us along the whole line.

'I continued at the head of the First Line of the Brigade, and led them up to and into the Battery – as I was leading them into it, one of the guns was fired

Above: Field Marshal Fitzroy James Henry Somerset, 1st Baron Raglan. Lord Raglan's written orders on the 24 October made little sense and required his ADCs to explain their exact meaning – this failing allowed Nolan to lead the Light Brigade in a death of glory Charge.

Below left: Lieutenant General George Charles Bingham, 3rd Earl of Lucan, General Officer Commander of the Cavalry. Brought out of retirement, Lucan had never commanded in the field and lacked tactical awareness. Once committed to attack along the North Valley, he failed to provide the support that could have led to victory.

Below right: Major General James Thomas Brudenell, 7th Earl of Cardigan, was given the order to Charge in-front of the troops. He advised Lucan of the enemy's disposition but had no option other than to obey.

Above: *The Charge of the Heavy Brigade* (William Simpson). The Heavies advanced across rough ground and through the edge of the Light Brigade's camp before attacking Russian cavalry many times their own strength. British artillery followed-up the Heavies' victory, demonstrating the importance of close artillery support.

Left: Captain Louis Edward Nolan, 15th Hussars, ADC to General Airey. It was Nolan's deliberate misinterpretation of Lord Raglan's Fourth Order to the cavalry which led to the immortal Charge.

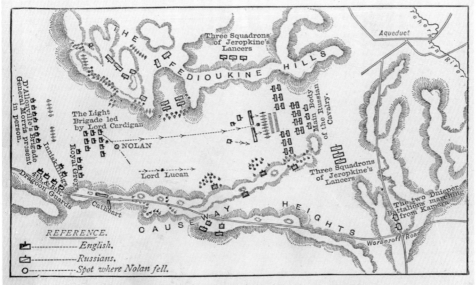

PLAN OF THE CHARGE OF THE LIGHT BRIGADE AT BALACLAVA..

Above: A map of the Charge of the Light Brigade. The Heavy Brigade was stationed in the opening to the South Valley immediately prior to the Fourth Order being delivered, Lord Lucan being half way between his two brigades.

Below: Lord Cardigan riding his mount 'Ronald' headlong into the ranks of No. 3 Don Cossack battery. Cardigan reportedly never looked back once the Charge began and maintained a steady pace. He passed through the gun line and faced the massed ranks of the enemy cavalry beyond.

A TRUMP CARD (IGAN).

'C'est magnifique, mais ce n'est pas la guerre: c'est de la folie' – General Bosquet. A panoramic view of the Charge as seen from the Fedioukine Heights (William Simpson). The Charge was made over an unprecedented distance of 1 1/4 miles. The heavy fire from three sides soon destroyed the cavalry's perfect formation, while elements of the Second Line veered off to the left and right.

Above left: The 17th Lancers at the guns. The survivors of the First Line cutting down and lancing the gun-crews, before pressing on to push back the enemy's cavalry support.

Above right: The 11th Hussars in combat at the guns. They are seen entering the left flank of No. 3 Don Cossack battery in support of the 17th Lancers, while in the background, the Russian battery on the Causeway Heights continues to fire upon the Second Line.

A Victorian 'scrap' depicting a scene from the Charge, with the 11th Hussars at the guns. The Russian gunners wore thick overcoats which could withstand a sword cut, the men quickly learned to use the 'point' to great effect.

Above: A view of the carnage at the gun line as the 11th Hussars hack at the Russian gun-crews. Moments later, elements of the 4th Light Dragoons arrived on the scene, while the 8th Hussars had veered off to the right and largely missed the guns.

Right: The 4th Light Dragoons at the guns. Men of the 4th Light Dragoons, part of the Second Line, enter the gun-line and tackle the surviving gunners of No. 3 Don Cossack battery.

The 4th Chasseurs d'Afrique silenced the Russian guns on the Fedioukine Heights, also reducing the effectiveness of their infantry support. The withdrawal of shattered remnants of the Light Brigade was covered by the 1st Chasseurs d'Afrique.

Above: Cossacks attempt to cut off the survivors. The Russians threw out Cossacks and Uhlans from each side of the North Valley in order to cut off the Light Brigade's retreat. The enemy expected the British to lay down their arms, but the survivors remained full of fight. (A pre-Charge image from *The London Illustrated News*, 26 November 1853).

Left: A 17th Lancer being mistreated at the hands of the Cossacks. There were many eyewitness accounts of Cossacks murdering the wounded and men who had been surrounded and had surrendered.

Above: The mare 'Butcher' being put out to grass at Colchester Cavalry Barracks. Survivors of the Charge are (from left to right): Private (later Sergeant-Major) Edwin Hughes, Private James Malanfy, Private Edward Hunt, 'Butcher', Private John Douglas, Private James Lamb, Private (later Sergeant-Major) William Eccles. (Photograph entitled 'Six Survivors of the Balaclava Charge of the 13th Light Dragoons, 1872').

Below: Survivors of the Charge marked the 21st anniversary of Balaclava with a banquet held at Alexandra Palace (1875). Two years later the Balaclava Commemoration Society was formed. (*The Illustrated London News*, 30 October 1875).

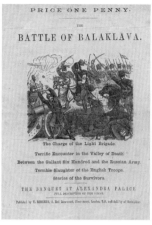

Above left: 'The 750 Guinea Balaclava Bugle'. The bugle sounded by Trumpet Major Henry Joy at Balaclava while at the head of the Heavy Brigade – it was only after the sale of his bugle that the controversy as to whether the Charge was sounded at the head of the Light Brigade.

Above right: A one-penny pamphlet sold in advance of the first Balaclava Banquet (1875), which included a number of first-hand accounts, including those of Private William Staden and Private Thomas Wroots of the 11th Hussars.

Below: Survivors of the Charge attending their annual reunion in 1890. Many of the men featured in the line-up left us personal accounts, some of which are quoted in this volume. (*The London Illustrated News*, 1890).

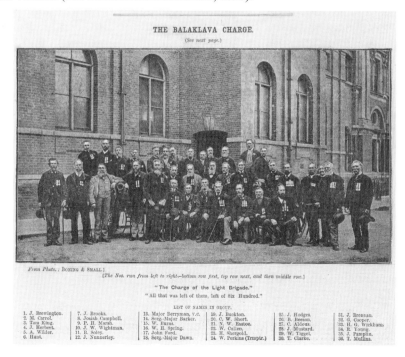

close to my horse's head, but I rode straight forward through the Battery at the head of the Brigade, and through and past the guns, till I came nearly up to a strong force of Russian Cavalry stationed behind the Battery and some distance in rear of the guns. I was then attacked by some Cossacks, slightly wounded, and nearly dismounted: I had difficulty in recovering my seat, and in defending myself against several Cossacks who attacked me – I was at this time nearly alone, for the First Line of Cavalry, which had followed me into the Battery, had been entirely broken up – some of them had borne away to the left by an open space (hereby avoiding the impediments of Russian Limber Carriages Ammunition wagons etc) and afterwards retreated.

'Upon disengaging myself from the Cossacks, and returning past the Guns, I saw the broken remnants of the First Line in small detached parties retreating up the hill towards our original position. As I was returning, I saw General Scarlett who commanded the Heavy Cavalry Brigade, and who was then about half way between the Russian Battery (on the right flank) and the place from which we commenced the Charge – I went up and said a few words to him, Lord Lucan being near him, and then as rapidly as I could joined the remains of my Brigade and reformed them.

'The whole affair from the moment we moved off until we reformed on the ground from which we started did not occupy more than twenty minutes – On my coming upon the Regiments which were reforming after their return, two or three of them gave me three cheers.

'On the troops forming up on their original ground, I had then counted by my Brigade Major, and found that there were one hundred and ninety five [*198*] [un] wounded men out of about six hundred and seventy [*673*], who had gone with me into action; and on the following day it was found that three hundred of the men who had gone into action were killed, wounded or missing; that three hundred and ninety-six horses were put hors de combat and thirty were obliged to be shot, and that twenty four officers were killed and wounded. It is my firm belief, that all Officers and men both of the leading and supporting Regiments did their duty well; and they were all exposed not only to the front fire of the Battery in the Valley, but also to the fire of the Batteries on each flank and of the Russian Riflemen.

'After counting the remains of the Brigade I rode off to Lord Raglan who disapproved entirely of the attack; stating to me that to attack a Battery in front, was contrary to all the usages of warfare – During this affair, I was not accompanied by any Aide-de-Camp, Lieutenant Maxse was wounded short of the Battery, and retreated – my excellent Aide-de-Camp Captain Lockwood I never saw at all from the moment of advancing; he was killed, and we never could discover where. My extra Aide-de-Camp Sir George Wombwell of the 17th Lancers had his horse killed on entering the Batteries [*sic*], and was taken Prisoner, but escaped afterwards by his Agility in jumping on a stray horse and galloping away with the 4th Light Dragoons on their return.'

4th Light Dragoons

Private John Edden, 4th Light Dragoons

'And then the slaughter began. The enemy opened fire from the batteries, and our men began to fall in half-dozens; and the guns were well aimed for emptying the saddles. They did not, however, aim so accurately for the First Line as they did for the Second. Directly we got into this fire, what with that from the guns and the infantry together, we could scarcely see where we were. Men and horses were fast falling around me. We lost sight of the First Line. I had not been in the fire long before a sergeant on my right had his head half blown off by a shell, which burst in front of me and killed almost half of our left hand troop.

'The officer who was leading the squadron I was in was Captain Brown [Captain John George Brown], a hasty tempered gentlemen. He kept telling us to "Keep back; hold your horses in hand." But the cry from the men was: "Loose out; get at them. We shall all be shot before we can strike a blow." We were then three-quarters of a mile from the guns, and a portion of the ground was cultivated. It was being torn up all the way in front of us with bullets and shot.

'As the Third Line came into action, commanded by Colonel Sewell [Lieutenant Colonel Frederick George Shewell], of the 8th Hussars, this line of cavalry just referred to wheeled round and hemmed us in. The First Line that had rushed into the enemy's camp charged back again by a whole host of Russian cavalry. The remark was passed from man to man. "Look at them Charging the 8th!" which we had mistaken in the excitement of the moment; but it was the Russians charging the First Line back.

'At this time our rear was cut off. Lord Paget, after enquiring for Lord Cardigan, ordered our men to rally, as they were scattered in all directions.

'An old soldier belonging to the 17th Lancers, Jack Penn, shouted "Rally be - - - ! a mob's the best to break our road through." After that we were all intermixed with Cossacks, Polish Lancers, and all descriptions of men together. We were that close that we could not point them. I struck three or four [in] the mouth with the hilt of my sword, and could not do it any other way.

'We were pressed closely and very strongly by the Cossacks all the time, when the battery that had been on our right going down opened fire into the lot of us; into their own men as well as into us. At that time the ground was being ploughed up by shots and bullets, and men were falling around us by dozens. Just at this moment my horse was shot from under me, and I was rather badly hurt in the fall. I was staggered for a bit, but I soon recovered. They were all making their way home to the lines where we started the best they could; every man for himself.

'The French cavalry had charged the battery on our left and had silenced the guns; and the dismounted men, seeing this, were making towards that battery. But I took the advice of an old soldier, who said "Keep here under this battery, and you will be under the range." There I saw nothing but dead and dying men and horses.

'I afterwards returned to our camp the best way I could on foot, and when I got there it was pitiful to see the remnants of the Light Brigade. I know that there had been great slaughter, but I never knew it was so bad until then.'[1]

From a speech made by John Edden, reported in the *Tamworth Herald* of 20 November 1897:

'But where the English were wrong was that we went too far, for when we got the advantage the result was that their whole army was poured on us. We were caught nicely in a trap.

'We were surrounded with a set of the deadliest cut-throats, the Cossacks and they – the cowardly brutes – could not do without piercing the wounded men.

'My horse was shot from under me and fell pinning me to the ground but in its wriggling and plunging with pain I was able to get loose. I was in an awful position. I could see that if I went one way I had a deadly fire to go through and I knew that if I went the other way I should be subject to the tender mercies of the Cossacks. My mind was made up and I decided to go through the firing.

'How I got through I don't know, I can't even think. The ground was ploughed up all along and the men and horses were cut down by the score. And I will say it now – and I wish others were here to bear me out – although it is not generally known – I was the last man that ever came out of the Charge to answer my name. One hundred and ninety eight answered to their names and a great proportion of them were wounded.'

Private Robert Stuart Farquharson, 4th Light Dragoons

'Lord Lucan gave his orders to Lord Cardigan, who ordered the brigade to move off at a walk. This pace we kept at until we were fairly off the hill and into a heavy, ploughed field below, where we broke into a trot, which we continued until getting on to grass, when we got into a gallop, all the time [*sic*] being exposed to a galling fire in front from an eight-gun battery which the enemy had placed in the centre of the valley.

'Now the order "Draw swords" was given, and, with a yell and shout of defiance such as is heard only from desperate men, we found ourselves careering over the ground as fast as our horses could carry us, onward towards the battery in front, and which all the time maintained a deadly fire. Presently, too, we came under a cross-fire from big guns, both to the right and the left, and also from small weapons used by thousands of infantry posted beneath these.

185

'Our officers were as cool as could be. Lord George Paget, as he rode in front of the regiment with his orderly (Parkes) and field trumpeter (Crawford) along with him, now and then called out, "Steady, men, steady!" he shouted, looking right and left of him to see that his injunctions were obeyed. The galling fire to which we had been subjected raised our worst passions, and we had all but one desire, and that was to silence the fellows who worked the fatal guns.

'At last, and despite the murderous fusillade, we were at the guns, and a slashing hand-to-hand fight followed with the men who served them. Up to this moment our colonel's sword had remained in its scabbard, which Parkes observing said to him "Come, my Lord, it is time you were drawing your sword – we are on top of the guns." His Lordship thereupon drew at once, and in another moment it was through the neck of a Russian gunner.

'I can't say how long we were here when the cry arose, "Fourth Light Dragoons to the assistance of the 11th." In response to this a young officer of ours, named Martin [Cornet Fiennes Wykeham Martin], who was acting-adjutant that morning, called off the right squadron, to which I belonged, and away we hurried round to the aid of the 11th Hussars, whom we found away on the other side of, and at some distance beyond, the now silent guns, engaged with a force six times their own number of Cossacks and Russian Hussars.

'Just as we got into the mêlée my horse dropped. He had been hit by a bullet; but in addition to that, a Russian gunner with whom I was engaged, in attempting to cut me down missed his mark, the blow falling on the horse and opening the poor brute's breast with an ugly gash. Before the fellow could recover from his miss I had him through the head with my point. No sooner was I on the ground and saw that it was all over with my horse than I found the skirmish was past. I was left alone on the field. I ran about, trying to find my way back, but could scarcely see where I was going, so dense were the clouds of smoke hanging over the ground.

'Presently a man of my own regiment came galloping towards me. When he got up I saw that he was wounded on the right arm, and seemed very faint and weak. All I could do for him was to tear a strip off my overalls and tie it tightly round the arm above the wound; and off he rode. Then a sergeant-major of ours named Fowler [Troop Sergeant Major William Fowler] came riding up and asked me if I knew where the regiment was. Of course I couldn't tell him; and away he went also. Then I saw, a little way off, the 11th Hussars galloping along, with Colonel Douglas [Lieutenant Colonel John Douglas] in front. When he saw me, he cried out to "halt," but his men couldn't hear him, and on they went. Following them up on his own account was a horse of the 17th Lancers, which I managed to catch by the bridle. I was in the act of mounting, when the beast reared up into the air and then fell heavily to the ground, bearing me along with it. As I lay there, somewhat stunned with the fall, a large body of Cossacks galloped past in pursuit of the 11th Hussars. One of them made a prod at me with his lance, but only succeeded in tearing the leg of my trousers and scratching my boot, without injuring me whatever.

'When they had passed on, I got up again and took to my heels; and as the Russian guns on either side of the valley still kept playing away, I had a lively run for it, dodging the round shot that kept bouncing about the ground. Again I managed to catch a stray horse – a little Cossack "mount" this time, and, jumping on his back, I urged him on towards the entrance to the valley. On the way I encountered a Russian Hussar, who made a well-meant cut at me then dropping the point of my sword over to my right rear I caught him a thrust on the right cheek which made him yell. I had no time, however, to see what he wanted further, and made off as fast as I could. Shortly I got clear of the cross-fire from the batteries, and came up to a party of men belonging to different regiments of our brigade, stragglers like myself. We kept together, and went on until, by-and-by, we saw the bannerols of a Lancer regiment fluttering above a bank of smoke in which we were enveloped. Thinking it was our own 17th Lancers we made straight for them – only discovering when too close that it was a regiment of Polish Lancers, together with a regiment of Russian Hussars, which had been formed up across the mouth of the valley, and were about to advance and sweep away all our men who were still left on the ground. Keeping well together, we went straight at the enemy and cut our way right through the crowd. We were not yet "out of the wood" though, for, galloping on, we immediately found ourselves confronted with a strong force of Cossacks, drawn up in line to the rear of the others. We had just to do the same by them – and did it; getting through both barriers, to the best of my recollection and belief, without the loss of a man.

'Pushing onward, we now saw, about a mile off, the Scots Greys [*sic*] – I think it was them – coming on to cover our retreat from the field. It was a welcome enough sight; but it wasn't to do me any good. A cannon shot put a sudden stop to my gallop. I saw the horrid thing bounding along the ground, but for the life of me I couldn't get out of its way, and it flew up and caught my borrowed Cossack steed on the head, killing it, of course, there and then. I fell to the ground along with it; and in two or three minutes thereafter I was surrounded by Cossacks and taken prisoner.'[2]

Private Joseph Grigg, 4th Light Dragoons

'As we got nearer the guns our pace was terrific; the horses were as anxious to go as we were; mine snorted and vibrated with excitement, and I could hardly keep my seat, for we seemed to go like the wind.

'The lines were about a hundred yards apart, so that when a man went down with his horse, the man behind him had time to turn his horse on one side or jump him over the obstacle. Every man thus had all his work to do to look before him, and there were not many chances to watch the dreadful work of the shots, shells, and bullets, which were showered at us from all directions.

'Men and horses began to fall fast; the man on my right hand went down with a crash, and soon afterwards the man on my left went down also. I remember, as we neared the guns, Captain Brown [Captain John George Brown], who was in command of our squadron, called out to the men in the Second Line, who were getting too near the front, "Steady, men, steady! you shall have a go in directly."

'Just before we got to the guns, we gave three loud cheers, and then, in a moment, we were among the enemy. As I passed the wheel of a gun-carriage the gun was fired, and I suppose some of the 8th Hussars got that shot, or shell, or whatever it was. The wind was blowing from behind us, and the smoke from the guns prevented us from seeing very well what work there was for us to do.

'The first man I noticed was a mounted driver. He cut me across the eyes with his whip, which almost blinded me, but as my horse flew past him, I made a cut at him and caught him in the mouth so that his teeth all rattled together as he fell from his horse. I can fancy I hear the horrible sound now. As he fell I cut at him again; and then I made for another driver, and cut him across the back of his neck and gave him a second cut as he fell. A few gunners stood in a group with their rifles, and we cut at them as we went rushing by.

'Beyond the guns the Russian cavalry, who should have come out to prevent our getting near the gunners, were coming down upon us howling wildly, and we went at them with a rush. I selected a mounted Cossack, who was making for me with his lance pointed at my breast. I knocked it upwards with my sword, pulled up quickly, and cut him down across the face. I tried to get hold of his lance, but he dropped it. As he was falling, I noticed that he was strapped onto the saddle, so that he did not come to the ground, and the horse rushed away with him. His lance, like all the others used by the Cossacks, had a black tuft of hair, about three inches from the blade, to hide a hook having a sharp edge, with which the reins of their enemies are cut when the lance is withdrawn after a thrust.

'Some of the men of the 4th and I made for several other Cossacks who were there in a body, cutting our way through them as through a small flock of sheep; and while thus engaged, the batteries on the slopes fired upon us, and their own men.

'Just then I heard Lord George Paget call out, "Rally on me!" I turned and saw him holding up his sword, and we all turned our horses towards where he had taken up a position in front of the guns. On arriving there, we noticed a regiment of Polish Lancers, which had come out from an opening in the hills behind us and was preparing to charge our rear; we thereupon charged through the guns again, killing several Russian hussars who were still there.

It seemed to me then, in the terrible din, confusion, and excitement, that all the gunners and drivers were on the ground either dead or wounded.

'Before the Polish Lancers had time to form line and attack us, the Chasseurs D'Afrique, who were coming down the valley at a sweeping pace, drove them back with great loss.

'After a short engagement with the Russian hussars, we turned our horses in the direction of our starting-place and rode back the best way we could, under fire of the infantry and the batteries on the hills. I was in company with a comrade belonging to my own troop, and all of a sudden down went his horse, and he pitched over its head and lay helpless on the ground. I immediately dismounted and picked him up, when I found his shoulder was dislocated. Regimental Sergeant-Major Johnson [Sergeant Thomas George Johnson] of the 13th Light Dragoons, who was coming up behind us, rode towards us, calling out, "What's the matter?" And between us we got him back in safety.'[3]

Private James Henry Herbert, 4th Light Dragoons

'Lord Cardigan shouted: "Stand to your horses, men! Prepare to mount! Mount!"

'The trumpeters of the different regiments sounded these orders, and we sprang into our saddles.

'The order was then given: "The Light Brigade will advance!"

'We knew one thing – we knew what was expected of us, for two or three days before the Charge Lord Lucan had addressed us, saying: "Keep your horses well in hand, men, and obey your officers; but when you get in amongst the Russians, *skiver* them well!"

'As he spoke he gave us with his own sword an illustration of what he meant – which was pointing and cutting with the weapon.

'We knew that we were going into something pretty desperate; but we did not realise what was in store for us. Not a soul suspected that.

'The batteries poured in a fearful fire from these three quarters – straight head and on our right and left: and, in addition, there must have been great numbers of Cossacks and infantry in ambush on our right, because from that direction also a murderous fire was coming.

'Our men dropped from their saddles by dozens. Some were wounded, some were killed on the spot, and fell out of their saddles. There were cases of man and horses being literally blown to pieces by shells.

'Soon after we had started, the wild rush of the living men was accompanied by maddened horses and empty saddles.

'Tom Fletcher [Private Thomas Fletcher] was shot. He was a brave soldier and a splendid horseman; but the heavy fire was disorganising us, and he got a little behind me in his dressing. I shouted: "Keep up, Tom!" The words were no sooner out of my mouth that I heard a whiz and a thud, and a bullet which had just grazed me struck him in the back of the head. But he held on, wounded though he was, and fought till he was taken prisoner.

'For the whole of the distance we rode through a perfect blaze of fire. So terrible was the flanking fire on our right and left, that when we had reached the bottom of the valley there were not more than one hundred men remaining mounted [*sic*].

'When we reached the battery we found that the gunners and drivers had limbered up their guns and were ready to retreat. We galloped up and surrounded them as well as we could with our shattered numbers, and stopped them from going.

'There the most terrible part of the whole mad business came. The gunners tried to escape from the fury of our men by crawling under the guns; but the drivers had not time to get away from their horses. They were sabred as they tried to dismount, and a good many of our own men dismounted and struck the Russians under their own guns or routed them out at the point of the sword. At such a time nothing could escape – men had no time to think, and the very horses were cut and stabbed and killed. So far as my own recollection goes there was not a man or horse who escaped alive in the whole of the battery.

'We had captured the guns fairly enough, and for a short time they were actually in our possession; but the Russians were seen to be hurrying up large bodies of troops. Lord George Paget shouted to Colonel Shewell, commanding the 8th: "We must rally on the Lancers, men!" evidently believing that a body of Lancers had advanced to our support. He was at that time looking up the valley.

'One or two of our men, amongst them a sergeant called Andrews [Corporal John Andrews], shouted back, "But they're Russian Lancers!" Then Lord George replied that we must hold together and cut our way through them; and the order was given to go about and retire.

'This, indeed, was the only thing we could do, because it was clear that the handful of men who were still lucky enough to be living could do nothing against the Russian masses who were now in motion against us.

'To stay where we were was to be cut to pieces – and for nothing – inasmuch as we had no support, and could not take the guns away.

'When we went about we made for the Lancers, whom we now saw clearly enough. They were drawn up in a line right across the valley, not far from the point at which the flanking batteries on our right and left were placed.

'Our horses were utterly winded, and terribly distressed with the galloping and charging down the valley for more than a mile. It was impossible to get them to go very fast; but the remnants of the five regiments obeyed the order to hold together and went at the Russian Lancers.

'As we came back I saw the officers commanding the Russians waving their swords as if they were trying to bring the flanks of the Lancers round, so as to hem us in; but they seemed to me to be afraid to move, or not to know what their officers were driving at. It was, of course, a disgraceful thing that they allowed a single man to get back again down [*sic*] the valley. Strictly speaking, not a soul in the Light Brigade should have been permitted to return, in view of the superior numbers of the enemy, their freshness and our own exhausted state. We rushed in amongst them, and there was a renewal of the cutting, slashing, pointing and parrying of the earlier part of the fight. There was no fancy work, but just hard, useful business, and it fulfilled its object, for we cut through the opposing lancers.[4]

'The Russian batteries continued to blaze away even when we were mixed up with their own people, and destroyed friend and foe alike. It was merciless butchery so far as their own soldiers were concerned, though it was fair enough in our case, as we were the object to be destroyed.

'In addition to this artillery fire we had to bear the fire of the hundreds of Cossacks who were hovering on our flanks. Many a man who had gone through the Charge in safety fell before the Cossacks' fire.

'The charge had caused us to be scattered and utterly disorganised and separated.

'Many a friend was missing, and some that I thought I should never see again were found. There was one amongst them, a member of my own troop, that I did not expect to set eyes on, but I overtook him during our retreat.

'I saw that something was wrong, as he was terribly pale, so I said: "Hello, Bill, what's the matter? Are you hurt?"

'He said: "Yes, I am, shot through the foot."

'"Here, old boy," I told him, "you must get out of this. Hang on to the saddle and give me the reins. I'll get you through."

'I did get him through luckily, and when we were safely back I saw him taken off his horse. He was removed to one of the hospital ships in Balaclava harbour, doctored and invalided home.

'A few lucky ones amongst us got safely back – and a melancholy return it was! We staggered in. Some singly, some in twos, and some in threes; and the way we were met and cheered and helped showed how stunned those were who had been left behind, and had seen us going on an undertaking that looked like sheer madness and certain death for every man and horse.

'That we should have suffered even more than we did at the finish is certain if it had not been for the action of some French cavalry, who advanced and silenced some of the Russian guns.

'There was a man in our regiment named Fox [Private Christopher Fox]. When the order to advance was given he was on duty in the camp. He rushed to his horse, rode in the Charge, and came safely back. And to what? The cat! He was court-martialled for leaving his post without orders and sentenced to receive fifty lashes.'[5]

8th Hussars

An anonymous private in the 8th Hussars

'I had three Russians to deal with at once. An hussar made a desperate slap at my head which I parried, and with a cut "number two" gave him so tremendous a slash in the neck that it almost sickened me to look on. I had now to wheel in order to meet a Polish lancer who was just charging me full tilt. I saw that the butt was fixed against his thigh, and that he gave his lance a slight quiver, and that he seemed to know how to use it. I bent down slightly on my saddle, received his lance on the back on my sword which passed over my shoulder, at the same instant that the point on my weapon, through the mere rush of the horses passing each other, entered his breast, and went clean through him, coming out at his back, so that I was forced to draw it out with a wrench as he rolled over the crupper.

'A Cossack was now upon me, but as I reined back in time his aim failed, and he shot my horse's head, and I then rode after him, wounding him in the shoulder, and knocking man and horse over with my own, so that I was all but unseated.'[6]

Lieutenant Daniel Hugh Clutterbuck, 8th Hussars

'As the line approached the Russian artillery, the smoke became so dense that we could see but little except the flashes of the guns, and I then lost sight of Lord Cardigan.

'At the part of the Russian line that I came in contact with, they were trying to limber up and carry off their guns, and I heard some of our soldiers propose to secure these guns; but as I at the moment perceived a line of Russian cavalry in rear of the guns, I directed these men, who belonged to the 17th Lancers, to leave the guns to be dealt with by the Second Line, and to charge the Russian cavalry. This they did, and drove them in on their second reserve. We were then within sight of the bridge over the aqueduct, and I should think 500 yards or more in the rear of the Russian guns. Finding the enemy then too strong to be dealt with by the few men that remained, I called out to the men to halt; and perceiving the 8th Hussars advancing. I further directed and led the men back to that corps, which on the moment was wheeled about by Colonel Shewell.

'I was induced to give these orders in consequence of not being able to see anything of Lord Cardigan on emerging from the smoke that hung over the Russian guns, and being the senior officer in his absence, until I joined Colonel Shewell. We were then completely cut off by the enemy, and after a momentary consultation among the senior officers, Colonel Shewell, who assumed the command, led us to the Charge. We broke through.'[7]

Private John Doyle, 8th Hussars

'We charged under a most terrific fire from cannon and musketry, so that the shot and shell, grape, canister, and musketry came upon us like hail. We had not advanced far, when a comrade on my right, named Hefferon [Private Thomas Hefferon], was struck by a shell which exploded at the time, blowing his body into the air, but his hips remained for a long time after in the saddle. I was covered with his remains. Lennan [Private Martin Lennon], who brought the dog Jemmy with him, was riding on my left, when a round shot struck him on the left side of the head, and I got another splash from him. His body remained in the saddle for some time.

'My horse got a bullet through his nose, above the noseband, which caused him to lose a great deal of blood, and every time he gave his head a chuck the blood spurted over me. That night when I opened my cloak, I found 23 bullets in it. There were five buttons blown off my dress jacket: the slings of my sabretache were cut off, but my sword belts were not touched. I also had the right heel and spur blown off my boot. It was a long and terrible Charge.

'When we arrived at the 13 guns [sic] which were placed in front of us, where the First Line had dashed through, we pulled up in rear of the guns for the purpose of keeping the passage open for the advanced line, which was composed of the 4th [sic] and 13th Light Dragoons and 17th Lancers. The Second Line consisted of the 8th and 11th Hussars [sic]. We, the few of us who got there, got the word from Colonel Shewell to come "left about," as we saw the Russian cavalry pouring down upon us in masses sufficient to devour us, for I do not think at that time we could have mustered 40 men, until we got the remnant of the First Line up to help us.

'A private named Dawan [Private William Dawn] had a mallet and spikes in his haversack; he dismounted and spiked two or three guns, but had not time to spike more, for the Russian cavalry had entirely surrounded us. At this moment Colonel Shewell gave the word – "Men stick together! – Cheer and Charge!" We gave a most terrific yell, and like tigers cut through the two regiments formed in front of us. There were three men of the 8th Hussars taken prisoners. As soon as we got through they broke up and pursued us, but there was no body of us, we were scattered, and there were from 40 to 60 Russians after or around one man. I can answer for myself, that there was a large number after me. Although my old friend (my horse) Hickabod had lost a deal of blood, there were none of the Russian cavalry could pass him, for if they could have got in front of me I should have been killed; but as they could not pass me, and being young, supple, and like an eel in the saddle, I could turn and twist as quick as lightning.

'As they were galloping nearly one on the top of another to see who would have me first, I must have wounded many of them, as I did nothing but parry their points and return my own as quickly as I could. There was an officer who dashed into the centre of us when the Russian lancers came down on our left, and wounded a man named Kennedy [Private Richard Kennedy]; he took the skin off one side of his head; he had also wounded or killed several others, but I could not say how many. I had pointed him with a "right-rear point," and just as the Russian retreat sounded I saw the same officer endeavouring to get in front of me; when he heard the sound he turned short to the left, and met me right hand to right hand, and made a terrible point at me; but I had my eye on him, for I knew I had pointed him in rear of the guns, and he would have me if he could, but, thank God, I was too quick for him! I parried off his point, and with a return point drove my sword through his mouth. I still kept on the swing, and saw nothing more of him. In less than two minutes the guns which we had ridden through in the morning again opened upon us.

'Soon afterwards I came in contact with Colonel Shewell, who was then in the ploughed ground. Knowing the ground well, as I used to pass over it every day, and being on a pathway, I shouted to Colonel Shewell to get on my track, or he would never get across. He took my advice, inclined to his right, and got on my track. Soon afterwards I came up with a sergeant-major of the 13th Light Dragoons [Regimental Sergeant Major George Gardner], and shouted to him to take hold of my left stirrup. He did so, and my horse and stirrup helped him along until we came close to the 6th French Hussars [*sic*], who were after charging the battery that first opened fire upon us on our ride into the "Valley of Death." They had lost 90 men [*sic*], but had silenced the battery, and come to cover our retreat. At this time the sergeant-major lost his hold and fell, but soon after he got back to our retiring place.

'When I got back no one knew me, for I was covered with blood from my head to my feet. Colonel Shewell called out to know who I was; and then told me to take my horse to the commissary officer (Mr Cruikshank) and shoot him! He thought he was done for. I got a quart of rum and bathed the wounds on his nose with it, and in a few hours there was a fine healthy scale over it.'[8]

Private Robert Owen Glendwr, 8th Hussars

'My horse was wounded near the first battery on the right. I dismounted, and caught a horse belonging to the 13th Light Dragoons, and rejoined the 8th.

'When wheeling to return at the end of the battery I charged the Polish lancers with the 8th, and my horse was wounded in the chest by a splinter of shell.

'I was taken prisoner, but was left on the ground while the lancers followed the 8th up the valley. I was slightly wounded, but managed to crawl some distance, and after great trouble and pain from my wound I caught a remount of the 4th Light Dragoons, which was riderless.'[9]

Private Charles Macaulay, 8th Hussars
'GALLANT SIX HUNDRED
'DYING VETERAN'S STORY OF A GREAT CHARGE
'On the morning of Balaclava I was in a tent with eight comrades, and only two of them returned at night. I rode through the Charge on the left file but one, the outside man being called Herbert [Private E. Herbert]. We had not gone far before Herbert was killed by a cannon-ball. A moment or two after my right-hand man had his head taken clean off by a round shot. His trunk kept upright on the horse for several yards, and then fell over near me. Men and horses now began to fall very fast, and we galloped as hard as ever we could. Some of the horses had their entire legs taken away and scudded on their stumps until the poor brutes fell over.

'We got among the guns at last, and if it was a proud moment for us the feeling was short-lived. We fully expected to be supported, but when the smoke cleared we discovered that what we took for British troops was in reality Russian cavalry. They came for us in a perfect cloud, and we faced about and rushed right into them. There was an awful clash of swords, and, almost before we could realise it, we had cut right through them. This opened a passage for the remainder of the brigade, and was the only real bit of fighting we had; the other was only slaughter.'[10]

Private Anthony Sheridan, 8th Hussars
'Well, we merely trotted at first, but when we came within cannon-shot we put our horses into a canter. The Russians met us with a heavy cannonade.

'It was almost dark, with smoke and fog, and you did not know where you were until you ran against a Cossack. You know your blood soon gets warm when you are fighting, and it didn't take long to find that we had nothing to do but give them a point as good as their cut. I got a cut with a sword on the forehead at the guns. It was not much, but it has left a scar. I remember it now. It was fearful. We were cut and shot at in all directions, and it was each man for himself.

'I gave the Cossacks a great deal more than I got. If those lancers had hemmed us in, it would have been all up with us. I was in the Second Line going out, but there were no lines coming in. As we were returning we saw the French on our left.

'It was a melancholy sight to see our poor fellows lying dead and dying all around us. I saw Lord Fitzgibbon, who was mortally wounded, pull out his purse and offer it to any one of us who would dismount and accept it, but Lord! we did not think of money at such a moment as that. Life and honour were more precious to us than money, so I suppose the Russians got the English gold after all.'[11]

11th Hussars

Private John Thomas Bambrick, 11th Hussars

'An aide-de-camp was dispatched from Lucan's staff to Lord Cardigan. His Lordship then came back, and gave the orders, "Light Brigade, stand to your horses!" "Prepare to mount!" "Mount!"

'We were ordered to advance in echelon of regiments from the right. Before us was a battery of Russian artillery, another on the right of us, and another on the left, with some squares of infantry to our right front, the guns being supported by masses of cavalry.

'After cutting our way through the batteries [*sic*], squares of infantry, and squadrons of cavalry, the command was still "On, on, forward boys!" till we reached the Tractir bridge at the bottom of the valley. Our horses were by this time pretty well blown, and it was there we noticed how fearfully thin our ranks had become. He [Colonel Douglas] then called out, "Threes about, and rally on the 17th Lancers." We did so, but on reaching them, found to our dismay, they were the Polish lancers, who came from the carry to the engage lance. We cut our way through them, when we were confronted by a second line. Here a few of us, with Colonel Douglas, of the 11th Hussars, at our head, skirted their right flank.

'Shortly after having done so a shell, fired from the Russian battery on the left (which was on our right going down) lodged in my mare's side and exploded, tearing her completely open. While trying to extricate myself, her whole weight being on my left leg, I was attacked by a Russian officer.

'He made a cut at me with his sword, which I guarded, having fortunately retained hold of my blade, at the same moment grasping his reins with my left hand, which caused his stallion to throw up his head, thus dragging me from under my own. On regaining my feet, still retaining hold of his horse, he made a cut (seven) at my head, which, guarding, I delivered, first point, which took effect under his waist-belt. He at once quitted hold of his sword, and seemed to be fumbling in his holster for his pistol. While in the act of doing so I ran him through about the same place, the blood spurting over me as I drew my blade, which I followed up with a well-delivered blow on the face, when he fell to earth dead.

'On trying to mount the charger thus gained I had gone some considerable distance and found that I had received two wounds in my late conflict, one just below the knee and the other in my arm, the Russian having given me a severe wound in the muscle of my right arm, but in the excitement I had felt neither at the time.

'I found them in a group – some lying down, others standing to their horses' heads. In their centre were Brigade-General Lord Cardigan, Colonel Douglas, Sir Roger Palmer, and other officers. As I rode up they greeted me with a cheer, for many of my comrades, some of whom saw my horse shot under me, thought I was lying with the lost majority.

'It seems little short of a miracle that any of us ever came out. The carnage was something terrible. I remember well the comrades on my right and left hand falling, while the one immediately behind me lived through it, although he, like myself, had those on each side of him stricken down.'[12]

Sergeant William Bentley, 11th Hussars

'During the Charge I was close to Colonel Douglas, who earnestly impressed upon us the necessity of keeping well together as we swept down the valley. After passing the guns which had been silenced, the colonel called upon us to attack the cavalry which was drawn up in the rear, saying, "Give them another charge." We followed them as far as the valley would permit us, and then came close upon them. The colonel then called upon us to retire and re-form upon the lancers in our rear. I drew his attention to the circumstances of their being Russians, and not our lancers, when we got his order "Fight for your lives." thereupon all retired. On passing them I was attacked by an officer and several of the men, and received a slight wound from a lance. I was pursued by them, and cut the officer across the face. Lieutenant Dunn came to my assistance. I saw him cleave one of them almost to the saddle and can bear witness to his admirable and gallant fortitude and determination.'[13]

Sergeant Seth Bond, 11th Hussars

'The reports from the guns and bursting shells were deafening. The smoke too was almost blinding. Horses and men were falling in every direction, and the horses that were not hurt were so upset that we could not keep them in a straight line for a time. A man named Allerad [Private Charles Allured] who was riding on my left fell from his horse like a stone. I looked back and saw the poor fellow lying on his back, his right temple being cut quite away and his brain partly on the ground. After moving on a short distance Lieutenant Trevellyn [Lieutenant Harington Astley Trevelyan], of ours, was shot through the foot and was in great agony. I begged him not to fall out, if so he would be done for.

'We now came to the Russians in front. Our orders were to cut them down. We did so as far as possible and pursued the remainder down the valley.

'Here we saw a thousand more Russians huddled together in great confusion and ready to retreat over [the] Tractir Bridge, no doubt, thinking the whole of the cavalry were coming down on them. Our Colonel (Colonel Douglas) ordered us to halt and wait for support.

'After waiting a short time the Colonel gave the orders "Threes about, we will fall back on the Lancers". One of the men in the ranks said "they are not our Lancers, Colonel." The Colonel's answer to this was "What! What!" and having had another look said "Quite right, men I can do no more, disciplines gone; keep together and cut your road through. Trot."

'As we moved off all the Russian troops there, finding only 60 or 70 of the 11th on the spot, gained courage, and getting into something like order, followed and fired into us until we got near the lancers. Just at that time a young man named James Elder (my servant who turned me out in the morning) fell from his horse, no doubt shot by some of the rifles pursuing us from the bottom of the valley. I looked back for a moment and saw three lancers in the act of piercing him, and heard him cry "Oh! Oh! Oh!" as the lances entered his body. I dare not look again, as at that moment I heard a voice, which proved to be Captain Dunn's [Lieutenant Alexander Roberts Dunn], say. "Look out, Bond, or that villain will cut you down." I turned my head at once to my left, and had no sooner done so than I received a tremendous blow from a sword on my left arm. The blow quite benumbed my whole arm, and I thought at first that it was off. It cut through my tunic, and also cut my arm a good deal, but after a short time I was able to use my fingers sufficiently to handle the reins. Almost immediately afterwards I received two more sword cuts on the same arm, one below the elbow and the other near the wrist. About the same time I received a heavy blow on the head, cutting through the bear skin and lining of my busby, but only bruising my head so as to raise a large lump. I also had several cuts on my back. My horse, which was naturally a rather slow one, was wounded in the rear fetlock joint by a bursting shell, and died a few days after the Charge, and to make matters worse, I had all the time been looking to my right for danger, not knowing that those [Russian] hussars were attacking us on our left until Captain Dunn called out to me.

'By this time we had got back to the battery, and as we passed it the Russian cavalry left us to the mercy of the guns and the Russian rifles, the latter running down in front of the battery and firing at anyone they saw. Just then I heard a voice call out, "Stop that horse." I looked back and saw a horse galloping close after me. I pulled up and caught it, and found it was a Sergeant of the 8th Hussars who had called out to me to stop it [probably Sergeant John Atkins Pickworth]. The moment I had done so, one of our own men [Private

Robert Briggs] came running up and says, "Let me have the horse, Sergeant". I told him I had stopped it for the Sergeant behind. He said he had lost his horse as well, and meant having it. He was mounted when the Sergeant who called to me first came up. The Sergeant said it was not quite fair, as he had asked me to stop it. I said in reply, that I could not refuse one of our own regiment, to which the Sergeant replied "Ah, well, I suppose all is fair in war, so let me have hold of each of your stirrups, and I'll run; the sooner we get out of this the better". We were then under fire, so the Sergeant ran between the horses, holding on by the stirrups until we were out of danger.

'On our return Lord Cardigan seeing a small group of eight or ten of the 11th asked if that was all that was left of the "poor eleventh". The men informed his Lordship that they did not know of any more having escaped, where at his lordship was visibly moved. Matters did not prove to be quite so bad, for others, in groups and singly (including myself) turned up. And so we presented a better muster, but the roll call, not only ours but of other regiments, was indeed a sorry spectacle, and one which I shall never forget.'[14]

Corporal John Buckton, 11th Hussars

'We went off at a trot... we soon found what we were in for. We saw great numbers of cavalry and infantry at the rear of the guns, while on each side of the valley there were skirmishers who, as soon as they could, began to pepper us. Bullets fell thick and heavy amongst us; indeed, it seemed as if every man of us was doomed to destruction.

'We fought desperately, and many a Russian fell to rise no more. Their gunners we cut and hacked in every way, and but very few minutes elapsed before we had captured the guns. My horse was shot near the girth, and so near my leg that my trousers were covered with blood. He kept up bravely but every now and then I felt he gave a sort of jerk or quiver in his side, and I half expected I should lose him. He took me back home, though, but he was shot in the camp the next morning. I also got shot in the cloak rolled on the horse's back in front of me.

'Every man was for himself. We were all higgledy piggledy, but fighting more like devils than men. We were being cut up in a dreadful way, and we could not stand it.

'On our way back from the Tchernaya river [Chernaya], whither we had driven the Russians, we saw, as we thought, the 17th Lancers, and we were going to retire under them, but we found that they were the Polish lancers who had been stationed to cut our retreat right off. On our way down the valley they had been behind a hill on our left, and now they had emerged and formed a line right in our front. How we got through them I don't exactly know, but certainly I don't think they opened purposely for us to pass. Our poor fellows – the mere handful that were left of them – hurrahed and hallooed as loudly as they could, and that apparently had an effect upon the Polish horsemen, for it was evident their horses had not, like ours, been trained to withstand the noise and din of battle; and when they heard the British "hurrahs" and saw our brave fellows rushing towards them at such a mad pace, they became restless and turned round and about and before they could form again in any kind of way our men had bobbed through their ranks.

'It was at this moment that the Russian guns reopened firing on friend and foe alike and several of their horsemen fell.

'Some of them pricked with their lances at our men as they passed, but they did not do much harm, owing to the fright and the manner in which the men surprised them. The Chasseurs d'Afrique came to our assistance after we had passed the Polish lancers.

'[The British were wounded] mostly with swords, but the shot did the mischief. It would take a good blow with a sword to kill a man, but a shot does it at once. When we reached the guns we had nothing but the Russian Cavalry to contend with, sword to sword; but all the way down the artillery and infantry, especially the latter, had slaughtered us terribly.'[15]

Private R.T. Chambers, 11th Hussars
'Camp near the Heights of Sevastopol, October 30th, 1854

'My Dear Mother,

'The plain was about two miles in length and two hundred yards wide, so you can form some idea how we were knocked over, and having no support from our own army of either infantry, cavalry, or artillery, we charged immense masses of Russian cavalry and artillery, and on our return up the plain to our main body their cavalry had reformed across the plain to intercept our passage, which, however, we broke through, when their batteries and infantry from the hills again opened on us, horses and men falling every stride.'[14]

Private Nathan Henry, 11th Hussars
'Just before reaching the battery a shell burst in front and part of the shell struck my horse on the near foreleg, shattering it to pieces, and as we were riding at the gallop the poor old horse suddenly came down. I went over its head, and dislocated my bridle-hand. My right hand man [Private William Cullen] leaping over me and saving me from being crushed to death no doubt.'[16]

'My horse was killed just before arriving at the guns. On recovering myself I saw Lord Paget leading the 4th but did not see him afterwards. Seeing my regiment a little distance beyond the guns, halted, I ran to them, when I was directed by Sergeant-major Smith to a riderless horse in the ranks, which I mounted. We then pursued the cavalry in our front to the bottom of the valley not far from the aqueduct bridge. No other regiment was with us or near us, and no word of command was given, except by Colonel Douglas. After passing the Lancers that were formed across the valley to intercept our retreat my second horse was killed and I was taken prisoner.'[17]

Lieutenant Roger William Henry Palmer, 11th Hussars

'A few nights before Balaclava I was orderly officer and going round the sentries at night, I found Private Jowett (afterwards Sergeant-Major in the 18th Hussars) [Private Gregory Jowett] sitting down (and I am afraid) asleep at his post. I did not like to confine him as I knew he would most certainly be flogged.

'While I was thinking, the Orderly Sergeant-Major [Sergeant Joseph Pickles] said to me in a very loud and dictatorial tone of voice, "You must confine this man, Sir, or the Colonel will be very angry."

'This determined me, so I turned on the Sergeant-Major, and said, "What the devil do you mean by speaking to me in that manner. If you say another word, I shall put you under arrest for insolence to your superior officer."

'So after cautioning Jowett not to sit down on his post again I left him.

'A few days after this occurrence the Battle of Balaclava took place, and in the evening after, I was talking to Lieutenant (later Colonel) Dunn, VC [Lieutenant Alexander Roberts Dunn], and he said to me, "You had a very near shave of it today, old fellow, as we were rallying after the first halt. A Russian came up behind you and put his carbine very close to your head. You did not see him, but Private Jowett charged and cut him down.'

'I then remarked to Dunn, "Lucky for me I saved him from getting flogged the other day, otherwise he might not have been in such a hurry to save my life at that time."'[18]

The contemporary writer Kinglake:

'The Russians who stood gathered in the most immediate proximity of the 11th Hussars were a confused number, including it seems, artillery and cavalry. They were in a state of apparent helplessness, and one of their officers, wearing the epaulettes of a full Colonel, came up bare-headed to the stirrup of Lieutenant Roger Palmer, and voluntarily delivered his sword to him.

'Palmer handed over his sword to a corporal or sergeant at his side, and did not, of course, molest the disarmed officer, although the condition of things was not such as to allow the taking and securing of prisoners. When the crowd cleared, however, it disclosed to the 11th Hussars some squadrons of Russian

Cavalry formed in perfect order. Douglas led forward his hussars at a charge, but the Russians all at once went about and retreated, far on and into the opening of the gorge which divides the Aqueduct from the eastern base of the Fedioukine Hills, the 11th moved down in pursuit.

[Lieutenant Colonel Douglas:] 'I saw in our rear two squadrons of lancers drawn up. I instantly proclaimed, "They're the 17th, let us rally on them." At that very moment Lieutenant Roger Palmer rode up and said, "I beg your pardon, Colonel, that is not the 17th, that is the enemy." "Well", I exclaimed, "We must only retire and go through them". So with the 4th Light Dragoons we charged the Russian Lancers and got past them with few casualties.'

Describing the scene during the retreat when the 11th Hussars and the 4th Light Dragoons suddenly stopped and faced their pursuers, thereby checking the Russians, Kinglake records an alternative version:

'But during the very moments that were occupied by this operation of fronting towards the pursuers, it was becoming known to our officers and men that the enemy had interposed a fresh body of cavalry in a new, and indeed, opposite quarter.

'Roger Palmer, that young Lieutenant of the 11th Hussars to whom the Russian Colonel had given his sword, was singularly gifted with long sight, and casting his glance towards our left rear, he saw in that direction, but at a distance of several hundred yards, a considerable body of cavalry, which he assured himself must be Russian.

'He reported this to his chief, Colonel Douglas, who at first scarce believed that the squadron thus observed could be Russian; and it being perceptible that the force considered of Lancers, men were able, for a little while, to indulge in a pleasant surprise, and to imagine the Lancers described in our rear, at a distance of several hundred yards, must be our own "Seventeenth."

'Presently however, Roger Palmer convinced Colonel Douglas that the headgear of the cavalry so described, was Russian; and in another moment, all doubt was at an end, for our officers and men could now see that the newly-interposed troops were formed up across the slope of the valley, with a front towards the Russian rear, as though barring the retreat of our people.

'So, there then being certain knowledge that the English were between two powerful bodies of Russian cavalry, it became necessary in the very next moments in determining how to meet the emergency.'

Proceeding to describe the manner in which the Dragoons and the Hussars forced their way out of this, the account continues:

'Lieutenant Roger Palmer, for one, became engaged at this point, in what can be called a personal combat.

'This brief combat ended however, as did all the other collisions, in the failure of every attempt to cut off the English, and without receiving much harm in the course of this singular traverse, our people got past.

'It is possible that men might have been unhorsed and killed by the Russian Lancers without it becoming known that the deaths were so occasioned, but my impression is that few such casualties resulted from this encounter.'[19]

Private Henry William Parker, 11th Hussars

'I was not many yards from Colonel Douglas during the Charge and retreat. None of the 11th remained at the guns for Colonel Douglas frequently called out, "Follow me men, and use the point." When we halted a short distance on the right rear of the guns, I heard Colonel Douglas call out, "What are we to do now Lord Paget?" He replied, "Where is Lord Cardigan?" and galloped away. I did not see him again.

'Colonel Douglas immediately gave the order for us to charge the Russian cavalry in our front, which consisted of hussars and Cossacks. They retreated and did not halt till we got to the bottom of the valley, not far from the aqueduct.

'The other regiments must have retired, for three squadrons of lancers formed across our rear; as we approached them their right squadron was thrown back, after passing them, the artillery opened fire on us, when my horse was killed and I was made prisoner.'[20]

Private William Henry Pennington, 11th Hussars

'As we galloped within range of the enemy's guns, it seemed impossible that a single man would return. The utter hopelessness of this movement was, indeed, obvious to every one present. Annihilation appeared inevitable. It was a case of selling life as dearly as might be. The enemy opened upon us with a terrific hail of round-shot, grape, shell, and canister.

'The guns lost by the Turks in the redoubts were also turned against us, while the Russian Infantry added to the carnage by withering volleys of musketry. An indescribable scene of slaughter and destruction ensued.

'My own comrades fell right and left of me; one with his right arm shattered by a shell, the other with a bullet through his heart. A ball passed through my right leg, and the black mare that I rode was shot dead beneath me. Men and horses lay heaped around! The rush of the still charging squadrons, the roaring of the guns, the smoke and dust, the whizzing of shot, the clatter of equipments, the clashing of swords, the groans of the dying, and the cries of the wounded for help, I can never forget!

'Dismounted and wounded, my situation was critical indeed. To my front the leading regiments, still pressing on (with ranks terribly thinned by this murderous fire), could not be seen for the smoke which enveloped them.

'To my right, and close at hand, clusters of the enemy's cavalry were hacking and spearing our dismounted, wounded, and disarmed men. I clutched my sabre with a firmer grasp, and braced myself to meet death like a soldier and a man. But my heart leaped with inconceivable joy and relief, as the gallant Irish Hussars (the Eighth) came spurring on, as steadily and undaunted, as at field-days of the Brigade.

'"Come on, my dear boys!" cried an Officer on their flank. Lieutenant [*sic*] Harrison, with a presence of mind which showed the coolness of his head and the goodness of his heart, was holding a riderless horse by the rein, in the hope of assisting some dismounted man.

'Though one leg was disabled, I contrived to mount, and thus I found myself with the noble Eighth.

'The firing slackened, for our Brigade had driven every Russian from the guns.

'We made the alarming discovery that a body of Russian Lancers had gathered in our rear; and that our isolation from the British lines was complete. For a moment we could not realize it to be true, and some enthusiast shouted "Hurrah, it is the Seventeenth!" forgetting in the confusion that the "Death and Glory Boys" were in front.

'Colonel Shewell shouted, "Regiment, right about wheel," – "break through them my lads." The "Irish Boys" answered with a cheer, and charged at the ranks which were drawn across the valley to intercept them. We dashed at the enemy with a determination which seems astonishing to me now. We cut and thrust at the Muscovite horsemen with a resolution which soon opened a lane for the return of the survivors of the Brigade, and thus secured a retreat for our shattered band. I had the bad luck to get separated and was pursued by the enemy's Lancers until I got in sight of our Heavy Brigade, parrying and returning the thrusts that were given. But the grey mare of the Eighth was equal to my need, and her speed enabled me to distance my pursuers. I rode into our lines; but the blood I had lost had left me so weak, that I was lifted from the saddle, and laid upon the ground.

'Of the Eleventh, I have heard, but thirty-three mustered to answer the roll'.[21]

Another account reads:
'My comrades in the 11th Hussars on my immediate right and left, met with a speedy death; and, in another instant, my mare "Black Bess," possibly like myself, seeing but dimly through the blinding dust and smoke, bent her knees upon the carcass of a dead horse right in her path.

'It must have been when about two thirds of the North Valley had been traversed, that my mare received a bullet, which lamed her very badly. This, of course, decreased her pace, and I found myself at some distance in the rear of my regiment, and quite alone.

'I received a ball through the calf of my right leg from the infantry concealed on the Causeway ridges, succeeded immediately by a grape shot, which just cleared the top of my skull by a hair's breadth, which tilted my busby to the right side; "Black Bess" fell prone to earth without a struggle; she having accepted the coup-de-grace with a bullet through her head. She dropped right down between my legs, leaving me standing over her though shaken by the fall.

'As I stood for the moment perplexed in the extreme with the bullets still making dust spots on the green (for the wound in my leg was bleeding somewhat freely) I observed on my right front several parties of the enemy's lancers engaged in the cruel and cowardly work of maltreating and murdering some of our dismounted men.

'One man of my own regiment, whose face was streaming with blood, was, in his wounded condition, ruthlessly attacked and slain by some half-dozen of these butchers.

'Nathan Henry had lost his sword, and was of course quite at the mercy of these fiends; but in his case they desisted in their murderous practice and made him a prisoner.

'I think it is probable that the appearance of an officer may have acted upon these ruffians as a deterrent; for I believe there were but few cases in which the enemy evinced unnecessary harshness when their officers were present.

'Tom Spring [Private William Henry Spring aka Pilkington] of ours, who was taken prisoner, however, had a cruel experience. He fell with his horse after passing through the battery, and was unable to extricate his foot from one of his stirrup-irons, which was over-pressed by his horse's dead body. His sword was discoloured with blood, and that this sight may have inspired the cruel ire of his assailant. But a Russian officer fired every chamber of his revolver at the prostrate form of the helpless hussar. These bullets directed at his breast; any one of which would doubtless have proved fatal, but for the resistance offered by the woollen padding of his hussar jacket.

'But, as I still stood dismounted, the sight of the atrocities in front of me, gave me nerve, and steeled my beating heart. I resolved to make something like a stand. I disencumbered myself of my waist-belts and scabbard, of course retaining my sword.

'My situation seemed desperate, for no one appeared in sight but these blood-thirsty Cossacks. I had not yet been seen by them, but could hardly expect, as I stood there detached and solitary, much longer to escape their observation. I had abandoned all hope of escaping with life, though resolved to sell it dearly, when I heard behind me the "thudding" of cavalry, and to my infinite and indescribable relief, I discovered it was the good old 8th.

'The regiment was led by Colonel Shewell; Troop Sergeant-Major Harrison was leading a riderless grey mare, in the belief that she might presently prove of use. He reined in close to me and cried, "Come on, my boy, mount her!" I needed but slight instigation, and contrived, wounded as I was, to scramble into the saddle; it was by the side of "Old Bags" [Harrison] that I continued to advance with the 8th Royal Irish Hussars.

'We had not ridden fifty yards under a now slackening fire, when we became aware of stragglers mounted and dismounted, badly disabled, making their way past us, as best they might, in the direction of our lines.

'We had to exercise considerable caution, for the valley was strewn with the helpless wounded, the dying, and the dead.

'It was about this time that some alert individual observed a body of lancers ranged across the valley in our rear, thus interposed between us and the British lines. In the excitement that prevailed, many mistook them for our own 17th. "Hurrah, the 17th Lancers!" But a more careful regard revealed the grey-coated Russian. "My God! cut off!"

'We were now halted by Colonel Shewell, who quickly decided upon his course of action; and gave the word "8th Hussars right about wheel," a manoeuvre which was completed as steadily as on a peace parade. "We must break through those men; keep together, and follow me," he commanded. The Russian cavalry remained stationary, until we had nearly reached them at the highest rate of speed we could attain; and, as if astounded by our determined rush, allowed one flank to fall back; though many of us had to break through their dense and deep formation. They offered but half-hearted opposition; as we cleared them, and flew free, they commenced a pursuit; but by no means one of set purpose. I found myself separated in the rush from my friends of the 8th, and was then singled out by half a dozen lancers, who kept me employed at my best in parrying their points; thus urging me to use all my efforts to encourage the pace of the mare. She went with a splendid stride, and I began to leave my pursuers behind. A few bullets raised the dust about her hoofs, but she escaped unhurt.

'Some good fellows assisted me to dismount, for my right leg was now stiff and useless; but when I reached the ground I contrived to get in front of that grey mare's head, and I kissed her on the nose. I rested at full length upon the ground, near the side of Lieutenant Trevelyan of "Ours"; indeed I belonged to his troop. He was hors de combat from a wound very similar to mine, a bullet having passed through the calf of his left leg. He very generously handed me his haversack, and invited me to partake of its contents.

'I must not quit that terrible North Valley without recording my admiring sense of the splendid service rendered to the Light Brigade, by the French Generals of Cavalry, Morris, and D'Allonville, with their magnificent squadrons of the Chasseurs d'Afrique. These gallant horsemen silenced the batteries and infantry on the Fedioukine ridges, and compelled the enemy to withdraw.'[22]

Private John Charles Purvis, 11th Hussars

'Scutari Hospital, December 11, 1854

'My dear Brother - I dare say by this time you have seen that I have been wounded severely. I must tell you the nature of my wound. It was a canister shot through between the two bones of the lower part of the left leg, about six inches above the ankle; one of the bones was quite shattered, and amputation found to be necessary. It was taken off in the temporary hospital we had in Balaclava. I was sent aboard ship that evening...

'Off we went, tearing towards destruction. The round shot came first killing many poor fellow. One most wonderfully came past my shoulder, striking my rear-rank man right in the chest. Onward we went. I could see the shell bursting over our heads, and hear the grape and canister hissing through us. The cross-fire was murderous – a square of infantry and guns with grape and canister pelting through us and shelling from the opposite heights. But I felt or feared nothing – a sort of wildness came over me, and I seemed to care not where I went or what I did, onward still. The First Line had retired, the guns were silenced, and retiring behind a large horde of Cossacks, they formed a front, but would not stand our charge, but galloped through guns and everything.

'We cut down the gunners and literally took the whole lot. The Cossacks came out by twos and threes, and kept firing away at us from their long pieces. We looked anxiously round for a support, when we perceived what we considered the 17th Lancers a good distance in the rear of us. "Hurra, my boys," sung out our brave Colonel Douglas, "let's give them another charge; the 17th will be up then, and we'll take [the] guns home with us." "Come on lads," said Lord Paget, colonel of the 4th Lights. I could find myself as excited as possible singing out "Come on boys;" anything is preferable to sitting quietly and being shot at. At last someone gave the alarm that it was a large body of Russian lancers formed up to cut our retreat. "There's no help for it," said Lord George Paget, "we must retire and cut our way through them as well as we can." We went threes about, and went calmly to the rear. They did not attempt to cross our front, but attacked our right flank and rear. I was pretty near the right flank, and of course, retiring in the rear rank.

'I had allowed my horse to flag a little, when one of the gentlemen came to attack me with his lance at a slanting position, and was making a poke for my back; I wheeled round in the saddle, parried his lance, and gave him a second rear point to the left of his right shoulder, which I expect will spoil his lancing for some time. I was quite chuckling to myself over this affair, when we came to the horrid fire again. I had not gone far through till I got a rap in the leg as if from a sledge hammer. I looked down and saw the blood gushing from a good-sized hole. "Now then, old horse" – he had carried me well through the campaign – save my life now. I had seen all over the field four or five Cossacks spiking any poor fellow who was down. I kept the right spur at work, and galloped a mile or more, when I began to get quite blind and faint.

'Old Cardigan was sitting, with the tears almost in his eyes, when he saw his smart brigade so cut up. Our fellows cheered him, when he said, "You must not think, men, that this is one of my mad-brained actions; I would have given almost anything rather than it had happened."

'I moved forward and asked to be taken to the rear; I was hurried off to the doctor (the assistant), who had a lot of our officers and men in the nice green ditch of a vineyard, where we could lie up the slope. I had lost a tremendous deal of blood, and one of the officers gave me a good swig of brandy out of his flask. The doctor stopped the bleeding, and we had to wait some time for the ambulance, which came at last, and took us off to the hospital.'[23]

Private John Richardson, 11th Hussars

'Every private soldier could see what a mistake was being made; but all we had to do was to obey orders. The order came. "Trot, gallop, charge;" and Lord Cardigan – he was a rough spoken man, sir, was Lord Cardigan, but good-hearted – he shouts, "Give em the points lads; it's no use slashing at em." And he was right because they all wore those long thick ulsters.

'The enemy were amazed. They thought we were followed by our army. There was a lot of smoke about, and I couldn't see much. I remember after we got among the artillery and came to the hand-to-hand work, my horse was killed, and fell with me under him. I struggled from under my horse, and used my musket [sic], reloading as fast as I could. I received a couple of lance wounds from the Cossacks. I fought my way from among the guns, and then set out to return to the British line on foot. It was all over ploughed fields, and the Russians kept on firing on us all the time. A couple of Cossacks intercepted me on the way, and I settled both with my carbine. They were big cowards, the Cossacks. You had only to point a gun at them, and whether it was loaded or not, they would run.

'There were 160 [*sic*] in my regiment when we rode out, but only 23 [*sic*] of us ever got back. If the Russians had only known what a handful of men we were, they could have cut us all to mincemeat.

'At the roll-call after it was all over, he [Cardigan] said it was certain that "every man who rode in that charge *would be provided for*".'[24]

Sergeant-Major George Loy Smith, 11th Hussars

'The trumpets now sounded the advance. The 13th and 17th moved off, and we, the 11th, were ordered to support them. As soon as they, the First Line, had advanced about 100 yards, we moved off, soon breaking into a gallop, but did not actually cover the 17th the whole way down, consequently we swept down the valley, much nearer the Fedioukine Hills than any other regiment. As we moved off [*sic*] the Russians opened fire from all their batteries, the round shot passed through us, and the shells burst over and amongst us, causing great havoc.

'The first man of my troop that was struck was Private Young [Richard Albert Young], a cannonball taking off his right arm, I being close on his right rear, fancied I felt the wind from it as it passed me, I afterwards found I was bespattered with his flesh. Before we had advanced many hundred yards Private Turner's [George Turner] left arm was also struck off close to the shoulder, and Private Ward [David Ward] was struck full in the chest, a shell too burst over us, a piece of which struck Cornet Houghton [Lieutenant George Powell Houghton] in the forehead.

'When Private Young lost his arm, he coolly fell back and asked me what he was to do, I replied: "Turn your horse about and get to the rear as fast as you can." I had scarcely done speaking to him when Private Turner fell back.

'We now came under a terrific fire, for the infantry in and about the Redoubts kept up a continual fusillade as we came opposite to them; but the men hung well together, keeping their line and closing in, as their comrades fell wounded or killed. Many riderless horses were now galloping along with us, forcing their way up into the ranks, and keeping their places as though their masters had been on their backs, many of these horses belonged to the First Line, for we now frequently met with their lifeless bodies. I was particularly struck with one of the 17th Lancers lying on his face with his arms stretched out, and a short distance from his right hand was his lance with the pole broken.

'When about a hundred yards in rear Colonel Douglas halted us. During the advance Lieutenant Trevelyan and Cornet Houghton had fallen out, being wounded, the latter mortally. Regimental Sergeant-Major [George] Bull, Trumpeters [William] Smith and [Joseph John] Keates had their horses killed or wounded, so that the only leader in front of the right squadron was Troop

Sergeant-Major Trevan [Patrick Rourke Teevan]; Sergeant-Major Joseph [Sergeant John Joseph] and I were the only two left as serrafiles. It now became my particular duty (the Regimental Sergeant-Major's horse having been wounded) to note every word of command the Colonel should give, as I now considered the Regimental Sergeant-Major's duty devolved on me. After halting, the word was "close in on the centre," so that the squadron interval was filled up. During the advance, which had not taken many minutes, we had lost, as near as I could calculate, about 50 men, so that we had about 80 left. I am sure we had quite this number from what I witnessed afterwards.

'Lord Paget at this moment galloped up to our right flank. Colonel Douglas seeing him, called out, "What are we to do now, Lord Paget?" He replied, "Where is Lord Cardigan?" and galloped away. Colonel Douglas, seeing that there was no time to lose, having no order to retire, and expecting every moment that we should be charged by this body of Cavalry in our front, called out, "Give them another charge men, Hurrah."

'Waving our swords over our heads, on we galloped, expecting the next minute to be amongst them, but to our surprise, when not more than 20 yards off, they wheeled about and galloped away in front of us, we, shouting and feeling rather amused, for they were 20 to one, there not being at this time more than about 80 of us, the Eleventh, left.

'After galloping a short distance, on looking round, I saw one of the guns some distance to our right being taken away; it was a large brass gun with carriage painted green, drawn by six horses, there were only three men, and [a] driver with it. Feeling that it had escaped from the battery, and knowing that the 4th Light Dragoons had possession, I at once formed the resolution to retake it, so seeing three men riding independently in the rear, they having just been crushed out, I called to them to follow me, saying, "Let us take this gun." I at once galloped off, [and] when within a short distance of it I saw a Hussar Officer and 3 Cossacks, who had detached themselves from the main body for its protection, and were coming rapidly between me and my regiment. On looking round I found I was alone, that the three men had not followed me as I expected. Feeling it would be madness to attempt the capture single-handed, I instantly halted, turned about and galloped off in the direction of my regiment. The first Cossack and the officer hesitated, calling out to the other two who were a little distance in their rear. This hesitation enabled me to rejoin my comrades. If there had been any other troops, either of ours or the Russians, any distance in rear of the guns at this time, I should have seen them for I went beyond the left flank of the battery.

'As I galloped up to the regiment, I noticed one of the 17th Lancers in our right squadron; his was the only flag that waved either with us or the cavalry we were pursuing, the Cossacks having no lance flags. I afterwards learnt there was one of the 13th Light Dragoons there as well. His name was Nicholson [Private William Nicholson], beyond these and one or two stragglers that joined us on our way back, we were not in any way mixed up at any time with any other part of the Brigade.

'We were now nearing the extreme end of the valley, about a mile and a half from our position, still pursuing this body of Cavalry.

'I looked anxiously round hoping to see our supports coming to our assistance, when instead I saw a body of Lancers in the act of forming across our rear; they must have formed the reserve, for they were out of sight when we passed down; they appeared to come out of the road leading to the Tractir Bridge which is between hills. I at once knew they were Russians by their lance flags, they being green and white. I inwardly said to myself, "none of us have many more minutes to live." Colonel Douglas at this moment caught sight of these Lancers, and supposing them to be our 17th, shouted out "Rally, men on the 17th Lancers." Someone immediately replied, "It is the Russian Lancers, Sir;" he, Colonel Douglas, shouted "Then fight for your lives."

'It was with great reluctance that the men turned their backs on those they had so lately been pursuing; at last one or two turned, then the remainder started off at a gallop to break through the squadrons of Lancers that barred our way. All order was now lost, we no longer resembled the steady line we had done in passing over the same ground a few minutes before and we assumed an oval shape, the best horses in front. Many men whose horses had been wounded, others whose horses were fagged and could not keep up, were taken and killed, for the Russian hussars were now pursuing us, and shouting "Bussu, bussu, English," so that we were driven onto the line of lancers in our front. I at this time was riding on the right rear, when turning and looking over my right shoulder, I saw several Russian officers leading their squadrons close to me; I at once formed the right rear guard, expecting to be attacked.

'We were driven on till about two hundred yards from the lancers; the Hussars then halted, and as it were handed us over to the lancers, who were waiting steadily for us, with their lances at the carry, instead of charging us as they ought to have done. This was the third time this day that I had seen the Russian Cavalry remain halted when they should have charged.

'I was about 50 yards in front of their right squadron, and on the right of our body, so drawing my reins a little shorter, and taking a firmer grip on the saddle, and clenching my teeth, I prepared to break through saying to myself, "I will go through here or fall!" At the same time fixing my eyes on the part of the squadron I intended to try to break through. When but a short distance from them, and expecting the next minute to have a lance or two through me, to my astonishment, the right squadron, went about, wheeled to the right, halted and fronted with the greatest precision, as though they had been on parade, their lances still on the carry. I now galloped along their front, looking at them as though I had been inspecting them; when near the centre of the squadron, I heard the leader give a word of command, in a moment their lances came to the guard, and they galloped on to our flank, then began a hand-to-hand fight, many of our men being killed.

'I, however, got past, and was congratulating myself, when the Russian Artillery opened fire on us. I now felt my horse limp. Sergeant-Major Joseph who was riding near me, said, "Smith, your horse's leg is broken." Feeling there was no time to be lost, I immediately dropped my reins, drew my feet out of the stirrups, and jumped clear out of the saddle, my horse falling at the same moment at her near side.

'Without hesitation I commenced running, our men passing me galloping for their lives, some saying "Come along Sergeant-Major" but no one could assist me, it being every man for himself. Fearing I should get knocked down if I kept up the same track the mounted men were going, I inclined to the left; in another minute I noticed that all the mounted men that had escaped had passed me and were fast disappearing. I was now about a mile from our position, so on I sped, sword in hand, still keeping well up the left side of the valley. I now found, that I could not be far from a square of infantry, for the bullets showered around me, sometimes striking the ground and driving the dust over me. The ordeal was something frightful, for I expected every moment to be struck.

'Presently I heard galloping, on looking round I saw the Russian lancers about eighty yards in my rear; and two men of my regiment about the same distance, running on my right rear; feeling they were in pursuit of us, I resolved to sell my life as dearly as possible. On looking round again I saw them circle to the right and meet the two men; when close in front of them, I saw their lances go down, both must have been killed.

'After a little time, I saw one of the 17th in front of me, I sped on. When I got near I found he was an officer, and wore his forage cap, much to my surprise. When within a few yards of him, I said, "this is warm work, sir," he looked round at me over his right shoulder but made no reply, his face was covered with blood. This officer was Captain Morris [Captain William Morris] who led the 17th Lancers, and behaved so gallantly.

'I now inclined to my right. When in the centre of the valley I halted, and listened attentively for bullets; not hearing any, I began to feel that I had escaped, so returned my sword, and took out of my haversack a little India rubber bottle that had a little rum in it and took a small quantity of it.

'Three of our riderless horses came to me. When the third came up [I] rode quickly on.

'As I neared the rear of my regiment I heard them numbering off, and someone said, "Number off, Sergeant-Major," so I called out 63, as 62 was the last number I heard. It is evident that the 11th was the last regiment, and I was the last man that returned up the valley [sic]. I then formed up with about half a dozen dismounted men in the rear.

'Colonel Douglas now came round, and ordered me to march the dismounted men down to the encampment, mount them on any spare horses I could find, and bring them back. On arriving at the encampment I found that all the horses left there had been wounded by the Cossacks.

'I found the orderly-room clerk; he shook hands with me, saying, "how glad I am you have escaped, George." I told him I had lost my horse, and how fearfully the regiment had been cut up, he then said – "what is this on your busby and jacket," on picking it off I found it to be small pieces of flesh that had flown over me when Private Young's arm had been shot off. I now sat down, and the feelings that came over me are not easy to describe, I was moved to tears when I thought of the havoc I had witnessed.

'As dusk drew on the remnant of the 11th returned to the camp. I then assembled the men of my troop and called roll: one-half were missing – 6 being killed, 10 wounded, and 2 were made prisoners; 3 of the 10 lost their right arms, and one his left, he died three days after, another his left leg, he died at Scutari; of the two prisoners one died in Russia of his wounds, the other returned, having lost a leg. Twenty-four horses were killed, and five wounded, two so severely that they had to be destroyed the following day. Captain Cook was wounded, and had his horse killed.'[25]

Smith was nominated to the Medaille Militaire by a decree dated the 6 March 1861. The citation reads: 'Recommended by the vote of his comrades, who with himself returned from the Crimea previous to the first issue of the French Medal. Served until the 25th January 1856 and was present at the battles of the Alma, Balaclava and Inkerman. Horse shot under him at Balaclava, where he behaved gallantly.'

Private William Staden, 11th Hussars

'Very soon the shot and shell that were poured in upon us began to have a visible effect on our number, weakening the lines to an alarming extent. Our lines were literally cut through by the enemy's firing, and I witnessed twelve horses fall at one time by cannon-shot.

'There was not much time to think; the command had come upon us suddenly, and we were ready to do or die. At every stride saddles were being emptied, or horses were shot from under the men. Many of the men who had been dismounted and wounded got ridden over; for in the exciting Charge this could not be helped. In that fatal ride no description could properly convey the awful sight that was presented. We were galloping as fast as our horses could go to keep in line together; and during the time it took to reach the [end of the] valley, which was about a mile and a quarter in length, where the guns were stationed, you had not much thought of anything around you.

'As we rode down the valley I overheard no conversation pass between the men; I believe the officers gave words of command, but in the din and confusion nothing definitely could be heard. The trumpets sounded the Charge, and after this the officers' or anyone's orders could not be heard unless you were close to them. The only thing was, to look before you to see what there was to do.

'Directly we got to the guns we found that we were a mixed company; but I believe the 8th Hussars kept their line all through. Men were pushing eagerly forward in their anxiety to go to the front. As soon as we reached the guns we killed many gunners, and afterwards attacked the Russian cavalry, who gave way.

'Some of the Light Brigade pursued them for some distance towards [the] Tchernaya Bridge [Chernaya], but these poor fellows never returned [*sic*]. Of course, those of our men who went after the cavalry were all killed [*sic*], for they had no chance with nearly the whole of the Russian army, who were behind the guns, upon them.

'We held the guns for a time, but were soon ordered to return, or there would have been but few of us left. We retired as best we could, mixing ourselves up in other regiments; and to the noble Chasseurs d'Afrique we owe a good deal, for they charged the Russian Horse Artillery, who were on the left of us as we went down the valley, and drove them away, so that, on returning, we had not to run the risk of their deadly shot. By this means many lives were saved. When we returned from where we started, our hearts were almost too full to speak. It was a sad cut-up for us to see so many poor fellows missing, and many anxious inquiries were made after comrades, for there was such a sprinkle of us who had returned.'[26]

Private Edward Richard Woodham, 11th Hussars

'I imagined I observed some of the officers protesting against the order. We advanced a short distance at a walking pace. The man next to me was named Wootten [Private George Wootton], and when the order was given to move, he says to me, "Ted, old fellow, I know we shall charge." I recollect looking round and replying, "Oh nonsense! Look at the strength in front of us. We're never going to charge there."

'Presently we got into a gallop, and then all was excitement. I remember looking at poor Wootten and saying, "Yes, we're going to charge, and with a vengeance, too." We increased in speed at every stride, and went down the valley at a terrific rate. He was shot down almost instantly, and I had the melancholy duty of reporting his death to his bereaved widow and family.

'The scene that presented itself as we proceeded was indescribable; from all sides the bullets came flying, and many a man had his arm shot off, while our gallant comrades were falling from their horses in all directions. A battery on our right was firing shell, but we were galloping at such a pace that we had time to get away before the shells burst, and of course that, in a great measure, saved many of us from being wounded or killed.

'As soon as we reached the guns the men began dodging by getting under them, and for a time they defended with the rammers; but it was no contest – they had no chance with us, and we cut them down like ninepins. Of course we captured the battery and many of our men dismounted to spike the guns.

'We had no hammers, but drove the spikes in with the hilt of our swords or our hands — in any way we could.

'Near to the end of the valley my horse was shot under me, and it fell with my left leg under it, so that I could not move. A corporal of the 13th Light Dragoons rode up and commenced pulling at my horse's head. The animal gave a bit of a struggle, which I took advantage of, and regained my feet. All then was smoke and confusion, and all of our men that I could see were cutting right and left, and making their way back to camp.

'I began running away as hard as I could, when a soldier belonging to the 8th Hussars, who was lying under his horse shouted; to me, "For God's sake, man, don't leave me here." At this time the firing from the guns was incessant — indeed it was murderous; still I returned and strove hard to release him, but without effect, the horse being dead. The enemy at this time were coming up the valley, and killing the wounded on their march, so I said to the man, "It's no use my stopping here; we shall both be killed." I then reluctantly left him to his fate, and joined three or four of my comrades who, like myself, had been unhorsed, and were trying to escape on foot. We threw away everything that in the least encumbered us; even our busbies – in fact, we retained nothing except our sword-blades.

'The enemy, seeing us together, concentrated a heavy fire upon us; and, in order that the gunners might direct their attention to something else, we lay flat down, and they did not pursue us further. Shortly afterwards I espied a riderless horse, belonging to the 17th Lancers, which I succeeded in capturing by seizing hold of its bridle, and mounting it, I rode at full gallop to the top of the valley.

'The valley presented a fearful scene at this time. Our poor fellows lay moaning and groaning everywhere, but with the greater number the bullets had told their tale. Those who had escaped were making their way, some on foot and some mounted, with wounded and limping horses. All those who were able at once formed, and it was a dreadful sight to see the havoc that had been made.'[27]

Private Thomas Wroots, 11th Hussars

'Just after we started my mare got pushed out of the line. I cried out, "Let me come up - let me come up." Just then the Russians commenced firing, and in half a second there was room enough for an omnibus to come up.

'I was near a man named Morton ['Morton' remains unidentified]. He was wounded in the right arm, and the pain was so great that he shrieked out fearfully. Another man near me was shot in the left side, and I should think he rode fifty yards, then all at once he tumbled to his left and came down on the ground like a lump of clay. His charger, like many others, galloped away.

'There was too much confusion to say what did take place at the guns. You may depend upon it we had to do something, or else not a soul of us ever would have got away. Some of the horses without riders held back, some went forward like mad, and some followed us right in.

'I recollect in our retreat hearing Lord George Paget say, "For God's sake, 11th and 4th, do halt, and show them a front" — that is when they were peppering us from the right and left. Someone said, "There's the lancers; let us go and form on them, and we will show them a good front." In place of that it turned out to be a Polish regiment of lancers. We got near them, but they did not seem to stir. I saw one fellow, however, run up behind one of our sergeants — I think his name was Hudson [Corporal Edward Hudson] – and catch him right in the middle of the back with his lance; the ambulance brought him in afterwards, but he soon died.

'I saw the captain of the lancers quite plain. He said something to his men, and they all turned threes right, and took up their places. It was then that their own artillery fired into them. We got past them. We were "beauties," being covered with blood, dirt, and grime when we got back again. Every man that [General] Cruikshank, one of our officers, met, he gave a glass of grog to.'[28]

13th Light Dragoons

George Badger, 13th Light Dragoons

'A comrade named Williams [Private George Williams or Private Thomas Joseph Williams] remarked, "We are going to have some warm work." I replied, "Yes, especially if we are going down there (pointing down the valley). See that line of guns staring at us, and look at those two guns unlimbering on our left."

216

'Lord Cardigan gave orders to the trumpeter, who sounded, "Stand to your horses," "Mount," "Draw swords," "Walk", "Trot", "Gallop", and "Charge". Comparatively few, however, heard the actual "Charge" sounded, on account of the deafening roar of the guns.

'Captain Nolan was right in front of us and was the first to fall. As he was struck he fell backwards. The involuntary pull which he gave the reins caused his horse to swerve right round and face us. The animal went off a little to the left or I should have been right against Captain Nolan. After the horse had gone a few paces its rider fell.

'As we charged down the valley the Russians rained grape and canister upon us – a perfect leaden hail. Three men on my left and two on my right were swept out of their saddles, and I received a wound. We continued the death ride, men falling thick and fast around, and the officers continually calling to the men to "Close in."

'At times we could not see the guns for smoke. Just as we got in front of them it was [then] that a piece of shell struck me on the side. We were now close to the guns.

'Some of the Russian gunners refused to budge an inch, and died fighting at their post, while others slipped, some under the guns, and some under horses, to avoid the fury of our onslaught.

'I was "pointing" at a Russian and had dropped my man, when I was attacked by one of his comrades, and, before I could recover my guard, the point of the sword entered my left side, between the ribs, but just in the nick of time one of our own men [a 4th Light Dragoon] cut my assailant down. It was lucky for me that he did.

'[The columns of Russians in the rear then rushed on us and we had to make the best of our way back, the Russians still keeping up the heavy fire. (*Shrewsbury Chronicle*, 15 January 1904.)]

'A miracle it was indeed how any of us came back from the Death Valley. I was the last man to return [*sic*]. The Russians, thinking to cut every one of us off, had sent a detachment to cut off our return.

'When a little distance from the guns a heavy shot struck my horse in the fore-quarters, and he fell while galloping, and in coming to earth I hurt my neck. There was a heavy musketry fire from the enemy in the redoubts, and balls whistled past my ears and dropped at my feet. On my right I saw Major Oldham [Captain John Augustus Oldham] resting his head on his elbow. He beckoned to me, and held out something that he wished me to take – a watch and chain and purse, and I was making towards him to see what I could do for him when a bullet struck him, and he fell back.

'As one of the 13th Light Dragoons rode by I caught hold of a stirrup iron of the saddle, but not being able to run along quickly enough, I was compelled to let go. The mounted men managed to get out of the [battle] field, dead and wounded men and horses being alone left behind.

'I saw a body of Russian lancers approaching from the top of the valley, and one of these made a point at the man whose stirrup iron I had to let go. I knew I had to run the gauntlet, and I managed to get under the hill on which was one of the redoubts. There I stayed till the Russian lancers came up, and then the firing from the redoubts ceased. Their lancers stopped when they reached Major Oldham, and while their doctor was examining him, I seized my opportunity to get away.

'I made for the top of the valley. Where I met Lord Cardigan, who, pulling up his horse, said, "Anyone else coming out of the valley?" and I replied, "No, I'm the last." "My man, are you badly wounded?" he asked, and I replied "No." He told me to go to the commissariat and get some liquor, as he thought I required it, and turning round he galloped off. I was admitted into the regimental hospital, and afterwards into the general hospital.'[29]

Cornet Denzil Thomas Chamberlayne, 13th Light Dragoons
'I received a lance thrust in the stomach from the right, which fortunately missed me, but broke my cap pouch and ripped up my revolver case. I also received a sword cut on the arm, but felt it very lightly, as I shot the Russian dragoon through the head when his arm was raised. My poor charger Pimento was shot through two places in the flank with Minié balls [sic], and one through the body on our retiring. He was only just able to carry me out of the range of the enemy's batteries when he fell to rise no more. The enemy's cavalry was in immense force. I had very many hairbreadth escapes. Returning was the worst part of the business. I was nearly the last out of about 35 that started together to return, but I only saw nine when we got out of range. Men and horses fell like nine-pins; it was an awful sight.'[30]

Private Joseph Doughton, 13th Light Dragoons
'When we came within five hundred yards of their Artillery, which had been hurling destruction upon us, we were in fact encircled and surrounded by a blaze of fire from all directions, in addition to the fire from the Russian Riflemen.

'We entered the Batteries [sic], cutting down the whole of the Russian Artillerymen, a portion having crept under the limbers of their guns for protection, but were shot by our Carbines: the remnant of our little band, which was then reduced to about 400 in strength, dashed through a mass of Russian Cavalry, 5,200 strong. Having broke through that mass, we came threes about, and returned in the same manner, doing as much execution as we could to the enemy's cavalry. We were completely surrounded by a massive Russian army, but they could not stand against the fury of our Charge, and they fled in all directions.

'On our return from the guns we were exposed to the same fire as we were going down. On nearing the summit of the hill, I received a gun shot through the right elbow joint, and also three lance stabs in my body: immediately after, my horse was shot from under me near to the same place that Captain Nolan fell going down. I was then left on foot, to get off the field as best I could.

'On nearing the English lines, I got a horse belonging to the 11th Hussars. With the assistance of a comrade, I was soon upon its back, and on my way to the hospital at Balaclava, where I remained till 5 o'clock the same afternoon; when I was put on board Her Majesty's ship *Australia*, for Scutari, where I arrived on the 30th of October.'[31]

Lieutenant Edward Lennox Jervis, 13th Light Dragoons

'On we went, the Lancers shaking their lances and waving them in the air like madmen, and all the time Cardigan bang in front, for all the world riding as if he were going down the park. And by this [time] the grape-shot was tearing holes in us. One of our seniors [Captain Oldham] was on a white horse, a rather curious mount, and he was literally blown up [*sic*] at this stage, so we found no trace of him afterwards.

'Once among the guns, gunners and Blue Hussars fled, but as we pulled around, a body of infantry stopped the way and some of the cavalry came up. However, they opened ranks to let us pass, yet we were soon mixed up again, and our fellows were now few and far between. One of my troopers for a moment confused the black and white Russian flags with the old Seventeenth's, and paid dearly for it. Then the guns on our left opened on the lot of us, Russians and all, and my mare's hock was shot away. I managed to catch another horse myself, although one of my brave fellows [Private William Gardiner] brought me one immediately. For that he got the Sardinian medal. The Chasseurs d'Afrique ere this had charged on our left flank to our assistance, and of course helped us materially in being able to ride safely back.'[32]

Private Robert Martin, 13th Light Dragoons

Several of us had our right arms shattered in an instant almost passing the Russian riflemen on our left. A man in front of me was blown to pieces. I turned to a comrade who was riding on my right to ask him to take my sword knot off, and just as I spoke to him his horse was killed under him. He got another horse, and that was also killed under him, but, strange to say, he came out of the affair without a scratch. When we went down at the guns, there was a terrible confusion, all the different regiments being mixed up.

'I got my medal for distinguished conduct in this way – A man named Glanister [Private James Glanister, 11th Hussars] made a cut at a Russian with his sword. The weapon broke off close to the hilt, and the blade flew up in the air. Just then a Cossack rode up to our left, and drawing his pistol aimed it at us. The bullet passed my face and caught Glanister in the jaw, carrying away the lower part of his face. He fell, face down on his cloak in front of him.

'Lord Paget then came up, and, holding up his sword, called out "Rally, men, get together as well as you can and retire." Putting the reins of my own horse in my mouth, I caught hold with my left hand of the reins of his horse, and turned it round to retire. Glanister was lying quite helpless, and his horse got into the ranks of his own regiment and brought him out.'[33]

Another version places the same events in a slightly different chronological order:

'Glanister [James Glanister] had unfortunately broken his sword off at the hilt by striking a Russian on the top of his helmet. The order to retire was then given by Lord George Paget, and on my turning I perceived a Cossack close to us. He immediately levelled his pistol and fired at Glanister and myself. The ball whizzed past my face and struck Glanister, shattering his under-jaw and causing him to fall forward on his cloak, which was rolled up in front of him. The Cossack bolted at once and I had the presence of mind to grasp the reins of my horse and put them in my mouth – at the same time seizing those of Glanister's horse and turning it into the ranks – by this means his life was no doubt saved.

'It was now every man for himself. I galloped back with the remnant of my regiment, and passed through the Polish lancers, who had formed across our line of retreat. I was now beginning to feel faint from loss of blood, and urged my horse at its utmost speed to get out of range of fire, but a bullet struck my ammunition pouch. The next thing I remember was being held up by an officer and his administering some rum to me which had the effect of bringing me round. I was then assisted off my horse, placed on a stretcher, and carried to the rear.

'My arm was afterwards amputated and I was sent to Scutari Hospital.'[34]

Private Henry Dyson Naylor, 13th Light Dragoons

'The men on the right and left of me did not believe that we were going to attack the enemy in front of us, but soon they found out that we were; poor fellows; for that was their last [battle] field. Both were killed [as] the shot and shell flew like hail about us, our line began to get terribly thin by this time. My horse began to limp and I could not manage him. My off reins were cut in two. I managed to tie them. I received a stinging sensation about my left shoulder. I got to the guns and passed through and got a tremendous blow with a sponge staff as I passed through.

'Then it was our turn. We drove the enemy into the River Tchernaya [Chernaya]; at this time we had lost all formation; it was everyone for himself. I was very near making a mistake in joining the enemy's Lancers but I saw my mistake in time. We were completely hemmed in by them and I was bleeding from two wounds myself and some men of the brigade dashed back again, I got to the guns when my horse fell down dead giving me a nice toss of his head; how I got from the guns it must have been a miracle, as the Cossacks were lancing our poor fellows all round.

'The agony of my wounds by this time began to tell on me, my lower jaw shattered and wounded in my left shoulder. I saw the surgeon of my regiment half way up the valley he got off his horse and put me on [it] and took me to the ambulance cart.

'The gallant Chasseurs d'Afrique did gallant service for us, they took and spiked the battery that was on our left. My regiment went in 125 men and 39 answered to the roll call.'[35]

A second version of events reads:

'A minute afterwards my bridle reins were cut by a shot, and my horse tore away with me. I found myself near to Lord Cardigan, who said, "What are you doing here?" I replied, "My reins are cut, sir." After the first onslaught my horse was shot under me and galloped nearly 100 yards before she fell. It might have been the same shell that struck me. My jaw and shoulder were broken, and I lay among the [wounded, there being a] heap around me till I was helped up. Four or five of us hobbled away out of "the fire".'

'Once only during the slaughter in front of the Russian guns did Private Naylor feel in peril of his life in combat, and this was in a hand-to-hand sword contest with a Russian officer, whom he finally cut down. The wounds received in the Charge were so serious that Naylor had to be sent home, the most painful injury being that caused by a blow from a cannon rammer, which struck him on the loins, and caused him pain until his death, which was due largely to the effects of the wounds.'[36]

17th Lancers

Troop Sergeant-Major William Barker, 17th Lancers
In a letter addressed to Lord Cardigan, and presumably to be used in his defence in the Calthorpe case, Barker wrote the following:

'I remember seeing, after your Lordship had led the attack, the whole length of the valley under a tremendous fire from the whole of the enemy's guns; that your Lordship was the first to enter the battery, the officers and men following your Lordship, and taking possession of the battery by cutting down and spearing the artillerymen at their guns, amidst a deadly fire from the enemy's flank batteries, and from a large body of infantry formed in the left rear of the battery, causing death and destruction all around.

'And, in consequence of the loss of officers as leaders and the ranks having to open out, so as to clear the guns, limber-carriages, etc., in the battery, the men became scattered, and all order lost, it being an impossibility to rally any number of men.

'I observed, after your Lordship had cleared the battery, and failed in restoring order, again dash forward, followed by about twenty or thirty men of both regiments mixed up together, and come in contact with a strong force of the enemy's cavalry advancing up the valley, at about two hundred yards in rear of the battery, when a hand-to-hand conflict ensued; but the men, seeing at once that there was no chance of success, turned their horses about and endeavoured to retire. I galloped away to the left, and came up to your Lordship as your Lordship, with sword in hand, was valorously resisting the attack, and putting to flight three or four of the enemy's Cossacks, a couple of squadrons of the enemy's cavalry advancing from their right flank across the valley at the same time, apparently with the intention of cutting off our retreat, your Lordship retiring at an easy canter up the valley under a fearful fire from all arms.

'I continued to ride near to your lordship to the end of the valley, your lordship halting frequently to make inquiries of the wounded. I wish to add that I am prepared to swear that when your Lordship retired, and I followed you from the battery, that no part of the Light Brigade was advancing, but had already advanced and passed the flanks of the battery.'[37]

Private Arthur Berkleman, 17th Lancers

'When halfway across the plain, the narrator [Berkleman] saw fire belch forth from the cannon in front, while thinking that the Russians had also cannon on the right and left, which opened up a cross-fire, soon after which a piece of shell hit his horse's chest, and he lay there for some time stunned.

'When he recovered he found his comrades had gone, and looking around saw the Cossacks busy and riderless horses everywhere, and with prostrated men on every side. He went to catch a horse and a cannon ball knocked the dust up at his feet.

'He caught a horse and when mounting him two Cossacks went for him. He kept them on the right, and one, the more daring, rushed him and the narrator's lance went right through his body and nearly unseated him. They were recalled, and though it was considered presumption for 600 men [sic] to tackle 35,000 [sic] their end had been accomplished, though with great sacrifice, for when they mustered there was only a handful [sic] of the gallant band remaining.

Others had been mown down by the relentless fire of the enemy. The narrator came out without a scratch. The narrator was attentively listened to and much applauded.'[38]

Berkleman gave a speech at an event in Windsor, New South Wales, stating his horse was killed by a shell fragment and he was knocked unconscious, recovered and caught a horse.

Roy Dutton in his *Forgotten Heroes* quotes a newspaper report of unknown origin (but believed to be from one circulating in the Canterbury area of New Zealand around May/June of 1890) and found in a 'scrap-book' formerly belonging to James W. Wightman of the 17th Lancers:

'The "Noble Six Hundred" – Now that so much painful interest has been revived in the famous "Charge of the Light Brigade", it will be interesting to learn the impressions made by that memorable affair upon one who actually took part in the Charge. We learn from the *Australian Star* that at an entertainment at Windsor, New South Wales, the other day Tennyson's poem was recited and at the close Mr M A Berilman (sic), a "Light Brigade" survivor, gave his personal experiences.

'He said that previous to the famous Charge, the Light Brigade was located adjacent to the Russian posts, and did all they could to make them commence hostilities. On the eventful morning the Russians came on and appeared to him to be in endless numbers. After various manoeuvres the order came for the Light Brigade to go at them, and all were surprised. The Six Hundred sat as firm as rocks, and had nought to do but obey the order and advance.'

Private Martin McGrath, 17th Lancers

'Poor Dick Dullan [Private Richard Dollard] was next to me in the ranks. Lord Lucan gave orders to charge the guns in front of us; we thought that was all there were, but when we got within shot of them they opened fire from about fifty guns [*sic*], thirteen of which were in front [*sic*], and the remainder on the hills at each side, so that they had a fine play at us.

'They completely blew men and horses to pieces before we knew where we were, but about fifty of us got up to their guns, and we cut the gunners all away.

'Then we were attacked by some of the cavalry, five of whom bore down on Dick Dullard and me. We killed four of them, and as Dick had his lance in the fifth, there came a shot from a twelve-pounder which swept the poor fellow's head off, so I had to make the best of my way out of that; and the next shot that was fired out of the same gun, as near as I can judge, blew away the hind quarters of my mare. Thus I was in a nice fix.

'I did not know which way to go, or the moment that I would be blown to pieces; but fortunately I got a Russian's horse, mounted him, and joined about twenty of ours and the 13th Light Dragoons. There was a line of their cavalry in front of us, so we had to cut our way through them; in doing so we lost about eight men more, and then the brutes opened fire on us again and picked down a few more. The horse that I had was struck by a ball about the eyes, and it only left a small piece of his skull and ears; the lower part of his head was completely taken away; so I was left to my legs again, and made the best of my way off the field with shot and shell whistling about me, and just as I got out, a shell burst on my right and a splinter struck me in the heel. I was obliged to lie down, and crawl on my hands and knees out of the way. That and a lance wound were all that I got, and I thought myself very lucky.

'Out of our regiment there were only thirty-five that came back safe. I never went near the doctor, and was all right in a week, ready for the next fight.'[39]

Captain The Hon. Godfrey Charles. Morgan, 17th Lancers

'We took the guns, cut up the gunners, routed the cavalry, and amid a storm of shot, found ourselves very soon surrounded on all sides by the enemy, though all that remained of us cut our way back to our position.'[40]

Private John Vahey, 17th Lancers

John Vahey spent the night of the 24th in the guard tent with Paddy Heffernan, of the Royals (who charged with the Heavy Brigade) under arrest for being drunk on duty. Awoken by the sound of cannon-fire the following morning they found the sentry absent and decided they would try to join the action, Vahey on a Russian horse.

This is Vahey's account of what transpired:

'On still, we went faster and faster as our horses got excited and warmed to their work, heedless of the torrent of shot that came tearing through us.

'Nearer and nearer we came to the dreadful battery, which kept vomiting death on us like a volcano, till I seemed to feel on my cheek the hot air from the cannon's mouth. At last we were on it. Half a dozen of us leaped in among the guns at once, and I with one blow of my butcher's axe brained a Russian gunner just as he was clapping the lintstock to the touch-hole of his artillery piece. With another I split open the head of an officer who was trying to rally the artillery detachment in the rear; and then what of us were left went smack through the stragglers, cutting and slashing like fiends, right straight at the column of cavalry drawn up behind the battery.

'They were round us like a stream of bees, and we, not more seemingly than a couple of dozen of us, were hacking and hewing away our hardest, each individual man the centre of a separate mêlée. I know I never troubled about guards myself, but kept whirling the axe about me, every now and then bringing it down to some purpose; and ever as it fell, the Ruskies gave ground a bit, only to crush denser round me a minute after. Still nothing seemed to touch me. They dursn't come to close quarters with the sword, for the axe had a devil of a long reach; and they dursn't use pistols, for they were too thick themselves.

'I'm hanged if I don't half think I should have been there till now, had I not chanced to hear above the din a trumpet from somewhere far in the rear sound "Threes about". Round I wheeled, still thrashing about me like a windmill, slap through the heart of the battery again, knocking over an artilleryman or two as I passed, and presently overtook a small batch of men of various regiments, who under Colonel Shewell of the 8th Hussars, were trying to retreat in some kind of order.

'The chances of getting back again on our own side of the valley looked very blue. The Russian cavalry were hard on our heels, and we suffered sorely from the devilish battery in our rear, which kept pelting into the thick of us, without much discrimination between friend and foe. The guns on those forts on our left were not doing us much good neither. Soon what little formation we had was knocked to pieces, and then the word was, "Every man for himself, and God help the hindmost".

'A young fellow of the 11th Hussars [Private Charles Macaulay, 8th Hussars] and myself hung together for a while, both of us trying to make the most of our blown and jaded horses; but at last down he went, his horse shot under him, and himself wounded. As the lad's busby rolled off when his head touched the ground, he gave a look up at me which went to my heart, rough as I was. God pity him, he was little more than a boy. I was out of the saddle in a twinkling, and had him across the holsters and myself in the seat again only just in time, for the damnable Cossacks were down upon us like so many wolves. Oh! he was a good plucky one, was that little Russian horse; right gamely did he struggle with the double load on his back, and hurrah! here were the heavies at last and we were safe.

'As I was riding to the rear to give the wounded man up to the doctor. I rode up to our own camp, and by and by a sergeant came and made a prisoner of me, for the crime of breaking out of the guard tent when confined thereto. The next day I was brought in front of Lord Lucan who told me, that although he had a good mind to try me by court-martial, he would let me off this time, in consideration of the use I had made of the liberty I had taken, and perhaps he would do more for me if I kept sober.'[41]

True to his word, John Vahey was later awarded the Distinguished Conduct Medal for his gallantry that day.

His account bears a striking resemblance to those of a private of the 13th Light Dragoons (believed to be Private John Keeley) recorded in an interview with Archibald Forbes in 1873 and published in his *Memories and Studies of War and Peace* (1895), and that of Private John Paine, 17th Lancers, published in a number of newspapers including the *Empire* New South Wales, 22 July 1868.

Private James William Wightman, 17th Lancers

'I belonged to the right troop of the 1st (the right) Squadron of the 17th Lancers; my squadron leader being Captain (now General) R. White, my troop leader Captain Morgan, now Lord Tredegar.

'I did not hear the "Gallop" but it was sounded. Neither voice nor trumpet, so far as I know, ordered the "Charge;" Brittain was a dead man [*sic*] in a few strides after he sounded the "Gallop."

'A body of Russian Hussars blocked our way. Morley, roaring Nottingham oaths by way of encouragement, led us straight at them, and we went through and out at the other side as if they had been made of tinsel paper. As we rode up the valley, my horse was wounded by a bullet in the shoulder, and I had hard work to put the poor beast along.

'Presently we were abreast of the Infantry who had blazed into our right as we went down; and we had to take their fire again, this time on our left. Their firing was very impartial; their own Hussars and Cossacks following close on us suffered from it as well as we.'[42]

Appendix III

Tables

The Commemorative Banquets of 1875

The Officer's Banquet

The following officers are believed to have attended the 1875 Balaclava Banquet held at Willis's Rooms, King Street, St James's, 1875 (gazetted rank 25th October 1854):

General the Earl of Lucan, Commander Cavalry Division

Colonel Lord George Augustus Frederick Paget, Commanded the Second Line

Lieutenant Colonel Edward Cooper Hodge, Commanded the 4th (Royal Irish) Dragoon Guards (Heavy Brigade)

Assistant Quartermaster General Thomas W. McMahon, 5th Dragoon Guards (Heavy Brigade)

Major George Calvert Clarke, 2nd (Royal North British) Dragoons (Heavy Brigade)

Major Robert Wardlaw, 1st Royal Dragoons (Heavy Brigade)

Captain Robert Portal, 4th Light Dragoons

Captain Edward D'Arcy Hunt, 6th (Inniskilling) Dragoon Guards (Heavy Brigade)

Lieutenant Frederick Hay Swinfen, 5th Dragoon Guards (Heavy Brigade)

Lord Tredegar, Captain The Hon. Godfrey Charles Morgan, 13th Light Dragoons

Captain Lord George Bingham, Coldstream Guards [son and], ADC to the Earl of Lucan

Lieutenant The Hon. Hedworth Hylton Jolliffe, 4th Light Dragoons

Cornet George Orby Wombwell, 17th Lancers

Lieutenant Alexander James Hardy Elliot, 5th Dragoon Guards, ADC to General Scarlett

Captain Robert White, 17th Lancers

Cornet William Mussenden, 8th Hussars

Captain Edward Fellowes, 11th Hussars

Assistant Surgeon William Richard Grylls, 19th Regiment of Foot

Cornet John Glas Sandeman, 1st Royal Dragoons (Heavy Brigade)
Lieutenant Sir William Gordon, 17th Lancers
Major C. McConnel
Captain William de Cardonnel Elmsall, 1st Royal Dragoons (Heavy Brigade)
Cornet George Gooch Clowes, 8th Hussars
Captain George Maxwell Goad, brother of Captain Thomas Howard Goad, 13th
    Light Dragoons
Assistant-Surgeon John Henry Wilkin, 11th Hussars
Captain Michael McCreagh, 4th Dragoon Guards (Heavy Brigade)
Lieutenant Edward Lennox Jervis, 13th Light Dragoons
Cornet John Stephenson Ferguson, 5th Dragoon Guards (Heavy Brigade)
Paymaster Henry Duberly, 8th Hussars
Captain Robert George Manley, 6th (Inniskilling) Dragoon Guards (Heavy Brigade)
Cornet Lennox Prendergast, 2nd (Royal North British) Dragoons (Heavy Brigade)
Cornet William Affleck King, 4th Light Dragoons
Captain Gole
Quartermaster William Scott, 1st Royal Dragoons (Heavy Brigade)
Captain George Campbell Henville Player Brigstock, 4th (Royal Irish) Dragoon
    Guards
Cornet George Warwick Hunt, 4th Light Dragoons
Surgeon James Mouat, 6th (Inniskilling) Dragoon Guards (Heavy Brigade)
    (Victoria Cross for assisting Captain Morris)
Lieutenant Francis Sutherland, 2nd (Royal North British) Dragoons (Heavy
    Brigade)
Assistant-Comptroller Murray
Mr E. Pepys
Sergeant John Atkins Pickworth, 8th Hussars
Troop Sergeant-Major Henry Harrison, 8th Hussars

The following officers were invited to attended the 1875 Balaclava Banquet
held at the Alexandra Palace (1875 ranks given):

Captain Daniel Hugh Clutterbuck (8th Hussars)
Major R. De Salis (8th Hussars)
Major Edward Lennox Jervis (13th Light Dragoons)
Colonel William Mussenden (8th Hussars)
Major General Edward Seager (8th Hussars)

Captain, the Hon. Godfrey Charles Morgan (Lord Tredegar) (17th Lancers)
Brevet-Colonel Roger William Henry Palmer (11th Hussars)
Captain Percy Shawe Smith (13th Light Dragoons)

Lieutenant Colonel Arthur Tremayne (13th Light Dragoons)
Colonel Harington Astley Trevelyan (11th Hussars)
Colonel Robert White (17th Lancers)
Major Sir George George Orby Wombwell (17th Lancers)

The Balaclava Banquet of 25 October 1875

It was decided amongst surviving veterans of the Charge of the Light Brigade, that it would be appropriate to mark its 21st anniversary by a special banquet for the rank and file. To this end a committee of Chargers was formed and a venue sought. Sir Edward Lee and the directors of the Alexandra Palace offered the venue and to provide free hospitality.

Suitable strenuous efforts had been made to prepare the palace. *The Illustrated London News* of five days later recorded:

'Along the hall... was a well arranged museum of relics consisting of arms and bullet-ridden and sabre-cut helmets and other portions of uniform. There was also in the collection articles found in the baggage of Prince Menshikov, which was abandoned by him on the field of battle. There was the head of the charger which carried the Earl of Cardigan while leading the charge. This was sent by the Countess of Cardigan. But a more remarkable object was a living horse, a high-caste chestnut Arab, the oldest charger that has survived the Crimea War, if not the oldest in the British service... As the beautiful little beast stood bridle and saddle at the Alexander Palace he looked quite young and fit for another campaign.'

The men came from all walks of life – some had been wounded and still bore their wounds, or found themselves on hard times, others had prospered since leaving the service.

The Illustrated London News further reported:

'It was gratifying to see that to a man they were dressed respectably and seemed to be occupying comfortable positions. Their hearty greetings of one another was in itself a sight to see. Some of them who had been companions in the same regiments had never met since they left the Army.'

All were proudly wearing their medals, not neatly mounted as today, but pinned on separately much as the wearer wished.

Although the occasion was an 'other ranks' celebration, some officers were invited. The 'chair' on the centre of the top table was occupied by Colonel

Robert White who as a captain had led the directing squadron of the 17th Lancers. Other officers included Major Sir George Wombwell of the 17th Lancers and Sir Godfrey Morgan. The Victoria Cross winners given pride of place were: 'Mr J. Malone, 6th Dragoons; Mr J. Wooden [*sic*], 104th Regiment [and] Mr J. Berryman'.

Mr Samuel Wilson late of the 11th Hussars rose to announce the first of numerous toasts including 'the Queen'. This 'was drunk with great cheering' and was succeeded by the *National Anthem*.

Amidst the speeches and entertainment, an especially penned song *The Light Brigade* was sung, with the band and choir giving up the struggle to be heard above the bellowing of the chorus. This was followed by William Pennington, who read Tennyson's poem.

The final toast, made by the chairman, reminded all gathered of the men left in the Valley of Death:

'The memory of the dead'. All stood solemnly, if not soberly, while the 8th Hussars' band played the *Dead March*.

An unknown survivor called out: 'Three cheers for Cardigan and Nolan!' Every man responded wholeheartedly.

A table indicating the NCOs and men of the 4th Light Dragoons known to have attended the 1875 Banquet and been members of the Balaclava Commemoration Society in 1877 and 1879.

Surname	Initials	Rank	No	Charger	1875	1877	1879
Armes	T.F.	Pte	1535	x	x	F. Armes	x
Baker	J.G.	Sgt	888	x	x	x	x
Balme	G.	Pte	1049	x	invited	x	x
Best	W.O.	Pte	1201	x	x		
Bolton	J.	Pte	868	x	x	x	x
Bowler	M.	Pte	1322	x		x	x
Boxall	J.	Pte	1550	x	x	x	x
Bradley	E.	Pte	1542	x		x	
Brewington	J.	Pte	1510	x		x	x
Butler	W.	Pte	1452	x	x	x	x
Carroll	P.	Pte	1515	x	x	Committee	
Coldwell	J.	Pte	1364			x	ABIS
Connor	D.	Pte	1125	x	invited	x	x
Cousins	C.	Pte	1482	x		Committee	ABIS

Surname	Initials	Rank	No	Charger	1875	1877	1879
Deering	D.	Pte	1302	x	x	x	x
Devlin	J.	Cpl	1447	x	x	x	x
Edden	J.	Pte	1481	x	x	x	x
Farquharson	R.	Pte	1277	x		R. Furguson	x
Farrell	J.	Pte	1420	x		x	x
Fletcher	T.	Pte	1271	x	x		
Forbes	J.F.	Pte	1330	x	x	x	x
Ford	J.	Pte	1547	x	x	x	x
Ferguson	R.	Pte	1192	x	x	x	x
Grant	R.	Cpl	817	x		x	x
Gray	J.R.	Pte	1485	x		J. Grey	ABS D. 21.06.91
Gregg	J.	Pte	1480	x			x
Goshall	J.	Pte	1085	x		J. Goswell	
Groves	H.	Pte	1466	x			x
Guthrie	T.	Pte	1316	x		x	D. 09.07.77
Hallaway	J.	Pte	1580	x	x	J. Holloway	x
Herbert	J.H.	Pte	1460	x	x	x	x
Heron	D.J.	Pte	1327	x	x	D. Heren	D. 09.01.95
Hickley	J.	Pte	1379	x	x		
Howes	J.	Sgt	1274	x	x	x	x
Jones	W.	Pte	1349	x		x	x
Keegan	H.	Pte	1446	x	H. Keagan	x	x
Kelly	J.	Sgt	1229	x		x	x
King	T.	Pte	1509	x	x	x	x
McGregor	G.	Pte	1382	x		x	x
Palin	J.	Pte	1381	x	x		
Phillips	J.	Pte	1404	x		x	
Pearson	W.	Pte	1353	x			x
Pitt	W.	Farrier	1193	x	x	x	x
Price	G.A.	Pte	1174	x	G.D. Price	x	x
Rogers	T.	Pte	986	x		x	x
Ryan	P.	Pte	1555	x	x	x	x
Short	F.	Cpl	1230	x	x	F. Shorto	x
Thomas	D.	Pte	1181	x		x	x

Surname	Initials	Rank	No	Charger	1875	1877	1879
Thorne	W.	Pte	1203	x	x	x	
Vick	J.	Pte	725	x		x	x
Welch	W.	Pte	1423			M. Welsh	AIS
Whitby	J.	Pte	1508	x	x	x	x
Whitehead	J.	Cpl	1289	x		x	x
Wilsden	H.	Pte	1361	x		x	x

A table indicating the NCOs and men of the 8th Hussars known to have attended the 1875 Banquet and been members of the Balaclava Commemoration Society in 1877 and 1879.

Surname	Initials	Rank	No	Charger	1875	1877	1879
Bevan	J.	Pte	1060	x		x	x
Bird	W.	Pte	1209	x	x	Committee	x
Chapman	R.	Pte	1182	May		x	ABIS
Cheshire	H.	Pte	1201	x		x	x
Clarke	M.	TSM	453	x		x	D. 27.12.78
Dalton	H.	Pte	1436	x		x	x
Dawn	W.	Pte	1180	x	x	x	x
Donoghue	J.	Tpt	1064	x		x	x
Doyle	J.	Pte	1131	x		x	x
Dwan	J.	Farrier	1079	x	J. Dewan	x	x
Fulton	W.	Pte	1153	x		x	x
Glendwr	R.O.	Pte	1192	x	x	x	x
Grey	W.	Tpt-Maj	392	x	x	x	x
Harrison	H.	TSM	370	x			x
Hefferon	J.	Tpt	1151	x	x	x	x
Hogan	J.	Pte	1006	x	x	x	x
Holmes	W.	Pte	1224	x		x	
Hurst	T.	Pte	1121	x		J. Hurst	
Johnson	R.	Pte	1126	x	x	x	x
McCausland	J.	Pte	1114	x	x	J.MacCauslan	x
Macaulay	C.	Pte	1057	x	x	x	x
Mortimer	P.	Pte	938	x	x	J. Mortimore	x
Nichol	R.	Pte	1077	x	x	R. Nicholls	x
Palframan	R.	Pte	1218	x		x	x
Perry	T.	Pte	597	x	invited	Committee	x

Surname	Initials	Rank	No	Charger	1875	1877	1879
Pickworth	J.A.	Sgt	684	x			x
Sheridan	A.	Pte	468	x	x		D. 23/01/78
Twamley	T.	Pte	1078	x	x	x	x
Williams	R.	Pte	732		x		AIS
Wilson	S.	Pte	911	x			x

A table indicating the NCOs and men of the 11th Hussars known to have attended the 1875 Banquet and been members of the Balaclava Commemoration Society in 1877 and 1879.

Surname	Initials	Rank	No	Charger	1875	1877	1879
Alliston	T.	Pte	1128		x	x	ABIS
Andrews	D.	Pte	1444	x	x		x
Ashton	R.	Pte	828	x	x	x	x
Barber	J.	Farrier	1298			x	ABIS
Barras	J.	Farrier	801			x	ABIS
Beeson	B.	Pte	1570	x	B. Beeson	x	x
Bentley	W.	Sgt	863	x	x	x	x
Bond	S.	Sgt	1091	x	x	x	x
Breese	J.	Sgt	1102	x	x	x	
Briggs	R.	Pte	1437	x		x	x
Brown	S.C.	Pte	1231	x		C. Brown	
Brown	R.	Pte	1453	x	x	x	x
Buckton	J.	Cpl	1413	x	x	x	x
Burling	J.	Pte	1526			x	ABIS
Bury	P.H.	Pte	1452			P.H. Burry	ABIS
Cart	C.	Pte	1046	x		x	
Chambers	R.	Pte	1252	x		x	x
Cork	C.	Pte	1437	x	x	x	x
Coultate	G.	Pte	752			x	ABIS
Cox	S.	Pte	1573			x	ABIS D.1877
Cullen	W.	Pte	1520	x		x	x
Davies	R.	Sgt	1495	x	x	x	x
Davis	R.	Cpl	1530	x		x	x
Dryden	J.	Pte	1617	x		x	
Eastoe	M.N.	Pte	1578	x	N.W.Easto	x	x

Surname	Initials	Rank	No	Charger	1875	1877	1879
Glanister	J.	Pte	1564	x	x	x	x
Grantham	D.	Pte	1486	x	x	x	x
Gusterson	J.	Pte	1618	x	x	x	x
Hampson	H.	Pte	1310			x	ABIS
Harvey	J.	Pte	1433			x	ABIS
Henry	N.	Pte	1584	x		x	x
Hodges	J.	Pte	1550	x	x	x	x
Holland	M.	Pte	1543	x	x	x	x
Jamieson	S.	Pte	1593	x	x		x
Jewell	H.	Pte	1403	x	x	x	x
Jowett	G,	Pte	1357	x	invited	Committee	x
Keates	J.	Tpt	914	x		x	x
Kelly	J.	Pte	1613	x			x
Kilvert	J.A.	Cpl	1513	x		R. Kilvert	x
Lawson	J.	Sgt	1415	x	x	Committee	x
Lovett	W.	Pte	1226			x	AIS
Martin	R.	Pte	1337	x	x	x	x
Maule	G.	Pte	1602	x		x	x
Middleton	I.	Pte	1422	May	x	J. Middleton	ABS
Parker	H.	Pte	1484	x	x	x	x
Parkinson	J.	Pte	1541	x		x	x
Pennington	W.H.	Pte	1631	x	x	x	x
Perkins	W.	Tpr	1304	x	W. Perkin	x	x
Phillips	W.	Pte	1370	x		x	x
Powell	C.	Pte	1587	x	x		x
Proctor	J.	Pte	1467	No	x	x	ABIS
Rhys	W.L.	Pte	1498	May	x	x	ABIS
Richardson	C.	Pte	1567	x		x	x
Roberts	T.	Pte	1198	x		x	x
Rust	J.	Pte	1320			x	AIS
Sheargold	H.	Pte	1704	x		x	x
Short	C.W.	Pte	1517	x			x
Smith	G.L.	TSM	766	x	x	President	x
Smith	W.	Tpr	1586	x	x	x	x
Spring aka Pilkington)	W.H.	Pte	1608	x		x	x

Surname	Initials	Rank	No	Charger	1875	1877	1879
Staden	W.	Pte	870	x		E. Staden	ABIS
Teevan	P.R.	TSM	1159	x		x	x
Twamley	T.	Pte	1078	x	T.Tremley		
Venables	E.	Pte	1561			x	ABIS
Warr	J.	Pte	1481	x		x	
White	G.	Pte	1420			x	ABIS
Wilder	A.	Pte	1445	x	x	x	x
Wilder	J.	Pte	1516	x	x	L. Wilder	AS
Williams	J.	Pte	663	x		x	
Williams	T.	Pte	1479	x	x	x	x
Williamson	W.	Sgt	1122	May	x		D.17.01.76
Woodham	E.R.	Pte	1355	x	x	Chairman	
Wroots	T.	Pte	1235	x	invited	x	x
Young	R.	Pte	1463	x	x	x	x

A table indicating the NCOs and men of the 13th Light Dragoons known to have attended the 1875 Banquet and been members of the Balaclava Commemoration Society in 1877 and 1879.

Surname	Initials	Rank	No	Charger	1875	1877	1879
Allen	J.	Cpl	1199	x	x		x
Allman aka Moore	J.	Pte	1562	x		J. Allmen	
Allwood	J.	Pte	1534	x	x		x
Andrews	L.	Pte	746	x	x	x	x
Badger	G.	Pte	1545	x			x
Brooks	J.	Pte	1516	x	x	x	x
Brown	H.	Pte	1168	x	x	x	x
Cameron	J.	Cpl	412	x	x	x	x
Campbell	A.H.	Pte	1366	x		x	
Colson	W.D.	Pte	1433	x	x	x	x
Cooke	T.	Pte	1048	x	x		
Cunningham	J.	Pte	1298	x		x	x
Deason	A.	Pte	1494	x		Committee	ABIS 1890 Dinner
Eccles	J.	Pte	1468	x			x
Ettridge	J.	Pte	1483	x	x	J. Etridge	x

235

Surname	Initials	Rank	No	Charger	1875	1877	1879
Evans	R.	Pte	1510	x	x	x	x
Gammage	G.	Tpt	1029	x	J. Gumage		x
Gardner	G.	Pte	1405	x			x
Garnham	G.	Pte	1480	x	x	x	x
Gibson (aka Pilmer)	G.	Pte	1471	x			x
Hanson	I.	Pte	1005		x		D. 10.25.78
Harding	J.H.	Pte	1382	x	x		x
Hindley	E.	Pte	1540	x			x
Hughes	E.	Pte	1506	x			x
Johnson	T.	Pte	1300	x	invited	x	x
Keen	T.	Pte	1529	x		J. Keen	x
Kimble	T.	Pte	1493	x		x	x
Lamb	J.	Pte	1406	x	x	x	x
Leaney	E.	Sgt	648	x	E. Leoney	R. Leney	x
Linkon	J.	TSM	762	x	x	x	x
Mahoney	D.	Pte	1319			x	AS D.31.12.78
Malanfy	J.	Pte	1276	x	x	x	D. Oct 1877
Malone	J.	Cpl	1440	x	x	x	x
Martin	E.	Cpl	1208	x	x	x	x
Mitchell	A.	Pte	1401	x	x	x	x
Naylor	H.D.	Pte	1460	x		x	
Pamplin	J.	Pte	1254	x	x		x
Peake	F.	Pte	1309	x	x	x	x
Powell	H.	Tpt	1228	x		x	x
Rhodes	J.	Pte	694	x	x	x	x
Sewell	W.	Pte	1452	x			x
Taylor	H.	Pte	1141	x	x	x	x
Veitch	J.	Pte	1431	x		x	x
Viner	F.	Pte	1464	x			x
Watlen	W.	Pte	1442	x	W. Watten		ABIS
White	T.	Pte	975	x		x	
Wickham	H.G.	Pte	1499	x			x
Wilde	G.	Pte	1119	x		G. Wild	x
Williams	G.	Pte	1348	x		Committee	x

TABLES

A table indicating the NCOs and men of the 17th Lancers known to have attended the 1875 Banquet and been members of the Balaclava Commemoration Society in 1877 and 1879.

Surname	Initials	Rank	No	Charger	1875	1877	1879
Aldous	C.	Pte	1064	x	x	Secretary	x
Allen	T.	Pte	807		x	x	ABIS
Baker	J.	Pte	828	x	J.G. Baker	x	x
Barker	W.	TSM	655	x	x	x	x
Beetham	W.	Pte	898	x		x	x
Berryman	J.	Sgt	735	x	x	x	x
Bloomfield	J.	Pte	484	x	x	x	x
Brennan	J.	Pte	636	x		x	ABIS
Brown	J.	Tpr	455	x		x	x
Brown	J.	Tpr	476	x	x		x
Buck	J.	Pte	1160	x		x	x
Burns	W.	Pte	796	x			x
Butler	W.	Pte	840	x	x	x	x
Cattermole	W.G.	TSM	483	x	invited	Committee	x
Clark	T.G.	Pte	1113	x	x	Committee	x
Comley	S.	Pte	705			S. Comerley	BIS
Dickenson	F.	Sgt	847	x	x	x	x
Dudley	T.	Pte	1134	x		x	x
Duggan	J.	Pte	579	x		x	x
Duncan	J.	Sgt	688	x		x	x
Dyer	T.	Pte	562	x	x		
Glannister	J.	Pte	1564	x	x		
Graham	W.W.	Sgt	961	x		x	x
Harpham	J.	Pte	1005	No		x	AS
Harris	R.	Pte	652	May	x	x	ABIS
Harriet	G.	Pte	803	No	G.Herriott	x	NOT F/D
Henderson	L.G.	Pte	1044	No		J.L. Henderson	Did not arrive in the Crimea
Hind	J.	Pte	854	No		x	AS
Holland	E.	Pte	1147	x	M.Holland	x	x
Ireland	J.	Pte	935		Portrait The Illustrated London News	x	ABIS

237

Surname	Initials	Rank	No	Charger	1875	1877	1879
Joy	H.	Tpt-Mjr	416	HEAVY/B		x	
Kennedy	S.	Pte	566	x	Sgt	x	D.26.09.77
Landfried	M.L.	Tpt	986	x	M.E. Landfred	T. Landfred	x
Lark	T.	Pte	1110	x		x	x
Manning	G.	Pte	1116			S. Manning	AIS
Marsh	P.	Pte	1025	x	x	x	x
Marshall	T.	Pte	1010	x	x	x	x
Morgan	C.	Farrier	988	x	x	x	x
Morley	T.	Cpl	1004	x	x	J. Morley	x
Mugg	H.	Pte	1085	x		x	x
Mullings	T.	Pte	1095	x	T. Mullins	x	x
Mustard	J.	Pte	1149	x	x	x	x
Nunnerley	J.I.	Cpl	870	x	x	x	x
Paine	J.	Pte	692	x		x	x
Pearson	W.	Pte	939	x			x
Penn	J.	Pte	1168	x	x	x	x
Phelan	J.	Pte	964	x		x	
Purvis	W.	Pte	868	x	x	x	x
Rafferty	P.	Pte	980	x		x	D. 16.03.77
Ramsey	G.D.	Pte	1029			W.G. Ramsey	AS
Reilley	J.	Pte	815	x	J. Reintly	J. Riley	x
Ryan	J.	Pte	1155	x	T. Ryan		x
Scarfe	J.	Sgt	481	x	x	Treasurer	x
Shenfield	J.	Pte	1156			W. Shenfield	AIS
Sherriff	G.	Pte				x	
Smith	J.	Pte	924	x		x	x
Soley	B.	Pte	1120	x		x	x
Stanley	D.	Pte	1009	x	x	E. Stanley	x
Swiney	J.	Pte	1036	x	x	x	x
Taylor	T.	Pte	1091			x	ABIS
Terry	G.	Sgt	721	x		x	x
Tiggell	W.	Pte	1178	x	J. Tiggell	x	x
Travis	W.	Pte	678	x	W.Travers	W.Travers	x
Waller	T.	Pte	1035	x			x
Webster	J.	Pte	902	x			x

Surname	Initials	Rank	No	Charger	1875	1877	1879
Weatherley	G.	Pte	673	x	x	G. Wetherley	x
Wightman	J.	Pte	1177	x		x	x
Williams	R.H.	Sgt	750	x		x	x
Wooden	C.	Sgt	799	x	J. Wooden		

A table indicating the NCOs and men whose names are listed as having attended the 1875 Banquet, but for whom no further details may be found

Surname	First Name	Rank	Serial no	Charged	1875	1877	1879
Batton	James				x		

Tables of Charger Status

4th Light Dragoons Table

4th Light Dragoons	Rank	No	Charged	Corroborating Evidence Supporting Charger Status
Andrews, John	Cpl	1262	UW	Nominated to the Médaille Militaire: 'Sergeant John Andrews - Gallant and distinguished conduct in the charge of the Light Cavalry Brigade on the 25th of October 1854. Served during the whole campaign 1854-55. Was present at the battles of Alma, Balaclava, Inkerman, Traktir, and the expedition to Eupatoria in October 1855'.
Armes, Thomas Frederick	Pte	1535	W	Shell fragments wounded both him and his horse, causing the loss of a finger. As he returned up the valley a round shot knocked him to the ground; a Cossack ran a lance into his leg. (*LG* 17.11.54 'slightly wounded'). To Scutari 26.10.54. To England 17.02.55. Discharged 16.10.55.
Armstrong, Joseph/Joshua	Cpl	1292	PoW-W	Wounded and taken PoW (*LG* 17.11.54). Rejoined the regiment 22.10.55. Honourably discharged by District Court-Martial 06.11.55. To England 25.12.55.
Bagshaw, James	Pte	1581	PoW	Rode on the right of the right-hand squadron in the rear rank. 'When within about forty yards of the guns my horse was killed, and I was taken PoW' (*LG* 17.11.54). Rejoined the regiment 26.10.55. Honourably discharged by District court-martial 06.11.55.

4th Light Dragoons	Rank	No	Charged	Corroborating Evidence Supporting Charger Status
Baker, John George	Sgt	888	UW	Obituary notes that he returned to bring in the wounded under fire: 'He was one of the comparatively few who came back scathless'. Obituary in *The Daily Telegraph* (Sydney) 24.06.93.
Balme, George	Pte	1049	UW	Member of the Balaclava Commemoration Society in 1879 (listed as 'Baum').
Barnes, Edward	Tpt	1236	KIA	Killed in action.
Best, Walter O.	Pte	1201	UW	'Came through without a scratch.' Source: Obituary in the *Western Mercury* 04.03.83. Attended 1875 Banquet. Received assistance from the T.H. Roberts Fund and the Light Brigade Relief Fund.
Bolton, James	Pte	868	PoW	Taken PoW (*LG* 17.11.54). Repatriated with other PoWs on the *Columbo* and 'Her Majesty's Ship' in October 1855.
Bowler, Michael	Pte	1322	UW	Member of the Balaclava Commemoration Society in 1879.
Boxall, John	Pte	1550	SW	Horse was shot under him and he was severely wounded, receiving a bullet in right leg and 12 lance wounds while on the ground and left for dead. Taken PoW (*LG* 17.11.54). Repatriated due to his wounds. To England 07.12.55. Discharged 26.05.56.
Bradley, Edward	Pte	1542	W	Slightly wounded (*LG* 17.11.54). To Scutari 26.10.54. Invalided to England 07.12.54.
Brewington, John	Pte	1510	UW	Witnessed the death of Lieutenant Sparke (account now lost).
Brown, John George	Cpt		SW	Wounded commanding 2nd Squadron (*LG* 17.11.54 'wounded severely'). Evidently fit for combat as wounded again at Inkerman. Appointed Brevet-Major (*LG* 12.12.54). Nominated a Knight of the Légion d'Honneur (5th Class) (*LG* 01.05.57), awarded the Order of the Medjidie (5th Class) (*LG* 02.03.58).
Burnett, James	Pte	1577	UW	To Scutari 26.10.54. Invalided to England 23.03.55.
Butler, William	Pte	1452	UW	Awarded the Distinguished Conduct Medal, recommendation 05.02.55.
Campbell, Edward	Sgt	1329	KIA	Killed in action.
Carroll, Peter	Pte	1515	W	Wounded by grape-shot (*LG* 17.11.54 'slightly wounded'). 'When we commenced to retreat my horse was killed and I was wounded with grape shot just in front of the guns. After running some

				little distance Lord George Paget and Colonel F.G. Shewell passed me riding together.' Source: *Lord Paget's Journal*. To Scutari 26.10.54. Rejoined regiment on the 14.12.54.
Carter, Joseph	Pte	1494	W	Wounded in the right arm by shell splinters (*LG* 17.11.54 'slightly wounded'). To Scutari 26.10.1854. Invalided to England 23.02.55.
Connor, Dennis	Pte	1125	UW	Portrait and account in *The Illustrated London News* 30.10.75.
Cousins, Charles	Pte	1482	UW	Member of the Balaclava Committee and the Balaclava Commemoration Society in 1877, but not in 1879. Obituaries confirm his Charger status, describing him as the last local Charger to die – a regular at the Chatham Army and Navy Club.
Crawford, Hugh	Tpt	1296	PoW	Lord George Paget's Field Trumpeter. Unhorsed. Assisted by Private S. Parkes, but taken PoW (*LG* 17.11.54). Rejoined the regiment 26.10.55. Honourably discharged by District court-martial 06.11.55.
Croydon, George	Pte	1440	W	Wounded (*LG* 17.11.54 'slightly wounded'). To Scutari 26.10.54. Re-joined the regiment 24.11.54.
Cuthbert, Joseph	Fa	1438	MAY	Possibly rode in the Charge. A letter in the Leicestershire Record Office inferring he Charged: 'I escaped thank God, my Horse was shot Dead with a Six Pound shot, fifteen men Killed and wounded out of my Troop…'
Deering (Deeran), Daniel	Pte	1302	UW	Member of B Troop. Rode in the right squadron in the front rank, and on the left of the regiment.
Devlin, James	Cpl	1447	SW	Sabre wound of the right hand, canister shot left shoulder (a fragment of his tunic was removed from the wound decades later), lance-wound left arm (*LG* 17.11.54 'severely wounded'). To Scutari 26.10.54. Invalided to England 21.01.55. Discharged 06.11.55. Awarded the Distinguished Conduct Medal, recommended 05.02.55.
Donaldson, James	Pte	961	K	Killed in action.
Downing, Frederick	Pte	1524	W	Received a severe sabre wound to right wrist (*LG* 17.11.54 'slightly wounded'). To Scutari 26.10.54. Invalided to England 21.01.55. Discharged from Chatham Invalid Depot 06.11.55.
Dray, James Edwin	Pte	1528	MAY	Believed rode in the Charge. Assumed name of John Davis post military service. Died 23.08.94 when it became known that he was a Charger. His tombstone recording his part in the Charge was created by public subscription.

4th Light Dragoons	Rank	No	Charged	Corroborating Evidence Supporting Charger Status
Edden, John	Pte	1481	UW	Rode with A Troop in the centre of the left squadron, in the front rank. Had two horses shot under him. Assisted Major J.T.D. Halkett. His affidavit in the Cardigan v. Calthorpe case states: 'My horse was shot just after this, and I did not get back until the remains of the regiment was formed up.'
				In the *Tamworth Herald* 22.10.98: 'In the charge his horse was shot from under him pinning him to the ground. Luckily the animal wriggled and he was able to free himself. He then had to make a decision whether to go back or go forward, he made up his mind to go into the firing.' He said that he was the last to come out of the charge and answer his name. Sergeant J. Howes and Private J. Palin claimed the same distinction.
Ellis, George	Lt & A		MAY	Probably rode in the Charge. 'On Board ship' 26.10.54 and invalided to England 31.03.55.
Farquharson, Robert Stuart	Pte	1277	PoW	Three horses killed under him and taken PoW, unwounded (*LG* 17.11.54). Re-joined the regiment 22.11.54. Honourably discharged by District court-martial 06.11.55. Wrote a detailed account.
Farrell, John	Pte	1420	UW	Assisted Private J. Ford who was pinned under his horse about 300 yards from the battery.
Ferguson, Robert	Pte	1192	UW	Rode in the centre of the front rank of the right-hand squadron and was the left guide of the right troop of the first squadron, under Captain Low. He stated that the troopers were not issued with gun spikes. Awarded the Distinguished Conduct Medal, recommendation 05.02.55.
Fletcher, Thomas	Pte	1271	MW	Mortally wounded (shot though the back of the head) and taken PoW (*LG* 17.11.54). Died either at Simferopol or on the road from Sevastopol. Mentioned in the account of Private J.H. Herbert. A 'James Fletcher' attended the 1875 Banquet.
Forbes, John Burghersh	Cpl	1330	W	Had two horses shot from under him but managed to return on a third horse. Promoted to corporal 25.10.54. 'Slightly wounded'. Death notice in the *Maitland Weekly Mercury* (New South Wales) 16.11.95.
Ford, John	Pte	1547	UW	Rode in G Troop, in the front rank, near the centre of the right squadron. Horse was shot under him about 300 yards from the guns, falling on his leg. Freed by Private J. Farrell. 'My horse was killed about

				150 yards from the guns… We had no gun spikes to disable the Russian guns.' Source: Affidavit in Cardigan v. Calthorpe.
Fowler, William	T.S.M	831	MW	Lance wound in the back and taken PoW (*LG* 17.11.54). Died 21.12.54 of wounds and dysentery at Simferopol having, according the *Memoirs* of James Wightman, 17th Lancers: 'To give more space in the carts to his fellow comrades, he walked every step of the fifty miles to Simferopol; his wounds mortified, and he died within a month of his being captured…'
Fox, Christopher	Pte	1314	UW	According to Private J.H. Herbert 'Survivor's Tales of Great Events' in the *Royal Magazine* Volume XIII: 'Fox left his post at camp to ride in the Charge and was afterwards given 50 lashes (only half the sentence being carried out)'. To Scutari 29.10.54.
Fredericks, Charles	Pte	1450	PoW-W	Wounded and taken PoW (*LG* 17.11.54 listed as 'Charles Frederick'). Rejoined the regiment 26.10.55. Honourably discharged by District court-martial 06.11.55. Fredericks stated: 'and in returning my horse was shot under me and injured me in its fall. I was at once surrounded and taken prisoner. The Russians then sent me to Simferopol where I remained in hospital for four months. I was afterwards sent twelve hundred miles into Russia, where I remained until the 27th of August 1855, when together with some other prisoners I was sent to Odessa from whence I was forwarded to Balaclava and reached that place on the 26th October 1855.'
Freestone, William	Pte	1544	MAY	May have ridden in the Charge. Obituary in a Portsmouth newspaper said he rode in the Charge and was wounded but there appears to be no evidence to support this. He served in the Metropolitan Police for some years.
Gilchrist, John	Pte	1312	MAY	Lummis and Wynn stated, 'Believed to have ridden in the Charge', but give no corroborating evidence for this statement. T. Brighton and A. Sewell stated he Charged.
Gillam, David J.	Cpl	1130	SW	Severely wounded by shell fragment at Inkerman. To Scutari 10.12.54. Invalided to England in March 1855. Promoted sergeant 25.10.54 and awarded the Distinguished Conduct Medal (DCM), recommendation 05.02.55. Nominated a Knight of the Légion d'Honneur (5th Class) (*LG* 04.08.56).

4th Light Dragoons	Rank	No	Charged	Corroborating Evidence Supporting Charger Status
Goshall, Joseph	Pte	1085	SW	Knee (R. Dutton says 'thigh') shattered by a 24lb shot, crawled a long distance from the field (*LG* 17.11.54 'severely wounded' and listed as 'Joseph Gosbell'). To Scutari Hospital 26.10.54. Invalided to England early in 1855. Discharged from Chatham Invalid Depot 06.05.55.
Gowings, George	Pte	1445	UW	Two horses decapitated. Mentioned too in the accounts of Private R. Grant and Private D. Connor. Gowing's letter to a friend in Exeter published in *The Daily News* 24.11.54: 'Our men fell by dozens – horses and men blown into the air, and we ran everyone through that we could get at. We had to cut our way through thousands of them. I cannot tell you the horrors we went through, but all I can say is we have only about fifty men left out of the regiment. We have lost half our officers. Poor Spence [Corporal Henry Spence] was killed, and in fact dozens that you have seen before we left England; but we were driven to desperation, and fought like madmen.'
Grant, Robert	Pte	817	UW	Rode in F Troop. Fought well beyond the guns and retired with the 11th Hussars. Horse shot from under him, falling on his leg and assisted by Private McGregor. Awarded the DCM, recommendation 05.02.55. An account of his rescue by Private George McGregor in *The Illustrated London News* 30.10.75.
Gray, John Richard	Pte	1485	W	Wounded (*LG* 17.11.54 'slightly wounded') and horse killed under him.
Gregory, James Alfred	Pte	1417	W	Wounded through the calf, the same bullet killing his horse under him (not on the official casualty list). To Scutari 29.11.54.
Grennan, Edward	Pte	1425	MAY	R. Dutton lists as a Charger. Had certificates from Lord Paget. Received assistance from the Light Brigade Relief Fund.
Grigg, Joseph	Pte	1180	UW	Saved an unhorsed comrade. Published an account.
Groves, Herbert	Pte	1466	UW	Member of the Balaclava Commemoration Society in 1879.
Guthrie, Thomas	Pte	1319	UW	Nominated to the Médaille Militaire: 'Gallant and distinguished conduct during the Charge of the Light Brigade on the 25th of October 1854. Served during the whole of the campaign in 1854-55. Present at the battles of the Alma, Balaclava, Inkerman, Traktir and the Expedition to Eupatoria in October of 1855.'

TABLES

Halkett, John Thomas Douglas	Maj		K	Killed riding with the 2nd Squadron (*LG* 17.11.54 'slightly wounded'). In the retreat after the Charge he was seen to fall wounded by a shell. Was assisted in a Victoria Cross action.
Hallaway, John	Pte	1580	W	Wounded. To Scutari 26.10.54. Rejoined the regiment 15.01.55.
Harling, Richard	Pte	1393	W	Wounded. To Scutari 15.12.54. Rejoined the regiment 11.03.55. Died 17.11.59, while still serving with the regiment. Death certificate states died as a result of an 'abscess resulting from wound he received in the light cavalry charge at Balaclava'.
Haxhall, Daniel	Pte	1536	K	Killed in action.
Herbert, Frank	T.S.M	1134	K	Killed in action while trying to prevent one of the guns being carried away. Death witnessed by Private George Alfred Price and Private Edward Grennan, both of 4th Light Dragoons.
Herbert, James Henry	Pte	1460	UW	Portrait and account in *The Illustrated London News* 30.10.75 and in *The Royal Magazine Volume XIII*.
Herbert, Thomas	Pte	1205	W	Slightly wounded (*LG* 17.11.54). To Scutari 26.10.54. Rejoined the regiment 11.05.55.
Heron, Dennis James	Pte	1327	W	With the aid of two other troopers captured a Russian gun but the six horses attached could not be moved, and had to be abandoned. When galloping back a bullet passed through his left arm (*LG* 17.11.54 'slightly wounded'). To Scutari Hospital 26.10.54. Invalided to England in March 1855.
Hickey, John	Pte	1379	W	To Scutari Hospital 27.10.54. Re-joined the regiment 14.12.54.
Howes, John	Sgt	1274	W	Rode as the 'left hand man of the regiment'. Assisted Cornet G.W. Hunt in trying to bring a Russian gun away – tried to cut the leather traces but found chain inside. Slight sabre cut on the side of his head: 'we were cutting our way through the Lancers I received a slight sword cut on the ear.' Source: *Lord Paget's Journal*. Said to be the last man to return to the lines. Privates J. Edden and J. Palin claimed the same distinction.
Hughes, John	Pte	1584	W	Gun-shot wound to right arm (*LG* 17.11.54 'slightly wounded'). To Scutari 26.10.54. Invalided to England in March 1855, and discharged from Chatham Invalid Depot 16.10.55.
Hulton, Thomas	Pte	1458	K	Killed in action. Private G.A. Price: 'The last two men I saw fall were poor Tommy Houlton [Private T. Hulton] and Charley Marshall.'

4th Light Dragoons	Rank	No	Charged	Corroborating Evidence Supporting Charger Status
Hunt, George Warwick	Crnt		UW	Attempted to bring away one of the cannons. Awarded the Order of the Medjidie (5th Class) (*LG* 02.03.58). Affidavit in the Cardigan v. Calthorpe case states: 'No officer wearing the uniform of the 11th Hussars passed through the 4th (going to the rear) except a Mr Houghton, who was wounded in the head. I think that was the officer who was taken for Lord Cardigan by the men of the 4th and 8th.'
Hutton, Thomas	Cpt		SW	Led E Troop of the 1st Squadron, which was commanded by Captain A. Low. Shot through the right thigh but continued to the guns, while shot through the other thigh during the retreat (*LG* 17.11.54 'wounded severely'). Horse had 11 wounds and collapsed and died on return. To Scutari 26.10.54. Invalided to England via Malta in December (arrived in England 21.03.55). Awarded the Order of the Medjidie (5th Class) (*LG* 02.03.58). Appointed Brevet-Major (*LG* 06.06.56).
Isaac, John	Pte	1219	MAY	Lummis and Wynn state the probability is that he did take part in the Charge, but give no corroborating evidence for this statement. Confined to Scutari Hospital 02.11.54-14.12.54. Died 08.10.55.
Jennings, Henry	R.S.M.	1102	W	'Slightly wounded' (*LG* 17.11.54).
Joliffe, The Hon. Hedworth Hylton	Lt		SW	Commanded a troop. Obituary Extract *Bath Chronicle* 02.11.99: 'He was badly wounded in the fighting and until the day of his death he carried a Russian bullet in his body.'
Jones, William	Pte	1349	W	Wounded (*LG* 17.11.54 'slightly wounded'). Horse shot under him. To Scutari 26.10.54 and rejoined the regiment on the 03.12.54. Funeral notice, *Sunday Times* (Sydney) 13.10.12: 'wounded in the leg by a cannon ball, and also received a sword cut on the hand. On the return from the 'valley of death' his horse was shot under him, but he caught a riderless steed, and succeeded in reaching the British lines.'
Keagan, Henry	Pte	1446	W	Rode in the same troop as Sergeant J. Howes. Received a sabre wound in the leg.
Keenan, William	Pte	1426	W	Gun-shot wound to right leg (*LG* 17.11.54 'slightly wounded'). To Scutari 26.10.54. Invalided to England 20.01.55. Discharged from Chatham Invalid Depot 14.10.55: 'Unfit for further service. Disabled by lameness of right leg from gun-shot wound – fracture of tibia – received at Balaclava.'

246

Kelly, James William	T.S.M	1229	W	Sabre cut across the right shoulder. Horse killed under him at the guns. Nominated to the Médaille Militaire: 'For gallant and distinguished conduct in the Charge of the Light Brigade at Balaclava on the 25th of October 1854.'
King, Thomas B.	Pte	1509	PoW	Served D Troop. Horse shot under him and taken PoW (*LG* 17.11.54). Saved the life of a Russian gunner, who he later shared a hospital ward with. Repatriated 25.10.55. Honourably discharged by District court-martial 06.11.55.
King, William Affleck	Crnt		UW	Rode in the Charge. Funeral recorded in the *Herts and Essex Observer* 04.09.86: 'was present at the "Balaclava" Charge, his horse and himself escaping quite unscathed, although a shot passed through his shako.'
Lang, Henry J.	Pte	1270	MAY	Possibly rode in the Charge. A. Sewell lists as a Charger, but gives no corroborating evidence for this statement.
Linser, George	Pte	1589	PoW-M	Mortally wounded and taken PoW (*LG* 17.11.54). Died either at Simferopol or on the road from Sevastopol.
Lovelock, Thomas	Tpt	1247	K	Killed in action. His last words were to Private Robert Farquharson: 'Well, Bob, you'll find that many of us will never get back to our lines again.'
Low, Alexander	Cpt		UW	Commanded 1st Squadron. Said to have killed 13 Russians in the mêlée. Brevet Lieutenant Colonel (*LG* 01.12.54), nominated a Knight of the Légion d'Honneur (5th Class) (*LG* 04.08.56), awarded the Al Valore Militaire, Order of the Medjidie (4th Class) (*LG* 02.03.58).
Lucas, Thomas	Pte	1540	PoW-W	Rode in the front rank to the left flank of the squadron. Five lance wounds to the body and two sabre wounds to the head, and a sabre cut to his left hand (arm later amputated), and taken PoW (*LG* 17.11.54). Repatriated with other PoWs on the *Columbo* and 'Her Majesty's Ship' in October 1855.
Lynch, Richard	Sgt	968	DoW	Troop Sergeant-Major John Linkon, 13th Light Dragoons: 'I saw Sergeant Lynch of the 4th Light Dragoons hacked about in a most dreadful manner.'
Marshall, Charles	Pte	1128	K	Private G.A. Price's letter in *The Daily Telegraph* 16.10.75: 'My comrades were shot right and left of me. The last two men I saw fall were poor Tommy Houlton [Private T. Hulton] and Charley Marshall'.

4th Light Dragoons	Rank	No	Charged	Corroborating Evidence Supporting Charger Status
Martin, Fiennes Wykeham	Crnt		UW	Rode as Acting Adjutant.
McGregor, George	Pte	1382	UW	Nominated to the Médaille Militaire: 'For gallant and distinguished conduct in the campaigns of 1854-55. Present at the battles of the Alma, Balaclava, Inkerman, Traktir, and the Expedition to Eupatoria in October 1855.' Lummis and Wynn note he assisted Private Robert Grant.
McVeagh, John	H.S.	906	W	Wounded and had his horse shot under him. Awarded the DCM, recommended 05.02.55.
Moody, Henry	Pte	1094	K	Killed in action.
Normoyle, James	Pte	918	PoW-M	Mortally wounded with a terrible cut to the face and taken PoW (*LG* 17.11.54). Died of his wounds in November 1854.
O'Brien, Michael	Pte	1461	PoW	Taken PoW (*LG* 17.11.54). Repatriated with other PoWs on the *Columbo* and 'Her Majesty's Ship' in October 1855.
Olley, James	Pte	1543	W	Horse shot under him, but directly caught another: 'I was with the 4th Light Dragoons and was wounded in the Charge, left eye shot out, sword cut across the forehead, a lance wound in the ribs, another on the back on my neck, another in the foot.' (*LG* 17.11.54 'slightly wounded'). To Scutari 26.10.54. Invalided to England 10.11.54.
Palin, John	Pte	1381	UW	Unwounded, although his rolled cloak was riddled with musket-balls and his water bottle twice holed. Thought to be the last unwounded man to ride back up the valley to make the roll-call. Private J. Edden and Sergeant J. Howes claimed the same distinction.
Parkes, Samuel	Pte	635	PoW	Taken PoW (*LG* 17.11.54). Repatriated with other PoWs on the *Columbo* and 'Her Majesty's Ship' in October 1855. Awarded the Victoria Cross *LG* 24.02.57.
Pearson, William	Pte	1353	W	Horse stumbled over a riderless horse and he mounted another. He had an epaulette shot from his shoulder and returned with a wound to the forehead. His cousin, Private T. Brown, 17th Lancers, was killed in action.
Phelan, Michael	Pte	1513	K	Killed in action.
Phillips, Joseph	Pte	1404	MW	Mortally wounded (*LG* 17.11.54 'slightly wounded') and died in the Regimental Camp on 09.12.54. However, Dutton states a 'J. Phillips' was a member of the Balaclava Commemoration Society in 1877.

Pitt, William	Far	1193	SW	Severely wounded. Funeral report in the *Army and Navy Gazette* 10.03.01: 'reached and spiked several of the Russian guns. While doing so he was severely wounded and remained on the field of battle until the next day.'
Potter, Samuel	Pte	1480	MAY	May have ridden in the Charge. Gravestone (Stapenhill Cemetery, Grave No. 1560) records his participation in the Charge: 'Honour the charge they made - The Noble Six Hundred'. A. Sewell lists as a Charger, but give no corroborating evidence for this statement.
Portal, Robert	Cpt		W	Commanded F Troop (left side of 2nd squadron). His horse 'Paddy', was hit in the shoulder by a Minié bullet and died after bringing Portal safely off the battlefield. Portal received a glancing blow on the back from a shell splinter but was not injured. Awarded the Al Valore Militaire, the Order of the Medjidie (5th Class) (*LG* 02.03.58), and nominated a Knight of the Légion d'Honneur (5th Class). Letters printed privately.
Price, George	Pte	1174	UW	Rode in E Troop in the Charge. Price, who rode in Captain T. Hutton's E Troop, states: 'Captain Hutton led us up to the guns; it was poor Cornet Sparks [Lieutenant H.A. Sparke] and Sergeant Herbert who dismounted to cut the traces of the horses attached to the Russian guns. I saw them both fall (the traces were leather-covered iron or steel chains). I was left quite alone once. My comrades were shot right and left of me.'
Reilly, John	R.S.M.	1398	UW	Horse was wounded three times. His younger brother, Joseph, rode with the 17th Lancers.
Robinson, George	Pte	1305	K	Killed in action.
Rogers, Thomas	Pte	986	W	Wounded (*LG* 17.11.54 'slightly wounded'). To Scutari 27.10.54 and rejoined the regiment 11.05.55.
Ryan, Thomas	Pte	1555	UW	Member of the Balaclava Commemoration Society in 1879.
Short, Frederick	Sgt	1250	UW	Rode on the extreme left of the right-hand squadron in the front rank. Horse died soon after returning from the field of battle. Awarded the DCM, recommended 05.02.55 for killing several drivers [six] and their horses, thereby preventing the enemy from removing the guns.
Sparke, Henry Astley	Lt		K	Killed in action commanding a troop (*LG* 17.11.54). See Private G.A. Price's account above. In a letter written by Cornet W. Martin to Canon Lummis

4th Light Dragoons	Rank	No	Charged	Corroborating Evidence Supporting Charger Status
				John Henry Sparke however provided a different version: 'Mr Sparke must, we all think, have been cut off by a regiment of Lancers that completely hemmed in the remains of the 4th'.
Spence, Henry	Cpl	1344	K	Killed in action.
Stanley, Frederick	Pte	1039	UW	His gravestone records that he was 'one of the Balaclava heroes.' Obituary in the *Manchester Evening News*, 09.04.94, confirms his Charger status but mentions no wounds.
Sutcliffe, William	Pte	1234	W	Mortally wounded (*LG* 17.11.54 'slightly wounded'). To Scutari Hospital 26.10.54, where he died 26.11.54.
Swan, George	Pte	1585	K	Killed in action.
Thomas, David	Pte	1181	UW	A member of E Troop, he rode in the right squadron about the centre of the front rank. Awarded the DCM, recommendation 05.02.55.
Thomas, William	Sgt	969	PoW-W	Wounded and taken PoW (*LG* 17.11.54). He must have escaped, as sent to Scutari 26.10.54. Invalided to England 26.04.55.
Thorne, William	Pte	1203	W	Wounded in the left foot by lance and musket ball (*LG* 17.11.54 'slightly wounded') and weakened from the loss of blood, was assisted back by Private J.H. Herbert who states in an interview published in 1912: 'Directly I got through I fell in with my old comrade named Thorne. He was shot through the foot and terribly weak through loss of blood. As I galloped past him I seized hold of his horse's reins, he himself [not] having command of his mount. I told him to hang on like grim death to the saddle and I would try to save his life. All this time the Russians were taking pot-shots at us; but I got him back alright.' To Scutari 26.11.54. Invalided to England via Malta 15.12.54. Discharged from Chatham Invalid Depot 06.11.55: 'Unfit for further service. Disabled by permanent lameness from gun-shot and lance wounds of the left foot.'
Tomset, Thomas	Pte	1586	K	Killed in action.
Turner, Henry	Pte	1263	MAY	Received assistance from the Light Brigade Relief Fund.
Tyler, James	Pte	1194	W	*LG* 17.11.54 'slightly wounded', although his papers say 'severely wounded'. To Scutari Hospital 26.10.54. Invalided to England in March 1855.

Vick, Joseph	Cpl	725	W	Parish Magazine of Great St Mary's Church, Sawbridge, notes in the Burials records: February 21st [1889] Joseph Vick; 'One of the Six Hundred,' aged 76 years. He 'was wounded in the face, and had a horse shot under him; rode out of the fight on a comrade's stirrup and on the way they stopped to release another who was trapped under his dead horse and brought him out with them.'
Waight, Charles	Pte	1257	K	Killed in action (*LG* 17.11.54).
Waterson, William	T.S.M	1215	UW	Awarded the Al Valore Militaire: 'Displayed very gallant conduct in the action at Balaclava in the Light Brigade Charge particularly in the retreat of the regiment after they had sabred the artillery men at their guns.'
Whitby, James	Pte	1508	UW	Member of the Balaclava Commemoration Society in 1879.
Whitby, Joseph	Pte	1493	W	Wounded (*LG* 17.11.54 'slightly wounded'). To Scutari Hospital on 03.11.54. Died at Scutari Hospital 25.02.55.
Whitehead, John	Pte	1289	UW	Horse killed under him by a bursting shell before reaching the guns. Thrown and suffered broken nose.
Williamson, Richard	Pte	1407	MAY	May have ridden in the Charge. To Scutari 26.10.54.
Wilsden, Henry	Pte	1361	UW	Member of the Balaclava Commemoration Society in 1879. Obituary in the *Oxford Times* 04.03.16: 'Mr Wilsden had an especial friend in the regiment, a man named John Edden, to whom, while in the heat of the Charge, he handed a bottle of water, which revived Edden, and enabled him to reach a place of safety.'

	Officers	NCOs	Trumpeters	Other Ranks	Total
Rode in the Charge and Killed-in-Action (K)	2	4	2	10	18
Rode in the Charge and Mortally Wounded (MW)	0	1	0	2	3
Rode in the Charge and Severely Wounded (SW)	3	2	0	3	8
Rode in the Charge and Prisoner of War (PoW)	0	0	1	5	6
Rode in the Charge and Prisoner of War – Wounded (PoW-W)	0	2	0	2	4
Rode in the Charge and Prisoner of War- mortally wounded (PoW-M)	0	0	0	2	2

	Officers	NCOs	Trumpeters	Other Ranks	Total
Rode in the Charge and wounded (W)	1	6	0	23	30
Rode in the Charge unwounded (UW)	4	6	0	28	38
May Have Ridden (MAY)	1	0	0	10	11
Identified Chargers	11	21	3	85	120
Unidentified Chargers					7
Total Number of Chargers					127

The following contemporary sources give details of the regiment's statistics for the 25 October 1854

The London Gazette 12 November 1854 - Return of Casualties from 22nd to 26th October, 1854, both days inclusive: 4th Light Dragoons

2 officers, 5 sergeants, 3 drummers, 24 rank and file, 50 horses, killed; 2 officers, 1 sergeant, 21 rank and file, wounded.

A contemporary source give the following:

The *Ipswich Journal* 18 November 1854 'That gallant regiment was led to the charge upon the Russian lines by Lord Cardigan, 118 strong – at the close but 39 returned in their saddles! In that terrible conflict Major Halkett fell at the head of his charging squadron...'

Only 39 members of the regiment answered the first Roll-call of mounted men made immediately after the Charge.

Daniell, D.S., 4th Hussars – The Story of the 4th Queen's Own Hussars 1685-1958 (Aldershot, 1959). p.195 states:

118 men set off for the guns. Now only 62 men answered their names. Two officers, 16 other ranks and 49 horses had been killed.

Two officers, 25 other ranks and 19 horses were wounded (12 of these had to be shot) and 16 other ranks were PoWs (five of the six wounded PoWs died).

8th Hussars Table

8th Hussars	Rank	No	Charged	Corroborating Evidence Supporting Charger Status
Adams, Joshua	Pte	899	K	Killed in action (*LG* 17.11.54).
Barry, John	Pte	1144	K	Killed in action (*LG* 17.11.54).
Bevin, John	Pte	1060	PoW-W	Wounded and PoW (*LG* 17.11.54 listed as 'John Berlin'). 'Sustained a contusion of the skull and slit ear.' – *Freeman's Journal* (New South Wales), 04.06.92. 'The only wound I have that will be discernible is a sword cut across my left ear. I had a great many lance wounds about my body, but they are all nearly well.' Source: *Lloyds Weekly Newspaper* 18.02.55. Repatriated with other PoWs on the *Columbo* and 'Her Majesty's Ship' in October 1855. Discharged from the regiment 1856.

Bird, William	Pte	1209	PoW-W	Two horses shot under him. A bullet-wound through the calf of the right leg and a lance-wound in the arm and taken PoW (*LG* 17.11.54 'PoW'). Repatriated with other PoWs on the *Columbo* and 'Her Majesty's Ship' in October 1855. Account in *The Illustrated London News* 30.10.75.
Bray, Francis	Pte	511	MW	Mortally wounded (*LG* 17.11.54 'dangerously wounded'). To Scutari 26.10.54 and died there or on-board ship.
Brennan, Michael	Pte	852	K	Killed in action (*LG* 17.11.54).
Brown, John	Pte	887	W	Wounded in both hands and musket-ball in back and saved from further attack by Lieutenant E. Phillips (*LG* 17.11.54 'severely wounded'). To Scutari General Hospital 26.10.54. PoW at Scutari 17.12.54. In a letter home, Lieutenant Phillips states: 'After his [Brown's] horse had been shot and he being thrown to the ground he started to run as quickly as possible – After going for some distance I found myself cut off by some Lancers who had got in my front. To some distance off from me was my servant, Brown, who was badly wounded in the arm and a musket-ball in the back, one of the Lancers cut at him when he was on the ground and wounded him in the hand.'
Chapman, Robert	Pte	1182	MAY	Possibly rode in the Charge. Member of the Balaclava Commemoration Society in 1877 but not in 1879. Obituary in the *Craven Herald* 16.08.84 and gravestone both make claim to his having Charged. A. Sewell lists as a Charger, but gives no corroborating evidence for this statement.
Cheshire, Henry	Pte	1201	SW	Gun-shot wound left leg (*LG* 17.11.54 'severely wounded'). To Scutari 05.11.54. Invalided to England via Malta 04.12.54. Discharged 15.03.55: 'Disabled by lameness from gun-shot wound of the left leg incurred at Balaclava.'
Clarke, Michael	T.S.M	453	SW	Personal papers say severely wounded (*LG* 15.11.54 'slightly wounded'). Awarded the DCM, recommended 12.01.55. Recommended for a commission by Colonel Rodolph de Salis 30.09.56: 'He has received a medal for distinguished conduct in the field and he was recommended for the Victoria Cross in consequence of his conduct at Balaclava.'
Clement, James	Pte	1189	SW	Severely wounded (*LG* 17.11.54). To Scutari General Hospital 26.10.54. Rejoined the regiment 03.12.54.

8th Hussars	Rank	No	Charged	Corroborating Evidence Supporting Charger Status
Clowes, George Gooch	Crnt		PoW-W	Affidavit in the Cardigan v. Calthorpe case: 'A body of Russian cavalry had formed in our rear with a view to cut off our retreat. By the orders of Colonel Shewell we were wheeled about, and charged through the Russian Lancers. After getting through them I was wounded by a grape shot, my horse was killed, and I was taken prisoner' (*LG* 17.11.54.) Later escaped but was too weak from blood loss and taken PoW again. Exchanged September 1855.
Clutterbuck, Daniel Hugh	Lt		W	Wounded in the right foot by a shell fragment, while commanding C Troop on the right of the Squadron (*LG* 17.11.54 'slightly wounded'). A medical certificate, signed by three doctors and dated 13.08.55, stated: 'Having carefully examined Captain D.H. Clutterbuck of the 8th Hussars, found that the wound he suffered at Balaclava on the 25th of October last has not perfectly healed and from the nature of the injury he is not likely to become efficient in a reasonable period of time.' He retired by the sale of his commission 14.09.55.
Dalton, Charles	Pte	1136	UW	Member of the Balaclava Commemoration Society in 1879.
Dawn, William	Pte	1180	UW	Horse killed under him and caught a riderless horse.
De Salis, Rodolph	Maj		UW	Commanded the right-hand squadron. Assisted Private P. Doolan off the field on his wounded horse 'Drummer Boy' to whom he had a Queen's Crimea Medal named: On the reverse is the inscription "Carried Lt Col de Salis 8th Hussars". Nominated a Knight of the Légion d'Honneur (5th Class) (*LG* 04.08.56), awarded the Order of the Medjidie (5th Class) (*LG* 02.03.58), and the Al Valore Militaire: 'Lieutenant Colonel Robert [*sic*] de Salis, served in the Eastern campaign of 1854-55, including the battles of the Alma, Balaclava, Inkerman, Tchernaya, and the Siege of Sevastopol.' De Salis wrote to his sister: 'I have reason to be thankful to Divine Providence in having been one of the few Light Cavalry officers who escaped the day before yesterday. We had a most serious disaster. We all of us went knowing it was to certain destruction as well as quite unavailing.' He added: 'Lord Cardigan has certainly evinced himself good in action but it requires an enemy before and a few cannon shells to make him bearable.' (R. Dutton, *Forgotten Heroes*).
Dies, James	Pte	1033	K	Killed in action (*LG* 17.11.54).

Donald, William	Cpl	579	K	Killed in action (*LG* 17.11.54).
Donoghue, James	Tpt	1064	UW	Donoghue acted as field trumpeter to Colonel Shewell, riding centre front of the regiment. His horse was shot under him after the remnants of the regiment had broken through the line blocking their retreat, and he was stunned in the fall. Making his way back with a comrade, they were attacked by several Polish Lancers. Nominated to the Médaille Militaire: 'Charged with the Light Brigade at Balaclava; was also present in the ranks at the Alma and Inkerman and served with the regiment throughout the war.'
Donovan, John	Pte	1067	UW	Gave evidence at the court-martial of Troop Sergeant-Major J. Linkon (13th Light Dragoons) following his return from Russian captivity, confirming that the latter was unhorsed but found a riderless mount and joined the 8th Hussars.
Doolan, Patrick	Pte	936	SW	He was badly wounded by a gunshot; fracturing the lower jaw on both sides and injuring several important nerves (*LG* 17.11.54 'dangerously wounded'). He was assisted back to the British lines by Major De Salis as noted by Fanny Duberly in her diary entry for that day: 'Horses able to move were given up to wounded men. Major de Salis of the 8th Hussars retreated on foot, leading his horse with a wounded trooper in the saddle.' To Scutari Hospital 27.10.54. Invalided to England on 10.01.55. Discharged from Chatham 23.04.55.
Doyle, John	Pte	1131	UW	'On going into the Charge I had the first finger of the bridle hand split in five places and a piece cut out of my thumb, and on coming out I got a fair point of a lance in the forehead,' but received no medical attention and 'did not know there was a hole in it for a week afterwards.' His horse 'Hickabod' received a bullet wound to the nose which bled heavily – Doyle was unrecognisable when he returned from the Charge. Published his account.
Dunn, John William	Tpt	1090	MW	Mortally wounded (*LG* 17.11.54 'severely wounded'). To Scutari 26.10.54, possibly dying on board ship en route.
Dunn, Patrick	Pte	931	MAY	Listed as a Charger by A. Sewell, although attached to Raglan's Staff. Awarded the DCM, recommended 12.01.55.
Dwan, James	Pte	1079	UW	Member of the Balaclava Commemoration Society in 1879.

8th Hussars	Rank	No	Charged	Corroborating Evidence Supporting Charger Status
Dyer, John	F.S.	431	UW	A. Sewell, E.J. Boys and R. Dutton all list as a Charger, but give no corroborating evidence for this statement.
Finnegan, Francis	Pte	385	MW	Mortally wounded and died at Balaclava Hospital on 26.10.54 (*LG* 17.11.54).
Fitzgibbon, John	Pte	1091	K	Killed in action (*LG* 17.11.54 'wounded and PoW').
Fitzgibbon, John Charles Henry Viscount	Lt		K	Commanded F Troop, on the left of the Squadron, and killed in action, shot twice in the chest and last seen encouraging his men (*LG* 17.11.54 'killed – doubtful').
Frevillier, William	Pte	661	MAY	May have ridden in the Charge. A. Sewell lists as a Charger, but gives no corroborating evidence for this statement.
Fulton, William Stephen John	Pte	1153	W	Wounded on the right wrist by grape-shot (*LG* 17.11.54 'slightly wounded') but assisted Captain White of the 17th Lancers. To Scutari 26.10.54. Invalided to England 20.12.54. Awarded the DCM, recommended 12.01.55. Account in *Answers* magazine 26.10.12.
Glendwr, Robert Owen	Pte	1192	SW	He had two horses shot under him and taken PoW by lancers, but managed to crawl his way back and found a horse. Two sabre wounds to his right arm (*LG* 17.11.54 listed as 'R.O. Glendire' and as 'severely wounded'). To Scutari 26.10.54. Invalided to England 23.12.54. Was discharged from Chatham Invalid Depot 26.10.55: 'Considered unfit for further military service. Impaired use of right hand from a sabre wound received at Balaclava, causing a stiffness of the wrist and inability to move the fingers. Likely to improve.' Served with the Metropolitan Police from 26.11.55 when his physical description was shown as before: 'having a sabre-cut on the right forearm and a partly paralysed right leg and arm.' Account in *The Illustrated London News* 30.10.75.
Gray, William	T.M	392	W	Rode in C Troop, with Lord Fitzgibbon deputising for Captain Lockwood. Slightly wounded in the shoulder. Nominated a Knight of the Légion d'Honneur (5th Class) (*LG* 04.08.56). Obituary in *Jackson's Woolwich Gazette* 01.01.84: 'Had his sword belt shot away, the ball entering his pocket, smashing his pipe, and lodged there. His trumpet was hit, his busby had two shots through it and he was slightly wounded in the shoulder.'

Hackett, Martin	Pte	1031	UW	Received assistance from the T.H. Roberts Fund and the Light Brigade Relief Fund.
Hanrahan, Denis	Pte	939	K	Killed in action (*LG* 17.11.54). Private W. Fulton of C Troop: 'My right-hand man, Denis Hanrahan, was shot in the head by one of the thousand grape-shot ringing about our ears, and sank on his saddle-bow his charger still going on with us.' Source: *The History of the VIII King's Royal Irish Hussars*, Rev. R.H. Murray.
Hanrahan, Thomas	Pte	979	MAY	A. Sewell lists as a Charger, but gives no corroborating evidence for this statement.
Harris, William	Pte	1159	MAY	May have ridden in the Charge, but died of dysentery at Scutari 24.02.55. Memorial in Harrietsham churchyard records him as a Charger.
Harrison, Henry	T.S.M	370	UW	Led a riderless horse back down the valley which he gave to Private W.H. Pennington, 11th Hussars. Promoted to cornet for gallantry at Inkerman, with effect from 05.11.54.
Hefferon, James Andrew	Tpt	1151	UW	Rode in C Troop, with Lord Fitzgibbon deputising for Captain G. Lockwood. Member of the Balaclava Commemoration Society in 1879.
Hefferon, Thomas	Pte	1152	K	Killed in action (*LG* 17.11.54), shot through the head early in the Charge, Private W. Bird's account refers. Private J. Doyle's Letter in the *Army and Navy Gazette* 03.01.91 gives a different version: 'Thomas, was shot on my right during the Charge; a shell met him and exploded and blew his body into the air.'
Heneage, Clement Walker	Crnt		UW	Horse unscathed during the Charge. Awarded the Victoria Cross by vote during the Indian Mutiny (action on the 17.06.58 at the Battle of Gwalior).
Herbert, Edmund	Pte	793	K	Killed in action (*LG* 17.11.54).
Hogan, John	Pte	1006	UW	Member of the Balaclava Commemoration Society in 1879.
Holmes, Henry	Pte	1224	SW	Horse shot from under him and severely injured in the fall. Discharged from Chatham Invalid Depot 24.06.55. Member of the Balaclava Commemoration Society in 1877, but not in 1879.
Horan, Patrick	Pte	808	PoW-W	Horse killed by round-shot injuring his legs as it fell. Taken PoW (*LG* 17.11.54). Repatriated 26.10.55. Discharged from Dundalk 21.10.56.
Hurst, Thomas	Pte	1121	UW	Member of the Balaclava Commemoration Society in 1877. Received assistance from the Light Brigade Relief Fund.
Johnson, Robert	Pte	1126	UW	Member of the Balaclava Commemoration Society in 1879.

8th Hussars	Rank	No	Charged	Corroborating Evidence Supporting Charger Status
Keating, Matthew	Pte	1031 or 1051	SW	Rode 'in the front rank rather to the right of the squadron.' Lost right arm and received nine lance wounds (*LG* 17.11.54 'killed or missing'). Medal Roll shown as being 'killed in action'. However the affidavit of Matthew Keating was filed on 02.06.63 in the Cardigan v. Calthorpe lawsuit.
Kennedy, Richard	Pte	1007	SW	Lance wound to the head during the retreat (*LG* 17.11.54 'severely wounded'). To Scutari 26.10.54. Rejoined regiment 14.12.54.
Kitterick, Patrick	Pte	1130	W	Slightly wounded in left heel (*LG* 17.11.54 'slightly wounded'). To Scutari Hospital 26.10.54. Invalided Home 24.03.55. Discharged from Chatham Invalid Depot 16.10.55.
Lennon, Martin	Pte	942	K	Killed in action (*LG* 17.11.54 listed as 'Martin Lemmion'). See Private J. Doyle's account.
Macaulay, Charles	Pte	1057	UW	*The Regiment* carried a letter from Macaulay describing how he was rescued by Private J. Vahey, 17th Lancers: 'I was lying under my second horse, a Russian one, my first having been shot from under me. He was on foot, in his shirt sleeves, and held his naked sword blade in his hand, not his axe. He assisted me from under the second horse and put me on another which was passing (being without a rider), and brought me off the field.' Nominated to the Médaille Militaire: 'Charged with the Light Brigade at Balaclava. Also present in the ranks at the Alma and Inkerman. Served with the Regiment throughout the war.'
Martin, John	Pte	992	UW	Two horses shot from under him. Nominated to the Médaille Militaire: 'Charged with the Light Brigade at Balaclava. Also present in the ranks at the Alma and Inkerman and served with the Regiment throughout the war.'
McCausland, John	Pte	1114	UW	Member of the Balaclava Commemoration Society in 1879. Received assistance from the Light Brigade Relief Fund.
McCluer, Harry	T.S.M	859	K	Killed in action (*LG* 17.11.54), shot through the head early in the Charge (see Private W. Bird's account) (*LG* 17.11.54).
McDonald, Edward	Pte	1272	K	Killed in action (*LG* 17.11.54).
Moneypenny, Robert	Pte	934	UW	Awarded the DCM, recommended 12.01.55: 'for praiseworthy and gallant service throughout the campaign'.
Morris, George	Pte	1136	K	Killed in action (*LG* 17.11.54).

Mortimer, John	Pte	938	UW	Member of the Balaclava Commemoration Society in 1879.
Mussenden, William	Crnt		UW	Horse killed by grapeshot. Awarded the Order of the Medjidie (5th Class) (*LG* 02.03.58).
Neal, James	Pte	1185	UW	Awarded the DCM, recommendation 12.01.55. L.W. Crider lists as a Charger, but gives no corroborating evidence for this statement.
Nichol, Robert	Pte	1027	UW	*The Newcastle Courant* 05.01.55: 'We had to charge some guns; we had to go through a triangle of fire, and there was infantry on the right, – that was how there were so many lost. When we got to the guns the Russian lancers were charging us in the rear. We came left about wheel, and charged them, and very soon mowed our way through them. I came out safe, but a ball had gone through the end of my cloak.' *Lloyds Weekly Newspaper* 14.01.55: 'This young man, only twenty-one years of age, was engaged in the deadly and heroic charge of the light cavalry at Balaclava and had his sword arm nearly chopped off just above the wrist [*sic*]. He fell amidst the dead and dying, Russian and English; and catching a trooper's horse without a rider, which came close to him, he jumped upon it, and holding the bridle with his left hand, managed to reach the English lines.' Member of the Balaclava Commemoration Society in 1879.
Palframan, Richard	Pte	1218	PoW	Horse shot, pinning him to the ground. Taken PoW (*LG* 17.11.54). Repatriated with other PoWs on the *Columbo* and 'Her Majesty's Ship' in October 1855.
Perry, Thomas	Pte	597	SW	Shot in both thighs, and through the right shoulder, received a lance wound to the thigh and left hand and two sword wounds to the head (*LG* 17.11.54). Exchanged 29.08.55. Found guilty of allowing himself to be taken PoW (despite receiving ten wounds) – 84 day's imprisonment followed by discharge due to vertigo, as a result of his head wounds.
Phillips, Edward	Lt		UW	Horse killed under him on the return, while commanding D Troop originally at the centre of the squadron. Defended himself and Private John Brown who was disabled in both hands, with his revolver until the enemy were called off by a trumpet call, when both made their escape.
Picking, William	Pte	1231	UW	Lummis and Wynn state taken PoW, but figures on the muster roll throughout. Deserted 14.08.56, possibly why never a member of the Balaclava Commemoration Society. Received assistance from the T.H. Roberts Fund.

8th Hussars	Rank	No	Charged	Corroborating Evidence Supporting Charger Status
Pickworth, John Atkins	Sgt	684	UW	Horse killed under him and held onto the stirrups of Privates R. Briggs and S. Bond to reach safety. Nominated a Knight of the Légion d'Honneur (5th Class). Recommended for the Victoria Cross (VC) during the Indian Mutiny.
Reilly, Michael	Sgt	917	K	Killed in action (*LG* 17.11.54). Lieutenant E. Seager's account mentions Sgt Reilly riding, apparently dead, beside him. His horse returned with him shot dead in the saddle.
Ross, Joseph	Pte	1222	K	Mortally wounded (*LG* 17.11.54 'severely wounded'). To Scutari Hospital 26.10.54, where he died 08.11.54.
Ryan, William	Pte	1004 or 1104	MW	Mortally wounded (*LG* 17.11.54 'dangerously wounded'). To Scutari Hospital 26.10.54, and died on board ship en route.
Seager, Edward	Lt		W	Seager took the place of Captain E. Tomkinson at Balaclava after the latter's horse had been killed. He rode as adjutant and was on the right of Lieutenant D.H. Clutterbuck. Commanded the right-hand squadron. In breaking through the lancers he received a lance's point which 'knocked off the skin of the knuckles of my second finger, and the point entered between the second and top joint of my little finger, coming out on the other side (*LG* 17.11.54). His mare, called 'Malta', received a ball through the neck, just above the windpipe, but carried on. Nominated a Knight of the Légion d'Honneur (5th Class), awarded the Order of Medjidie (5th Class) (*LG* 02.03.58). Promoted to Captain on day after the Charge.
Sewell, Edward	Sgt	1104	MW	Mortally wounded. To Scutari 26.10.54. Died 'of his wounds' 26.12.54.
Sewell, John	Cpl	1197	MW	Mortally wounded (*LG* 17.11.54 'severely wounded'). To Scutari 26.10.54. Died 26.12.54.
Sheridan, Anthony	Pte	468	W	Rode in E troop. Sword wound on the forehead at the guns. Account in *The Illustrated London News* 30.10.75.
Shewell, Frederick George	Lt Col		UW	Commanding, rode at left of squadron. His horse, along with that of Cornet Heneage's, said to be the only ones to return completely unscathed. Rallied the 8th Hussars and 17th Lancers in the retreat and was the first to engage the Cossacks attempting to cut off the retreat of the Brigade. Nominated a Knight of the Légion d'Honneur (4th Class) (*LG* 04.08.56), mentioned in despatches (*LG* 30.11.54), appointed Commander of the Bath (*LG* 10.07.55).
Spain, Christopher	Pte	568	W	Slightly wounded in left hand by lance, and shell splinter to left leg (*LG* 17.11.54 'slightly wounded'). To Scutari Hospital 26.10.54. Invalided to England 01.05.55. Discharged from Chatham Invalid Depot 12.06.55.

Steele, Hugh Massey	Pte	954	MAY	Possibly rode in the Charge. At Scutari Hospital late 1854. An account in the *Windsor and Richmond Gazette*, published October of 1888, credits him as a Charger.
Taylor, William	Cpl	872	MW	Mortally wounded and taken PoW (*LG* 17.11.54). Died either in hospital at Simferopol or on the road there. An account by an unknown private: 'Corporal Taylor on my left, mounted on a horse either startled or mad with the noise of the firing – couldn't stop him at all; he had no control over his mount. He shot past me like a rocket, bang into the heart of the Russian cavalry in the rear of the guns, which opened up and then closed upon him. I heard he was wounded and taken prisoner.' *History of the VIII King's Royal Irish Hussars*, Murray.
Tomkinson, Edward	Cpt		W	Wounded and had his horse shot under him, while commanding a Squadron. Brevet-Major (*LG* 12.12.54). Awarded the Al Valore Militaire, the Order of the Medjidie (5th Class) (*LG* 02.03.58).
Turner, Edward	Pte	1238	K	Killed in action (Wounded and PoW *LG* 17.11.54)
Twamley, Thomas	Pte	1078	SW	Wounded in seven places, with four lance wounds in the left side and three in the left arm (*LG* 17.11.54 listed as 'Thomas Tovamley', and as 'severely wounded'). To Scutari Hospital 26.10.54. Discharged 25.02.55. Awarded the DCM, recommended 12.01.55.
Waterer, Charles	Pte	1228	K	Killed in action (LG 17.11.54).
White, John	Pte	1011	K	Killed in action (*LG* 17.11.54).
Whyte, Charles	Pte	981	SW	*The Regiment* of 17 December 1898: 'At one time Whyte says he was surrounded by a score of armed Russians who ferociously hacked and jabbed at him with their sabres and lances. He received four severe wounds, in cutting his way through them, on his head, a lance wound on his breast, one in his leg and a bullet wound in another part of his body. 'Whyte was also a spectator of the extraordinary leap by Lord Cardigan over a Russian battery. 'As soon as the Charge had been accomplished, the Russians were observed carrying off an English sergeant as a prisoner. A number of our men at once volunteered to form a party to effect a rescue. Whyte was one of the party, and the object was obtained. In this hazardous service Whyte was again surrounded by Russians and had to defend himself as well as he could. Having despatched one or two opponents he thrust his sword through the body of an antagonist, but was unable to draw back.

8th Hussars	Rank	No	Charged	Corroborating Evidence Supporting Charger Status
				'One of the Russians close by observed this and made up to Whyte, when Lord Bingham [*the only reference to Lord Bingham as a possible Charger although the act occurred immediately after the Charge*], the gallant son of the Earl of Lucan, parried off the lance with a cut of his sword, and another cut brought the Russian to the ground, thus saving the life of Whyte.
				'After lying some time in a dangerous state at Scutari, where he experienced the kind attention of Miss Nightingale, he returned to England partially restored, but his injuries were so severe he was never fit for active service again.'
				At Scutari early 1855.
Williams, Samuel	T.S.M	420	UW	Awarded the Distinguished Conduct Medal.
Williams, William	Sgt	804	K	Killed in action (*LG* 17.11.54). See Private J. Doyle's account of his death. Doyle said he was the brother of 420 Troop Sergeant Major S. Williams.
Wilson, Samuel	Pte	911	UW	Member of the Balaclava Commemoration Society in 1879. Awarded the DCM.
Wilson, William	Pte	1204	UW	Awarded the Al Valore Militaire: 'Charged with the Light Brigade at Balaclava, and evinced great coolness and courage, being then only sixteen years of age.'

	Officers	NCOs	Trumpeters	Other Ranks	Total
Rode in the Charge and Killed in action (K)	1	4	0	15	20
Rode in the Charge and Mortally Wounded (MW)	0	3	1	3	7
Rode in the Charge and Severely Wounded (SW)	0	1	0	9	10
Rode in the Charge and Prisoner of War (PoW)	0	0	0	1	1
Rode in the Charge and Prisoner of War – Wounded (PoW-W)	1	0	0	4	5
Rode in the Charge and Prisoner of War – mortally wounded (PoW-M)	0	0	0	0	0
Rode in the Charge and wounded (W)	3	1	0	5	9
Rode in the Charge unwounded (UW)	5	4	2	19	30
May Have Ridden (MAY)	0	0	1	6	7
Identified chargers	10	13	4	62	89
Unidentified Chargers					26
Total Number of Chargers					115

TABLES

The following contemporary sources give details of the regiment's statistics for the 25 October 1854

The London Gazette 12 November 1854 – Return of Casualties from 22 to 26 October, 1854, both days inclusive:

8th Hussars

2 officers, 3 sergeants, 23 rank and file, 38 horses, killed; 2 officers, 2 sergeants, 1 drummer, 14 rank and file, wounded.

Lieutenant E. Seager, 8th Hussars, wrote, 'We had 26 men killed and 17 wounded, 36 horses killed and a number wounded' (Seager, Letter from the Crimea dated 26 October, 1854, NAM).

Only 38 members of the regiment answered the first roll-call of mounted men made immediately after the Charge

Ken Horton in editing *One Hussar The Journal of James Rawlins*, wrote: 'On rallying on their return, only 44 men turned up from the 104 that began the charge. 2 officers, 3 sergeants and 16 men dead; six taken prisoner. Thirty-eight horses dead in the valley and twenty-four seriously wounded left on the ground. Of the many wounded of the regiment, seven men later died of their wounds at Scutari.'

A terrier named Jenny, the mascot of the 8th, accompanied the regiment during the Charge and was wounded by a splinter in the neck. On her return to England Colonel de Salis presented the dog collar with the five clasps attached to it for Alma, Balaclava, Inkerman, Sevastopol and Central India; this is still in the Officer's mess.

11th Hussars Table

11th Hussars	Rank	No	Charged	Corroborating Evidence Supporting Charger Status
Allured, Charles	Pte	1340	K	Killed in action (*LG* 17.11.54). Sergeant S. Bond: 'A man named Allurad [*sic*], who was riding on my left, fell from his horse like a stone. I looked back and saw the poor fellow lying on his back, right temple cut away, and his brains lying half on the ground.' *Leamington Courier* 26.06.97.
Alliston, Thomas	Pte	1128	UW	Member of the Balaclava Commemoration Society in 1877 but not in 1879. Account: *The Sketch* 31.02.94 – image of T.J. Alliston *The Story of Balaclava Told by One of the Survivors* (TJA).
Andrews, David	Pte	1444	W	*LG* 17.11.54 'slightly wounded'.
Andrews, William	Pte	1028	MAY	Listed by R. Dutton as a Charger, but Private G. Wilde 13th Light Dragoons stated that he was not.
Archer, George	H.S.M	707	MAY	L.W. Crider lists as a Charger. He attended the 1892 Dinner. Awarded the DCM.

263

11th Hussars	Rank	No	Charged	Corroborating Evidence Supporting Charger Status
Ash, Henry	Pte	1121	MAY	His name appears on a confidential memo (along with Private J.T. Bambrick) from Horse Guards dated 31.12.55 recommending him for the Légion d'Honneur – the reason for the recommendation, which came to nothing, is not known. Served as orderly to Lord Cardigan.
Ashton, Robert	Pte	828	UW	Claimed to have ridden alongside Private R. Martin: 'We belonged to the same troop. We lived in the same room, and we rode side by side together in the Charge, but he had his arm shot off. I had my horse shot under me in less than half a minute, and my busby was shot off my head. My first horse was shot under me after a very short time.' He caught hold of Private Fleming's bridle, later the horse's tail, before catching a horse from the 4th Light Dragoons and reaching the guns. Died June 1860.
Bambrick, John T.	Pte	1465	W	Nominated a Knight of the Légion d'Honneur (5th Class) (*LG* 04.08.56): 'Rode next to 1495 Sergeant Robert Davies at Balaclava and endeavoured to help him capture a Russian gun that the crew was trying to get away from the field of battle. His horse was later killed under him.'
Bassett, William Walter	Cpl	1027	MAY	Promoted to corporal the day after the Charge (26.10.54). Died 18.11.54 at Balaclava.
Barber, John Clement	Far	1298	MAY	May have ridden. Member of the Balaclava Commemoration Society in 1877 but not in 1879.
Baynes, Henry	Pte	1029	MAY	May have ridden. Listed as a Charger by A. Sewell, but without corroborating evidence.
Beeson, Benjamin	Pte	1570	UW	'Rode in the centre of the right squadron.'
Bentley, William	Sgt	863	W	Rode on the left of the first squadron. When Lieutenant Colonel J. Douglas ordered the remnants of the 11th to form on the 17th Lancers, Bentley drew his attention to their being Russians. 'We got his order "fight for your lives"'. Unseated beyond the guns when he received a lance wound to back of the neck. Later his calf was grazed by a bullet after his horse flagged due to the exertions of the charge (*LG* 17.11.54 'slightly wounded'). Assisted by Lieutenant A. Dunn who was awarded the VC.
Berry, John	Pte	1306	PoW-W	Wounded and taken PoW (*LG* 17.11.54), died either at Simferopol or on the road from Sevastopol.

Bingham, John	Pte	1412	W	Wounded (*LG* 17.11.54 'slightly wounded').
Blissett, Edward	Pte	1430	UW	Received assistance from the Light Brigade Relief Fund.
Bond, Seth	Sgt	1091	W	Rode in the centre of the first squadron. Unhorsed and wounded by three sword cuts to his rein arm, also cuts to his back and head. Assisted by Private R. Briggs. Nominated to the Médaille Militaire by decree dated 16.04.56: '1091 Sergeant Seth Bond, Served in the Campaign in Bulgaria in 1854. Was present at the affair of Bulganak, and Battles of Alma, Balaclava and Inkerman. At the Alma, when ordered to pursue and capture prisoners, he exhibited great subordination in sparing (at the suggestion of a Staff Officer) a Russian, who had wounded him, and also at the action at Balaclava, his coolness and gallantry were noted. He also served in the whole of the Campaign from 1854 to 1856.' The *Tasmanian* (Launceston) 25.12.75 states he was 'surrounded by the Russian Hussars, and received several sword cuts on the left arm, head, &c.'
Breeze, John	Sgt	1102	UW	Lost his right arm at Inkerman. Awarded the DCM, recommendation 10.01.55.
Briers, Daniel Regan John	Pte	1539	MAY	Lummis and Wynn list as a Charger, although no clasp. Received assistance from the T.H. Roberts Fund. Attended dinners in 1903, 1906, and 1909-10. Account and portrait in *Answers* magazine, October 1912. Private J.S. Parkinson of the 11th stated it was very doubtful whether this man rode in the Charge. He was in the Commissary Department, but under fire.
Briggs, Robert	Pte	1473	UW	Horse shot from under him. Saved the life of Sergeant S. Bond (Lummis & Wynn), although Bond claimed that it was the other way around. Member of the Balaclava Commemoration Society in 1879.
Brown, Richard	Pte	1153	UW	Rode in centre of his squadron. Horse shot under him whereupon he was attacked by two Cossacks, both of whom he despatched, riding back on one of their horses. Lieutenant Colonel John Douglas's servant and later the favourite orderly of Lord Cardigan. On 16.05.86 Brown wrote to Pennington giving him the sword carried by Douglas during the Charge. It had been given to Brown on the Colonel's return from the Crimea.

11th Hussars	Rank	No	Charged	Corroborating Evidence Supporting Charger Status
Brown Samuel Charles	Pte	1231	UW	A member of the Balaclava Commemoration Society in 1877. Received assistance from the T.H. Roberts Fund. Attended Annual Dinners in 1894, '95, '97 and '99.
Brunton, Joseph	Pte	1176	K	Killed in action (*LG* 17.11.54).
Bubb, Robert	Pte	1588	K	Killed in action (*LG* 17.11.54).
Buckton, John	Cpl	1413	UW	Rode with C Troop. Unwounded, but horse destroyed the following day. 'I rode within a few files of the right of the regiment in the rear rank – several men on my right were killed in the advance' (*Lord Paget's Journal*). An account in *The Illustrated London News* 30.10.75.
Bull, George	S.M	1057	UW	Rode on the left of D Troop. Horse shot under him. Gazetted cornet in the 11th Hussars 15.12.54.
Canning, Walter	Pte	1604		May have ridden in the Charge according to R. Dutton, but he gives no supporting evidence.
Cart, Charles	Pte	1046	MAY	Member of the Balaclava Commemoration Society in 1877, but not in 1879. Received assistance from the Light Brigade Relief Fund.
Chambers, Richard Thompson	Pte	1252	UW	Member of the Balaclava Commemoration Society 1879. An account in a letter home 30.10.54.
Cook, Edwin Adolphus	Cpt		W	Commanded the 2nd Squadron. Rallied survivors and led them through the lancers where he was slightly wounded (*LG* 17.11.54). Appointed Brevet-Major (*LG* 12.12.54). Nominated a Knight of the Légion d'Honneur (5th Class) (*LG* 01.05.57).
Cooper, Charles B.	Pte	1603	K	Killed in action (*LG* 17.11.54).
Cork, Charles	Cpl	1437	W	Wounded (*LG* 17.11.54 'slightly wounded').
Crocker, Rowland	Pte	1551	MAY	Possibly rode in the Charge. His papers came into the hands of the Kensington workhouse master and led him to believe that he was a Charger. Funeral attended by a detachment of 11th Hussars from Ireland. Listed by Lummis & Wynn and A. Sewell who state, 'May have Charged', but give no corroborating evidence.
Cullen, William	Pte	1520	UW	Rode to the left of Private N. Henry. Assisted Privates J. Fleming and R. Layzell during the retreat.
Davies, Robert	Sgt	1495	W	Horse shot under him and a lance wound on the right thigh while trying to prevent one of the guns being carried away (*LG* 17.11.54 'slightly wounded'). At Scutari from 30.10.54 to 29.12.54. Awarded the Al Valore Militaire: 'After having passed through the battery in the Light Brigade Charge and perceiving a Russian field-piece limbered up ready for retreat, Sergeant Davies

				called to Private John T. Bambrick, who was riding next to him, to follow and endeavoured to capture it. In going to perform this duty he was attacked by two Russian lancers, one of whom he shot down, the other shot his horse; when on the ground he received a lance wound in the right thigh. He then caught a loose horse and rejoined his regiment.'
Davies, William	Pte	1406	K	Killed in action (*LG* 17.11.54 listed as 'W. Davis'). *The History of the Eleventh Hussars* (Williams, 1908) lists as 'William Davis'.
Davis, Richard	Cpl	1530	W	Muster roll shows him 'In hospital (wounded)', but he is not shown as so recorded on any other official casualty roll. Lummis and Wynn lists as a Charger. Member of the Balaclava Commemoration Society in 1877, but not 1879. Received assistance from the T.H. Roberts Fund.
Douglas, John	Lt Col		UW	Douglas commanded the regiment during the Charge. Troop Sergeant Major J. Joseph: 'After charging the Russian artillery, and arriving at the extreme end of the valley Colonel Douglas ordered us to save ourselves, and then led the remnants of the chargers so gallantly and coolly against the enemy's cavalry until we could proceed no further.' Nominated a Knight of the Légion d'Honneur (5th Class) (*LG* 01.05.57), awarded the Order of the Medjidie (4th Class) (*LG* 02.03.56), mentioned in despatches (*LG* 30.11.54), appointed a Commander of the Bath (*LG* 10.07.55).
Dryden, John	Pte	1617	W	A sabre wound on the upper part of the left arm and the bridge of the nose, 26 lance wounds on back, the right side of the body and the right thigh and taken PoW (*LG* 17.11.54). R.S. Farquharson: 'Dryden of the 11th Hussars, who had no fewer than thirty-six wounds'. Repatriated with other PoWs on the *Columbo* and 'Her Majesty's Ship' in October 1855. Invalided to England 23.01.56. Discharged from Chatham Invalid Depot 20.05.56.
Dunn, Alexander Roberts	Lt		UW	Commanded F Troop on the right of the 2nd Squadron. Awarded the VC for going to the assistance of Sergeant W. Bentley and Private R. Levett (*LG* 27.02.57).
Dyke, John	Pte	1265	UW	Rode on 'Old Bob'.
Eastoe, Nehemian William	Pte	1578	UW	Horse shot under him. Caught a loose Russian horse and retired unwounded.

267

11th Hussars	Rank	No	Charged	Corroborating Evidence Supporting Charger Status
Elder, James	Pte	1140	K	Killed in action (*LG* 17.11.54). Sergeant S. Bond's account in the *Leamington Courier* 26.06.96: 'Just at that time a young man named James Elder fell from his horse, no doubt shot by the rifles pursuing us up the valley. I looked back for a moment and saw three Russian Lancers in the act of piercing him and heard his cry, "Oh, Oh, Oh,' as the lances entered his body. I dared not look back again.'
Ellis, William	Pte	1456	MAY	Lummis interviewed Ellis and listed him as having 'Probably Charged', claiming to have ridden next to Private Thomas Warr. Pennington thought his claim possible, but queried why he had not come forward earlier.
Firth, Wilson	Pte	1612	SW	*LG* 17.11.54 'severely wounded'. To Scutari Hospital 04.11.54, where he died of fever 03.03.55.
Fleming, John	Pte	1156	W	Wounded in the left thigh by a lance thrust. Name is not included in the list of casualties in the *LG* 17.11.54, but obituary *Birmingham Daily Post* 23.05.92 confirms.
France, Thomas	Cpl	1334	K	Killed in action (*LG* 17.11.54).
Fry, William A.	Pte	1562	MAY	The inscription on the gravestone reads: 'A Crimean Hero. In Loving Memory of WILLIAM AUGUSTUS FRY of the 11th Hussars who died July 18th 1860, aged 25 years. He was one of the Gallant Six Hundred in the Charge of Balaclava.'
Glanister, James	Pte	1564	SW	At the guns a Cossack shot his pistol at him, the bullet shattered his lower jaw (*LG* 17.11.54 'dangerously wounded'). Assisted by Private R. Martin. After being invalided home he was discharged on 03.04.55 as unfit for further service. Awarded the DCM.
Grantham, David	Pte	1486	W	Horse shot under him and shot through the calf and wrist (not included in *LG* casualty list).
Groome, Henry	Pte	1569	W	Slightly wounded (*LG* 17.11.54). Sick at Scutari Hospital late 1854. Invalided to England early 1855.
Gusterson, James	Pte	1618	UW	Member of the Balaclava Commemoration Society in 1877, but not in 1879. Died 08.06.80.
Guttridge, George G.	T.S.M	1329	UW	'I well remember that Sergeant Gutteridge was on the right guide of the 2nd Squadron' - *Strand Magazine*, March 1891. 'I rode in the front rank on the extreme left of the regiment in the Charge.' (*Lord Paget's Journal*). Nominated a Knight of the Légion d'Honneur (4th Class) (*LG* 04.08.56).
Gwinnell, Reuben	Pte	1616	K	Killed in action (*LG* 17.11.54).

Hampson, George Henry	Pte	1310	MAY	May have ridden in the Charge.
Harrison, Robert	Pte	1389	UW	Nominated to the Médaille Militaire by decree dated 21.08.56: 'Present at the battles of Alma and Balaclava, where he behaved very gallantly in galloping to the rescue of several comrades who were fighting against overwhelming odds. Was also present at the Battle of Inkerman, and through the whole of the Campaign from 1854 to 1856.'
Harvey, James	Pte	1433	MAY	May have ridden in the Charge. Member of the Balaclava Commemoration Society in 1877, but not in 1879.
Hellett, Amos	Pte	1365	MAY	Possibly rode in the Charge. Listed as a Charger by A. Sewell. Extract from *Army and Navy Gazette* January 1890 announcing his death on 17th states that: 'He took part in the Charge of the Light Brigade at Balaclava.'
Henry, Nathan	Pte	1584	PoW	Had two horses shot under him and taken PoW (*LG* 17.11.54). It was said he was kept by a Russian Lady until after the Armistice and was reluctant to return. Repatriated with other PoWs on the *Columbo* and 'Her Majesty's Ship' in October 1855.
Hoarne, George	Pte	1590	K	Killed (*LG* 17.11.54 listed as 'G. Horne'). Private Nathan Henry witnessed his death: 'I had not gone many yards when I overlook one of my own regiment, also on foot, whose name was Horne but together we had not advanced many paces more when a shell fell and burst close to us, a piece of shell striking my comrade in the left side, knocking him down. I attempted to raise him, but he waved me away with one hand, pressing the other to his side. I noticed that the blood was flowing freely from his chest, and after giving a deep sigh, he fell back dead.' *History of the Eleventh Hussars* (Williams, 1908) lists as 'George Horne'.
Hodges, James	Pte	1550	UW	To Scutari 18.12.54. Invalided to England 27.02.55. Member of the Balaclava Commemoration Society 1879.
Holland, Matthew	Pte	1543	UW	'I rode in the front rank of the right troop of the regiment at Balaclava, I heard no word of command given by anyone except Colonel Douglas, either going down the valley or returning' (*Lord Paget's Journal*).

11th Hussars	Rank	No	Charged	Corroborating Evidence Supporting Charger Status
Houghton, George Powell	Lt		MW	Commanded C Troop on the right of the 1st Squadron. Mortally wounded (*LG* 17.11.54 'severely wounded'). Struck in the forehead by a fragment of a shell bursting and, riding a chestnut horse with white stockings, wearing similar uniforms and bearing some physical resemblance to Lord Cardigan, was mistaken for the Brigade commander. Died Scutari General Hospital 22.11.54.
Hudson, Edward	Cpl	1142	W	*LG* 17.11.54 'slightly wounded'. Private T. Wroots mentions him as follows when they engaged with a regiment of Polish Lancers: 'I saw one of these fellows run up behind one of our Sergeants, I think his name was Hudson, and catch him right in the middle of the back with his lance. He was not killed then, but I heard that he died some time later.' Admitted to hospital in early January 1855, died 31.01.55 near Kadikoi.
Hyde, Walter	Pte	1601	PoW-W	Wounded and taken PoW (*LG* 17.11.54). His name is not listed among those exchanged and may have died in captivity.
Jackman, John	Pte	1476	K	Killed in action (*LG* 17.11.54).
Jamieson, Samuel (aka S.J. Murdock)	Pte	1593	UW	Unwounded. Member of the Balaclava Commemoration Society 1879. Real name Samuel Jamieson Murdock.
Jewell, Henry	Pte	1403	SW	Severely wounded (*LG* 17.11.54). To Scutari Hospital 29.10.54. Invalided Home 24.03.55. Depot troop on 01.06.55.
Jones, John	Sgt	1423	K	Killed in action (*LG* 17.11.54).
Jordon, Thomas	Sgt	1209	K	Killed in action (*LG* 17.11.54).
Joseph, John	Sgt	1127	W	Rode as a serrefile left of E Troop during the Charge, possibly acting as Troop Sergeant Major. Wounded by a sabre cut in an encounter with a Russian officer: 'After charging the Russian artillery, and arriving at the extreme end of the valley Colonel Douglas ordered us to save ourselves, and then led the remnants of the chargers so gallantly and coolly against the enemy's cavalry until we could proceed no further' (*Lord Paget's Journal*).
Jowett, Gregory	Pte	1357	W	Wounded (*LG* 17.11.54 'slightly wounded'). Cut down a Russian holding a gun at Lieutenant R.W.H. Palmer's head.

Keates, Joseph John	Tpt	914	UW	Orderly trumpeter to the Earl of Cardigan. Horse killed under him.
Kelly, James	Pte	1613	UW	Member of the Balaclava Commemoration Society in 1879.
Kilvert, John Ashley	Cpl	1513	W	Wounded by a musket ball through his right leg and a slight sabre cut on the head (*LG* 17.11.54 'slightly wounded'). The ball passed through his saddle flap into his horse, but the animal did not fall. At close quarters he received a slight sabre cut on the head. His horse brought him back but had to be shot as soon as Kilvert was lifted off. His leg was bandaged and he was to have been taken away immediately but the ambulances were full so he was left in a ditch until darkness came. He was then discovered by an ambulance party nearly frozen to death. Promoted sergeant 26.10.54. To Scutari Hospital and subsequently invalided Home via Malta in February 1855.
Larkin, James	Pte	1270	K	Killed in action (*LG* 17.11.54).
Lawson, John	Sgt	1415	SW	Rode on the right of the 2nd Squadron, front rank, just behind Lieutenant Colonel Douglas. During the retreat wounded by canister shot in the right arm 'after passing the lancers' (amputated 3 inches below the elbow) (*LG* 17.11.54 'severely wounded'), and his horse shot under him. At Scutari 05.11.54 until 20.12.54. Discharged from Chatham Invalid Depot 10.07.55. Awarded the DCM, recommended 01.02.55.
Layzell, Robert	Pte	1335	K	Killed by several Cossacks while lying wounded beside his horse (*LG* 17.11.54 listed as 'R. Lazell'). Mentioned in the account by Private W. Cullen.
Levett, Robert	Pte	1260	K	Killed in action (*LG* 17.11.54), despite Lieutenant A. Dunn's efforts to save his life by disarming a Russian who was attacking him. For his actions Lieutenant Dunn was awarded of the Victoria Cross (*LG* 27.02.57).
Martin, Robert	Pte	1337	SW	Gun-shot wounded to right arm (amputated) (*LG* 17.11.54 'severely wounded'). Assisted Private J. Glanister of the 11th Hussars. To Scutari 30.10.54. Invalided Home 11.02.55. Discharged from Chatham Invalid Depot 24.07.55. Awarded the DCM.
Maule, George Frederick	Pte	1602	UW	Rode about the 5th file from the right of the regiment. Member of the Balaclava Commemoration Society in 1879.
McGeorge, John	Pte	1385	K	Killed in action (*LG* 17.11.54 listed as 'J.M. George').

11th Hussars	Rank	No	Charged	Corroborating Evidence Supporting Charger Status
Middleton, Isaac	Pte	1422	MAY	Lummis and Wynn stated 'May have ridden in the Charge,' but give no evidence.
Milburn, Silvester	Pte	741	SW	Wounded through right arm by a musket ball (*LG* 17.11.54 'severely wounded'). To Scutari 29.10.54. Invalided to England on the 26.01.55. Discharged from Chatham Invalid Depot 24.04.56.
Newman, Charles	Pte	1505	MAY	May have Charged. Received assistance from the Light Brigade Relief Fund.
Palmer, Roger Henry William	Lt		UW	Commanded E Troop on the left of the 2nd Squadron. Palmer's life was saved by Private G. Jowett, whom he had, a few days before, only cautioned for being asleep at his post. One of his stirrup-leathers was shot away and his busby shot off his head.
Parker, Henry William	Pte	1484	PoW-W	Rode on the left of the rear rank of the 1st Squadron, covering Sergeant Bentley. Horse shot under him, wounded and taken PoW (*LG* 17.11.54 'PoW'). Repatriated with other PoWs on *Columbo* and 'Her Majesty's Ship' in October 1855. Rejoined regiment at Scutari 26.10.55.
Parkinson, John Smith	Pte	1521	W	Account in *Answers* magazine 26 October 1912: 'I got through very well, until just as we reached the Russian guns [when] my horse was shot under me, my left leg being injured in the fall – but I was fortunate enough to secure a rider-less horse and followed on with the rest down the valley. On my return I received a slight lance wound in the neck from one of the Polish lancers sent to try to cut off our retreat. I also received a slight wound in the right leg [a spent bullet in the calf], but how or why I could not say, for I was about done up when we arrived back at our starting place.' His account in *The Royal Magazine* Vol. XVII, pp. 167 et seq. He modelled for Lady Butler's picture *Roll Call* or *After the Charge* and can be seen to the right of G.L. Smith reaching out his right hand.
Pennington, William Henry	Pte	1631	W	'Wounded by a musket ball through the calf of my right leg' (*LG* 17.11.54 'slightly wounded'). His horse went lame and was killed. He was saved from capture by being given a horse by Troop Sergeant Major Harrison of the 8th Hussars.

					He modelled for the figure of the dismounted hussar standing right of centre in Lady Butler's picture *After the Charge*. Autobiography *Sea, Camp and Stage*, also *Left of Six Hundred*. Account in *From the Fleet in the Fifties* by Mrs Tom Kelly. 'The British Soldier as he was at Balaclava and as he is today' in *Answers* magazine 25 October 1918. Biography in the *Hussar Journal*, vol. III.
Perkins, William	Tpt	850	UW		'I was trumpeter to [Lieutenant-] Colonel J. Douglas and rode close to him in the Charge and retreat, until my horse was killed after passing the lancers.' (*Lord Paget's Journal*). 'He was ordered to sound the "Reform" to form up with the 17th Lancers but at that moment it was seen that the lancers were Russian and Perkins sounded the 'Rally". He was wounded by a spent ball and got out of the "Valley of Death" on foot, his horse having been killed.' Source: *Army and Navy Gazette* 29 July 1899.
Phillips, William	Pte	1370	UW		Member of the Balaclava Commemoration Society in 1879.
Powell, Charles	Pte	1587	UW		Unwounded.
Purcell, David	Pte	1591	K		Killed in action (*LG* 17.11.54).
Purvis, John Charles	Pte	1441	MW		Mortally wounded 'having lost a leg' (*LG* 17.11.54 'severely wounded'). To Scutari General Hospital 29.10.54. Died 2.01.55. A letter written from Scutari on 11 December 1854 by a dragoon to his brother and published in *The Times* 17.01.54 is believed to have been written by Purvis.
Rhys, William Llewellyn	Pte	1498	MAY		May have ridden in the Charge. Attended the first Balaclava Banquet 1875. Member of the Balaclava Commemoration Society in 1877, but not in 1879. Died 05.05.81 buried Cathys Cemetery. Tombstone inscribed, 'When shall their glory fade. Honour the Charge they made, O' the wild charge they made, Honour the Light Brigade. All the world wondered, Noble Six hundred.' Death notices maintain he was a Charger.
Richardson, John	Pte	1567	W		Served in Lieutenant R. Palmer's Troop where he fought beyond the Russian guns, receiving two wounds in his left arm from Cossack lances.

11th Hussars	Rank	No	Charged	Corroborating Evidence Supporting Charger Status
Roberts, Thomas	Pte	1198	SW	Gun-shot wound to the right thigh (horse shot under him and wounded while remounting a second) (*LG* 17.11.54 'severely wounded'). To Scutari Hospital 26.10.54. Invalided to England 21.01.55. Discharged from Chatham Invalid Hospital 26.06.55: 'Severe gun-shot wound on the right thigh at Balaclava causing injury of the femur and contraction of the knee joint.'
Russell, Archibald	Pte	1120	K	Killed in action. *The History of the Eleventh Hussars* (Williams, 1908) lists as 'Archibald Rupell'.
Samer, Samuel	Pte	1364	W	Gun-shot wounded to right arm (*LG* 17.11.54 'slightly wounded'). Invalided to England via Scutari and Malta, he was discharged from the Invalid Depot at Chatham in May of 1855. Spent last 39 years of his life in Kew Lunatic Asylum, Melbourne, where he is reported to have suffered terrible nightmares. A press report noted, 'Samer had a large scar on the left shoulder, apparently a slash from a sword, a bullet wound distorting the bones of his right forearm, a stab wound in the left temple, in all probability the injury which caused him to lose his reason, a stab wound on the outer part of the left thigh and other small wounds over his body and arms. What a stirring picture could be conjured up by these scars, and yet the records are silent on the matter.'
Sheargold, Henry	Pte	1556	W	*LG* 17.11.54 'slightly wounded'. To Scutari where he is shown on the musters for November, although he returned to perform 'letter duty' in February 1855.
Sheppard, William	Pte	1580	PoW-W	Notes accompanying his medal state he had 'three horses shot from under him and received 14 wounds and taken PoW (*LG* 17.11.54)'. Repatriated in April 1855. Discharged in December 1855 having been 'rendered unfit for service from [a] grape shot wound on [the] outer and lower part of the left leg, followed by exfoliation of a portion of the fibula, resulting in weakness of the limb and union of the soft parts to the bone.'
Shoppee, Leonard	Pte	1528	K	Killed in action (*LG* 17.11.54).
Short, Charles Wiltshire	Pte	1517	UW	Death notice makes no mention of his being wounded or losing his horse.

Shrive, Thomas	Pte	1523	K	Killed in action (*LG* 17.11.54).
Smith, George Loy	S.M	677	UW	Took over as regimental sergeant major when RSM George Bull's horse was shot in the Charge. Rode on the left of F Troop. Horse shot under him, breaking a leg. He had to run to evade the Cossacks. He mounted a riderless horse of the 4th Light Dragoons and returned to the British lines. He numbered off as 63: 'Thus it is evident that the 11th was the last regiment and I the last man that returned up the valley.' Awarded the DCM, recommended 07.02.55, nominated to the Médaille Militaire by decree dated 06.03.61: 'Recommended by the vote of his comrades, who, with himself, returned from the Crimea previous to the first issue of the French Medal. Served until 25 January, 1856, and was present at the battles of the Alma, Balaclava and Inkerman. Horse shot under him at Balaclava, where he behaved Gallantly.' He modelled for Lady Butler's picture *After the Charge* and can be seen mounted on the left of the picture reaching out with his left hand.
Smith, William	Tpt	1586	UW	Horse shot from under him. Injured when his horse fell on him 'but still found time to bind up a wound in the thigh which one of his comrades had received and bought him safely out of the field' (*Guardian* 16.10.75). Wrote poem *Balaclava Heights 1854*.
Spring, William Henry (aka W. Pilkington)	Pte	1608	PoW-W	Rode in the centre of the 2nd Squadron's front rank. Horse shot under him during the retreat. Taken PoW after breaking through the lancers, having received 11 wounds, including every chamber of a Russian officer's revolver as he lay wounded (*LG* 17.11.54 'killed or missing'). Mentioned in an account by Private Pennington. In a statement made some years later, Spring recalled: 'We pursued the Russian cavalry to the bottom of the valley. When returning after passing the lancers my horse was killed and I was made prisoner.' Spring remained a prisoner of the Russians for twelve months, undergoing even worse privations than before, until he was exchanged in October 1855 for 20 Russians, that being the current rate of exchange. He was discharged from the army 16.01.63.

11th Hussars	Rank	No	Charged	Corroborating Evidence Supporting Charger Status
				'Spring, in the wild charge, had his horse shot under him, and received eleven wounds from sabre-cuts, bayonet thrusts, and bullets. One Russian officer emptied his five chambered revolver into him as he lay helpless upon the ground. He remained there until the morning, and for the next two days and nights was kept in a bullock waggon-house, which was without a roof, before his removal to hospital. Afterwards he was held a prisoner by the Russians for twelve months, when an exchange took place, and he regained his liberty.' Source: '*The London Daily Telegraph* of the '27th ult.' – post 1867.'
Staden, William	Pte	870	UW	Member of the Balaclava Commemoration Society in 1877, but not in 1879. Account in *The Illustrated London News* 30.10.75 under the name 'William Charles Stanton'.
Stephenson, James	Pte	1538	K	Killed in action (*LG* 17.11.54).
Strutt, John	Pte	1421	W	*LG* 17.11.54 'slightly wounded'. In hospital in January 1855 and died at Kadikoi 01.02.55.
Taylor, William	Pte	1541	W	*LG* 17.11.54 'slightly wounded'. Died 'in Camp Kadikoi' 18.01.55. Some sources say died as a PoW.
Teehan, Cornelius	Pte	1339	UW	Nominated to the Médaille Militaire, recommendation dated 16.05.56: 'Private Cornelius Teehan - Battles of the Alma and Balaclava, where he behaved gallantly. Was also at the Battle of Inkerman. Also served in Bulgaria in 1854, and was present at the affair of Bulganak and throughout the campaign in the Crimea from 1854 to 1856.'
Teevan, Patrick Rourke	T.S.M	1159	W	Commanded D Troop (the left troop of the 1st Squadron). 'I was surrounded by Russian lancers who had formed up to obstruct our return, but I passed through them, receiving a lance wound through my right thumb' (*Lord Paget's Journal*). Nominated to the Médaille Militaire: 'Present at the battles of the Alma and Balaclava, in which latter he led a troop and behaved gallantly. Was also present at the Battle of Inkerman, and throughout the Campaign from 1854 to 1856'. *Service Historique* of France confirmed the appointment under a decree 16.08.56.

Trevelyan, Harington Astley	Lt		W	Commanded the 1st Squadron. Gun-shot wound in calf of left leg while making his way back to the lines. He had a second shot through his shako, and a shell fell on his saddle (*LG* 17.11.54 'slightly wounded'). Awarded the Order of Medjidie (5th Class) (*LG* 02.03.58).
Turner, George	Pte	1358	MW	Mortally wounded. Left arm severed at the shoulder by a cannon ball during the early phase of the Charge (*LG* 17.11.54 'severely wounded'). Died 'on passage to the Hospital' 28.10.54. Account by Troop Sergeant Major G.L. Smith.
Wakelin, Henry John	Pte	1526	K	Killed in action (*LG* 17.11.54).
Walker, William	Pte	1621	W	Gunshot wound in his left shoulder (*LG* 17.11.54 'slightly wounded').
Ward, David	Pte	1080	K	Killed in action (*LG* 17.11.54). Death witnessed by Troop Sergeant Major G.L. Smith. 'Private Ward was struck full in the chest', and by Private R. Martin: 'Ward in front of me was blown to pieces.'
Wareham, William	Pte	938	K	Killed in action (*LG* 17.11.54). *The History of the Eleventh Hussars* (Williams, 1908) lists as 'William Warsham'.
Warr, Thomas	Pte	1481	SW	Warr's charger was badly wounded, and he had to lead it back to the rear, where it had to be shot. Member of the Balaclava Commemoration Society in 1877, but not the 1879 revised list. Received assistance from the T.H. Roberts Fund. Private W. Sheppard, 11th Hussars: 'A man named Warr who was in the Charge. I had not seen him since the Crimea, but I knew him at once.'
Wilcox, Edward	Pte	1202	W	Wounded (*LG* 17.11.54 'slightly wounded').
Wilder, Anthony	Pte	1445	UW	Member of the Balaclava Commemoration Society in 1879.
Wilkin, John Henry	A.S		UW	Took the place of Adjutant, Cornet J. Yates, who is said to have returned to camp (although Yates could equally have been acting as Brigade Major, hence the need for Wilkin to stand in. However, Mayow is believed to have returned to duty as Brigade Major, for the Charge). He had the honour of being called to the front of the Regiment and thanked by Lord Raglan for services in the field. Awarded the Order of the Medjidie (5th Class) (*LG* 02.03.58).
Williams, James	Cpl	663	PoW-M	Mortally wounded and taken PoW (*LG* 17.11.54). Died at Simferopol or on the road to Sevastopol.

11th Hussars	Rank	No	Charged	Corroborating Evidence Supporting Charger Status
Williams, Thomas	Pte	1479	UW	Member of the Balaclava Commemoration Society in 1877 and 1879. An account 'Personal Reminiscences of the Crimean War', being a lecture delivered by him on the eleventh anniversary of the Balaclava charge. 'I and my poor horses got through without a scratch, although I had one or two narrow escapes' (*Essex Standard* 26.01.55). 'My sword scabbard had two or three severe knocks; in fact, a ball caught it above the centre, and nearly cut it in two. How my leg escaped seems to me to be a miracle.'
Williamson, William J.	Sgt	1122	MAY	Possibly rode in the Charge. Listed by A. Sewell, who gives no corroborating evidence. Attended the first Balaclava Banquet in 1875. Obituary in *Leighton Buzzard Gazette* c.17.01.76: 'While charging the Russian guns he received two bayonet wounds in his legs which, from neglect at the time, never perfectly healed and eventually facilitated his death.'
Wilson, J	Pte	1741	PoW-W	Wounded, taken PoW and died at Simferopol or on the road from Sevastopol.
Woodham, Edward Richard	Pte	1355	UW	Helped spike the guns before his horse was shot under him but he was assisted free. Caught a 17th Lancer's horse.
Wootton, George	Pte	1533	K	Rode next to Private E.R. Woodham who witnessed his death: 'He was shot down almost immediately and that he [Woodham] had the melancholy task of reporting his death to the bereaved widow and family.' (*LG* 17.11.54). Account of Private J.S. Parkinson mentions him in 'Survivor's Tales of Great Events, retold from Personal Narratives', by Walter Woods in *Royal Magazine* Volume 17, 1909: 'Poor George! He was killed in the Charge of the Light Brigade... it was said amongst us that his excitement was his undoing, for, overcome by it, he rode out of the ranks, and rushed to meet the doom which was certain to any solitary horsemen in that fatal valley.'
Wroots, Thomas	Pte	1235	UW	Rode in D Troop. Account in *The Illustrated London News* 30.10.75.

Yates, John	Crnt Adjt		May	*The History of the Eleventh Hussars* (Williams, 1908) lists as a Charger. Pennington wrote in a letter that 'Yates was temporarily indisposed', but recovered sufficiently to meet the returning troopers who he rebuked for their dress and demeanour. According to Pennington, Cardigan remonstrated: '*They* have done their duty.' Yates is said to have retired to camp during the Battle of Inkerman and on rejoining the regiment was hauled out in front of them by Colonel Douglas. Troop Sergeant Major G.L Smith confirms this opinion, but both appear to have held grudges against Yates who had been transferred from the 17th Lancers to be appointed cornet 22.09.54 ahead of several candidates from within the regiment.
				Awarded the Al Valore Militaire: 'He was present in the Crimea from the commencement until August 1855; was present at the battles of the Alma, Balaclava and Inkerman and behaved gallantly. Acted as Brigade Major to Major General the Earl of Cardigan at Balaclava, and for a fortnight previously.'
Young, Richard Albert	Pte	1463	SW	A cannon ball took off his right arm (*LG* 17.11.54 'severely wounded'). Troop Sergeant Major G.L. Smith: 'When Young lost his arm he coolly fell back and asked me what he should do. I replied "Turn your horse about and get to the rear as you can."' To Scutari. Invalided to England in early 1855. Discharged from Chatham Invalid Depot 11.12.55. Awarded the DCM, recommended 10.01.55.

	Officers	NCOs	Trumpeters	Other Ranks	Total
Rode in the Charge and Killed in action (K)	0	3	0	22	25
Rode in the Charge and Mortally Wounded (MW)	1	0	0	2	3
Rode in the Charge and Severely Wounded (SW)	0	1	0	8	9
Rode in the Charge and Prisoner of War (PoW)	0	0	0	1	1
Rode in the Charge and Prisoner of War – Wounded (PoW-W)	0	0	0	5	5
Rode in the Charge and Prisoner of War – mortally wounded (PoW-M)	0	1	0	1	2

	Officers	NCOs	Trumpeters	Other Ranks	Total
Rode in the Charge and wounded (W)	2	9	0	17	28
Rode in the Charge unwounded (UW)	4	5	3	25	37
May Have Ridden (MAY)	1	3	0	12	16
Identified Chargers	8	22	3	93	126
Unidentified Chargers					18
Total Number of Chargers					144

The following contemporary sources give details of the regiment's statistics for the 25 October 1854

The London Gazette 12 November 1854

Return of Casualties from 22 to 26 October, 1854, both days inclusive:-

11th Hussars
2 sergeants, 30 rank and file, 72 horses, killed; 3 officers, 3 sergeants, 20 rank and file, wounded.

Only 25 members of the regiment answered the first roll-call of mounted men made immediately after the Charge.

State of the Regiment on October 25, 1854.

The Regimental Record gives the strength of the regiment, including officers, as 128.

13th Light Dragoons Table

13th Light Dragoons	Rank	No	Charged	Corroborating Evidence Supporting Charger Status
Adams, Adam	Pte	1464	W	Discharge papers note: 'scar on right cheek, scar on back of neck, two small scars on left arm and scar on outside of right fore-arm.' These were possibly the result of combat injuries.
Allen, John	Cpl	1199	W	Rode in the front rank and had his horse killed under him. Awarded the DCM. From his obituary report comes an account of how he is said to have won it: 'After his horse had been shot and he himself wounded in the knee (he is not shown as such in any of the "official" casualty lists) he was endeavouring to make his way back when he found a fellow trooper engaged in rescuing a wounded officer. He stopped to help and between them they managed to mount the officer on a riderless horse that was fortunately at hand.

				For this act, Corporal Allen received the much-prized medal for "Distinguished Conduct in the Field", his comrade in bravery receiving the Victoria Cross.'
Allwood, Job	Pte	1534	UW	Obituaries state he 'had two horses shot under him, but was uninjured.'
Andrews, Lewis G.	Pte	746	UW	Member of the Balaclava Commemoration Society in 1879.
Badger, George	Pte	1545	W	Rode 'in the front rank of the 13th [Light] Dragoons, and just on the left of Lord Cardigan.' He was nearly unseated by the mount of Captain L. Nolan. Sword wound to chest, horse shot under him. 'A piece of shell struck me on the side [which tore away part of my clothes and took a piece of flesh away with it]'. (*Shrewsbury Chronicle* 15 January 1904). Not included in *LG* list of casualties. Badger was the last to see Captain Oldham alive at the guns, unhorsed, wounded and bleeding badly, his sword in one hand, pistol in the other and defending himself against several Russians.
Bainton, William Henry	Pte	830	PoW-M	Mortally wounded and taken PoW (*LG* 17.11.54 listed as 'William Benton'). Mentioned in the account of Harry Powell: 'I had a brother who lost a leg and was taken prisoner and afterwards died at Simferopol. I received a letter from him stating how kind the Russians were and how well he had been looked after by the Sisters of Mercy. His name was William Baynton.'
Blackett, Thomas	Pte	1426	K	Killed in action (*LG* 17.11.54). However, R. Dutton states that both he (lost a finger) and his horse were wounded during the Charge when a shell exploded. During the retreat he broke through the wall of Cossacks. As he returned up the valley a round of shot knocked him to the ground, his horse finally collapsing, and as he lay helpless on the ground a Cossack ran a lance into his leg. To Scutari 26.10.54, nursed by Florence Nightingale and Miss Stanleyh. Invalided Home.
Braithwaite, Ernest Lucas	Sgt	1355	UW	Rode in the Charge. Received assistance from the Light Brigade Relief Fund.
Brooks, John (aka J. Withers)	Pte	1516	SW	'Wounded in the head and his horse blown to pieces by a shell. Carried off the field by a surgeon and a farrier.' (*LG* 17.11.54 'severely wounded'). To Scutari 26.10.54 and rejoined regiment 14.12.54.

13th Light Dragoons	Rank	No	Charged	Corroborating Evidence Supporting Charger Status
Brown, Henry	Pte	1168	UW	Two horses shot under him, but passed through the battle unscathed. Member of the Balaclava Commemoration Society in 1879.
Brown, John	Pte	2076	MAY	May have charged.
Bruce, John	Pte	1022	MAY	At the auction held in the salerooms of Debenham and Storr's 30.01.08, Lot 587 was a 'Pistol taken from a Russian Officer during the Charge of the Light Brigade at Balaclava by John Bruce, late 13th Light Dragoons.' His wife erected a stone over his grave 1855, so presumably was with the regiment in the Crimea. Received the Queen's Crimea Medal with four bars.
Cameron, James	Pte	412	W	Wounded (*LG* 17.11.54 'sent on-board ship without being seen by the Regimental Surgeon'). To Scutari General Hospital 26.10.54. Invalided to England 27.03.55, joining the Regimental Depot at Dorchester 22.06.55.
Campbell, A. Hutchinson	Pte	1366	MAY	Member of the Balaclava Commemoration Society in 1877, but not in 1879. Received assistance from the T.H. Roberts Fund.
Chadwick, Richard	Cpl	1448	MAY	Possibly rode in the Charge. Promoted from corporal to sergeant 25.10.54. Lummis and Wynn state that Chadwick attended the Annual Dinner in 1899.
Chamberlayne, Denzil Thomas	Crnt		UW	Rode in E Troop during the Charge, in the front row under the command of Captain A. Tremayne (another source says he commanded D Troop). Horse 'Pimento' shot three times through the body before collapsing.
Colson, William D.	Pte	1433	UW	Horse shot under him at the beginning of the action 'with twenty or thirty others' and escaped on another mount. 'It was a case of cut and thrust the whole time. My horse was shot almost at the onset of the battle and I fell in a heap with about twenty or thirty other riders. I picked myself up and found another horse, mounted, and rode out of the engagement without receiving a scratch.' Source: unattibuted press article. Member of the Balaclava Commemoration Society in 1879.
Cooke, Thomas	Pte	1048	W	Gunshot wound to the chest (the bullet drove one of Cooke's buttons into his chest, which was only removed decades later) and taken PoW (*LG* 17.11.54). Exchanged at Odessa 05.10.55.

Cooper, A. George	Pte	1526	PoW-W	Severely wounded (R. Dutton says eighteen wounds) and taken PoW (*LG* 17.11.54). Repatriated with other PoWs on the *Columbo* and 'Her Majesty's Ship' in October 1855. Honourably discharged by District court-martial 05.10.55. Mentioned in an account by R.S. Farquharson: 'Week after week, while in Veronitz, our numbers were increased by new arrivals of prisoners from the Crimea, including some of our wounded comrades whom we had left at Simferopol. Among these were Dryden of the 11th Hussars, who had no fewer than thirty-six wounds; Cooper and Duke of the 13th Light Dragoons, who had each been desperately wounded. All of these fellows seemed to have been well cared for in hospital, for their hurts were well and solidly healed up.'
Coulter, Joseph	Pte	1390	UW	Mentioned in an account by A. Mitchell: 'Another man, Coulter... his horse was shot under him in the early part of the action. He made his way back to the lines and took a sick horse and re-joined the regiment and went safely through the Charge, horse and man.'
Court, Charles	Pte	1421	K	Killed in action (*LG* 17.11.54). In an undated newspaper interview Private W. Dumayne, 13th Light Dragoons, mentions the manner of his death: 'This happened during our retreat down [*sic*] the valley. Our men at this time were falling on all sides by the fire of the flank batteries. As I passed on I heard a cry, and saw Private Court, of ours, fall from his horse: he had been hit by a round-shot.'
Cresswell, Josiah	Pte	1240	UW	Cresswell's name is included on a list of Balaclava survivors which appeared in a pamphlet by Nunnerley of the 17th. Charger status confirmed by Trumpeter Harry Powell, the two residing in the same accommodations in Sheffield. Received assistance from the Light Brigade Relief Fund.
Cunningham, James	Pte	1298	W	Wounded (*LG* 17.11.54) and 'sent aboard ship without being seen by the Regimental Surgeon'. To Scutari 26.10.54.
Davis, Richard	Tpt	1108	UW	Rode near Captain J.A. Oldham, commanding officer, throughout the Charge. Horse killed under him during the retreat. Nominated to the Médaille Militaire: 'Served in the Eastern Campaign, including the affairs of Bulganak and McKenzie's Farm, Balaclava and Inkerman, siege of Sevastopol and expedition to Eupatoria.'

13th Light Dragoons	Rank	No	Charged	Corroborating Evidence Supporting Charger Status
Dearlove, George	Pte	1055	UW	Nominated to the Médaille Militaire: 'Served the Eastern campaign, including the affairs of Bulganak and McKenzie's farm, battle of the Alma, Balaclava and Inkerman, Siege of Sevastopol and Expedition to Eupatoria.'
Deason, Alfred	Pte	1494	MAY	Member of the Balaclava Commemoration Society in 1877, but not in 1879. Attended the 1899 dinner.
Delworth, James	Pte		MAY	May have ridden in the Charge. Died at Scutari 25.05.55. The wider family had always understood that J. Delworth had ridden in the Charge.
Dorell, William	Pte	1503	K	Killed in action (*LG* 17.11.54).
Doughton Joseph	Pte	1422	W	Gunshot wound through the right elbow joint and three lance stabs (*LG* 17.11.54 listed as 'Joseph Douglas'). Sent to Balaclava Hospital and then to Scutari 25.10.54. Invalided to England 11.01.55. Discharged from Chatham Invalid Depot 16.10.55: 'Disabled from wound of right elbow from gun-shot fracture.' Published an account.
Douglas, John	Pte	1410	W	Wounded (*LG* 17.11.54 'sent on-board ship without being seen by the Regimental Surgeon'). Photographed on the occasion of the retirement of 'Butcher' 1872, the image entitled *Six survivors of the Balaclava Charge of the 13th Light Dragoons*.
Duke, Robert William	Pte	1340	PoW-W	Wounded and taken PoW (*LG* 17.11.54). He rejoined the regiment 26.10.55. Discharged from Kilmainham 28.06.58 as a result of a head wound from a shell splinter, gun-shot wound to right wrist, two sword wounds on knee and ten lance wounds in body and arm.
Dumayne, William Allen	Pte	1429	MAY	May have ridden in the Charge. Received assistance from the T.H. Roberts Fund and the Light Brigade Relief Fund.
Eccles, William	Pte	1468	UW	Member of the Balaclava Commemoration Society in 1879. Photographed at the retirement of 'Butcher' 1872, *Six survivors of the Balaclava Charge of the 13th Light Dragoons*.
Ettridge, John	Pte	1483	SW	Wounded (*LG* 17.11.54 'severely wounded'). To Scutari 26.10.54. Invalided to England via Malta, 16.12.54. Discharged from Chatham Invalid Depot 23.10.55: 'Disabled by loss of power in left hand after gun-shot wound through the arm at Balaclava.'
Evans, John	Pte	1217	MAY	May have ridden in the Charge. To Scutari 26.10.54 and the Hospital muster roll shows him as being there at the October-November musters. Entitled to the Balaclava bar.

Evans, Robert	Pte	1510	W	Wounded when his horse was killed under him. (*LG* 17.11.54 'Sent on-board ship without being seen by the Regimental Surgeon.') On the General Hospital, Scutari, rolls from 30.10.54, sent to Malta 25.12.54 and from there to Chatham 16.01.55. Discharged from the Chatham Invalid Depot 08.01.56: 'Found unfit for further service. Disabled from the service, having suffered amputation of the lower left extremity from a severe contusion of both lower extremities by a horse which was killed under him having fallen upon him. The right leg is quite recovered and the left has full use of it.' *The Times* 05.01.56 'In the charge at Balaclava a shell entered the chest of his horse, which rolled completely over, falling upon Evans, when the shell burst inside the animal, tearing it open from shoulder to hind-quarters, the weight of the horse nearly caused suffocation, while its death struggles inflicted severe confusions on the legs of Evans, who would have expired if not a man of his own troop and two lancers not released him.'
Farrington, Stephen	Pte	1316	UW	*The History of the 13th Hussars*, by C.R.B. Barrett: 'Pte Farringdon [*sic*] of Captain Goad's own troop said that he had seen the Captain sitting or half-lying, with his revolver in his hand. He was then wounded in the lower part of the face or neck.'
Fenton, John	Pte	1218	UW	Nominated to the Médaille Militaire: 'Served during the Eastern campaign, including the affairs of the Bulganak and MacKenzie's Farm, the battles of the Alma, Balaclava and Inkerman, Siege of Sevastopol, and Eupatoria.'
Firkins, Edward John	Pte	1477	UW	Letter from Firkins dated 'Camp before Sevastopol, 27 December 1854' describes his part in the retreat from the Don Cossack battery: 'I had only got a few yards when I saw two Russian Lancers coming towards me with clenched teeth and staring like savages. I prepared to meet them with as much coolness and determination as I could command, the first one made a thrust at me with his lance, it is a heavy weapon and easily struck down, which I did with my sword, thrusting it at the same time through the fellow's neck... The shock nearly brought me from my saddle...' (NAM. 1986-02-75). Firkins lost his sword and was saved by a 17th Lancer who put his lance through the Russian's back. Moments later Firkins' mount was killed by a shell and he was forced to make the British lines on foot.

13th Light Dragoons	Rank	No	Charged	Corroborating Evidence Supporting Charger Status
Fitzgerald, John	Sgt	1232	UW	'I had one horse shot under me at the very commencement and of course was running back to our own army the same as dozens of others when I saw a trumpeter of the 11th Hussars shot dead. He fell off his horse, poor fellow so I "borrowed" his mount and jumped on, the only chance you had then for they stopped the play of their big guns and sent 13 hundred cavalry down on us, every poor fellow they met dismounted 4 or 5 of them got about them and cut them to pieces. There was another Sergeant of the 11th Hussars [J. Jones or T. Jordan] running for this horse the same as I was, but I got there first and hopped into the saddle. I knew him well, poor fellow, and I can remember him saying, "Fitz, that horse belongs to us", but I paid no attention to him. I was sorry to hear they killed him, but everything is fair in war time.'
Foster, Charles Moore	Sgt	935	MAY	May have Charged. Promoted to troop sergeant major 26.10.54. He was further promoted to quartermaster 05.01.55, but died on the 25th of the same month.
Frazer, Richard	Pte	825	UW	Extract from *The Regiment* 24.10.96: 'A Balaclava Hero: On the other side of the Tweed, in the village of Forres resides one of the few remaining survivors of the gallant Six Hundred and the pride and glory of the British Empire and the wonder of nations... Mr R. Frazer, formerly a sergeant of the 13th Light Dragoons.'
Frazer, Robert	Pte	1435	K	Killed in action (*LG* 17.11.54).
Gammage, Joseph	Tpt	1029	UW	Attended the first Balaclava Banquet in 1875. Member of the Balaclava Commemoration Society in 1877. Signed the Loyal Address to the Queen in 1887. *Croydon Advertiser* 22.10.87: 'He rode into the Valley of Death with Lord Cardigan and his gallant Six Hundred, he came out of the struggle unscathed, although during the day he had three horses shot under him. Private Gammage was also the possessor of a photograph of the famous charger ridden by Lord Cardigan at Balaclava. He received it from Lady Cardigan.'
Gardner, George	R.S.M.	1091	UW	'Got as far as the mouth of the Russian guns, when a shell burst in the chest of his horse and threw the rider into the air. When he recovered he found he was laid out on a Russian gun; he scrambled to

				his feet and ran a mile and three-quarters through a storm of shot and shell before he reached his comrades.' A similar quote adding at this point, 'He had a distance of a mile and three-quarters to run through this deadly storm and in the stories that he told of that terrible three-year campaign he used to say that the shot seemed so close and thick around him that it seemed impossible for a rat to escape.' Awarded the Order of the Medjidie (5th Class) (*LG* 02.03.58).
Gardiner, William	Pte	1405	UW	Awarded the Al Valore Militaire: 'Corporal William Gardiner – Distinguished conduct in the Light Cavalry Brigade Charge at Balaclava on the 25th of October 1854.' Member of the Balaclava Commemoration Society in 1879.
Garnham, George	Pte	1480	UW	Horse shot under him. Attended the first Balaclava Banquet in 1875. Member of the Balaclava Commemoration Society in 1879.
Gibson, George (aka Plimmer)	Pte	1471	W	Rode in B Troop, wounded in the leg and his horse killed under him. Not in the *LG* casualty list. Assisted Lieutenant Sir William Gordon and Private J. Keen. Short account and portrait in *Answers* magazine, 26.10.12: 'I got down the valley right enough until I came to the guns. When we were retiring, I came across Sir William Gordon of the 17th Lancers. He was bleeding from the face, and making straight for the Polish lancers. I joined him and together we got through them. Then the Russians opened up on us and some Poles with them. I somehow evaded them and picked up Trumpeter Keen, who was wounded through the leg. We had not gone far when a grape-shot caught my horse on the shoulder and killed him instantly. I was stunned by the shock, and lay in the field for some time. I got up to where they were mustering about three or four o'clock. But I knew nothing about it, for I was blind and stupid.'
Glynn, William H.	Cpl	1345	MAY	May have ridden in the Charge, as promoted sergeant 26.10.54.
Goad, Thomas Howard	Cpt		K	Killed while commanding the 2nd Squadron (*LG* 17.11.54 'missing'). Captain S. Jenyns wrote to Charles Goad: 'We were half down before we reached the guns but the men... never wavered an inch, grape and shells cutting them to pieces. The last I saw of Howard was galloping about 100 yards from the guns, but after that there was so much smoke etc that I did not see him.

13th Light Dragoons	Rank	No	Charged	Corroborating Evidence Supporting Charger Status
				From all I can learn, he was seen wounded on the ground with his revolver in his hand.' In a letter Lieutenant Shawe Smith wrote: 'The last I saw of poor Goad was just going into the guns on my left. He was killed dead, as the Russians sent back a bill of exchange found on his body.'
Gorman, James	Pte	1538	W	He rode up to the guns, very close after the Earl of Cardigan, when a 24lb shot struck him on the leg, breaking it above and below the knee. He was knocked completely out of his saddle, and two heavy cavalry regiments charged over him, but the men humanely leapt their horses over his body, the officers shouting out 'Mind the poor fellow on the ground.' Made his way for over a mile to British lines, while avoiding the Cossacks who were murdering the wounded. Death notice in the *Inverness Courier* 30.11.97: 'He had his horse shot under him, and was struck between the eyes by a spent bullet. Besides that, he narrowly escaped being pierced by a Cossack spear while lying defenseless on the ground.' Gorman testified at the special inquiry held after the campaign.
Hanlon, Christopher Edward	Pte	1334	PoW-W	Severely wounded in the neck by a lance, and a rifle bullet passing through his clothing across his breast passed out through his bridle arm (total of 9 wounds). Taken PoW (*LG* 17.11.54). Repatriated with other PoWs on the *Columbo* and 'Her Majesty's Ship' in October 1855. Honourably acquitted by a garrison court-martial at Scutari 10.11.55.
Hanson, Isaac	Pte	1556	MAY	May have ridden in the Charge. Portrait in *The Illustrated London News* 30.10.75.
Harding, John Henry	Pte	1382	UW	Attended the first Balaclava Banquet, 25.10.75, was a member of the Balaclava Commemoration Society 1879, and attended the Annual Dinner in 1897.
Harris, Amos	Pte	1346	PoW-W	Wounded and taken PoW (*LG* 17.11.54). Exchanged 26.10.55. Honourably acquitted by a garrison court-martial at Scutari on 10.11.55.
Hindley, Edward	Pte	1540	UW	Member of the Balaclava Commemoration Society in 1879.
Holliday, Algernon	Pte	1365	K	Killed in action (*LG* 17.11.54).
Howarth, Willaim	Tpt	669	PoW-M	Mortally wounded and taken PoW (*LG* 17.11.54). According to Troop Sergeant Major J. Linkon he suffered 19 wounds and died either at Simferopol or on the road from Sevastopol, November 1854.

Hughes, Edwin	Pte	1506	W	Rode 'fifth file front rank, right first of line.' Horse shot under him, injuring his face and leg: 'I was damaged about the face and left leg but not seriously.' Assisted onto another horse, he was placed in charge of some Russian prisoners for the remainder of the day. 'We just did our duty without any thought of glory, and, of course, as in all wars many of our lot paid the supreme price. I was glad I was in it, and I'm glad that I am here to tell the tale.'
Hunt, Henry	Pte	1495	UW	Lummis and Wynn state he 'May have ridden in the Charge'. Photographed on the occasion of the retirement of 'Butcher' 1872, the image entitled *Six survivors of the Balaclava Charge of the 13th Light Dragoons*. In a photograph taken at the time of the Annual Dinner in 1890 is pictured a man dressed in the uniform of a Chelsea Pensioner and wearing three medals, but named merely as 'Hunt'. Rode in a carriage in the Lord Mayor's Show 09.11.90.
Jenyns, Soame Gambier	Cpt		UW	Commanded the 1st Squadron. When his superiors were killed he was left in command of the regiment and formed up the remainder of his troops for the return to British lines: 'I only brought nine mounted men back! Poor Moses (Jenyns' charger) was shot through his shoulder and through the hip into his guts, but just got me back. I had some narrow shaves, as indeed we all had. My cloak roll in front had three canister-shot through it, besides a piece of shell knocking off the end of it, and catching me on the knee, but only a severe bruise. In another account he adds: 'We retired in broken detachments through the guns. My horse was so badly wounded that I had to dismount and lead him. I then observed Lord Cardigan walking his horse between me and some broken detachments of the Light Brigade.' Appointed Brevet-Major (*LG* 12.12.54), awarded the Order of Medjidie 5th Class (*LG* 02.03.58), mentioned in despatches (*LG* 30.11.54), appointed a Commander of the Bath (*LG* 10.07.55).
Jervis, Edward Lennox	Lt		UW	Commanded B Troop on the left of the 1st Squadron. Horse shot under him (unwounded).
Johnson, Thomas George	Sgt	1300	UW	Nominated a Knight of the Légion d'Honneur (5th Class) (*LG* 04.08.56): 'Served during the Eastern campaign, including the reconnaissance on the Danube under the Earl of Cardigan, battles of Balaclava and Inkerman, Siege of Sevastopol, and

13th Light Dragoons	Rank	No	Charged	Corroborating Evidence Supporting Charger Status
				the Expedition to Eupatoria.' Another document adds, 'Was present at the Charge of Balaclava 25th Octr 1854, horse severely wounded.' Also nominated to the Médaille Militaire according to Roy Dutton.
Keeley, John	Pte	1363	UW	Lummis & Wynn states, 'May have ridden in the Charge', but gives no corroborating evidence. Affidavit of Sergeant Thomas George Johnson in the Cardigan v. Calthorpe case, 1863 refers. Awarded the DCM, recommended 13.02.55. In *War Correspondent* Vol 20 No 2, July 2002, Brian M. Best states he was 'The only man to charge with both the Heavy and Light Brigades.'
Keen, John	Pte	1529	SW	Severely wounded by canister shot in the right leg, was assisted by Private G. Gibson (*LG* 17.11.54). To Scutari 27.10.54. Invalided to England 23.02.55. Awarded the Distinguished Conduct Medal, recommended 13.02.55. Discharged from Cahir 18.10.56 as: 'Unfit for further service. This man suffers from gun-shot wounds of the right leg sustained in action at Balaclava on the 25th of October 1854 - from the nature of the wounds, a canister-shot entered the lower and outer part of the leg, winding around the leg and coming out at the upper third of the leg and in its course injuring the fibula. He is liable to have them re-opened and pieces of bone come away. Consequently his ability of earning a living is greatly impaired.'
Kimble, Thomas	Pte	1493	UW	Member of the Balaclava Commemoration Society in 1879.
Lamb, James	Pte	1406	W	Wounded by a shell in the right leg 'carrying away a good deal of the fleshy part'. Horse shot under him. Claimed to have drawn lots with Corporal J. Malone for the Victoria Cross. Account in the *Strand Magazine*, October 1891.
Lawson, William	Pte	1041	K	Killed in action (*LG* 17.11.54).
Leaney, Edward	Sgt	648	W	Rode in E Troop on the right of the line and had his horse shot under him. Was assisted back to the British lines by Private W. Dumayne. To Scutari 27.10.54 and invalided to England 20.12.54. At the Invalid Depot at Chatham from the 27.01.55 to 30.06.55. Discharged from Dorchester Barracks 05.09.55. Victoria Cross register 03.05.68 his claim for consideration for the award of the VC (addressed to The Right

				Honourable the Earl of Eglington and Wilton). In October 1902 a *Northampton Daily Reporter* newspaper gave his account of the Charge, William Dumayne refers to him: 'The event occurred when passing through the flank fire of the Russian guns when coming back up the valley... And I saw on the ground, struggling to rise, Sgt Leany [*sic*]. He called to me and I passed my sword into my bridle hand, caught hold of his and dragging him from under his horse, assisted him back to our lines, which when the muster was called, showed a poor count of the men.'
Linkon, John	T.S.M	762	PoW	Served in Captain Goad's Troop. Horse shot under him early on in the Charge. Caught a riderless horse (he stated this was Nolan's) and went down the valley with another regiment but taken PoW when this horse was killed (*LG* 17.11.54, listed as 'John Lincoln'). Repatriated with other PoWs on the *Columbo* and 'Her Majesty's Ship' in October 1855. Exchanged 26.10.54. Honourably acquitted by a garrison court-martial at Scutari 10.11.55 for 'having been taken a prisoner of war at Balaclava during the Charge of the Light Brigade'.
Long, Matthew	Cpl	1123	UW	Awarded the Distinguished Conduct Medal, recommended 13.02.55.
Malanfy, James	Pte	1276	W	Was wounded by a musket-ball, and owed the preservation of his life to a sixpenny piece which he had in one of his pockets. This coin caused the bullet to pass in an oblique direction and in the course of which a less serious wound was inflicted. Presented to Queen Victoria during her visit to Aldershot 05.07.72, as the only survivor of the Charge then on duty on the camp. After being presented to Her Majesty he was ordered to follow in the rear of the Regiment so that the Royal Family might recognise him as he passed by on the horse (Butcher) that had been for so many years his companion in both peace and war. Photographed on the occasion of the retirement of 'Butcher' 1872, the image entitled *Six survivors of the Balaclava Charge of the 13th Light Dragoons*.
Malone, Joseph	Cpl	1440	UW	Rode in Captain A. Tremayne's E Troop. Assisted Captain A.F.C. Webb for which he was awarded the Victoria Cross.

13th Light Dragoons	Rank	No	Charged	Corroborating Evidence Supporting Charger Status
Martin, Edward	Sgt	1208	W	Shell wound to the head (*LG* 17.11.54 'sent on board ship without being seen by the surgeon'). To Scutari 26.10.54. Invalided to England 21.01.55 and at Chatham Depot from the 12.02.55. Discharged from Chatham Invalid Depot 02.10.55.
				On Monday morning, about one o'clock, the Cunard steamship *Cambria* arrived in the Mersey, having on board ten officers, 213 rank and file from the hospitals at Scutari. 'One poor fellow, who belonged to the 13th Light Dragoons, and who was in that memorable charge at Balaclava, said as he saw the Russians about a mile and a half down the valley, which valley was flanked by batteries, he audibly uttered a prayer. Captain Jarvis, known in the regiment as "little" Jarvis, son of Chief Justice Jarvis, overheard him, and turned round to look; whereupon the soldier said, "May God protect you through the fight, officer," to which the captain assented, and said he hoped he would, "soldier." They went as quickly as their poor horses would go, scarcely noting how many fell by the way. This soldier warded off the Cossack lances, like sticks, and after some hairbreadth escapes was on his way back. When he had nearly returned, breathless, a shell burst in the air and a piece struck him behind the head. He fell senseless; but, in ten minutes or so, he awoke to consciousness, and seeing a Russian horse close by, he mounted it, and rode back' (*Liverpool Journal* 20.01.55).
Martin, William	Pte	1068	PoW-W	Wounded and taken PoW (*LG* 17.11.54). Died 26.11.54.
Mayhew, James Robert	Pte	1153	UW	Listed as a Charger by Lummis and Wynne and in subsequent lists. Never a member of the Balaclava Commemoration Society. Assisted by the Patriotic Fund and accepted by T.H. Roberts as a survivor and invited by him to attend the Jubilee celebrations organised by him at his Fleet Street offices in June of 1897.
McCann, John	Pte	1341	PoW	Taken PoW (*LG* 17.11.54). Repatriated with other PoWs on the *Columbo* and 'Her Majesty's Ship' in October 1855. Rejoined the regiment 26.10.55. Honourably acquitted by a garrison court-martial at Scutari 10.11.55 for 'having been taken a prisoner of war at Balaclava during the Charge of the Light Brigade'.
McGorrine, Thomas	Pte	1332	W	Wounded (*LG* 17.11.54 'killed or missing').

Mitchell, Albert	Pte	1401	UW	Published an account.
Montgomery, Hugh	Crnt		K	Commanded A Troop on the right of the 1st Squadron. Killed in action (*LG* 17.11.54 'missing'). *Memoirs of the Brave* by James Gibson states: 'Montgomery was seen in combat with six Russian hussars of whom he shot four and chased off the other two with his sword. He retreated with the last straggling groups, but seeing two of his men outnumbered, he returned to assist in their rescue. He received a fatal pistol shot in the neck.' Captain S.G. Jenyns wrote: 'Montgomery was my right troop leader (First squadron) and I saw him safely into the guns: after that, on returning, he was seen dead on his face, poor fellow.'
Moore, Joseph	Pte	1224	SW	Gun-shot wound to the left arm (amputated) (*LG* 17.11.54 'severely wounded'). To Scutari Hospital 26.10.54. Invalided to England 16.12.54. Discharged from Chatham Invalid Depot 23.10.55. Awarded the DCM, recommended 13.02.55.
Morrisey, Patrick	Sgt	1248	MAY	Possibly rode in the Charge (listed by R. Dutton).
Mulcahy, John	Sgt	1230	UW	Promoted from sergeant to troop sergeant-major 26.10.54. Awarded the DCM, recommended 13.02.55.
Nagle, Benjamin	Sgt	1315	UW	Rode as a corporal in the Charge. Briefly mentioned on Powell's account immediately post-Charge with reference to the muster and counting off the survivors.
Naylor, Henry Dyson	Pte	1460	W	Fracture of lower jaw, gun-shot wound of shoulder, and struck in the loins by a ram-rod (*LG* 17.11.54 'Sent on-board ship without being seen by the Regimental Surgeon'). Invalided to England 16.12.54. Discharged from Chatham Invalid Depot 23.10.55: 'Unfit for further service from disfigurement of the face by fracture of lower jaw at Balaclava. Also from gun-shot wound of shoulder.'
Naylor, James	Pte	697	W	Wounded (*LG* 17.11.54 'Sent on-board ship without being seen by the Regimental Surgeon'). Invalided to England 19.06.55. Discharged at Kilmainham 29.11.58.
Nicholson, William	Pte	1378	W	Rode in the First Line of 13 Light Dragoons and horse shot under him. Caught a riderless horse and charged the guns with the 11th Hussars. Lance wound in the side and the butt of a lance in the chin (*LG* 17.11.54 'Sent on-board ship without being seen by the Regimental Surgeon'). To Scutari 26.10.54. Returned to regiment mid-December 1854. Account and portrait in *The Illustrated London News* 30.10.75.

13th Light Dragoons	Rank	No	Charged	Corroborating Evidence Supporting Charger Status
Oldham, John Augustus	Cpt		K	Commanded the regiment (Lieutenant Colonel C. Doherty being sick) riding his second charger – a white mare – his first charger being unfit for work. This horse was notoriously a brute, and on the occasion of the Charge bolted and Oldham was the first to enter the Russian battery. He was thrown from his horse and rose to his feet only to be hit by shell fragments. He was last seen wounded and bleeding with his sword in one hand and his pistol in the other (*LG* 17.11.54 'killed'). Captain Jenyns described Oldham's final moments in what appeared almost a race between Oldham and Cardigan to reach the guns first: 'Oldham I saw killed by a shell which burst under his horse and knocked over two or three others. It blew his mare's hind legs off, and he jumped up himself not hit, when next moment he threw up his hands and fell dead on his face.' (R. Dutton, *Forgotten Heroes*, p. 255) Shortly after the battle a Russian officer came in under a flag of truce to arrange the burial of the dead. In the presence of Sir Fitzroy Maclean, who was standing close by, he asked, 'Who was the officer who rode a white horse and led the charge of Balaclava?' He was told that the officer was Captain Oldham, and at once replied, 'a brave man.' Sadly, his burial-place was not recorded.
Pamplin, Kames	Pte	1254	UW	Lummis and Wynn list as a Charger, but give no corroborating evidence for this statement.
Peake, Frederick	Sgt	1309	SW	Upper right arm was broken by a canister shot (*LG* 17.11.54 'severely wounded'). To Scutari Hospital 26.10.54. Invalided to England 26.12.54. Discharged from Chatham Invalid Depot 08.01.56: 'Disabled from canister-shot wound of upper right arm received in the cavalry charge at Balaclava. Ball appears to have broken the outer surface of the humerus. Arm is weak. Found unfit for further military service.'
Pedrick, John	Pte	1071	MAY	Lummis and Wynn state 'May have Ridden', but give no corroborating evidence.
Pegler, Henry	Pte	1436	SW	Wounded (*LG* 17.11.54 'severely wounded'). To Scutari 26.10.54, where he died 'in the General Hospital' 10.02.55.
Percival, Enoch	Pte	1469	MAY	Possibly Rode in the Charge. Lummis and Wynn state, 'May have ridden in the Charge,' and Sent to Scutari Hospital the day after the Charge 26.10.54.

				However, appears to be with the Service troop for the entire period 01.01.54 to 01.01.55. No trace can be found on the Hospital muster roll.
Pollard, Thomas	Pte	478	MW	Horse killed under him and made his way back with Private A. Mitchell (See his published account). To Scutari Hospital 09.12.54 and probably died on-board ship as not recorded at Scutari.
Powell, Harry	Tpt	1228	W	'I had a very narrow escape, a ball hitting the right top button of my jacket which glanced it off, and cut the jacket down as if it had been done with a sharp knife, and slightly grazing my throat; my horse was shot in the off fore leg in the upper part; however she managed to go down with me and carry me out.' Published an account. His horse 'Butcher', the last surviving mare to have taken part in the Charge, was presented to the regiment (put out to grass) at Colchester, 1872.
Rhodes, Joseph	Pte	694	SW	Gun-shot wound to right forearm (*LG* 17.11.54 severely wounded). To Scutari Hospital. Invalided to England 16.12.54. Discharged from Chatham Invalid Depot 02.10.55.
Robinson, John Daniel	Cpl	1449	UW	Letter to a friend in Doncaster (*Leeds Mercury* 30.12.54) indicated he assisted the Earl of Cardigan at the rear of the guns.
Rowley, Richard	Pte	984	SW	Wounded (*LG* 17.11.54 'severely wounded'). Awarded the DCM, recommended 13.02.55.
Sewell, William	Pte	1452	SW	Severely wounded in the head (shell fragments) and had a silver plate fixed over this wound (*LG* 17.11.54 'severely wounded'). Horse killed under him and had to mount an enemy horse. To Scutari 26.10.54. To Malta 15.11.54, and to England 04.01.55. Presented before Queen Victoria at Brompton Barracks 03.03.55. Discharged at Chatham 05.09.55: 'Unfit for further service from severe wound of the head from fragments of shell at Balaclava – four fractures of the skull and four foliations of bone behind the left ear. Suffers from headaches and vertigo.'
Slattery, James	Pte	1247	K	Killed in action (*LG* 17.11.54).
Smith, E.W. Aubrey	Cpl	1491	K	Killed in action (*LG* 17.11.54 'missing or killed in action'). '[A] Corporal on the right was struck by a shot or shell full in the face, completely smashing it - the blood bespattered us who rode near.' (Mitchell *Recollections*). L.W. Crider believes this man would have been Corporal Smith – E.J. Boys disagreed.

13th Light Dragoons	Rank	No	Charged	Corroborating Evidence Supporting Charger Status
Smith, George	T.S.M.	1106	PoW-W	Two horses shot under him. Sabre wound on the right forearm, eight minor sabre and lance wounds to body, taken PoW (*LG* 17.11.54). Exchanged and rejoined regiment 26.10.55. Repatriated with other PoWs on the *Columbo* and 'Her Majesty's Ship' in October 1855. Honourably discharged by garrison court-martial at Scutari 10.11.55 for: 'having been taken prisoner of war at Balaclava during the Charge of the Light Brigade.' Received nine wounds – reported as being 'seriously wounded.' To the Depot in England from Scutari on the 15.12.55.
Smith, Percy Shawe	Lt		UW	Rode (unarmed) as acting adjutant on the extreme right of the front rank. His horse was one of only two that were unwounded. Awarded the Al Valore Militaire, with a citation: 'For distinguished conduct in the Light Cavalry Charge at Balaclava on the 25th October 1854'. Awarded the Order of the Medjidie (5th Class) (*LG* 02.03.58). Promoted captain 26.10.54. Smith rode unarmed in the Charge. His right hand had been maimed in a shooting accident, but he was accepted for active service. Although he could only cheer his men on, he charged through the Russian guns and escaped with only a slight wound. He normally wore an iron guard on his maimed arm, presented by his brother officers, but it was mislaid on the morning of the Charge and he rode without it.
Taylor, Henry	Pte	1141	UW	Horse shot under him but he escaped unscathed. Death notice in the *Leytonstone Express and Independent* 21.12.07 refers.
Tremayne, Arthur	Cpt		W	Commanded E Troop on the left of the 2nd Squadron. Wounded early in the Charge and horse shot under him (held the stirrup straps of one of his men). Made Brevet-Major (*LG* 21.08.55 with effect from 17.07.55) and awarded the Order of Medjidie (*LG* 02.03.58). Nominated a Knight of the Légion d'Honneur (5th Class) (*LG* 04.08.56).
Veitch, John	Pte	1431	W	Wounded (*LG* 17.11.54 'sent on-board ship without being seen by the Regimental Surgeon'). To Scutari 26.10.54.

Viner, Frederick	Pte	1454	UW	Death notice in the *Norfolk Annals* 10.09.90: 'Died at Costessey, Frederick Vine, formerly of the 13th Light Dragoons. He took part in the light cavalry charge at Balaclava and his name was officially recorded in the list of survivors.'
Warren, Charles	Pte	1515	PoW	Taken PoW (*LG* 17.11.54). Repatriated with other PoWs on the *Columbo* and 'Her Majesty's Ship' in October 1855. Rejoined the regiment 26.10.55. Honourably discharge by garrison court-martial at Scutari 10.11.55 for 'having been taken prisoner of war at Balaclava during the Charge of the Light Brigade.'
Watlen, William	Pte	1442	MAY	Lummis and Wynn state 'May have ridden in the Charge', but give no corroborating evidence for this statement. Attended the 1875 Banquet.
Watson, James	Pte	1413	K	Killed in action (*LG* 17.11.54).
Weston, John	T.S.M	715	K	Killed in action (*LG* 17.11.54 listed as 'John Webster'). Extract from the obituary of Sergeant Edwin Leaney in the *Kent Messenger* 27.01.94: 'His comrade in the Charge was Sgt. Major Weston, but he fell a victim to the Russian guns.'
White, Thomas	Pte	975	W	Wounded (*LG* 17.11.54) 'sent on-board ship without being seen by the Regimental Surgeon'). To Scutari 26.10.54. Discharged from Cahir 18.10.56: 'At the battle of Balaclava he was struck by a piece of shell just above the forehead. The wound was only trifling, and no inconvenience to him has arisen from it.'
Wickham, Henry George	Pte	1499	SW	Severe lance wound.
Wilde, George	Pte	1119	W	Horse killed under him (the *Norfolk Annals* 12.05.87 refers) and wounded (*LG* 17.11.54 'slightly wounded').
Williams, George	Pte	1348	W	Gun-shot through the sword hand (*LG* 17.11.54 'severely wounded'). To Scutari 27.10.54. Returned to the regiment 01.01.55. His brother, Private T.J. Williams, killed in the Charge beside him.
Williams, Thomas Joseph	Pte	879	K	Killed in action (*LG* 17.11.54). Brother of Private G. Williams.
Wright, Edmund	Pte	1458	W	Shell splinter, right thigh (*LG* 17.11.54 'Sent on-board ship without being seen by the Regimental Surgeon'). To Scutari 26.10.54. Discharged from Chatham Invalid Depot 25.12.55: 'Was also wounded on the exterior surface of the right thigh by a piece of shell at the battle of Balaclava. Femur uninjured.'

	Officers	NCOs	Trumpeters	Other Ranks	Total
Rode in the Charge and Killed in action (K)	3	2	0	9	14
Rode in the Charge and Mortally Wounded (MW)	0	0	0	1	1
Rode in the Charge and Severely Wounded (SW)	0	1	0	9	10
Rode in the Charge and Prisoner of War (PoW)	0	1	0	2	3
Rode in the Charge and Prisoner of War – Wounded (PoW-W)	0	1	0	5	6
Rode in the Charge and Prisoner of War – mortally wounded (PoW-M)	0	0	1	1	2
Rode in the Charge and wounded (W)	1	3	1	21	26
Rode in the Charge unwounded (UW)	4	9	2	23	38
May Have Ridden (MAY)	0	4	0	10	14
Identified Chargers	8	21	4	81	114
Unidentified Chargers					14
Total Number of Chargers					128

The following contemporary sources give details of the regiment's statistics for the 25 October 1854

The London Gazette 12 November 1854: - 13th Light Dragoons

3 officers, 3 sergeants, 1 drummer, 20 rank and file, 76 horses, killed; 2 sergeants, 12 rank and file, wounded.

'We went 110 into it and lost 76 horses killed 10 wounded, 7 officers horses killed, 46 men killed and missing and wounded'. Source: Letter to Charles Goad, brother of Thomas Howard Goad (killed in the Charge) written 10-27-54 British Library, ref Additional MS 78157

Only 61 members of the regiment answered the first Roll-call of mounted men made immediately after the Charge.

After being rested a little, we were ordered to mount and muster to see how many there were able to mount. I was told by Corporal Nagle [Sergeant B. Nagle] the muster was twenty-seven [mounted men]. Source: Powell, *Recollections*.

Lieutenant Percy Smith, who was acting adjutant, in a letter, writes, 'the number of horses on parade was 108, exclusive of officers.'

From a letter to Colonel Anstruther-Thomson, written by Captain Jenyns, we get another figure: 'We had 110 horses and eight officers when we went into action (young Goad's horse, the one he jumped the timber on, was knocked over by a round-shot early in the day, and the young un hurt in the fall).'

The total loss of the regiment was three officers killed—Captains Oldham and Goad and Cornet Montgomery; Troop Sergeant Major Weston, and ten rank and file were also killed.

Thirty rank and file were wounded, and two Troop Sergeant Majors, while ten rank and file were taken prisoners.

Trumpeter Powell, on the authority of Corporal Nagle (both of the 13th), places the strength as low as 103.

These numbers are elsewhere stated thus: killed and missing, 69; roll call, 61.

From: C.R.B. Barrett, *History of the XIII Hussars*.

Cornet Cleveland, 17th Lancers, recorded: The 13th went in 125 strong, and only mustered 29 horses.

Sergeant T.G. Johnson, 13th Light Dragoons: 'As to the opinion that we aught to have reformed, why sir, there were none to form had it been possible. Instance in my own regiment. We turned out 112 of all ranks, and lost 84 horses; in fact only 10 of us assembled on the spot from whence we charged. We had 26 men wounded, 13 taken prisoner and 12 killed.' Source: Kinglake, *The Invasion of the Crimea*, volume 2.

The History of the 11th Hussars gives the parade state of the 13th Light Dragoons on 25 October as 130.

17th Lancers Table

17th Lancers	Rank	No.	Status	Corroborating Evidence Supporting Charger Status
Aldous, Charles	Pte	1064	W	Gunshot wound to the hand (*LG* 17.11.54 listed as 'Charles Aldows' and as 'killed or missing'). To Scutari Hospital 26.10.54, and to England 10.01.55. Discharged from Chatham Invalid Depot 24.07.55. Portrait in *The Illustrated London News* 30.10.75.
Allen, Thomas	Pte	807	MAY	Member of the Balaclava Commemoration Society in 1877 but not 1879. Death notices in the *Army & Navy Gazette* of June 1884 and *The Globe* 07.06.84 state he Charged. Included in the Balaclava roll in the Balaclava Centenary 17/21 Lancers Regimental Journal in 1954. A. Sewell lists as a Charger but gives no evidence.
Alexander, Joseph	Pte	989	UW	Survivor's account in *Pocket Hercules*. Swore an affidavit in Morris's claim for the VC for his actions. Received assistance from the Light Brigade Relief Fund.
Andrews, John	Pte	516	SW	Shell wound to left arm (*LG* 17.11.54 'severely wounded'). To Scutari Hospital 26.10.54. Invalided to England 10.01.55. Discharged from Chatham Invalid Depot 11.07.55.

17th Lancers	Rank	No.	Status	Corroborating Evidence Supporting Charger Status
Baker (aka Bacon), John	Pte	828	UW	Lummis and Wynn lists as a Charger, but without providing corroborating evidence. All subsequent lists include his name. A headstone in the graveyard of All Saints Church, Collingham, Notts, is inscribed: 'William Bacon of the village who was Killed in action at Balaclava.' 'In memory of William Bacon a native of this parish who fell in the battle Oct 25th 1854 aged 30 years. And George Broome his brother-in-law, Who met a soldier's death at the same time and place, Aged 35 years. They were privates in the 17th Lancers and fell in the Death Ride at Balaclava, John Bacon their brother of the same regiment escaped unhurt from the same desperate charge.'
Baker (aka Bacon), William	Pte	749	K	Killed in action (*LG* 17.11.54). Real name Bacon brother of John Bacon and brother-in-law of 486 G. Broom according to a headstone in the graveyard of All Saints Church, Collingham, Notts: 'William Bacon of the village who was Killed in action at Balaclava (See entry for Private John Baker).
Barker, William	T.S.M	655	UW	Witnessed every officer of his troop killed or wounded and assumed command. Horse shot under him, probably with the final volley, crushing his left knee and ankle. He caught another horse and resumed command. Member of the Balaclava Commemoration Society in 1879.
Barker, William	Pte	983	K	Killed in action (*LG* 17.11.54).
Beetham, William	Pte	898	UW	At Scutari 13.12.54 to 11.05.55. Member of the Balaclava Commemoration Society in 1879.
Berkleman, Arthur	Pte	871	UW	Several newspaper accounts claim that he Charged.
Berryman, John	Sgt	735	UW	Awarded the VC for assisting, along with Sergeant J. Farrell and Corporal J. Malone, Captain A.F.C. Webb to a place of relative safety.
Bloomfield, James	Pte	484	W	Obituary in the *Brighton Guardian* 16.05.83 records he received 'several wounds in the Charge.'
Bow, John	Pte	1039	SW	Severely wounded by a shell fragment (*LG* 17.11.54 listed as 'killed or missing'). To Scutari Hospital 26.10.54. Invalided to England 16.02.55, due to head wound and resulting vertigo.

Brennan, James	Pte	636	MAY		May have ridden in the Charge. Member of the Commemoration Society in 1877, but not 1879. Attended the Annual Dinner in 1887 and 1890 and the Lord Mayor's Show 1890, when he shared a carriage with Privates C. Aldous, H. Mugg, and T. Mullins, all known survivors.
Brooks, Walter	Pte	747	K		Served in No 4 Troop (Troop Sergeant Major D. O'Hara). Killed in action (*LG* 17.11.54). Mentioned in the account of Private W. Butler: 'Just as we got to No. 1 Redoubt [*sic*], my right-hand man Walter Brooks, was also shot.'
Broom, George	Pte	486	K		Killed in action (*LG* 17.11.54). Brother-in-law of John and Willam Bacon (aka Baker) a headstone in the graveyard of All Saints Church, Collingham, Notts: 'William Bacon of the village who was Killed in action at Balaclava' (see above).
Brown, John	Pte	455	SW		Slightly wounded. To Scutari 27.10.54. Invalided to England 16.02.55.
Brown, John	Tpt	476	UW		Boot and spur carried away by a musket ball, and had his coat-tail cut off by a Cossack lance. Source: his obituary in the *Inverness Courier* 04-01-98. Nominated a Knight of the Légion d'Honneur (4th Class) (*LG* 04.08.56). He claimed that he saved the life of Lieutenant Sir William Gordon. Brown was riding close behind Gordon (who was already wounded by several sabre cuts about the head) as the survivors of the Charge returned, when they found their way barred by Russian cavalry. A Russian Colonel was about to strike Gordon when Brown interposed and killed the Russian. Gordon then turned to Brown and shouted: 'Damn you man, why didn't you leave him to me?' See Lady Butler's painting *The Return from Balaclava* wherein Brown is depicted mounted & carrying a wounded lancer. Brown claimed, as regimental trumpeter, to have sounded the 'Charge'.
Brown, John	Tpt	926	W		Orderly trumpeter to Captain R. White at Balaclava. His horse's leg carried away by a cannon shot and his own thigh pierced by a bullet (*LG* 17.11.54 'slightly wounded'). To Scutari 26.10.54. Re-joined regiment 11.05.55.

17th Lancers	Rank	No.	Status	Corroborating Evidence Supporting Charger Status
Brown, Peter	Pte	862	SW	Shell wound to right hand (*LG* 17.11.54 'severely wounded'). To Scutari 26.10.54. Invalided to England 20.12.54 and discharged 18.10.55.
Brown, Thomas	Pte	714	PoW-M	Served in No. 4 Troop (TSM D. O'Hara). Mortally wounded and taken PoW (*LG* 17.11.54). Mentioned in the account of James Wightman: 'Poor Brown died two days after his admission to the hospital at Alexandrovaska [*sic*].' Possibly in early 1855.
Buck, James	Pte	1160	W	Wounded (*LG* 17.11.54 'slightly wounded').
Burns, William	Pte	796	UW	Horse shot under him.
Butler, William	Pte	840	W	Sword wounds to face and hands. Horse shot under him and he passed out, returning the following day. Published an account.
Carter, Henry	Pte	1145	SW	Shell fragment wound to right thigh and grape-shot wound to mouth (*LG* 17.11.54 listed as 'killed or missing'). To Scutari 26.10.54, invalided to England 26.04.55.
Cattermole, William George	T.S.M	483	W	'I proceeded with my squadron as a troop serre-file to the left troop of the left squadron.' Grazed knuckles of right hand. Spent shell fragment hitting thigh on return. Awarded the DCM, recommended 02.02.55
Chadwick, John	C&A		PoW-W	A member of Captain Morris's Troop but rode as adjutant. He was struck by a lance thrown by a Cossack and tried to defend himself with a revolver but was surrounded and taken PoW (*LG* 17.11.54 'killed or missing'). 'My horse was seriously wounded by a ball received in the animal's neck and this had the effect of covering me with a shower of blood from the wound. After this I felt my chance of returning alive was hopeless.' He was exchanged in September 1855. Affidavit of Troop Sergeant Major W.G. Cattermole in the Cardigan v. Calthorpe case states: 'The Adjutant (Mr Chadwick) rode on my right until we advanced to the Russian guns, when we got separated, and I did not see him again – he was taken prisoner.'
Clark, Thomas Gibson	Pte	1113	UW	Member of the Balaclava Commemoration Society 1879.
Cleveland, Archibald	Crnt		W	Rode as serre-file. His horse, 'Druid', was wounded twice before and at the guns and run through the leg at the guns. He was bruised by a lance blow to the side during his return. Mortally wounded at Inkerman, died 05.11.54.

Clifford, Frederick	Pte	1088	MW	Mentioned in Morley's account: 'I ordered Private Clifford of my own troop to halt, instead of which he charged into the solid column and was cut and pierced to death before my eyes.' (*LG* 17.11.54 'dangerously wounded'). To Scutari 26.10.54. Died of wounds 28.11.54 at Scutari.
Collin, John	Pte	1163	UW	Account in *Pocket Hercules*. Swore an affidavit in support of Morris's claim for the VC for his actions during the Charge.
Cope, James	Pte	1034	UW	Retired in the company of Corporal T. Morley, reaching British lines after the roll call. Mentioned in Morley's account: 'There were no more of the enemy in front and I told the men to separate. James Cope, 17th Lancers and George McGregor 4th Light Dragoons opened out each side of myself and we made the best way back up the valley. Cope and I reported together to the regiment which had assembled, numbered off, and then was complimented by Lord Cardigan. Before we got there we were the last squad to return and the only squad that rallied through the guns.'
Corcoran, Thomas	Pte	643	K	Served in No. 4 Troop (TSM D. O'Hara), killed in action (*LG* 17.11.54).
Davis, Thomas	Pte	772	UW	Listed by Lummis & Wynn and all subsequent writers as a Charger. but without providing corroborating evidence. In a letter written 09.11.54, Davis spoke of his haversack being taken from his side by a piece of shell at Balaclava.
Dickenson, Francis	Sgt	847	UW	With others helped to reverse some of the Russian guns.
Dimmock, William	Pte	653	W	Returned to the field of the Charge and carried away Captain White who was severely wounded. To Scutari 26.10.54, and to England 09.12.54 with Captain White. Appears in photograph with three other Chargers taken at the Brighton Cavalry Depot, August 1855.
Dollard, Richard	Pte	916	K	Killed in action (*LG* 17.11.54). Private M. McGrath's letter in the *Patriotic Found Journal* 24.02.55 states he was decapitated by cannon ball during retreat: 'Poor Dick Dullan [*sic*] was next to me in the ranks...we cut the gunners all away... Then we were attacked by some of the cavalry, five of whom bore down on Dick.

17th Lancers	Rank	No.	Status	Corroborating Evidence Supporting Charger Status
				Dullard and me. We killed four of them, and as Dick had his lance in the fifth, there came a shot from a twelve-pounder which swept the poor fellow's head off, so I had to make the best of my way out of that; and the next shot that was fired out of the same gun, as near as I can judge, blew away the hind quarters of my mare. Thus I was in a nice fix.'
Dowling, Patrick	Pte	1027	K	Killed in action (*LG* 17.11.54).
Doyle, William	Pte	576	W	Wounded (*LG* 17.11.54 'slightly wounded'). To Scutari 08.11.55 and invalided to England. Died on furlough 27.07.56.
Dudley, Thomas	Pte	1134	SW	Mentioned in Private J.W. Wightman's account: 'I have mentioned that my comrade, Peter Marsh, was my left-hand man; next beyond him was Private Dudley.' Collar-bone shattered by ball (*LG* 17.11.54 'severely wounded'). 'I thought it (the shot) a very lucky hit for me in two respects; first, if it had been an inch further to my neck, it would have been all up with me [for] certain' (*The Daily News* 26.01.55).
Duggan, John	Pte	579	SW	Wounded (*LG* 17.11.54 'severely wounded'). To Scutari 26.10.54. Invalided to England 02.05.55. Discharged at Brighton 21.04.56. Obituary in the *Drogheda Argus* 26.03.81: 'A lance thrust pierced his bridle arm, through which it dropped powerless to his side. He also received a couple of sabre cuts and his bridle rein was cut by bullets.'
Duncan, James	Sgt	688	UW	Horse killed. Awarded the Al Valore Militaire: 'Served the eastern campaign of 1854-5 to the end of the war, including the affair of the Bulganak, the battles of Alma, Balaclava (horse killed), and Inkerman (horse killed), and the Siege of Sevastopol, was never absent from the regiment.' Also awarded the Order of the Medjidie (5th Class) (*LG* 02.03.58), recommended for a nomination as a Knight of the Légion d'Honneur with similar citation.
Dyer, Thomas	Pte	562	UW	Listed by Lummis & Wynn and all subsequent writers as a Charger, but without providing corroborating evidence. Portrait in *The Illustrated London News* 30.10.75.

Edge, Robert	Pte	969	PoW-M	Mortally wounded and taken PoW (*LG* 17.11.54). Died either at Simferopol or on the road from Sevastopol. In a letter written to Thomas Morley by James Wightman in March 1889 he said that 'Robert Edge… died of his wounds.'
Ellis, Henry	Pte	1022	PoW-M	Mortally wounded and taken PoW (*LG* 17.11.54), probably dying soon afterwards.
Farrell, John	Sgt	795	UW	Horse killed under him. Awarded the Victoria Cross (*LG* 30.11.57) for assisting Sergeant J. Berryman of the 17th and Corporal J. Malone of the 13th Light Dragoons in removing the mortally wounded Captain A.F.C. Webb to a place of relative safety (all three were awarded the VC).
Fegan, Patrick	Pte	333	W	Wounded when a spent cannon ball damaged left foot (*LG* 17.11.54 'slightly wounded'). Discharged from Chatham Invalid Depot 27.11.55: 'Disabled by rheumatism pains and slight […] from contusion of a spent cannon-shot at Balaclava.'
Ffennell, Charles James	R.S.M.	699	UM	Lummis and Wynne include as a Charger, as do all subsequent Charger lists, but without evidence.
Flowers, George	Pte	524	K	Served in No. 4 Troop (TSM D. O'Hara). Killed in action (*LG* 17.11.54).
Foster, Thomas	Pte	1108	SW	Wounded in thigh by grape-shot (*LG* 17.11.54 'dangerously wounded'). To Scutari 26.10.54. Invalided to England 10.01.55. Photograph in the Royal Collection taken at Brighton August 1856.
Friend, James	Pte	982	W	Wounded (*LG* 17.11.54 'slightly wounded').
Garland, William	Sgt	954	UW	Garland's letter in *The Morning Chronicle* 21.11.54 states his horse was 'slightly wounded by grape-shot'.
Gordon, Sir William	Lt		SW	Commanded E Troop on the left of the 2nd Squadron and was on the extreme left of the First Line and his troop overshot the Russian guns altogether, passed through the guns and pursued the retreating Russian cavalry when he received five sabre wounds to the head. He was described by doctors as being their only patient 'with his head off'. The surgeon held his skull together using gold plates. (*LG* 17.11.54 'severely wounded'). Promoted captain 26.10.54. Nominated a Knight of the Légion d'Honneur (5th Class) *LG* 04.08.56), awarded the Order of the Medjidie (5th Class) (*LG* 02.03.58).
Graham, William Wallace	O.R.C	961	UW	Cornet 02.05.56: 'specially recommended for a Cornetcy on account of his distinguished gallantry at Balaclava.'

305

17th Lancers	Rank	No.	Status	Corroborating Evidence Supporting Charger Status
Gravenor, John	Pte	1157	W	Wounded in action. At the Scutari Depot from 31.10.54. Re-joined regiment 23.11.54.
Grey, Henry	Pte	1058	K	Served in No. 4 Troop (TSM D. O'Hara). Killed in action (*LG* 17.11.54).
Hall, James	Cpl	1051	PoW-M	Wounded by a ball below the right knee (horse also wounded) and PoW (*LG* 17.11.54 'killed or missing'). Probably died in captivity after the amputation of a leg either at Simferopol or on the road from Sevastopol. In October 1875, in a newspaper report of an interview given by David Stanley, he said, 'Corporal Hall, who was on my other side, had a leg blown off and his horse was shot under him. He fell and was taken prisoner, and died a prisoner.'
Harris, Robert	Pte	652	MAY	Lummis and Wynn state, 'May have ridden in the Charge.' Attended 1875 Banquet and a member of the Balaclava Commemoration Society in 1877 (died 1878 so not on the 1879 revised list). Name appears on the roll of Chargers in the Balaclava Centenary number of the *17th/21st Lancer Regimental Journal* in 1954.
Harrison, William	Pte	1131	PoW-M	Mortally wounded and died as a PoW (*LG* 17.11.54 'killed or missing').
Hart, Walter John	Pte	1143	W	Wounded (*LG* 17.11.54 'slightly wounded'). To Scutari 26.10.54. Invalided to England 28.03.55.
Hartopp, John William Cradock	Lt		W	In a letter to his wife Captain Morris mentions that Hartopp was wounded in the Charge. Not on medal roll for the clasp.
Herriott, George	Pte	803	W	Wounded in the left leg (*LG* 17.11.54 'slightly wounded'). To Scutari.
Holland, Edward	Pte	1147	UW	Account in *Lord Paget's Journal*: 'rode in the front rank of the right troop of the regiment' at Balaclava, but 'heard no word of command given by anyone except Colonel Douglas, either going down the valley or returning.'
Hughes, James	Pte	905	MAY	To Scutari after 05.11.54 reason unknown. A. Sewell lists Hughes as a Charger.
Hunscott, Samuel	Pte	944	UW	Swore an affidavit in support of Morris's claim for the Victoria Cross for his actions. Survivor's account *Pocket Hercules*.
Ireland, Joseph	Pte	935	MAY	May have ridden in the Charge. The Balaclava Centenary number of the 17/21 Lancers in 1954 includes his name in a list of all known Chargers. His gravestone is inscribed to 'One of the Six Hundred'. Portrait in *The Illustrated*

				London News 30.10.75. A letter appeared in the *Morning Post* 21.11.54 from a C.R. probably Charles Randall, in which he mentions 'Joe I...' as a fellow Charger.
Jackson, Robert	Pte	915	K	Killed in action (*LG* 17.11.54).
Jenner, Alfred	Pte	1118	PoW-M	Mortally wounded and taken PoW. (*LG* 17.10.17 listed as 'Alfred Tanner'). Died either at Simferopol or on the road from Sevastopol.
Kennedy, Stephen	Pte	566	UW	Member of the Balaclava Commemoration Society in 1879.
Kirk, William	Pte	842	PoW	Taken PoW (*LG* 17.11.54). Mentioned in J.W. Wightman's *Balaclava & The Russian Captivity*.
Lanfried, Martin Leonard	Tpt	986	W	Shot through the right arm (*LG* 17.11.54 'slightly wounded'), the bullet glancing off his pouch and killing his horse. Brought out of action by Private J. Mustard. To Scutari on 26.10.54. To Chatham Invalid Depot 21.12.55.
Lark, Thomas	Pte	1110	W	Wounded in action. Promoted corporal 26.10.54 following Corporal J.I. Nunnerley's promotion to sergeant.
Lees, John	Pte	841	K	Killed in action. His death is mentioned in J.W. Wightman's account.
Liles, George	Pte	1197	PoW- W	Wounded and taken PoW (*LG* 17.11.54 'Wounded and PoW'). Private J.W. Wightman's letter of March 1889 states: 'Lyle [*sic*] died, right leg amputated.' Died in Russia in September 1855.
Ling, Robert	Pte	1136	K	Private T. Wright states Ling was 'shot dead by his side' (*LG* 17.11.54).
Loftus, Edwin	Pte	389	K	Killed in action.
Magee, Thomas	Pte	934	W	Wounded in the left thigh by grape shot (*LG* 17.11.54 'slightly wounded'). To Scutari 26.10.54, invalided to England circa January 1855.
Mansell, George	Pte	1106	UW	Swore an affidavit in support of Captain W. Morris's claim for the Victoria Cross for his actions during the Charge.
Marsh, Robert H.	Pte	1025	UW	Rallied under Corporal Morley and managed to get back to the British lines. Private J.W. Wightman wrote: 'Peter Marsh, was my left-hand man... when, after John Lee had been shot out of the saddle, Private Thomas Dudley shouted "What a hole that bloody shell made" to which Marsh responded "Hold your foul mouth tongue. Swearing like a blackguard when you may be knocked into eternity next minute".'

17th Lancers	Rank	No.	Status	Corroborating Evidence Supporting Charger Status
Marshall, Thomas	Pte	1010	PoW-W	Lance wound to back and horse fell on him (total of nine wounds). Taken PoW (*LG* 17.11.54). Mentioned by J.W. Wightman as having rallied under 1004 Corporal T. Morley. Rejoined the regiment on 26.10.55 (returned with other PoWs on the *Columbo* and 'Her Majesty's Ship'). Discharged, 'invalided, and to pension', from Dublin on the 13.03.57: 'Unfit for further service from an injury to his back from a lance-wound and from contusions. This soldier also stated that his horse fell on him and hurt his back, but, which he has now recovered.'
McCallister, James	Pte	997	PoW	One of twelve lancers taken PoW (*LG* 17.11.54), and one of the three who survived captivity. Repatriated autumn 1855 (returned with other PoWs on the *Columbo* and 'Her Majesty's Ship'). Honourably acquitted by a garrison court-martial at Scutari.
McGrath, Martin	Pte	925	X	Extract from a letter by McGrath published in the *Patriotic Fund Journal* 24.2.55: 'Lord Lucan gave orders to charge the guns in front of us; we thought that was all there were, but when we got within shot of them they opened fire from about fifty guns, thirteen [*sic*] of which were in front, and the remainder on the hills at each side, so that they had a fine play at us.'
McNeill, David	Pte	684	SW	Wounded (*LG* 17.11.54 'severely wounded'). To Scutari (date unknown).
McNeill, Robert	Pte	901	K	Served in No. 4 Troop (TSM D. O'Hara). Killed in action (*LG* 17.11.54).
Melrose, Frederick	Pte	975	K	Writing in the *Strand Magazine*, March 1891, Sergeant J. Berryman recalled that Melrose was killed by a cannon ball as they closed in on the guns (*LG* 17.11.54): 'James Melrose calling out, "What man here would ask another man from England?" Poor fellow, they were the last words he spoke, for the next round from the guns killed him and many others. We were then so close to the guns that the report rang through my head, and I felt I was quite deaf for a time.'
Mitton, John	Pte	881	K	Served in No. 4 Troop (TSM D. O'Hara). Killed in action (*LG* 17.11.54).

Morgan, The Hon. Godfrey Charles	Cpt		W	Commanded B Troop on the right of the 1st Squadron. Riding 'Sir Briggs', who suffered a sabre cut over the right eye, he led a party of his regiment and the 13th Light Dragoons through Cossack lancers, receiving a few minor wounds.
Morgan, Charles	Pte	988	MAY	Probably rode in Captain G.C. Morgan's Troop. Listed as a Charger, wounded and mentioned on the Casualty Roll.
Morley, Thomas	Cpl	1004	UW	Rallied around twenty survivors leading them through the enemy cavalry. Returned after the roll call. Petitioned for award of the VC. Published an account.
Morris, William	Cpt		SW	Commanded the regiment and rode with the 2nd Squadron. Horse ('Old Treasurer' according to Kinglake, 'Old Trumpeter' according to E.J. Boys) shot under him at the guns. Three deep wounds in the head, a fractured right arm and broken ribs (*LG* 17.11.54 'severely wounded'). Nominated a Knight of the Légion d'Honneur (4th Class) (*LG* 04.08.56), awarded the Order of the Medjidie (4rd Class) (*LG* 02.03.58), mentioned in Lord Lucan's despatches 30.11.54, appointed Brevet Major for 'distinguished conduct' (*LG* 12.12.54), and appointed a Companion of the Bath (*LG* 10.07.55).
Mugg, Henry	Pte	1085	UW	Member of the Balaclava Commemoration Society 1879.
Mullins, Thomas	Pte	1095	SW	Served in No. 4 Troop (TSM D. O'Hara). Severely wounded (*LG* 17.11.54 as 'Thomas Mullen' 'dangerously wounded'). At Scutari from 03.11.54 and rejoined the regiment on the 14.12.54.
Mustard, James	Pte	1149	W	Rode with No. 4 Troop (TSM D. O'Hara). 'During retreat hit by canister shot in my left side (*LG* 17.11.54 'slightly wounded'). All I know is that we started at a trot, then at a canter, and finally at a mad gallop in which horses and men were wedged together in one great mass. I was in the front rank. It was hell. Cannon belched forth shot and shell all around us and I saw many a comrade fall, but I got through all right. Then we turned. We came back in extended order but the ride was just as awful, just as maddening. I got a canister shot in my left side that cut my belt and sent my sword rattling to the ground.' Aided Trumpeter R.M.L. Lanfried to safety. To Scutari 29.10.54. To England 26.02.55 and sent to the Brighton Depot from Chatham Invalid Depot 12.05.55.

17th Lancers	Rank	No.	Status	Corroborating Evidence Supporting Charger Status
Nicholson, John	Pte	1026	MAY	May have ridden in the Charge. Claimed in a press article to have been a PoW and to have been interviewed by General Liprandi. Received assistance from the Light Brigade Relief Fund.
Nunnerley, James Ikin	Cpl	870	UW	Horse shot under him before reaching the guns. Later assisted Corporal J. Malone, Captain A.F.C. Webb, and Trumpeter W. Brittain. Promoted sergeant 26.10.54. Nominated to the Médaille Militaire: 'Present at the Alma, Balaclava, Inkerman and Sevastopol. Was never absent from his duty.' During the Charge of the Light Brigade he was in the First Line on the right squadron of his regiment. He had several potentially fatal episodes during the charge, which lasted barely half an hour. These included his horse having a foreleg blown off within yards of the Russian guns, he having to force his way through shot and shell on foot and then being attacked by Russian Cavalry, his more than ordinary height and powerful frame proving most advantageous, and then being ridden over by riderless horses. He eventually caught a stray horse and returned. Before the Charge there were thirteen men in his tent, after only he remained. Promoted to sergeant the day after the charge. Published an account.
O'Gorman, James	Pte	882	W	Wounded. At Scutari General Depot aboard a hospital ship from the 31.10.54 and sent to rejoin the regiment 14.12.54.
O'Hara, Dennis	T.S.M	600	UW	After reaching the guns he rallied some of the remnants of the 17th Lancers in an effort to prevent the guns being carried away. Assisted in bringing in Captain W. Morris under fire and tried to stop the bleeding from a head wound until assistant Surgeon Cattel arrived.
Paine, John	Pte	692	W	Wounded (*LG* 17.11.54 'slightly wounded'). To Scutari 13.12.54 and invalided to England 23.06.55. An account identifying Paine with the story of 'Butcher Jack' appears in a number of newspapers including the *Empire* (New South Wales) 22 July 1868. However, it is considered that 'Butcher Jack' was actually Private John Vahey.

Pearce, Henry	Pte	790	K	Served in No. 4 Troop (TSM D. O'Hara). Killed in action (*LG* 17.11.54).
Pearson, William	Pte	939	W	Rode in Sir George Wombwell's Troop. Severe lance wounded in the side during retreat. To Scutari 26.10.54. Invalided to England 07.12.54. To Brighton Cavalry Depot 25.05.55, where he was photographed for Queen Victoria.
Penn, John	Cpl	1168	UW	His horse 'Nancy' was shot in the right shoulder. Retired with the Second Line. Awarded the DCM, recommended 19.02.55. Published an account.
Perkins, James	Pte	850	MAY	Listed by Lummis and Wynne as 'May have ridden in the Charge', but no evidence. Also listed as a Charger by A. Sewell and R. Dutton.
Phelan, William	Pte	964	W	Wounded. To Scutari in November 1854.
Purvis, William	Pte	868	W	Horse shot under him, suffered three broken ribs when his horse rolled on top of him, was knocked unconscious and when he came round was unable to get up, but was able to escape by hanging onto the stirrups of the horse ridden by Corporal R. Chadwick, 13th Light Dragoons. Purvis later remembered seeing Sergeant E. Talbot, 17th Lancers, riding headless for a considerable distance. He also recalled Captain John Winter, who had his arm in a sling from a badly gathered [*sic*] finger, being asked by his men not to get involved in the mêlée and said: 'Where my men go, I go', and he was shot to pieces, his riderless horse returning to the British lines.
Pyne, John	Cpl	928	W	Wounded (*LG* 17.11.54 'slightly wounded'), presumably the 'cut on left cheek' mentioned in his discharge papers. Letter in *The Morning Chronicle* 21.11.54 written by Sergeant W. Galand erroneously reported him as killed: 'Of all the non-commissioned officers we only lost Sergeant Talbot, shot dead; and three corporals, Hall, Pyne, and Wrigley.' Discharged 27.11.56.
Rafferty, Patrick	Pte	980	W	Horse shot from under him in front of the guns and wounded. To Scutari 26.10.54. Rejoined the regiment 10.11.54. Affidavit in the Cardigan v. Calthorpe case: 'The Earl of Cardigan, who was in command, led the Brigade by the centre of the First Line, just in front of me. That on nearing the Battery in our front my horse was killed, and about six other men and horses were at the same time disabled. That at about the same time I distinctly saw Lord Cardigan ride into and through the Battery, and that some short time after,

17th Lancers	Rank	No.	Status	Corroborating Evidence Supporting Charger Status
				when the remainder of the Brigade had passed us, and I had extricated myself, and was looking about to catch another horse, I noticed the General, Lord Cardigan, come away from where the guns were, and ride off at a hard canter up the Valley on the left-hand side going back – in which direction having remounted myself, I also followed.'
Randall, Charles H.	Pte	1062	UW	Rode with D Troop in the front line of the regiment. Letter written by Randall in the *Morning Post* 21.11.54 describing the Charge: 'The Light Brigade charged down a valley, between the fire of Russians. Captain Nolan, of the 15th Hussars, led us and he got shot himself, and nearly the whole Light Brigade was cut up. We had two officers killed, four wounded, and one taken prisoner; 22 men killed, 69 wounded, and seven taken prisoners. In fact, the whole regiment is nearly cut up, for when we came out of the field we could only mount 42 men. But, thank God I came out safe myself.' In a letter signed 'Charles Randall, messenger, City Union Offices, 51, St Mary's Axe' he claimed to have assisted Corporal H.I. Nunnerley to carry 726 Trumpeter W. Brittain to safety (R. Dutton). Swore an affidavit in the Calthorpe v. Cardigan case.
Ranson, Abraham	T.S.M	493	UW	Awarded the Al Valore Militaire, citation reads: 'Was present at the battles of the Alma, where he distinguished himself; Balaclava, where he again distinguished himself by engaging and cutting down a Russian officer; and Inkerman; siege of Sevastopol. Was never absent from the Regiment.' Swore an affidavit in support of Morris's claim for the VC.
Reilly, Joseph	Pte	815	UW	A member of the Balaclava Commemoration Society in 1879.
Ryan, James	Pte	1155	UW	Member of the Balaclava Commemoration Society in 1879.
Ryan, John	Pte	631	UW	Listed by L.W. Crider and A. Sewell as a Charger.
Scarfe, James	Sgt	481	SW	Rode with No. 4 Troop (TSM D. O'Hara). He had been unhorsed and rode off the field on a Cossack horse. Ten sabre wounds on forehead, back of the head, neck, both wrists, and thigh (*LG* 17.11.54 'severely wounded'). To Scutari Hospital 26.10.54. Invalided to England

				25.12.54. Presented before Queen Victoria at Brompton Barracks 03.03.55. The Queen later described in her Journal how Sergeant Scarff [*sic*] of the 17th Lancers 'told us how he had received his sabre cuts - one on his head and one on his two hands - which he had put up to save his head.'
Sewell, Johnson	Pte	1111	K	Killed in action (*LG* 17.11.54).
Sharpe, Thomas	Pte	940	PoW-M	Taken PoW (*LG* 17.11.54). The *Glasgow Daily Mail* gives extracts of a private letter from a resident in St Petersburg, dated 25.02.54, which states that he died in the hospital at Kharkoff 27.02.55. Buried at the expense of the English residents.
Shearingham, John	Sgt	539	W	Horse shot under him. Received sword and lance wound. Nominated to the Médaille Militaire, the citation for which states: 'Never absent from his duties.' Swore an affidavit of Morris's claim for the VC. Extract from the *Falmouth and Penryn News* 20.07.67 reporting the funeral of an old Veteran at Charlestown: 'Mr Shearingham served for twenty-four years in the 17th Lancers and was with his regiment in the Crimea during the whole of the campaign. He had his horse killed under him at the Battle of Balaclava, and while extricating himself from under the dead animal was wounded, first by a sword cut, and then by a lance wound in the thigh, by a Cossack. He, however, contrived to catch, and mount, a rider-less horse of the Brigade, which carried him safety within British lines. Afterwards, while gallantly attacking a party of 20 Cossacks escorting a Russian officer with dispatches, and a lady, he was wounded in the head by a pistol shot fired from the carriage, which scarred his left eye and caused him blindness for some considerable time.'
Smith, George	Pte	1003	UW	Served in No. 4 Troop (TSM D. O'Hara). Reported the whereabouts of the wounded Captain W. Morris to O'Hara. Awarded the DCM, recommendation 19.02.55. Swore an affidavit in favour of Morris's claim for the VC.
Smith, John	Pte	924	UW	Member of the Balaclava Commemoration Society in 1879. Portrait in *The Illustrated London News* 30.10.75. *The Daily Telegraph* 04.02.99: 'During the Charge of the Light Brigade he found that the thick coat worn by the Russian soldiers was almost proof against his sword-cuts, so he used the point of his blade. Seeing a fellow trooper slashing for all

17th Lancers	Rank	No.	Status	Corroborating Evidence Supporting Charger Status
				he was worth at the enemy, he called out, "Don't cut em man, give em the point." Many a comrade acted on this good advice, thereby lessening the number of the foe.' Mentioned in Thomas Morley's account: 'Private John Smith mounted one of the horses attached to the gun.' Known as 'Blood Smith' or 'Fighting Smith'. Mr Robert Davies who assisted Mr T.H. Roberts in his work annotated his copy of the book by D.H. Parry, *The Death or Glory Boys*: 'He often told me of his service during the Charge and how he had been splashed with the blood of Captain Nolan when he was struck.'
Smith, Thomas	Pte	531	MAY	May have ridden in the Charge. Served in A Troop. To Scutari 26.10.54. Invalided to England 02.03.55. Appears in photograph with three other Chargers taken at the Brighton Cavalry Depot August 1855.
Soley, Benjamin	Pte	1120	SW	Received three wounds (*LG* 17.11.54 'severely wounded'), although qualified for Inkerman bar.
Stanley, David	Pte	1009	W	Wounded.
Stannage, James	Pte	1016	K	Killed in action (*LG* 17.11.54).
Stewart, Thomas	Pte	974	W	Served in No 4 Troop (TSM D. O'Hara). Wounded. To Scutari 03.11.54 and rejoined regiment 03.02.55.
Swiney, John	Pte	1036	UW	Wounded at Inkerman. Member of the Balaclava Commemoration Society in 1879.
Talbot, Edward	Sgt	556	K	Decapitated by a cannon ball (*LG* 17.11.54). A Sheffield Newspaper interview with David Stanley in 1875 included the following: 'Sergeant Talbot rode next to me in the front rank. When we were half-way down he had his head blown off, and he rode sixty yards in the saddle before he fell off.'
Taylor, George	Cpl	405	SW	Served in No. 4 Troop (TSM D. O'Hara). Wounded (*LG* 17.11.54 'severely wounded'). To the General Hospital Scutari 26.10.54, where he died 16.01.55. Awarded the DCM, recommended 19.01.55.
Terry, George	Sgt	721	UW	Rode in the Charge.

Thompson, John Henry	Lt		K	Commanded C Troop on the left of the 1st Squadron. Killed in action about 80 yards from the guns when the final salvo was fired (*LG* 17.11.54 'Killed or missing'). Sergeant Major Barker of the 17th said in an interview in 1897: 'I then assumed the command of Lieutenant Thomson's troop, whom I had seen but a few moments before, shot, and falling from his horse.'
Tiggle, Samuel William	Pte	1178	UW	Member of the Balaclava Commemoration Society in 1879.
Travis, William	Pte	678	UW	Member of the Balaclava Commemoration Society in 1877. Listed by Lummis and Wynn as a Charger, but without corroborating evidence for this.
Trowman, Edward	Pte	923	UW	Received assistance from the T.H. Roberts Fund and the Light Brigade Relief Fund.
Toulson, Thomas	Pte	838	May	838 Private Thomas Toulson is remembered on a memorial in Beeston Churchyard, Nottinghamshire, along with 841 Private John Lees. Both are said to have Charged.
Vahey, John	Pte	598	UW	Served in Captain Morris's Troop. 'Butcher Jack' awarded the Distinguished Conduct Medal, recommendation 19.01.55. According to the Rev W.H. Fitchett: 'The regimental Butcher of the 17th Lancers was engaged in killing a sheep when he heard the trumpets sound for the charge. He leapt on a horse in shirt sleeves with bare arms and a pipe in his mouth, he rode through the whole charge and slew it is said six men with his own hands and came back pipe still in mouth.'
Waller, Frederick	Pte	1035	UW	Member of the Balaclava Commemoration Society in 1879.
Watson, Charles	Pte	872	UW	Nominated to the Médaille Militaire.
Watts, James	Pte	1153	SW	Served in No. 4 Troop (TSM D. O'Hara). Severely wounded in the Charge (leg amputated at Balaclava Hospital without anaesthetic).
Weatherley, George	Cpl	673	UW	Portrait in *The Illustrated London News* 30.10.75.
Webb, Frederick Cavendish	Cpt		MW	Commanded D Troop on the right of the 2nd Squadron. Mortally wounded (leg amputated below the knee) (LG 17.11.54 'severely wounded'), and was assisted by Sergeant J. Berryman and Sergeant J. Farrell of the 17th and Corporal J. Malone of the 13th. All three were awarded the Victoria Cross. Died Scutari 06.11.54.

17th Lancers	Rank	No.	Status	Corroborating Evidence Supporting Charger Status
Webster, James	Pte	902	UW	Member of the Balaclava Commemoration Society in 1879.
White, Robert	Cpt		SW	Commanded 1st Squadron, and rode with C Troop on the left of the directing squadron in the Charge and was checked by Lord Cardigan in the early stages for 'forcing the pace'. Private James Wightman recalled as the regiment closed in on the guns: 'There crashed into us a regular volley from the Russian cannon. I saw Captain White go down and Cardigan disappeared into the smoke.' He suffered a 'severe flesh wound to the leg, and his horse shot.' Wounded before reaching the guns and brought off the field by Private W. Dimmock some three hours after the Charge (*LG* 17.11.54 'severely wounded'). To Scutari 26.10.54. Invalided to England 13.01.55. Awarded the Order of the Medjidie (5th Class) (*LG* 02.03.58).
Wightman, James William	Pte	1177	PoW-W	His horse was wounded and he was cut down suffering 13 wounds and taken PoW (*LG* 17.11.54). In support of Lord Cardigan's role he states: 'after passing the guns, I distinctly heard his Lordship give the order to rally inside the Guns in the space between those Guns and the Russian Cavalry in the rear.' Wightman was one of the Chargers that railed to 1004 Corporal T. Morley on hearing his bellowing rough voice. Wightman's horse was now showing the signs of the Charge, and finally, riddled with bullets, fell to the ground, its rider also shot through the forehead and the top of the shoulder. Then while struggling out from under the dead horse, a Cossack standing over him stabbed him with a lance in the neck, also sticking him many times in the ribs and back, on trying to rise to his feet as he tried to draw his sword a final thrust by the lance went through the palm of his hand. This was the end for our gallant fighter. Falling to the ground he was later to be taken prisoner. Repatriated Autumn 1855 (returned with other PoWs on the *Columbo* and 'Her Majesty's Ship'). Wrote an account.
Williams, Richard Hall	Sgt	750	UW	During the Charge he was suffering from a painful boil on his nose, a factor to which he later referred: 'My visage was so fearsome that the Russians even held their fire. But the pain

				was so great that on the following day I had to report to the Regimental Surgeon – a step not to be lightly taken then... Two orderlies held me and I received a smart buffet on the nose, which dispersed the fluid.'
Wilson, John	Pte	1017	K	Rode with No. 4 Troop (TSM D. O'Hara). Wilson was Lieutenant Sir William Gordon's servant in the Crimea and was probably with him during the Charge. Killed in action (*LG* 17.11.54).
Winter, John Pratt	Cpt		K	Commanded the 2nd Squadron (*LG* 17.11.54 'killed or missing'). He was last seen half a mile beyond the guns; his horse severely wounded in several places by grape shot but returned to the British lines. Another source claims he was seen to fall close to the enemy's guns just as the retreat was sounded. Affidavit of Troop Sergeant Major W.G. Cattermole in the Cardigan v. Calthorpe case: 'I saw [Winter] falling from his horse when struck – I would think – by a piece of shell.'
Wooden, Charles	Sgt	799	UW	Horse shot under him, but made his way back to British lines unwounded. Returned to the battlefield and assisted Dr Mouat in rescuing Captain Morris and successfully petitioned for the award of the Victoria Cross, which was awarded (*LG* 26.10.58). Nominated to the Médaille Militaire.
Wright, Thomas	Pte	1097	UW	Horse shot under him. He saw 926 Private J. Brown whose horse lost a leg to cannon-fire. Brown was limping towards him after being shot in the ankle and called out for assistance to which Wright replied: 'It is every man for himself today.'
Wrigley, Constantine	Pte	469	K	Killed in action (*LG* 17.11.54 listed as 'Corporal Constantine Wrigley').
Yates, John	Pte	1102	UW	Wounded in the right hand. He eventually arrived at Scutari Hospital on 12.12.54. To England 22.03.55.
Young, Henry M.	Pte	1078	PoW-W	Wounded and taken PoW (*LG* 17.11.54). Believed died at Simferopol, between 05.05.55 and 09.06.55, when his death was reported in *The Illustrated London News*. J.W. Wightman notes: 'Private Melrose was killed on his right and Young, who rode on his left, was taken a prisoner of war and died at Simferopol November 12 1854 from his wounds.'

	Officers	NCOs	Trumpeters	Other Ranks	Total
Rode in the Charge and Killed in action (K)	2	1	0	19	22
Rode in the Charge and Mortally Wounded (MW)	1	0	0	1	2
Rode in the Charge and Severely Wounded (SW)	3	2	0	11	16
Rode in the Charge and Prisoner of War (PoW)	0	0	0	2	2
Rode in the Charge and Prisoner of War – Wounded (PoW-W)	1	0	0	5	6
Rode in the Charge and Prisoner of War – mortally wounded (PoW-M)	0	1	0	6	7
Rode in the Charge and wounded (W)	3	3	2	23	31
Rode in the Charge unwounded (UW)	0	16	1	32	49
May Have Ridden (MAY)	0	0	0	8	8
Identified Chargers	10	23	3	106	143
Unidentified Chargers					4
Total Number of Chargers					147

The following contemporary sources give details of the regiment's statistics for the 25 October 1854:

The London Gazette 12 November 1854

Return of Casualties from 22nd to 26th October, 1854, both days inclusive.

CAVALRY.

17th Lancers

3 officers, 1 sergeant, 32 rank and file, 99 horses, killed; 4 officers, 1 sergeant,

2 drummers, 31 rank and file, wounded.

Only 35 members of the regiment answered the first roll-call of mounted men made immediately after the Charge.

Cleveland wrote in a letter to his uncle, dated 'Balaclava, Oct 26, 1854': 'The 17th Lancers went into battle 145 strong. When we mustered, we only had 34 horses not wounded: 99 were killed; 79 men killed or wounded; seven out of ten officers killed and wounded. We have now only three officers. Thank God I am one.'

Thomas Morley in *Man of the Hour*: 'I am only certain of the figures for my own regiment. The 17th Lancers went into the engagement 145 and came out 45 mounted. Every officer of my squadron was killed or wounded. We lost 13 prisoners, only one of them unwounded, and he was dismounted, his horse having been killed. Of these only three lived to return to the English ranks.'

Nunnerley: 'Out of the 145 belonging to the regiment who went into the Charge only 35 could report for active duty'

Captain The Hon. Godfrey Charles Morgan, 17th Lancers: 'I numbered the regiment off 34 when we returned. The other regiments suffered nearly as much' (*Goulburn Herald and County of Argyle Advertiser* 24 March 1855).

Identified Chargers Table (from the five regiments engaged)

All Chargers	Officers	NCOs	Trumpeters	Other Ranks	Total
Rode in the Charge and KIA	11	15	2	65	93
Rode in the Charge and Severely Wounded	6	7	0	40	53
Rode in the Charge and Mortally Wounded	1	4	3	7	15
Rode in the Charge and PoW	0	1	1	10	12
Rode in the Charge and PoW (Wounded)	3	3	0	22	28
Rode in the Charge and died in Captivity	0	2	1	10	13
Rode in the Charge and Slightly Wounded	13	22	3	90	128
Rode in the Charge unwounded	22	40	8	131	201
May Have Ridden unwounded	3	7	1	47	58
Total	59	101	19	422	601

Although only 198 mounted men (out of 673 engaged) were able to muster on the afternoon following the Charge, some 500 men of all ranks, including the wounded made it out of the valley, with 58 men taken as PoWs.

Adkin states that about 306 men returned unwounded (out of 664 he gives as charging).

Lord Cardigan states that '396 horses were put hors de combat', and 'in the two following days, I had upwards of 30 of the horses of the Light Cavalry Brigade shot, being desperately wounded in the affair.'

Whinyates gives 366 horses lost in total.

Staff Table

Staff	Rank	Unit	Charger Status
Bingham, Lord George	Cornet in the Coldstream Guards	Aide-de-Camp to his father, the 3rd Earl of Lucan	Mentioned in the account of Private Charles Whyte, 8th Hussars, as having saved his life in the aftermath of the Charge. Therefore, he may have ridden and be a new Charger.
Brittain, William	726 Tpr	17th Lancers Attached to staff as Brigade trumpeter	Mortally wounded by a large ball in the thigh early in the Charge (*LG* 17.11.54 'dangerously wounded'). To Scutari where he died 14.02.55. As orderly trumpeter to Lord Cardigan, he sounded 'Walk', 'Trot', 'Gallop,' but was wounded before being able to sound the 'Charge'.
Brudenell, James Thomas	Maj-Gen	G. Staff Commanding	Rode 'Ronald' in front of 1st Squadron 17th Lancers (the squadron of direction). Slightly Wounded. Mentioned in despatches (*LG* 30.11.54), nominated a Knight of the Légion d'Honneur (4th Class) (*LG* 04.08.56),

Staff	Rank	Unit	Charger Status
			Awarded the Order of the Medjidie (2nd Class) (*LG* 02.03.58), appointed a Knight Commander of the Bath (*LG* 10.07.55)
de la Tour, Louis Gabriel Aymard	Col	French Staff	Cannonball broke his horse's leg. Returned unwounded.
Govone, Giuseppe	Maj	Attached to the French Headquarters Staff	Wounded.
Landriani, Giuseppe	Lt	Unattached	Leg fractured by grape-shot and horse killed half way down the valley. Taken prisoner. Rode on the right with the 13th Light Dragoons. Repatriated but died of his wounds. His death was reported in the *Morning Post* of 30 June 1858.
Lockwood, George	Cptn	8th Hussars Aide-de-Camp	Henry Joy, 17th Lancers, as trumpet major of the cavalry division, sounded the Charge for the Heavy Brigade as they advanced in support of the Light Brigade: 'Some time afterwards Captain Lockwood, aide-de-camp to the Earl of Cardigan, rode up to me in a state of great excitement, without his busby, asking if I had seen Lord Cardigan. I replied, "Yes; he has just passed me," and I pointed in the direction which he had taken. The captain rode away, and I never saw that officer again.' (*LG* 12.11.54 'killed or missing').
Maxse, Henry Fitzhardinge Berkeley	Lt	21st Regt Aide-de-Camp to Lord Cardigan	Shot in the foot and ankle, and was carried on board Cardigan's yacht the *Dryad* (*LG* 12.11.54 'wounded slightly'). Awarded the Order of the Medjidie (5th Class).
Mayow, George Wynell	L.C.	Unattached, Major of Brigade	Sick in the days leading up to the Charge, his place as Brigade Major was taken by Cornet John Yates, Adjutant 11th Hussars. (In his affidavit sworn on 30 May 1863 and filed on 2 June 1863, claims to have acted as Brigade Major during the Charge). Mayow rallied men of the 17th Lancers under Troop Sergeant Major D. O'Hara who joined forces with the remnants of the 8th Hussars under Colonel F.G. Shewell, which Lieutenant E. Seager, 8th Hussars, had ordered to right about wheel to attack the Lancers who were blocking their path. Mentioned in despatch (*LG* 30.11.54), nominated a Knight of the Légion d'Honneur (5th Class) (*LG* 04.08.56), awarded the Al Valore

			Militaire, the citation for this states: 'Brevet Lieutenant Colonel George Wynell Mayow, (Unattached) Served as a Staff Officer to the Cavalry in the campaign of 1854-55 and was present at the battles of the Alma, Balaclava, Inkerman and the Siege of Sevastopol.' Order of the Medjidie (4th Class), (*LG* 02.03.58).
Nolan, Louis Edward	Cptn	15th Hussars Aide-de-Camp to Brigadier General Airey	Aide-de-Camp to Brigadier General Airey. Rode in front of the 2nd Squadron, 17th Lancers. Killed in action. Lord Raglan's ADC, Lieutenant Calthorpe, was ready to take the fateful order, but Raglan told Airey to hand it to Nolan. Raglan and Airey passed on verbal instructions to clarify the contents of the written order.
Paget, George August Frederick	Col Lord	Commanding Second Line	Rode 'Exquisite' in the 1st Squadron 4th Light Dragoons. Mentioned in despatch (*LG* 30.11.54), nominated a Knight of the Légion d'Honneur, 4th Class (*LG* 04.08.56), awarded the Al Valore Militare and the Order of the Medjidie (3rd Class) (*LG* 02.03.58), appointed a Companion of the Bath (*LG* 10.07.55).
Wombwell, George Orby	Cornet	17th Lancers Extra Aide-de-Camp to Lord Cardigan	Rode as orderly officer to Lord Cardigan. Had two horses shot under him. Taken prisoner but, encouraged by Captain W. Morris, he caught a riderless horse and escaped in the company of the 11th Hussars, afterwards receiving a blow to the arm. Promoted lieutenant 26.10.54.

The London Gazette 12 November 1854

Return of Casualties among officers from 22nd to 26th October, 1854, both days inclusive.

27th October, 1854.

Staff

Lieutenant General the Earl of Lucan, wounded slightly; Brigadier General the Hon. J.Y. Scarlett, wounded slightly; Captain the Hon. W. Charteris, killed; Captain George Lockwood, killed or missing; Lieutenant H.F. Maxse, wounded slightly; Lieutenant A.I. Elliot, wounded slightly.

The London Gazette 12 November 1854

Return of Casualties from 22nd to 26th October, 1854, both days inclusive.

CAVALRY

Staff

2 officers killed; 4 officers wounded.

Bibliography

Original Documents

Blunt, Sir John (Lord Lucan's interpreter), personal papers, National Army Museum, London.

Joliffe, Hedworth, Letter, National Army Museum, London.

Raglan, Lord, Papers, National Army Museum, London.

Seager, Edward, Letter, National Army Museum.

Tremayne, Arthur, Letter, National Army Museum.

Wombwell, George, Letters, The Queen's Royal Lancers Museum.

Books

Abbott, P.E., *Recipients of the Distinguished Conduct Medal 1855-1909* (1975).

Adkin, Mark, *The Charge, The Real Reason Why the Light Brigade Was Lost* (Pen & Sword, 1996).

Anonymous, *Aldershottana: or Chinks in My Hut* (London, Ward & Lock, 1856).

Anonymous, *The Charge of the Light Brigade by one who was in it*, United Services Journal, April 1856.

Anglesey, the Marquess of, *A History of the British Cavalry 1815 to 1919, Vol. II, 1851-1871* (Leo Cooper, Barnsley, 1975).

Anglesey, the Marquess of, *'Little Hodge', being extracts from the diaries and letters of Colonel Edward Cooper Hodge written during the Crimea War, 1854-1856* (Leo Cooper, London, 1971).

Bancroft, James W., *Echelon, The Light Brigade Action at Balaklava, A New Perspective* (Spellmount, Stroud, 2011).

Baron Bazancourt, (translated by Robert Howe Gould) *The Crimean Expedition, to the Capture of Sevastopol, Chronicles of the War in the East* (Sampson Low, London, 1856).

Barrett, C.R.B., *The History of the 13th Hussars*, 2 volumes (London, 1911).

Barthorp, M., *Heroes of the Crimea* (Blandford, 1991).

Beauchamp Walker, Charles Pyndar, *Days of a Soldier's Life, being letters written by the late General Sir C.P. Beauchamp Walker, KCB* (Chapman and Hall, London, 1894).

Bentley, Nicholas, [ed], *Russell's Despatches from the Crimea* (Panther, London, 1970).

Brighton, Terry, *Hell Riders, The Truth About the Charge of the Light Brigade* (Penguin, London, 2005).

Butler, William, *A Descriptive Account of the Famous Charge of The Light Brigade* (Privately published, c.1890).

Buttery, David, *Messenger of Death, Captain Nolan and the Charge of the Light Brigade* (Pen & Sword, 2008).

Calthorpe, Captain S.J.G., *Letters from Headquarters; or, The Realities of the War in the Crimea, by an Officer on the Staff*, 2 volumes (John Murray, 1858).

Cardigan, James Thomas Brudenell, 7th Earl of, *Eight Months on Active Service* (William Clowes and Sons, London, 1855).

Calthorpe v. Cardigan, *Affidavits filed by Lieutenant Colonel The Honourable Somerset John Gough Calthorpe (5th Dragoon Guards) The Respondent* (John Murray, 1863).

Cattell, Assistant Surgeon, W., MS Autobiography, NAM.

Cleveland, Cornet Archibald, *Letters to his Uncle from Balaclava* (1854).

Clifford, Henry VC, *His letters & Sketches from the Crimea* (Michael Joseph, London, 1956).

Cornwallis, Major Fiennes, *Letters Written from the Crimea* (1868).

Crider, Lawrence, *In Search of the Light Brigade: A Biographical Dictionary of the Members of the Five Regiments of the Light Brigade from January 1, 1854 to March 31, 1856* (Eurocommunica, 2004).

Dallas, Lieutenant Colonel G.F., (ed Michael Hargreaves Mawson), *Eyewitness in the Crimea: The Crimean War letters of Lieutenant Colonel George Frederick Dallas* (Greenhill, London, 2001).

Daniell, D.S., *4th Hussars – The Story of the 4th Queen's Own Hussars 1685-1958* (Aldershot, 1959).

Dawson, Anthony, *Letters from the Light Brigade* (Pen & Sword, 2014).

David, Saul, *The Homicidal Earl, The Life of Lord Cardigan* (Abacus, London, 1998).

Doughton, Joseph, *Narrative of Joseph Doughton, Late of Her Majesty's 13th Light Dragoons, One of the Heroes Wounded at the Battle of Balaclava, in the Gallant Cavalry Charge* (Birmingham, 1856).

Doyle, John, *A Descriptive Account of the Famous Charge of the Light Brigade at Balaclava* (Privately published, Manchester, 1877).

Drummond, K., *Letters form the Crimea* (Norris & Son, London, 1855).

Duberly, Frances, *Journal Kept During the Russian War*: from the Departure of the Army from England in April, 1854, to the fall of Sevastopol (Longman, Brown, Green & Longman, London, 1856).

Falls, Cyril (ed.), *A Diary of the Crimea by George Palmer Evelyn* (Gerald Duckworth & Co, London 1954)

Dutton, Roy, *Forgotten Heroes, The Charge of the Light Brigade* (InfoDial, Oxton, 2007).

Dutton, Roy, *Forgotten Heroes, The Charge of the Heavy Brigade* (InfoDial, Oxton, 2008).

Ewart, J.A., *The Story of a Soldier's Life* (Sampson Low, London, 1881).

Farquharson, Robert, *Reminiscences of Crimean Campaigning And Russian Imprisonment* (Privately published, Glasgow, 1882).

Fay, Charles Alexandre, *Souvenirs de la Guerre de Crimee, 1854-1856* (Paris, 1867).

Figes, Orlando, Crimea: *The Last Crusade* (Penguin, London, 2010).

Fortescue, Sir John, *A History of the British Army* (Macmillan, London, 1899).

Fortescue, The Hon. J.W., *A History of the 17th Lancers (Duke of Cambridge's Own)* (London, 1895).

Fox-Strangeways, Brigadier General Thomas, Balaclava chapter in *From Coruna to Sevastopol* by Colonel F. Whinyates (W.H. Allen, 1884).

Franks, Henry, *Leaves from a Soldier's Notebook* (Thirst, 1904).

Grehan John, *Voices From the Past: The Charge of the Light Brigade*, (Frontline Books, 2017).

Grigg, Joseph, *Told From the Ranks - Recollections of Service by Privates and Non-Commissioned Officers of the British Army 1843-1901*. Collected by E. Milton Small (London, 1901).

Hamley, General Sir Edward, *The War in the Crimea* (Seeley and Co., London, 1891).

Harrison, John, *The Gallant Six Hundred* (Hutchinson, London, 1973).

Herbert, James Henry, his account of the Charge in 'Survivors' Tales of Great Events', *Royal Magazine*, volume xiii (1906).

Hibbert, Christopher, *The Destruction of Lord Raglan, Tragedy of the Crimean War 1854-55* (Penguin, 1985).

Higginson, General Sir George, *71 Years of a Guardsman's Life*, 1916.

Hughes, T.S.M. Edwin, his account in the *Blackpool Gazette* (1912.

Jocelyn, Colonel J.R.J., *History of the Royal Artillery (Crimea Period)*, 1911.

Kelly, Christine, *Mrs Duberly's War: Journal & Letters From the Crimea* (OUP, 2007).

Kelly, Mrs Tom, (an account by Pennington in) *From The Fleet in the Fifties* (1902).

Kinglake, A.W., *The Invasion of the Crimea: Its Origin, and An Account of its Progress Down to the Death of Lord Raglan*, 8 volumes (William Blackwood & Sons, 1878).

BIBLIOGRAPHY

Lambert, Andrew and Badsey, Stephen, *The War Correspondents, The Crimea War* (Bramley, Stroud, 1997).

Lummis, William M., and Wynne, Kenneth G., *Honour the Light Brigade* (Hayward, 1973).

McGuffie, T.H., *Rank and File* (St. Martin's, New York, 1966).

Mallinson, Alan, *The Making of the British Army, From the English Civil War to the War on Terror* (Bantam, 2009).

Massie, Alastair, *A Most Desperate Undertaking, The British Army in the Crimea, 1854-56* (National Army Museum, 2009).

Mitchell, Albert, *Recollections of One of the Light Brigade* (R. Pelton, Tunbridge Wells, 1885).

Mollo, John and Boris, *Into the Valley of Death* (Windrow & Greene, 1999).

Morley, Thomas, *The Cause of the Charge of Balaclava* (Privately published, Nottingham, 1899).

Morley, Thomas, *The Man of The Hour* (Privately published, 1892).

Moyse-Bartlett, H., *Nolan of Balaclava, And his influence on the British Cavalry* (Leo Cooper, 1971).

Murray, Rev. R.H., *The History of the VIII King's Royal Irish Hussars*, 2 volumes (Cambridge, 1928).

Nolan, E.H., *Illustrated History of the War against Russia* (James Virtue, 1857).

Nolan, Edward Louis, *Cavalry Journal* (1911).

Nunnerley, James Ikin, *Short Sketch of the 17th Lancers and Life of Sergeant-Major J.I. Nunnerley* (Privately published, Liverpool, 1884).

Paget, C.S. (Ed.) *The Light Cavalry Brigade in the Crimea: Extracts from the letters and journal of the late General Lord G. Paget... during the Crimea War. With a map* (John Murray, 1881).

Parkinson, John Smith, his account of the Charge in 'Survivors' Tales of Great Events', *Royal Magazine*, vol xvii (London, 1909).

Parry, D.H., *The Death or Glory Boys* (1899).

Pemberton, W. Baring, *Battles of the Crimean War* (Batsford, 1962).

Pennington, William, *Left of Six Hundred* (Privately published, Bristol, 1887).

Pennington, William, *Sea, Camp, and Stage* (Privately published, Bristol, 1906).

Portal, Robert, *Letters from the Crimea* (Privately published, Winchester, 1900).

Powell, Harry, *Recollections of a Young Soldier During the Crimean War* (Oxford, 1876).

Richardson, Private John, account in *Spy* magazine (1892).

Richardson, Robert G. (Ed), *Nurse Sarah Anne – with Florence Nightingale at Scutari* (John Murray, 1977).

Russell, William Howard, *Despatches from the Crimea* (Frontline, 2008).

Russell, William Howard, *The British Expedition to the Crimea* (Routledge, 1858).

Russell, William Howard, *The Great War with Russia, the invasion of the Crimea: A Personal Retrospective* (Routledge, 1895).

Russell, William Howard, *The War to the Death of Lord Raglan* (1855).

Ryan, George, *Our Heroes of the Crimea* (1855).

Ryzhov, Lieutenant-General Ivan Ivanovic, *O Srazhenii pod Balaklave* from *Russkii Vestnik* (1870).

Seaton, Albert, *The Crimean War, A Russian Chronicle* (Batsford, 1977).

Sewell, Andrew, *The Cavalry Division in the Crimea.*

Shavshin, Vladimir, *The Valley of Death* (Sevastopol, 2005).

Small, E., *Told From the Ranks, Recollections of service during the Queen's reign by privates and non-commissioned officers of the British Army* (A. Melrose, 1897).

Smith, George Loy, *A Victorian RSM, From India to the Crimea* (D.J. Costello, Tunbridge Wells, 1987).

Spilsbury, Julian, *The Thin Red Line, An Eyewitness History of the Crimea War* (Weidenfeld & Nicolson).

Stuart, Brian (Ed.), *Soldier's Glory, being 'Rough Notes of an Old Soldier' by Major General Sir George Bell* (G. Bell & Sons, 1956).

Stephenson, Frederick Charles Arthur, *At Home and on the Battlefield: Letters from the Crimea, China and Egypt, 1854-1888* (John Murray, 1915).

Sweetman, John, *Balaclava 1854, The Charge of the Light Brigade* (Osprey, London, 1990).

Sweetman, John, *Raglan, From the Peninsula to the Crimea* (Pen & Sword, 2010).

Thomas, Donald Serrel, *Charge! Hurrah! Hurrah! Life of Cardigan of Balaclava* (Routledge & Kegan Paul, 1974).

'Thormanby', *Kings of the hunting-field*, (Hutchinson, 1899).

Trow, M.J., *The Pocket Hercules, Captain Morris and the Charge of the Light Brigade* (Pen & Sword, 2006).

Walker, Beauchamp, *Days of a Soldier's Life, being letters written by the late General Sir C.P. Beauchamp Walker, KCB,* (Chapman and Hall, 1894),

Warner, Philip, *Letters Home from the Crimea, A young cavalryman's campaign from Balaclava and Sevastopol to victory* (Windrush, Moreton-in-Marsh, 1999).

Warner, Philip, *A Cavalryman in the Crimea: Letters of Temple Godman, 5th Dragoon Guards* (Pen & Sword, 2009).

Whinyates, Francis Arthur, *From Coruna to Sevastopol. The History of 'C' Battery, 'A'Brigade (late 'C'Troop), Royal Horse Artillery* (W.H. Allen, 1884).

White-Thompson, Sir Robert, *A Memoir of Lieutenant Colonel William Morris* (1903).

Wightman, James William, 'One of the Six Hundred' (*Nineteenth Century Magazine*, May 1892).

Williams, Captain G.T., *Historical Records of the Eleventh Hussars* (London, 1908).

Wood, Evelyn, *The Crimea in 1854, and 1894* (Chapman & Hall, 1896).

Wombwell, Captain George, *Letters from Sevastopol* (1854).

Woodham-Smith, Cecil, *The Reason Why* (Constable, 1953).

Wolseley, Field-Marshal Viscount, *The Story of a Soldier's Life* (Archibald Constable, Westminster, 1903).

Periodicals

17th/21st Lancer Regimental Journal in 1954

4th Hussars Journal

Answers magazine, Portraits and Accounts of 14 Survivors (1912)

Army and Navy Gazette of 29 July 1899

Army and Navy Gazette of 10 March 1901

Canadian Legion Magazine (1954)

Patriotic Fund Journal of 24 February 1855

The London Gazette (various issues)

The Regiment of 24 October 1896

The Strand Magazine issue Nos. 1 and 2 (1891)

The War Correspondent: The Journal of the Crimean War Research Society, Special Balaclava Issue 1996.

Anonymous, The Charge of the Light Brigade by one who was in it, *United Services Journal*, April 1856.

Newspapers

Bath Chronicle of 2 November 1899

Birkenhead and Cheshire Advertiser and Wallasey Guardian of 28 October 1899

Birmingham Daily Post of 23 May 1892

Brighton Guardian of 16 May 1883

Brisbane Courier, Queensland of 19 June 1890

Cardiff and Pontypridd Glamorgan County Times (1908)

Cheshire Observer of 26 September 1896.

Coburg Leader of 27 March 1897

Craven Herald of 16 August 1884

Croydon Advertiser of 22 October 1887

Daily Telegraph (Sydney) of 24 June 1893

Daily Telegraph of 4 February 1899

Empire (New South Wales) of 22 July 1868

Express and Telegrap (Adelaide, Australia) of 25 February 1905

Falmouth and Penryn News of 20 July 1867

Glasgow Daily Mail 1854

Goulburn Herald and County of Argyle Advertiser (New South Wales) of 24 March 1855

Herts and Essex Observer of 4 September 1886

Inverness Courier of 30 November 1897

Inverness Courier of 4 January 1898

Kalgoolie Miner

Kent Messenger of 27 January 1894

Leamington Courier of 26 June 1897

*Leighton Buzzard Observe*r of March 18, 1894

Leeds Mercury of 30 December 1854

Lloyds Weekly Newspaper of 14 January 1855

Lloyds Weekly Newspaper of 18 February 1855

Maitland Daily Mercury (New South Wales) of 21 March 1896

Manchester Evening News, of 9 April 1894

Narracoorte Herald of 7 March 1876

Norfolk Annals of 12 May 1887

Norfolk Annals 10 September 1890

Northampton Daily Reporter undated

Oldham Chronicle of 27 March 1869

Oxford Times of 4 March 1916

Reynolds Newspaper of 26 November 1854

Sheffield Daily Independent of 24 December 1902

Tasmanian (Launceston) 25 December 1875

The Coolgardie Miner of 1 December 1897

The Daily News of 24 November 1854

The Daily Telegraph of 16 October 1875

The Examiner of 9 December 1854 and 20 January 1855

The Illustrated London News of 30th October 1875

The Mercury (Hobart, Tasmania) of 5 December 1896

The Monmouthshire Merlin of 1 December 1854

The Morning Chronicle of 21 November 1854

The Morning Chronicle of 23 November 1854

The Newcastle Courant of 17 November 1854

The Times

The Warwickshire Advertiser and *The Leamington Courier* of 26 June 1896

The *West Australian* of 28 March 1894

The *Western Australian Times* of 25 January 1876

BIBLIOGRAPHY

Vancouver News Advertiser of 16 September 1892
Wellington Journal & Shrewsbury News of 16 January 1904
Western Mercury of 4 March 1883
Windsor and Richmond Gazette of October 1888
Yorkshire Evening Press of 14 June 1909.
Zeehan and Dundas Herald (Tasmania) of 20 December 1894

Muster Rolls

4th Light Dragoons	WO 12/657 to WO 12/663
8th Hussars	WO 12/843 to WO 12/848
11th Hussars	WO 12/1011 to WO12/1023
13th Light Dragoons	WO 12/116 to WO 12/1123
17th Lancers	WO 12/1337 to WO 12/1343

Medal Rolls

4th Light Dragoons	100/24 pp. 197-229
8th Hussars	100/24 pp. 279-312
11th Hussars	100/24 pp. 389-421
13th Light Dragoons	100/24 pp. 456-888
17th Lancers	100/24 pp. 490-523

Soldiers Discharge Documents (WO 28)

On-line sources include:

ancestry.uk

marksrussianmilitaryhistory.info

Hansard archive – debates of the House of Lords and House of Commons

Lives of the Light Brigade, The E.J. Boys Archive

The Letters of Queen Victoria, Volume III, 1854-1861, by Queen Victoria of Great Britain, Victoria (edited by Arthur Benson and Viscount Reginald Baliol Brett Esher), Project Gutenberg, 2009.

Trove – The online Newspaper Source (Australia)

Endnotes

Introduction

1. News correspondent for *The Times*, William Howard Russell had arrived on Sapouné Ridge in time to witness the later stages of the battle, although he had missed the defence of No. 1 Redoubt. In the immediate aftermath of the Charge he rode down to interview the survivors. His notes formed the basis of his despatch, the first in-depth public report of the catastrophe, published on 13 November.

Chapter 1. The Road to War

1. A mastery of drill was crucial in combat, and giving the wrong order to effect a manoeuvre could be costly, as had proved the case at the Battle of Aliwal (28 January 1846) when an incorrect order led to the cavalry retiring when at the point of victory.
2. Source: *The National Army [Museum] Book of the Crimean War: The Untold Story* by Alistair Massie, pp. 24-5.

Chapter 2. The Invasion of the Crimea and the Battle of the Alma

1. Calthorpe, *Letters from Headquarters*, p. 73
2. Mitchell, *Recollections*.

Chapter 3. The March to Balaclava

1. Kinglake, *The Invasion of the Crimea*, pp. 237-8
2. National Army Museum 1989-06041, *Journal of Captain Louis Nolan*.
3. Some sources place these events on the 19th and early morning of the 20th, but 'The Destruction of Sir George Cathcart' in *The Crimea War Society Journal* confirms that it was on the 20th and 21st.
4. Massie, *The Crimean War, The Untold Story*, p. 78
5. Moyse-Bartlett, *Edward Nolan*, p. 141.

Chapter 4. The Fall of the Redoubts to the Signing of the Fourth Order

1. Paget, *The Light Cavalry Brigade in the Crimea*, p.162.
2. Smith, *A Victorian RSM*, p. 125.

3. Letter home by an NCO on the 1st Dragoon Guards published in the *Reynolds Newspaper* of 26 November 1854.

4. The following extracts are from a letter from Sergeant C. McGregor of the Scots Greys, to his brother in Greenock. The letter, dated 2 November 1854, is typical of how the British Cavalry interpreted the action: 'The whole of the cavalry paraded every morning at five o'clock, and on that morning, as usual, we were in front of our lines, when the enemy opened fire upon one of the batteries which was manned by Turks, who fled, leaving the enemy to possess himself of the same. Emboldened by their success, in the course of twenty minutes the Russians came cheering over the hills in thousands – both horse artillery, cavalry, and infantry – driving the poor Turks all in front of them.'

5. Ewart, *A Soldier's Life*, vol. 1, p. 104.

6. Paget, General George, *The Light Cavalry Brigade*, p.1642.

7. *Brisbane Courier*, Queensland of 19 June 1890, p. 5.

8. Kinglake, *Invasion of the Crimea*, vol. 4, p. 209 fn. 10.

9. Earl of Cardigan, *Eight Months on Active Service*, p. 88.

10. Charles Dickens wrote in his journal *All the Year Round*: 'It is not a thing that should be suffered to die away. When he cut off a soldier's head at a blow, and disabled and dispersed several other, he had no very exciting motives of self-devotion. Pay, promotion, or popularity could not well enter his head, for he knew too, that the British public rarely asks the names of the poor privates and non-commissioned officers who fall. What John Grieve did, then, was an act of the purest and most unselfish heroism.' Grieve was awarded the Victoria Cross, *The London Gazette*, 24 February 1857: 'Balaclava, Crimea, 25 October 1854, No. 774 Sergeant Major John Grieve, 2nd Dragoons. Saved the life of an officer in the Heavy Cavalry Charge at Balaclava, who was surrounded by Russian cavalry, by his gallant conduct of riding up to his rescue and cutting off the head of one Russian, disabling and dispersing others.'

11. Massie, *The Crimean War: The Untold Story*.

12. Warner, *A Cavalryman*, p. 75.

13. Whinyates, *From Coruna to Sevastopol*.

14. *Goulburn Herald and County of Argyle Advertiser*, NSW, Saturday 24 March 1855, p. 4 (via the *Edinburgh Courant*).

15. Harrison, *The Gallant Six Hundred*, p. 189.

16. Captain The Hon Godfrey Charles Morgan of the 17th Lancers: 'I perfectly remember Captain Morris, in a moment of excitement, suggesting to the Earl of Cardigan that he should attack the retreating enemy.' Lord Cardigan's recollection was that Morris advanced independently with the 17th Lancers and was ordered back: 'Captain Morris broke away from the column with his regiment without orders, upon which I asked him sharply why he did so, and

desired him to fall again into column.' (Affidavit submitted in the Cardigan v. Calthorpe case, filed 2 June 1863).

17. Woodham-Smith, *The Reason Why*, p. 232.
18. Paget, *The Light Cavalry Brigade in the Crimea*, p. 174.
19. Higginson, *71 Years of a Guardsman's Life*, p. 185.
20. Kinglake, *The Invasion of the Crimea*, vol. 4, p. 208.
21. Kinglake, *Ibid*, p.178.
22. Mitchell, *Recollections*. In fact there were no indications at this time that the Russians were carrying off the Royal Naval guns in the lost redoubt, although those in No. 4 Redoubt were spiked and later discarded. Only after the battle were the captured guns from from Nos. 1 to 3 Redoubts removed and paraded through Sevastopol.
23. Doyle, *A Descriptive Account of the Famous Charge of the Light Brigade*.
24. Paget, *The Light Cavalry Brigade in the Crimea*, p. 205.
25. In *A Review of the Crimean War*, p. 109.
26. Is quoted in Whinyates, *From Sevastopol to Corunna*, p. 162.
27. *The Homicidal Earl*, p. 298.
28. Dawson, *Letters from the Light Brigade*, p. 127.
29. Kinglake, *The Invasion of the Crimea*, 4th Ed, vol. 2, p. 400.

Chapter 5. The Charge to the Guns

1. *Nineteenth Century* magazine, May 1892, 'Balaclava and the Russian Captivity'.
2. Although all of those directly involved were certain that Nolan had directed that the Cavalry Brigade should redeem itself and charge No. 3 Don Cossack battery, there were those not present but who knew Nolan and who were adamant that he would never have conceived such a plan. A letter from an Officer in defence of Nolan was published in *The Daily News* shortly after the battle: 'I cannot help but remembering that Captain Nolan was one of our most distinguished cavalry officers – a man who …. Had acquired a thorough knowledge of his arm, and who, more than anyone else, was able to make a fair estimate of its capabilities … he had also been a deep thinker on his profession, and was the author of one of the best books on cavalry service. To lead cavalry, unsupported by foot, through a cross-fire of two batteries, in order to cut down the support and gunners of the third, is so adventurous and unmilitary a proceeding that Captain Nolan is the last man whom I can believe of so much thoughtfulness and folly. (*The Daily News* of 18 November 1854).
3. Knowing that there were enemy batteries in position on the Fedioukine Heights and at the eastern end of the North Valley, leading an assault on the redoubts

via the valley would subject them to a heavy barrage. The more direct approach would have been along the line of the Woronzoff road and the South Valley, in the direction to which the 4th Division were advancing. For the Heavy Brigade to move into the North Valley to join the Light Brigade would only make any sense if they were to attack No. 3 Don Cossack battery. Therefore it must have been perfectly apparent to Nolan that Lord Lucan believed this to be the intended objective.

4. On 22 June 1868 he wrote: 'I also take the opportunity of here stating my impression that Captain Nolan (though I cannot think he realised their position) intended to charge the guns we did charge, and no other.'

5. Lord Lucan later confirmed that from his position he could see both the guns on the Fedioukine Heights and those at the end of the North Valley, but not those on the Causeway.

6. Lieutenant Colonel A. Tremayne, quoted in the *Journal of the 13th/18 Hussars*, April 1964, p. 67.

7. Butler, *A Descriptive Account*.

8. Morris died in Poona, India, murdered by his servant, before the plethora of books and newspaper articles began to rewrite the events of the 25th. He never divulged what, if anything, was said between Nolan and himself, but one would have expected that had he been aware that his directions had been misunderstood by Lord Lucan, then he would have made this fact known at the earliest opportunity. He did not, tantalizingly, reveal the details of the brief conversation between the pair that occurred when Nolan asked for permission to Charge with the 17th Lancers – surely Morris would have wished to know what they were to Charge in order to consider his best plan of action once their objective was reached?

9. Nunnerley, *Short Sketch of the 17th Lancers*.

10. Kinglake, *The Invasion of the Crimea*, vol. 2, p. 401. Lord Lucan's recollections of the event were also reported by Kinglake: 'With General Airey's order in my hands I trotted up to Lord Cardigan, and gave him distinctly its contents so far as they concerned him. I would not say on my oath that I did not read the order to him. He at once objected, on the grounds that he would be exposed to a flanking battery. I told him that I was aware of it. "I know it," but that "Lord Raglan would have it," and that we had no choice but to obey. I then said that I wished him to advance very steadily and quietly, and that I would narrow his front by removing the 11th Hussars from the First to the Second Line. This he strenuously opposed; but I moved across his front and directed Lieutenant Colonel Douglas not to advance with the rest of the line, but to form a Second Line with the 4th Light Dragoons.'

11. Beauchamp Walker, *Days of a Soldier's Life*, p. 136. Walker added, when referring to the artillery fire during the Charge: 'I hope I shall not soon again get such a pelting. Luckily a great many of their shells burst too high.'

12. Morley, *The Man of the Hour*.

13. NAM: 07-288-2, Lord Cardigan's Memorandum on the Charge of the Light Brigade.

    Lord Lucan's actions followed Queen's Regulations for a Cavalry attack, in that he divided both brigades into three elements; a 'First Line', a 'Support Line', and a 'Reserve'. Regulations, however, give the separation as 400 yards, whereas eyewitnesses quote either 100 or 200 yards.

14. Paget, *The Light Cavalry Brigade in the Crimea*, p. 247.

15. Godfrey Trevelyan Williams, *Historical Records of the 11th Hussars*.

16. Letter written at Balaclava 27 October 1854 to his mother, from *Letters from the Crimea to several members of his family* by Mrs Wykeham Martin. This said, General Cathcart had no intention of retaking the redoubts, which he felt were too exposed to hold.

17. Godfrey Trevelyan Williams.

18. Daniell, *4th Hussars*.

19. Letter from De Salis to a Major Howard Vyre quoted in *Reynolds Newspaper* 10 December 1854.

20. *Nineteenth Century* magazine, May 1892, 'Balaclava and the Russian Captivity'.

21. Walk: not to exceed four miles per hour; Trot: not to exceed eight and a half miles per hour; Gallop: eleven miles per hour; Charge: not to exceed the utmost speed of the slowest horse.

22. The regulations also stated: 'Whatever distance a Line has to go over, it is desirable, if the nature of the ground will permit, that it should move at a brisk trot, till within two hundred and fifty yards of the enemy, and then gallop, making a progressive increase, till within forty or fifty yards of the point of attack, when the word "Charge" will be given, and the gallop made with as much rapidity as the body can bear in good order.' (*Regulations For The Instruction, Formations, and Movements of The Cavalry*, May 1852, Sections VIII and IX). The advance and Charge at Balaclava took seven minutes, which was in line with regulations.

23. *Nineteenth Century* magazine, May 1892, 'Balaclava and the Russian Captivity'.

24. The usual rate of fire was about two rounds per minute as reloading and realignment procedures were tiring and time-consuming. This meant that the Fedioukine guns were able to fire about seven times each before their target disappeared down the valley. Perhaps 70 shots, around 30 shells and

40 roundshots, were fired at the Light Brigade from this battery over the first 875 yards of its advance.

25. Wightman, 'One of the Six Hundred' *Nineteenth Century Magazine*, May 1892. For Morley's account to be correct, Nolan must have ridden across the 17th Lancer's front rather than across Cardigan. In which case Cardigan would not have been unaware of his actions, as he did not look back during the whole time his brigade advanced. Morley also says that there arose 20-30 yards separation between the 17th Lancers and the 13th Light Dragoons, resulting from the aborted change of direction. This was clearly not so, and would have been remarked upon by survivors.

26. Morley, *The Man of The Hour*.

27. Nunnerley, *Short Sketch of the 17th Lancers*, p. 18.

28. Marquess of Anglesey, *A History of the British Cavalry*, p. 34.

29. Extract from a letter sent to his brother dated Scutari, 8 November 1855.

30. Calthorpe, *Letters from Headquarters*.

31. Paget, *The Light Cavalry Brigade in the Crimea*, p. 178.

32. Godfrey Trevelyan Williams, *Historical Record of the 11th Hussars*.

33. Trumpeter John Louden later claimed to have sounded the advance of the Heavies: 'I was alongside General Scarlett when he gave the order, 'The heavy Brigade will support the Lights.' These were, I believe, his exact words. The Lights had then broken into a gallop, and were close to 'The Valley of Death.' I sounded, and soon myself and general Scarlett were some 30 yards in front of the advancing squadron.'

34. Letter written by a member of the 1st Dragoon Guards and published in the *Manchester Times* of 22 November 1854.

35. Walker, *Days of a Soldier's Life*, pp. 135-6.

36. *Strand Magazine*, October 1891.

37. Trevelyan Williams, *11th Hussars*. This places their attack as taking place within five minutes of the Charge i.e. at 11.15 am.

38. A member of Scarlett's staff recalled the events in a letter which was later quoted in the press: 'Suddenly he [Scarlett] turned around in the saddle and exclaimed, "Why! The Heavies are retiring! The Heavies are retiring! Have you sounded retire?" He was very much excited, I replied, "No, General."'

39. Letter published in the *Vancouver News Advertiser* of 16 September 1892.

40. Jocelyn, *History of the Royal Artillery (Crimea Period)*, p. 213.

41. *Maitland Daily Mercury* (NSW), Saturday, 21 March 1896, p. 4.

42. *Leighton Buzzard Observer*, March 18, 1894.

43. William Butler, *A Descriptive Account of the Famous Charge of the Light Brigade*.

44. *The Coolgardie Miner* of 1 December 1897.

45. Letter mounted and framed and displayed in the 17th Lancers Museum at Belvoir Castle.

46. Roy Dutton, *Forgotten Heroes of the Charge of the Light Brigade*, p. 254.

47. Albert Mitchell, *Recollections of One of the Light Brigade*.

48. Paget, *The Light Cavalry Brigade in the Crimea*, p. 179.

49. Affidavit of James Donoghue, Cardigan v. Calthorpe, sworn 29 May 1863, filed 2 June 1863.

50. Extract from a manuscript account entitled 'The Charge of the Light Brigade', signed by James Olley and dated 'Holt Norfolk, July 29th 1897'.

51. Letter written at Balaclava 27 October 1854, to his mother, from *Letters from the Crimea to several members of his family* by Mrs Wykeham Martin (privately printed, 1868).

52. Affidavit of Matthew Keating, Cardigan v. Calthorpe, sworn 29 May 1863, filed 2 June 1863.

53. *The Illustrated London News*, 30 October 1875, p. 439.

54. Letter in the *Goulburn Herald and County of Argyle Advertiser* of 24 March 1855.

55. *Nineteenth Century* magazine, May 1892, 'Balaclava and the Russian Captivity'.

56. Pennington, *Sea, Camp, and Stage*, p. 55.

57. Murray, *The History of the VIII King's Royal Irish Hussars*.

58. Lieutenant E. Seager's letter from the Crimea dated 26 October 1854, NAM.

59. Dutton, *Forgotten Heroes*, p. 170.

60. *The Illustrated London News*, 30 October 1875.

61. Morley, *The Man of the Hour*.

62. *The Coolgardie Miner* of 1 December 1897.

63. Adkin p 161 note - quoted by McGuffie, *Rank and File*, p. 385.

64. McGuffie, *Rank and File*, p. 385.

65. Affidavit made in connection with the Cardigan v. Calthorpe case.

66. Letter dated 31 October 1854, in the *Monmouthshire Merlin* of 1 December 1854, p.5.

67. *Zeehan and Dundas Herald*, Tasmania, 20 December 1894 (via *The Illustrated London News*).

68. Mitchell, *Recollections of One of the Light Brigade*.

69. Portal, *Letters from the Crimea*. Letter to his mother dated 26th October, pp. 49-51.

70. Extract from a letter from Baker to his parents in the *Leeds Mercury* of 2 January 1855.

71. Letter to his brother-in-law of 28 October 1854 quoted in the *Irish Hussar* of October 1933, p. 49.

72. Letter written to a comrade and later published in *The Daily Telegraph* of 16 October 1875.

73. Barthorp, *Heroes of the Crimea*, p. 51.

74. Barrett, *The History of the 13th Hussars*, p. 364.

75. *Zeehan and Dundas Herald*, Tasmania, 20 December 1894 (via *The Illustrated London News*).

76. Daniell, *4th Hussars – The Story of the 4th Queen's Own Hussars*.

77. *Answers* magazine of 26 October 1912.

78. *Nineteenth Century* magazine, May 1892, 'Balaclava and the Russian Captivity'.

79. *Cardiff and Pontypridd Glamorgan County Times* (1908).

80. Sweetman, *Balaclava 1854*, p. 82.

81. *Lord Paget's Journal.*

82. W. Cattell, Assistant Surgeon, MS Autobiography, NAM, p. 14.

83. *Recollections of One of the Light Brigade* by Albert Mitchell, (1887).

84. Adkin, *The Charge: The Real Reason Why the Light Brigade was Lost*, p. 149.

85. The Earl of Cardigan, *Eight Months on Active Service*, p. 90.

86. *Eight Months on Active Service*, p. 90.

87. Brighton, *Hell Riders*, pp. 145-6.

88. Nunnerley, *Short Sketch.*

89. Letter dated 31 October 1854, published in *The Monmouthshire Merlin*, 1 December 1854.

90. Mitchell, *Recollections* (1887).

91. Godfrey Trevelyan Williams *Historical Records of the 11th Hussars.*

92. Paget: *The Light Cavalry Brigade in the Crimea*, pp. 182-3.

Chapter 6. Behind the guns

1. Private John Smith, *The Daily Telegraph*, 4 February 1899.

2. Morley, *Man of the Hour.*

3. Dutton, *Forgotten Heroes*, pp. 290-1.

4. *Oldham Chronicle* of 27 March 1869.

5. *The Coolgardie Miner* of 1 December 1897.

6. Sir Evelyn Wood, *The Crimean War*, p. 120.

7. Mitchell, *Recollections.*

8. Affidavit made in the Cardigan v. Calthorpe case.

9. Affidavit of Lieutenant Colonel Mayow made in the Cardigan v. Calthorpe case.

10. *Nineteenth Century* magazine, May 1892, 'Balaclava and the Russian Captivity'.

11. Kinglake, *The Invasion of the Crimea*, p. 402.

12. Morley, *Man of the Hour*.
13. *Nineteenth Century* magazine, May 1892, 'Balaclava and the Russian Captivity'.
14. Ibid.
15. *Leeds Mercury* of 30 December 1854.
16. 'Extracts from a letter from a private in the 8th Hussars', *Leeds Intelligence* of 13 January 1855.
17. Extract from a manuscript entitled 'The Charge of the Light Brigade', signed by James Olley and dated 'Holt Norfolk, July 29th 1897'.
18. Affidavit of Thomas George Johnson in the Cardigan v. Calthorpe case.
19. Morley, *The Cause of the Charge of Balaclava*, p. 10.
20. This blast had caused 'Ronald' to pull round and left Cardigan believing for a few moments that he had lost a leg.
21. Buttery, *Messenger of Death*, p. 138.
22. Trow, *The Pocket Hercules*, p. 107.
23. Kinglake, *The Invasion of the Crimea*.
24. *Ibid*.
25. Sweetman, *Balaclava 1854*, p. 76.
26. *Nineteenth Century* magazine, May 1892, 'Balaclava and the Russian Captivity'.
27. Bancroft, *Echelon, The Light Brigade Action at Balaklava*, p. 5.
28. *Lord Paget's Journal*
29. *The Illustrated London News*, 30 October 1875.
30. Paget, *Extracts*, p. 248.
31. Godfrey Trevelyan Williams.
32. *The Daily Telegraph* of 16 October 1875.
33. Dutton, *Forgotten Heroes*, p. 254.
34. Paget, *Extracts*, p. 195.
35. Extract from a manuscript 'The Charge of the Light Brigade' signed by James Olley and dated 'Holt Norfolk, July 29th 1897'.
36. *The Illustrated London News* of 30 October 1875.
37. *Lord Paget's Journal*.
38. *Ibid*.
39. Tremayne's account as quoted in Dutton *Forgotten Heroes*, p. 264.
40. Affidavit of Troop Sergeant-Major Frederick Short in Cardigan v. Calthorpe, filed on 2 June 1863.
41. Private Robert Ferguson, affidavit, in the Cardigan v. Calthorpe case.
42. Marquess of Anglesey, *A History of the British Cavalry*, p. 95.
43. *Lord Paget's Journal*.
44. Letter written to a comrade and later published in *The Daily Telegraph* of 16 October 1875.

45. *The Mercury*, Hobart, Tasmania, 5 December 1896.

46. *Gundagai Times and Tumut, Adelong and Murrumbidgee District Advertiser*, Friday 28 February 1913. The quote begins: 'We were standing to our horses, when the order came to advance. The man who said the trumpet was sounded is a liar. We increased our pace as we went along until we were in the thick of it.'

47. *Nineteenth Century* magazine, May 1892, 'Balaclava and the Russian Captivity'.

48. Murray, *History of the VIII King's Royal Irish Hussars*.

49. *Lord Paget's Journal*.

50. Paget, *Extracts*, p. 248.

51. Extract from a letter sent to his brother dated Scutari, 8 November 1855.

52. Affidavit of Trumpeter William Perkins, 11th Hussars in the Cardigan v. Calthorpe case.

53. Source: Pennington, *Left of Six Hundred*.

54. *The Illustrated London News* of 30 October 1875, p. 439.

55. Pennington, *Sea, Camp, and Stage*, p. 57.

56. Murray, *The History of the VIII King's Royal Irish Hussars*.

57. *The Illustrated London News* of 30 October 1875, p. 439.

58. Paget, *Extracts*, p. 248.

59. Interview published in *The Nottingham Evening Post* of 4 December 1912.

60. *The Illustrated London News* 30 October 1875. Private Robert Ashton's account begins: 'The odds were too much against us. Colonel Douglas gave the order to re-form the line, and join the 17th Lancers, initially with the object of recharging the guns; but, upon finding out that he had made a mistake in thinking they were our comrades...'

61. *Lord Paget's Journal*.

62. Letter dated 31 October 1854 in *The Monmouthshire Merlin* of 1 December 1854.

63. *The Daily Telegraph* of 16 October 1875.

64. Dutton, *Forgotten Heroes*, p. 178.

65. *Lord Paget's Journal*.

66. Sir William Gordon's reminiscences as quoted in the *Coburg Leader* of 27 March 1897, p. 3.

67. Private Robert Ferguson, DCM, affidavit filed in the Cardigan v. Calthorpe lawsuit.

68. Interview later published in *The Mercury*, Hobart, Tasmania, 5 December 1896.

69. Adkin, *The Charge: The Real Reason Why the Light Brigade was Lost*, p. 200.

70. Paget, *Extracts*, p. 190.

71. *Ibid.* p. 191.

72. Affidavit in the Cardigan v. Calthorpe case.
73. Portal, *Letters from the Crimea*. Letter to his mother dated 26th October, pp. 49-51.

Chapter 7. A Fighting Retreat

1. *Leighton Buzzard Observer*, 18 March 1894.
2. Letter to his brother-in-law of 28 October 1854 quoted in the Irish Hussar of October 1933 p. 49.
3. Portal, *Letters from the Crimea*. Letter to his mother dated 26th October, pp. 49-51.
4. *The Illustrated London News*, 30 October 1875.
5. Mitchell, *Recollections*
6. Crider, *In Search of the Light Brigade*, p. 494.
7. Grehan, *Voices From the Past*. The fuller quote reads: 'We were now through [the battery] and on the further side a considerable body of Russian cavalry, and so near the bottom of the valley that we could well discern the Tchernaya [Chernaya] river. But we were all three wearied and weakened by loss of blood; our horses wounded in many places; there were enemies all about us, and we thought it was about time to be getting back.'
8. *The Illustrated London News*, 30 October 1875, p. 439.
9. Extract from a letter sent to his brother dated Scutari, 8 November 1855.
10. *The Daily Telegraph* of 16 October 1875.
11. Clifford, *His letters & Sketches*, pp. 72-3.
12. Letter to Mr Berkeley, MP, 'General Hospital, Scutari, Constantinople, 3 November 1854' in *The Daily News*, Dec 1854.
13. Pennington, *Left of Six Hundred*.
14. Mitchell, *Recollections*.
15. Seager, Lieutenant E., Letter from the Crimea dated 26 October, 1854, NAM
16. Massie, *The Crimean War*, p. 93.
17. Clifford, *His letters & Sketches*, p. 74.
18. Extract from a manuscript account entitled 'The Charge of the Light Brigade' signed by James Olley and dated 'Holt Norfolk, July 29th 1897'.
19. *The Mercury*, Hobart, Tasmania, 5 December 1896.
20. *Sheffield Daily Independent* of 24 December 1902.
21. Mitchell, *Recollections*.
22. Godfrey Trevelyan Williams, *Historical Records*.
23. Whinyates, *From Coruna to Sevastopol*.
24. Marquess of Anglesey, *A History of the British Cavalry*, vol. II, p. 101.
25. Harris, *The Gallant Six Hundred*, p. 251.

26. In the hours after reaching the British lines, Lord Cardigan made a point of going over to General d'Allonville to thank him for the support provided by the Chasseurs d'Afrique.

27. Whinyates, *From Coruna to Sevastopol*, p. 170.

28. Harris, *The Gallant Six Hundred*, p. 249.

29. Nunnerley, *Short Sketch* (1884).

30. Dutton, p. 170.

31. Whinyates, *From Coruna to Sevastopol*.

32. Mitchell, *Recollections*.

33. *Yorkshire Evening Press* of 14 June 1909.

34. *The Newcastle Courant* of 17 November 1854, under the title 'Accounts from various sources'.

35. There was later controversy as to whether the Charge was actually sounded, and if so, by whom. It is assumed that Brittain was wounded early in the Charge, before he had the opportunity to sound the 'Charge' which order would only have been given when closing in on No. 3 Don Cossack battery. The debate as to whether the Charge was actually ever sounded arose in connection with the sale of the bugle, claimed at one time by Trumpet Major Joy to have sounded the Charge. The sale of Joy's bugle and medals, took place on 30 March 1898, raised the not considerable sum of 750 guineas. The new owner, Mr Middlebrook, displayed the bugle and other relics in Edinburgh Castle, Regent's Park, until his death in 1908, when they were sold in Messrs. Debenham Storr and Co.'s salerooms in February of that year.

 Almost immediately following the first sale, William Bird, 8th Hussars, came forward and stated that Joy had not taken part in the Charge, but had charged with the Heavy Brigade, and that Joy had subsequently agreed to quietly withdraw from the Balaclava Commemoration Society, which he did.

 Further controversy then arose between veterans, as to whether the Charge was actually sounded at all. There were strong arguments on both sides and opinion remained divided. It does, however, seem unlikely that Trumpeter William Brittain, duty trumpeter to Lord Cardigan, was still in the saddle as the Brigade neared No. 3 Don Cossack battery – the regimental trumpeters would have taken up the call from Brittain. Lord Cardigan did not look back during the advance and may have been unaware of Brittain having been brought down, while his personal account does not refer to command.

36. Letter from Mrs Farrell, the wife of a 5th Dragoon who was at Scutari unofficially on nursing duties, to a Mrs Powell.

37. Richardson, *Nurse Sarah Anne*.

38. Vicomte de Noé.
39. *The Illustrated London News* of 30 October 1875.
40. Dawson, *Letters*, pp. 150-1.
41. Butler, *A Descriptive Account*. The quote begins: 'Going back was worse than coming, for a regiment was drawn across our path, and guns were playing upon us.'
42. Pemberton, *Battles*, p. 113.
43. Massie, *A Most Desperate Undertaking*.
44. Morley, *Man of the Hour*.
45. *Nineteenth Century* magazine, May 1892, 'Balaclava and the Russian Captivity'.
46. *Zeehan and Dundas Herald*, Tasmania, 20 December 1894, via *The Illustrated London News*.
47. Letter to his Land Agent, dated 'Heights before Sevastopol, December 2nd, 1854'.
48. Butler, *A Descriptive Account*.
49. Extract from a letter sent to his brother dated Scutari, 8th November 1855.
50. There was later some controversy as to whether Lockwood had indeed Charged, or had been on despatch duty at the beginning of the Charge and only gone in search of Cardigan after the event. Lieutenant Maxse wrote to the editor of *The Times*, published on 28 June 1868: 'Captain Lockwood started in front of the Light Brigade from the moment of its advance about four horses' length to my left and some five or six to the right rear of Lord Cardigan. The loud ringing cheer and gallant bearing of poor Lockwood, as he turned in his saddle about three parts of the way down can never be effaced from my memory, and is doubtless in the recollections of others. This is the last time I saw him; he was not near me on passing the Russian battery.'
51. 'The Destruction of Sir George Cathcart' in *The Crimea War Society Journal*.
52. Daniell, *4th Hussars*.
53. Private Robert Ferguson DCM, affidavit filed in Cardigan v. Calthorpe, sworn 20 May 1863, filed 2 June 1863.
54. Account by Troop Sergeant Major William Barker, 17th Lancers, in The *Leighton Buzzard Observer*, 18 March 1894.
55. Morley, *The Cause of the Charge*. The actual figure for mounted survivors is 198, as three men arrived a little after this roll call, while the generally accepted total of Chargers, including staff officers, is 673.
56. National Army Museum 1983 – 11 – 9 Captain Seager.
57. *The Morning Chronicle* of 23 November 1854 (which it sourced from the *Kilkenny Moderator*).

ENDNOTES

Chapter 8. After the Battle

1. Kinglake, *The Invasion of the Crimea*.
2. Russell, *The War to the Death*, p. 159.
3. Whinyates, *From Coruna to Sevastopol*, p. 142.
4. *Ibid*.
5. Hamley, *The War in the Crimea*.
6. Adye, *Recollections of a Military Life*, p. 49.
7. Source unknown.
8. Doyle, *A Descriptive Account of the Famous Charge of the Light Brigade*.
9. Smith, *A Victorian RSM*, p. 147.
10. Massie, *The Crimean War*, p. 92.
11. *Extracts from the Letters and Journal of General Lord George Paget*.
12. At Simferopol Hospital, Kirk was roomed with Russian wounded from Inkerman. He was spat on by two of them, retaliated with his fists and had to be restrained. William Kirk died the following day, probably poisoned.
13. *Lloyds Weekly Newspaper* of 18 February 1855.
14. *A Diary of the Crimea by George Palmer Evelyn* (edited, with a preface by Cyril Falls) (Gerald Duckworth & Co, London 1954), pp. 95-6.
15. Harris, *The Gallant Six Hundred*, p. 262. Lord Lucan later observed that the order had come from Lord Raglan who from his elevated position on the Sapouné Ridge had a far better overview of the battlefield; it was therefore possible that the cavalry action, although unlikely to succeed, might be one action in a wider plan – the Cavalry was to be sacrificed to save the Army. Interestingly Lucan did not, at any point, tear Lucan's written order to pieces line by line – the order was nonsensical and needed to be explained by the ADC who carried it. Unfortunately the ADC, Nolan, used this looseness to direct the Cavalry against No. 3 Don Cossack battery in a death or glory charge.
16. Woodham-Smith *The Reason Why*, p. 264.
17. *Extracts from the letters and journal of the late General Lord G. Paget*, p. 73.
18. Moyse-Bartlett, *Nolan of Balaclava*, p. 144.
19. Lucan was made KCB on 1855 and Colonel of the 8th Hussars. He was promoted a general and made Gold Stick and colonel of the 1st Life Guards in 1865, and in 1869 he was made GCB and in 1887 promoted field-marshal, but his reputation was damaged.
20. Woodham-Smith *The Reason Why*, p. 272.
21. Ronald got caught in the crossfire when a statement came out that he had shied at the blast of cannon close by at the final volley and carried Cardigan back to the British lines at a gallop.

Conclusion

1. The only evidence comes in the memoirs of Corporal Nunnerley (1884) and Corporal Thomas Morley (1892) who claimed that Nolan had called out 'three's right' and that the some of the 17th Lancers wheeled to the right but their direction was corrected by the former. However, Morley who heard the order, was at that time seventy yards from Nolan. No staff officer, regimental officer, NCO or other members of the rank and file, who were much closer to Nolan, ever came forward with evidence of either hearing this command, or of this manoeuvre having been performed.

Appendix I: Medals

1. Stories of the Victoria Cross printed in *The Strand Magazine*, March 1891, based on an article in the *Morning Post* of 1 February 1855 – the two combined in the above.
2. *Strand Magazine*, October 1891. Lamb later claimed that he and Corporal Malone drew lists for the Victoria Cross and that Malone drew first and won.
3. *Heroes of the Crimea* by M. Barthorp (Blandford, 1991), p. 54.
4. Cyril Falls (1954), p. 95-6.
5. Affidavit, filed in the Cardigan v. Calthorpe lawsuit. The statement was sworn on 27 May 1863. Filed on 2 June 1863.
6. 'An order came to the Commanding Officer of [the] regiment to send in the name of an officer, non-commissioned officer and private, for the Légion d'Honneur. Captain Jenyns and Captain Tremayne, to their credit, wished Captain Percy Smith to be recommended, instead of either of themselves, they having already received the rank of Brevet-Major. The Commanding Officer thought that Captain Phillips had already been rewarded by getting a Troop, and would not send in the name of the above-mentioned officer, whereupon Captain Tremayne allowed his name to go in.' (*Recollections of a Young Soldier* by Harry Powell, 13th Light Dragoons.)

Appendix II: Personal Accounts by Regiments

1. *Tamworth Mercury* of 15 November 1890.
2. Farquharson, *Reminiscences*.
3. Source: Grigg, *Told from the Ranks*, pp. 64-9.
4. *The Illustrated London News* of 30 October 1875.
5. *The Royal Magazine* vol. XIII (1879) 'Survivor's Tales of Great Events No. II – The Charge of the Light Brigade from the narrative of Mr H. Herbert, 4th Light Dragoons'.

ENDNOTES

6. Anonymous, *United Service Journal*, April 1856, p. 554.

7. Affidavit filed in the Cardigan v. Calthorpe lawsuit, sworn 30 May 1863, filed 2nd June 1863.

8. John Doyle: *A Descriptive Account of the Famous Charge of the Light Brigade*.

9. Letter from Glendwr quoted in *The Daily Telegraph* of 16 October 1875 and the *Sheldrake's Aldershot and Sandhurst Military Gazette* of 30 October 1875.

10. *Express and Telegraph*, Adelaide, Australia, 25 February 1905, p. 4.

11. *The Illustrated London News* of 30 October 1875.

12. *Narracoorte Herald* of Tuesday 7 March 1876, p. 3.

13. *Lord Paget's Journal*.

14. *The Warwickshire Advertiser* and *The Leamington Courier* of 26 June 1896.

15. *The Illustrated London News* of 30 October 1875, p. 438.

16. An unpublished biography *A Chequered Life*.

17. *Lord Paget's Journal*.

18. Williams, *Historical Records of the Eleventh Hussars*.

19. Kinglake, *The Invasion of the Crimea*, vol. 2.

20. *Lord Paget's Journal*.

21. Pennington, *Left of Six Hundred*.

22. Kelly, *From the Fleet in the Fifties*, pp. 192-206.

23. *The Morning Chronicle* of 18 January 1855 'a letter from a dragoon' (previously in the *Globe*).

24. 'A Balaclava Hero: 'Fifty Lashes with the Cat' an article published a penny paper known as the *Spy*, in June 1897, and based on an interview with Richardson conducted at Crumpsall Workhouse.

25. Godfrey Trevelyan Williams, *Historical Record of the 11th Hussars*.

26. *The Illustrated London News* of 30 October 1875.

27. *Ibid*.

28. *The Illustrated London News* of 30 October 1875, p. 439.

29. *Wellington Journal & Shrewsbury News*, 16 January 1904.

30. Letter written by Cornet Denzil Thomas Chamberlayne of the 13th Light Dragoons to his father published in the *York Herald* of 16 November 1854.

31. *Narrative of Joseph Doughton, late of her Majesty's 13th Light Dragoons, one of the heroes wounded at the Battle of Balaclava, in the Gallant Cavalry Charge* (Birmingham, 1856).

32. *Zeehan and Dundas Herald*, Tasmania, Thursday 20 December 1894 (via *The Illustrated London News*).

33. *Cheshire Observer* of 26 September 1896.

34. Reminiscence of the Charge appeared in the *Birkenhead and Cheshire Advertiser and Wallasey Guardian* of 28 October 1899.

35. The *Western Australian Times* of 25 January 1876.
36. The *West Australian* of 28 March 1894, p. 3.
37. *Not Published* (John Mitchell, London, 1864), pp. 14-15.
38. Newspaper clipping in James Wightman's scrapbook quoted in *The Australian Graves of Crimean War Light Brigade Veterans* by Edward J. Boys from *Sabretache* vol. LXI, June 2000.
39. Anthony Dawson's *Letters from the Light Brigade*.
40. *Goulburn Herald and County of Argyle Advertiser*, 24 March 1855.
41. *Soldiering and Scribbling* magazine.
42. *Nineteenth Century* magazine, May 1892, 'Balaclava and the Russian Captivity' and *The West Australian*, 6 June 1892.

Index

INDEX